For Health and Beauty

For Health and Beauty

Physical Culture for Frenchwomen,

1880s–1930s

MARY LYNN STEWART

The Johns Hopkins University Press

Baltimore & London

—◦❧ • ❧◦—

The Johns Hopkins University Press
2715 North Charles Street
Baltimore, Maryland 21218-4363
www.press.jhu.edu

Library of Congress Cataloging-in-Publication Data
Stewart, Mary Lynn, 1945–
    For health and beauty : physical culture for Frenchwomen, 1880s–1930s /
Mary Lynn Stewart.
    Includes bibliographical references and index.
    ISBN 0-8018-6483-6 (alk. paper)
    1. Women—France—History. 2. Women—France—Physiology.
3. Women—Health and hygiene—France. 4. Body, Human—Social
aspects—France—History. 5. Beauty culture—France—History.
6. Physical education and training—France—History. I. Title.
HQ1613 .S68 2000
305.4´0944—dc21   00-041258

A catalog record for this book is available
from the British Library.

To my mother,
Mary Cecilia Stewart

Contents

Illustrations

Acknowledgments

$\mathscr{T}$HIS BOOK is the product of more than a decade of research, writing, and revising, aided at each stage by administrators, archivists, librarians, and scholars in several fields. I am grateful to every one of them and hope that I have conveyed my appreciation, where appropriate, in the text or endnotes. I want to acknowledge here only those people and institutions that made essential contributions at key moments in the process.

I am deeply indebted to Angus McLaren, Marlene LeGates, and Elinor Accampo for reading a very rough first draft of the manuscript and managing to make both practical and creative suggestions for revision. I owe a great deal to Linda Clark and Judith Stone, who made equally constructive suggestions to improve the second draft of the manuscript. Similarly, I appreciate the specialized commentary on two chapters by my colleagues Hannah Gay, in history, and Meredith Kimball, in women's studies, and the careful critique of the first part of the manuscript by Karen Offen. I also want to thank the anonymous reader for Johns Hopkins University Press; Henry Tom, executive editor at the press; and freelance editor Suzanne Bastedo for their thoughtful assistance in the difficult task of cutting and polishing the manuscript.

The Social Science and Humanities Research Council of Canada funded several research trips, including a two-semester sabbatical spent in France, between 1987 and 1990. I am also very grateful to the administrators and colleagues at Simon Fraser University who enabled me to continue and deepen my research at times when I might otherwise have been overly preoccupied with a personal health problem and later with administrative duties as chair of women's studies. The university offered me the luxury of a year to reflect, write, and, as it happened, reconceive the entire project as a university research professor in the academic year 1992–93. The dean of arts helped support three further research trips through the program of chair's research grants in 1994, 1995, and 1996. Finally, the University Publication Fund subsidized reproduction, permissions, and indexing costs.

In writing this book, I have been influenced by Michel Foucault's ideas about the social body's investment in regulating individual bodies through the imposition of biomedical norms upon those individual bodies and through the "seduction" of individuals into desiring these norms and adopting the behaviors associated with them.[1] This book focuses on the diffuse efforts of hygienists to inculcate corporeal discipline through mother-daughter and conjugal relations and of the school system and private business to supplement the family in this endeavor. Perhaps less obviously, this book is informed by Pierre Bourdieu's ideas that sexual identity is formed by cultural reproduction of models of sexuality, by observation of others, by repetition and practice.[2]

Finally, this book also owes a debt to feminist anthropologists who explicate the construction of gendered bodies. Most of these researchers are cited where appropriate in the text, but one who contributed to the conceptual framework of this book must be acknowledged here. Before I began researching this book, I read Emily Martin's *The Woman in the Body*. Her demonstration of how processes such as menstruation, birth, and menopause—so often construed as "natural" and universal varied in their metaphoric meaning and hence in women's understanding and experience of them—laid the foundation for this book.[3]

Despite my debts and gratitude to all of the above and to many others cited in the text, I alone am responsible for any errors or omissions in the text.

For Health and Beauty

Introduction

*F*OR HEALTH AND BEAUTY looks at physical culture for Frenchwomen in several ways. First it analyzes scientific, esthetic, medical, and hygienic expertise about women's bodies between the 1880s and 1930s to understand how and why experts designed a sexual and reproductive image allegedly for all, but actually for bourgeois Frenchwomen. Second, it examines girls' science, health, and physical education curricula and women's health, beauty, and sexual advice manuals that taught French girls and women how to achieve these not necessarily compatible corporeal ideals. Comprising personal hygiene, deportment, exercise, and beauty regimens, this kind of instruction was called *physical culture*. Third, the book assesses how some Frenchwomen received this contradictory discourse not only on their physical but also on their psychological being.

It is trite, indeed, to argue that medical science, education, journalism, and advertising modify women's body images and bodily care. Instead, this book demonstrates that these disciplines, institutions, and media had to alter their appeal, and specifically, had to promise to improve health and beauty, to persuade Frenchwomen to change some of their corporeal standards and practices. Finally, the book shows how internal contradictions in expert advice and women's sense of self-preservation contributed to the experts' failure to convince Frenchwomen to follow their most persistent counsel—to have more babies.

Periodization

Between 1880 and 1940, the introduction of cell theory into human biology, of endocrinology into gynecology, and of germ theory into hygiene transformed scientific and medical visions of women's bodies. In these six decades, the implementation of free, compulsory public education, the proliferation of women's self-help literature, and the commercialization of health, beauty, and fitness products disseminated new scientific and commercial representations of the female body. Bodily ideals and aspirations mutated from rounded, plump contours to straighter, slimmer figures and from relatively immobile to more dynamic bodies. Charting these changes is one objective of this book. Accounting for them is a second objective.

The time frame for these changes coincides with the Third Republic, which was consolidated by 1880 and fell in 1940. This republic confronted two widely perceived problems involving health and reproduction. One problem emanated from a theory that human beings had degenerated through accumulating inherited defects. This theory gained credence after military defeat in the Franco-Prussian War (1870) was interpreted as a sign of declining vigor as well as decreased military prowess. French politicians realized that expenditure on public hygiene entailed private hygiene, which required teachers, nurses, housewives, and mothers to inculcate the routines of personal cleanliness. Although degeneration theory lost scientific ground in the 1890s, crusaders against prostitution, alcoholism, syphilis, and tuberculosis began a chorus about a societal version of degeneration.[1] Antivenereal and antitubercular lobbies kept up the refrain after the First World War.

The second and more general concern was depopulation. The birth rate, which had been falling longer in France than in any other nation, continued to fall after the Franco-Prussian War. By the early 1890s, the political nation confronted the disturbing (although temporary) phenomenon of lower natality than mortality rates. As Karen Offen discovered, fear of *dénatalité* affected feminist, antifeminist, and nationalist positions in the *fin de siècle*.[2] A decline in the sex ratio for live births exacerbated the perceived problem. Long before losing a generation of young men in the First World War, France had 650,000 fewer men than women. Robert Nye demonstrates that a consensus emerged "on the relation of sex to the population problem that cut across most other ideological differences."[3] Although the legislative response was negligible before the Great War, rhetoric about depopulation was ubiquitous. For instance, republicans defended the divorce law of 1884 as a way of dissolving childless unions and facilitating fruitful marriages.[4] The annihilation of two million men in the Great War and the flu epidemic of 1918 revived demographic apprehensions. In the 1920s and 1930s, widely distributed hygiene handbooks reported that France had a birth rate and sex ratio lower than those of other European countries.[5] The prewar consensus now extended to legislative action. A symbolic law, passed by a huge majority in 1920, raised the penalties for abortion and for disseminating female-controlled contraception.[6]

Evidently, the First World War served as a watershed in the Third Republic. Specifically, this war accelerated some changes in youthful behavior and conjugal relations which are discussed in this book. However, changes in biological knowledge and everyday physical life rarely occur in lockstep with particular political events or cultural crises. Part Two discusses the "crisis of masculinity" in the *fin de siècle* and the "crisis of femininity" in the 1920s as two phases of ongoing debate about gender. One thesis of this book is that biologically based conceptions of masculinity and femininity imply constant debate about sex and gender.

Bioreasoning

At the heart of French discourse on women's bodies is "the sheer physicality that seems to attend being in Western culture." According to Oyeronke Oyewumi, an anthropologist who studies African women, this specifically Western phenomenon means that Western identities are shaped by biological thinking, and Western gender identities cannot exist without sex.[7] Part One of this book charts this kind of reasoning in French biological, medical, and hygienic thinking from the mid-eighteenth to the mid-twentieth centuries. As historians such as Thomas Laqueur, Londa Schiebinger, and Geneviève Fraisse have disclosed, natural scientists, physiologists, and physicians sexualized the body in new and more extensive ways between the early 1700s and the 1830s. These pioneers and their followers influenced biomedical theories about women's bodies in the late nineteenth and early twentieth centuries, so several chapters of this book begin with synopses of their ideas. Because the forefathers and their intellectual progeny in the Third Republic drew upon longstanding religious and scientific ideologies about the sexed body, these ideologies are introduced in the following paragraphs.

Aristotelian or natural philosophy was the wellspring of bioreasoning. Aristotle focused on heat as the essential quality of life. Aristotle, and legions of Aristotelians from the later Middle Ages on, envisioned women as less hot than men and hence as imperfect men. Because women were cooler, their genitals had to be located inside their bodies. Both sexes produced seminal liquid, but women, being cooler, could only produce catemenia, or menstrual blood, which was more passive than semen. Like their seminal liquids, women were passive, men active.[8] The association of sexual with gender characteristics, the distinction between active and passive sexual emissions and therefore genders, and assumptions about the superiority of the active gender would recur throughout Western history.

Deeply rooted in the Hellenized Christian tradition are bipolar oppositions between body and soul, body and mind, desire and reason, men and women. For Hellenized Christians, the body was the seat of passion and had to be subordinated to reason in the interests of social order. As Barbara Duden comments, "This dichotomous way of thinking in opposite categories of nature and culture is shot through with sexual references and metaphors in which woman is equated with nature" (because of women's reproductive role).[9] The female body, closer to nature, was a challenge to social order. Also rooted in Judeo-Christian theology were inferences about biological and social differences between men and women based on the Genesis account of Eve's creation from Adam's rib. Church fathers from Augustine on regarded the later and contingent creation of women as proof of their subordinate status and reproductive purpose: woman was made for man and for procreation. According to Margaret Miles, the Church fathers' recognition of Adam's desire for Eve left considerable anxiety about the seductive female body.[10]

After a millennium of representing women's bodies as similar, if inferior, versions of men's bodies, eighteenth-century medical science declared them essentially different. As Thomas Laqueur describes it, instead of visualizing sex difference as one of vertical degree, medical theorists viewed it as "horizontally ordered opposites." The reversal reflected new perceptions of female sex organs and the "biologizing of gender differences."[11] Londa Schiebinger criticizes Laqueur's emphases on sex organs and a shift from hierarchically ordered to incommensurable sexes. She demonstrates that European anatomists also sexualized the skeleton and represented the male and female bodies as "each having a distinct telos—physical and intellectual strength for the man, motherhood for the woman." This conception of essential difference did not preclude the arrangement of difference hierarchically.[12]

Another operating premise of this book is that gender—the socially constructed categories of men and women—is not an outgrowth of sex differences but of hierarchical thinking. Scholars who endeavored to base gender roles on anatomical or physiological sex differences always ordered any difference they discovered hierarchically, with man as the prototype and woman as the deficient variant. I am indebted to Christine Delphy for introducing me to this idea.[13] My research on women's bodies only confirmed that hierarchical gender assumptions permeated the search for sex differences. Even Laqueur concluded that political considerations informed biomedical discourse on sexual dichotomy. "When time-immemorial custom became a less and less plausible justification for social relations [during the eighteenth-century Enlightenment], the battleground of gender roles shifted to nature, to biological sex."[14] In the century and a half following the Enlightenment, the study of sex differences was conducted in an environment of political debate about gender.

Biopolitics

In the Enlightenment, philosophes refused to accept ideas or institutions on the basis of religious or political authority. They claimed to understand the world through reason, which would discover natural laws governing the world by the study of history, anthropology, and biology. A radical extension of this position postulated that in a state of nature, all men had rights. Radicals used natural rights theory to critique hierarchical states and societies but disagreed about how this applied to women. For instance, in the *Encyclopedia* (1751–80), one article on women contends that men and women were equal before civilization, so that female subordination was the result of civil, not natural, law. Another article states that "the laws and customs of Europe unanimously and decisively give authority to the male because he is the one with the greatest strength of mind and body."[15] Enlightened ambivalence revolved around the pivotal question of what was natural in humans. One answer was the body, which, in Christianity, had been aligned with femininity. Even though the motifs of the *Encyclopedia* were social utility and productive activity, it contained far more articles on women's bodies than on their social or economic roles. Lieselotte Steinbrugge explains that the reigning economic theory, physiocracy, sought power and prosperity in population growth as well as in productivity. Population growth required reproduction, which was also associated with women's bodies.[16] Natural rights and physiocratic theories placed women's bodies at the heart of political and economic discourse.

Given the egalitarian potential of natural rights theory, philosophes worried about how to ensure social and political stability. Many of them thought that the solution would be mothers instilling moral and civic responsibility in a domestic family. Bothered by what would happen if women claimed natural, individual, and political rights, philosophes preempted the possibility by proclaiming corporeal inequality and social complementarity.

Jean-Jacques Rousseau's *Emile*, published in 1762, makes the seminal statement. When Rousseau describes the education of Emile's intended mate, Sophie, the reader learns that Sophie had "to submit to the strictest and most enduring restraints, those of propriety." Being closer to nature and more instinctual, she is at a more primitive level of civilization and must never develop her passions. Although Rousseau maintains that, except for sex, woman differs from man only in degree, sex differences had many ramifications. Like the moral physiologists discussed in Chapter 1, Rousseau claims that "resemblances and differences must have an influence on moral nature. . . . In the union of the sexes each contributes to the common end, but in different ways. From this diversity springs the first difference. . . . The man should be strong and active; the woman should be weak and passive." This Aristotelian distinction between active and passive sex set off a familiar exposition of gender differences with enormous social and political implications. For instance, Rousseau argues that the state needs a domestic patriarchal family in which the mother nurtures a bond between father and children. Without a mother to preserve a united family, the "human race is doomed to extinction. . . . Will the bonds of convention hold firm without some foundation in nature? Can devotion to the state exist apart from the love of those near and dear to us? Can patriotism thrive except in the soil of the miniature fatherland, the home?"[17]

Rousseau assured his readers that sexual inequality was not a matter of prejudice, but of reason. Thereafter, few political theorists acknowledged any uncertainty about the roots of sexual inequality (although some admitted that certain inequities might be caused by prejudice). Geneviève Fraisse documents how women's exclusion from democratic politics between 1770 and 1830 was naturalized by moral physiologists through the elaboration of a reductively sexual and reproductive vision of women's bodies. By asserting a relationship between reproduction and feminine identity, these physiologists ensured the natural foundation of sex difference. Their linkage of physical constitution and social convenience was the lifeblood of an extended political discourse.[18] The first two chapters of this book trace the circulation of this biological and medical discourse into the twentieth century. The following paragraphs introduce the major political issues.

According to Joan Wallach Scott, with the emergence of liberal individualism, women "came into being as political outsiders through the discourse of sexual difference." To justify broader political participation, revolutionaries imagined an abstract individual who transcended earlier social and political distinctions between Frenchmen. This abstract individual was established through a contrast to women, defined as "naturally" different and dependent.[19] The first political test of natural rights came in the Declaration of the

Rights of Man of 1789, which embodied the rights-bearing individual as a man.[20] When revolutionary politicians defined enfranchisement, they excluded poor men, servants, colonial subjects, slaves, and women. Debate swirled around the exemption of poor, colonial, and slave men, all of whom were granted "inactive"—or limited—citizenship.[21]

Nearly a century separated the declaration of manhood suffrage in 1848 and the proclamation of universal suffrage in 1944. This lengthy hiatus was not the result of feminist indifference about the vote. Hubertine Auclert directed a movement for female enfranchisement from 1876 until her death in 1914, Madeleine Pelletier led a smaller activist group from 1906 until her institutionalization in the 1930s, and Louise Weiss conducted a more constitutional campaign in the 1930s. Caught in the conundrum of having to evoke their difference from the abstract rights-bearing individual in order to object to their exclusion from citizenship, these feminists engaged in complex intellectual maneuvering. Auclert employed egalitarian arguments, based on women's equal capacity for reason and morality, and essentialist arguments, based on women's special knowledge of children, the family, health, and welfare. Madeleine Pelletier took an individualist approach, denying that sex differences had any implication for citizenship.[22]

Resistance by the Catholic Church has been the traditional explanation for the failure to grant female enfranchisement. Certainly the Church posed as a defender of women's interests against the Republic long after the Papacy ordered Catholics to accept the Republic in 1892.[23] However, the traditional explanation ignores two pertinent facts: elements in the Church favored women's suffrage by the turn of the century, and Catholics on the extreme right accepted it as a bulwark against communism after the Russian Revolution in 1917.

A more persuasive interpretation of French paralysis on women's suffrage is republican procrastination, for republicans controlled all legislative assemblies after 1880. Anticlerical republicans not unreasonably feared that women voters would be under the influence of the Church. Women constituted nearly two thirds of French communicants at Easter mass in 1900, and Catholic women's groups organized against anticlerical republicans in the 1902 and 1905 elections. Between 1909 and 1914 when republicans introduced into the Chamber of Deputies bills allowing women to vote in local elections, only 40 percent of the deputies supported this attenuated form of suffrage.[24] Ideologically, the republican dilemma devolved from their commitment to natural rights individualism. For many republicans, the right to vote issued from the principle of equality between individuals, and women had been defined as reproductive beings, not individuals.

Although few biologists entered the formal political arena, their theories about sexual and therefore gender dichotomies informed political opposition to female suffrage. One conduit was the large contingent of doctors in the legislature. French physicians constituted between 10 and 12 percent of each legislature between 1880 and 1914, a higher proportion than in England, Germany, and other European states. Doctors held leadership positions and many seats on parliamentary committees, notably those on public health and population issues, and they dominated powerful pronatalist lobbies.[25]

Rationales about women's physical weakness and reproductive function featured in opposition to women's suffrage. Responding to feminist pressure and women's contributions to the war effort, the Chamber of Deputies approved a bill granting women the same voting rights as men.[26] Senator Alexandre Bérard's report on this bill, presented to the Senate in 1919, blocked passage until the end of the Republic. Bérard began with political and procedural objections such as the timing, when France, "stupefied" by the war, would have an electorate dominated by women. To counter the maternal feminist position that women needed the vote to pass maternal and child protection laws, he cited France's respectable record of legislation in this area but concluded with familiar bioreasoning: "You *cannot* make men and women have the same nature: they complement one another." Women must return to their social duty, maternity. "Are women's hands made for the battle of the public arena? Rather than handling the ballot, women's hands are made to be kissed."[27]

In the next decade, poet and critic Paul Valéry denounced "this curious mix of cynicism and devotion with which men deny women the vote." Yet Valéry based his support for enfranchisement on biological function. After dismissing opposition on the basis of the inequality of physical strength, because strength was losing importance in modern industrial societies, he dealt with "the final obstacle," maternity. "Here the inequality is imposed by nature. And here the law should give women the right to legislate on motherhood issues."[28] His biofunctional rationale approximated maternal feminist arguments. Other feminists, such as journalist Thérèse Pottecher, rejected this kind of rationale: "It is not clear just how the maternal specialization of women, which is only temporary, lasting fifteen to twenty years at most, could constitute any incapacity or inferiority whatsoever."[29]

Science, Culture, and Commerce

In the Third Republic, science operated in conjunction with cultural and commercial interests to communicate ideals and standards about women's bodies. Biologists and physicians studying woman's body (with adjective and noun in the singular) borrowed freely from art criticism and popular history; physicians wrote beauty advice books and sold cosmetics. Medical and lay authors of the burgeoning subgenre of women's health, beauty, and sexual advice literature cited biomedical experts on women's physical being. The beauty industry with its ubiquitous publicity appealed to the authority of science. Women's advice literature and health and beauty advertising helped re-educate women about their bodies.

Anxieties about degeneration and depopulation directed the attention of French physicians and psychologists to heterosexual reproduction. Robert Nye uncovered an extensive prewar literature on men's sexual potency and perversion.[30] French physicians troubled about young men having homosexual contacts prescribed early marriages as a preventive measure.[31] The idea of pushing homosexuals into marriages was still debated between the world wars, with some discomfort about reproducing "other unbalanced beings."[32]

Lesbianism attracted less attention, except in salacious erotic and pornographic literature.[33] Many prewar studies of "perverts" ignored or dismissed lesbians as hysterics or menopausal depressives.[34] After the war, there was more apprehension about lesbianism in medical circles, and some of this concern was transmitted to a wider reading public. Dr. Maurice Boigey wrote *Sylvie*, an update of *Sophie* which went through several editions in the 1920s. Although Boigey was progressive in certain regards, he simply modernized Rousseau's moralizing vision of women. He accepted career women if they remembered that they were "above all, consolers of men and ministers of human love." Boigey contrasted Sylvie to "those fearful monsters of women, . . . who abandon themselves to certain . . . perversions" and to Suzanne, a feminist, with feminists being characterized as women who "lack men."[35]

Simultaneous with the scientific and popular discourse on sexuality, there were literary and journalistic debates about gender. In the *fin de siècle*, single women pursuing higher education and preparing for careers inspired novels such as *The Future Eve* (1888) and *The New Eve* (1896), which predicted a new age of independent women. However, the male authors were denigrated as *vaginards*. Literary and dramatic caricatures of *garçonnettes* who either died childless or reformed and had children were popular. As Elaine Showalter argues, "In periods of cultural insecurity, when there are fears of regression and degeneration, the longing for strict border controls around the definition of gender, as well as race, class, and nationality, becomes especially intense."[36] By the early twentieth century, feminists drew fire. Journalists and public lecturers attacked feminist dress reformers (*bloomeristes*) for menacing the ideal Frenchwoman—the mother of a family—and threatened that women swayed by feminist crusades would become "hybrid beings, clothed in a grotesque masculinity."[37]

More literary and journalistic furor about gender followed in the wake of the First World War. Deconstructing journalism, novels, and natalist propaganda, Mary Louise Roberts discerns much angst about independent, single, childless women, balanced against admiration for married mothers of large families. Roberts shows that novels such as the best-seller *La Garçonne* released anxieties about women who wore masculine clothing and sported boyish hairstyles becoming mannish, only to reassure readers by revealing the unhappy and sterile lives of these women.[38] Well into the 1930s, doctors told cautionary tales about feminists wanting independence and ending up alone and unhappy. Dr. Vauchet explained why: "The enigmatic character of the woman is not only a product of collective culture; above all, it is rooted in a very special physiological economy, very different from the man." This economy was unstable because of nerves and menstrual cycling.[39]

Ideals of feminine beauty intruded in this scientific and cultural discourse. In Europe, as in other patriarchal civilizations, beauty ideals are defined primarily for men's pleasure and are camouflaged as "natural." In medieval Europe, scholastic literature made no distinction between physical beauty and moral goodness. The Church Fathers treated cosmetics as the devil's invention because they embellished appearance. As Ben Love remarks, "For women of medieval and early modern Europe, beauty was, therefore, not so much a physical trait as a behavioral one, tied to the twin notions of morality and moderation."[40] Even in the 1930s, remnants of this conception of feminine beauty remained in church-inspired manuals for married women. By then, however, manuals written by Catholic laywomen put as much emphasis on cosmetically enhanced external appearance as they did on the "soul."[41] In the seventh edition of the authoritative French dictionary, published in 1879, the entry for *beauty* mentioned *bonté* or the moral quality of kindness but concentrated on visible manifestations that "please the eyes." By the eighth edition, published in 1933, moral qualities had disappeared from the definition of *beauty*.[42]

Since the Middle Ages, physical appearance and cosmetics had been re-evaluated several times. In the sixteenth century, etiquette books reinterpreted the creation story to mean that women were placed on earth to please men and hence should cultivate their physical attractiveness. In the seventeenth and eighteenth centuries, aristocrats of both sexes powdered their faces as well as their wigs; their obvious cosmetics, along with their luxurious clothing, distinguished them from other social groups. Scorning aristocratic idleness and ostentatious display, the eighteenth-century philosophes encouraged "natural" beauty, but only for women.[43] For most of the nineteenth century, bourgeois people associated conspicuous white powder and colored cosmetics with actors,[44] who were treated as pariahs, and actresses, who were presumed to be promiscuous.[45]

In the 1860s, as part of his critique of the philosophes' reification of nature, the poet Baudelaire declared that women had a duty to improve nature, and it did not matter if the "artifice" was apparent.[46] His decadent reputation and philosophical approach made little impression on "decent" women. In the 1880s and 1890s, cultural critics such as the Goncourt brothers and Octave Uzanne delineated the idea of "fatal" beauty, in which cosmetics were a necessary if mildly fraudulent element. According to Miraille Dottin-Orsini, these literary men popularized terms such as the *eternal feminine* and *femininity*,[47] and according to Rose Fortassier, they and their peers elevated the *Parisienne* into an alluring archetype.[48] Giovanni Boldini painted and exhibited portraits of fashionable *Parisiennes* such as Mme. Charles Max, who seemed, to aesthete and critic of the day Robert de Montesquiou, a "modern universal feminine" of elegance and chic[49] (see Fig.1.).

Although aesthetes' nebulous ideas about the eternal feminine confused even intelligent women such as Clara Malraux,[50] popular novels and plays conveyed the significance of physical appeal to women. In the last two decades of the nineteenth century, French plays and novels about *Parisiennes* presented their heroines as naturally plain yet alluring thanks to their attire, accessories, and cosmetics.[51] In 1913 and 1923, Charles and Anne-Marie Lalo published studies of the heroines of French novels which showed that all, even "feminist" heroines, had to look lovely to be loved.[52] In response to the Lalos's thesis, journalists interviewed attractive women on what constituted true beauty. One popular stage actress, Mlle. Polaire, modestly and properly attributed her beauty to personal cleanliness, good health, and grooming. In her autobiography, *Polaire By Herself* (1933), she was more honest about the role of her youthful looks, smooth complexion, and slender waist.[53]

1. Portrait of Madame Charles Max (1896)
by Giovani Boldini. *Musée d'Orsay*

Beginning in the 1880s, a new genre of advice literature explicated the new beauty ideals for bourgeois women. In *The Woman in Paris* (1894) Octave Uzanne argued that the *Parisienne* "pleased" through elegance, fashion, and style. Although Uzanne was part of the revival of the *style moderne,* with its penchant for aristocratic women as objets d'art, he reassured bourgeois women that they could manage on fifteen hundred francs a year. In *The Art and Artifice of Beauty* (ca. 1900), Uzanne flattered bourgeois women by asserting that they were "healthier, cleaner, less made up than their ancestors" and absolved cosmetics of moral turpitude by calling them health as well as beauty products.[54] Many physicians published health and beauty guides that stressed cleansing for complexion care but grudgingly accepted powder and rouge (which contained toxic ingredients).[55] Concurrently, women with genuine or bogus aristocratic titles wrote beauty books rehabilitating powder and rouge as distinguished (as it had been on aristocratic women) if discreet (as it would have to be on bourgeois women).[56] More democratic beauty guides appeared in the following decades. By the 1930s, a Dr. Payot was claiming (with considerable exaggeration) that "all working women wear makeup. For the first time in history, beauty is not the preserve of a privileged class."[57] The conflation of comeliness with cosmetics is striking.

Beauty contests, beauty institutes, and cosmetics companies flourished alongside this publishing phenomenon. The first French contests and institutes emerged in the 1890s. Unlike earlier pageants in the United States, which involved stage presentations, an illustrated magazine published photographs of the faces of beautiful women (mainly actresses and dancers) and asked readers to vote for their favorites.[58] In the same decade, many women ceased to concoct all their cosmetics at home or to have them specially prepared in pharmacies. An 1899 catalog listed 16 lip rouges and 14 eyebrow and eyelid darkeners.[59] By 1936, Paris alone had 66 beauty institutes and 101 cosmetic companies.[60] Their advertisements filled the pages of women's magazines, constituting another source of information about women's bodies for this book.

This swell of beauty consciousness coincided with and commented upon the second wave of feminism and "new women." Like many antifeminists, Octave Uzanne labeled feminists and "bluestockings" ugly and unfeminine.[61] The most positive beauty counselor—the Baroness d'Orchamps—stated that feminism was a "revolt of the feminine soul against some abuses of masculine power," whereas the most hostile—the Countess Tramar—warned that feminists wanted to make women into hermaphrodites.[62] In the interwar, most beauty advisors, such as Lucie Delarue-Mardrus, took an intermediary line. Delarue-Mardrus admitted the progress of feminism but denied that it satisfied "woman": "her power and happiness are still and will long remain, to please."[63]

Many feminists were drawn into the discourse about beauty.[64] In the 1890s, when the feminist daily *La Fronde* canvassed readers about the meaning of beauty, most respondents emphasized that *beauté* implied *bonté*. Already, however, *La Fronde* accepted advertisements for hair dyes, perfumes, and an (already discredited) thyroid extract to stay thin. A decade later, another feminist journal asserted that "moral elegance produces physical elegance" yet ran a regular column on beauty secrets.[65] By 1914, a supporter of women's suffrage wrote a beauty guide justifying cosmetics: "if we are happier because we are prettier, more masterful, and more gracious."[66] In response to greater emphasis on youth and physical appeal after the war, feminist journalists such as Suzanne Balitrand continued to express interest in "keeping up our physical attractions."[67]

Method

This book began with a paradox. While reading industrial hygienists' studies of women's work for a previous project on labor legislation in Third Republic France, I noticed internal inconsistencies, even within single-authored studies. Most of these experts declared women weak and sickly yet described them putting in long hours of paid labor as well as doing unpaid housework and childcare. In the book I wrote on labor legislation, I account for this anomaly by the experts' predilection for sex-specific standards, their status as bourgeois men, and their projection of the bourgeois ideal of femininity onto working-class women. Without doubting the importance of ideological, class, and gender blinders, I decided to explore medical perspectives on women's bodies. My first foray into the secondary literature compounded the problem. Edward Shorter's *A History of Women's Bodies* claimed that women were sickly because they were "victimized" by faulty reproductive systems and their own stubborn traditionalism.[68] Even after compensating for Shorter's denial of women's agency, I remained disturbed by his passive depiction of women's bodies as well as his contention that modern medicine emancipated women.

Subsequent histories of medicine in relation to women relieved me of the necessity to refute Shorter, although comparison of his treatment of any subject also covered in this book would reveal significant differences. Few passages of this book discuss illness; no passage scorns popular or folkloric understanding of the female body. Wherever possible, I have avoided passive, often geographical, metaphors about women's bodies. These metaphors are endemic in medical texts and in many studies of women's body based upon biomedical evidence.[69] Most of this book is not organized anatomically, by body part, or physiologically, by organic process. Instead, Part One analyzes types of knowledge about the female body, and Parts Two and Three are arranged phenomenologically and culturally, according to stages in the reproductive cycle and other physical abilities as experienced by girls and women and as understood in their time.

To get an idea of what literate Frenchwomen learned about their bodies between the 1880s and 1930s, I studied the school texts and self-help manuals available to girls and women. Once again, I discovered contradictions, mainly about sexuality and reproduction. At the suggestion of Linda Clark, I read dozens of textbooks in natural science, domestic economy, and hygiene at the Institute Pédagogique. These textbooks gave detailed instructions about all aspects of personal hygiene except intimate or pubic care. Although the texts alluded to girls' future maternity, and the curriculum eventually included infant care, the school system did not provide information about sex or birth. Similarly, women's health and sexual advice literature stressed women's reproductive role but offered little practical information about sexual intercourse. To learn about the physical abilities of girls and women, I explored the physical education texts and the voluminous debate about gymnastics for girls and sports for women at the Institute d'Education Physique et Sportive. Even the most supportive texts and tracts expressed doubts about the abilities of girls and women because of their reproductive functions.

Still seeking what women might have absorbed from experts, I focused on popular fiction and autobiographies written by and for women. After much sifting, many of the anecdotes and quotations came from semiautobiographical novels by Colette, who also wrote nonfiction on feminine beauty and physical culture. Guided by Philippe Lejeune and Leah Hewitt,[70] I chose twenty-four autobiographies and journals written between 1880 and 1940 by Frenchwomen. Although most of the autobiographies written for publication were reticent about the authors' bodies, their reserve seems to reflect the mixed and often negative messages prevalent in the Third Republic about female bodies.

The most candid texts were private journals, especially those written by Catherine Pozzi between 1896 and 1934 and edited and published by Claire

Paulhan in 1987 and 1995.[71] Catherine Pozzi's upbringing as the daughter of the first chair in gynecology at the Paris Medical Faculty and her advanced studies in physiology informed her observations of the female body. She also related to her body as a girl and woman suffering from tuberculosis, a common but socially unacceptable disease. Her body awareness and less than deferential attitude toward medicine and physiology provided astute commentary on many subjects in this book.

The first two volumes of Simone de Beauvoir's memoirs recounting the story of her girlhood and early adulthood broke the silence about intimate bodily experiences. She was mute about her abortion, which was still illegal when she published these two volumes in 1957 and 1966. (For these generations of women, abortion, like family violence, remains the body's secret.)[72] Beauvoir's unhappy memories of her first menstruation and her comparative optimism about forthcoming menopause are noted in Part Two as examples of negative attitudes toward the female reproductive cycle. Elsewhere, I analyze Beauvoir's survey of biology in *The Second Sex*. Like historians before me,[73] I find that her famous statement—that one is not born, but becomes a woman—fails to deliver the promised cultural interpretation of the female body. According to philosophers, her commitment to individual consciousness did not allow for cultural any more than it allowed for biological determinism.[74] I would add this: although she challenged the most egregious forms of reproductive reductionism, she never seriously interrogated the profoundly natalist biomedical scholarship of her era. Ironically, the most famous egalitarian feminist in the world viewed the female body through a very conventional, natalist lens. Conversely, if contemporary French feminists such as Julia Kristeva and Luce Irigaray (who are often labeled essentialists) are only dealing with the female body metaphorically and symbolically,[75] they do not uncouple their analysis of femininity from the European tradition of fixating upon certain, primarily reproductive parts of the female body.

PART I

Carnal Knowledge

—◦❧ • ❧◦—

IT IS NAIVE to believe that historians can flesh out the sizes and shapes of human bodies in the past from the idealized images in visual art or the incomplete records of height, weight, and corporeal dimensions. The difficulties multiply when the subjects are nineteenth- or early twentieth-century women. Artistic anatomy and morphology, which compared the human figure with "real" bodies, only focused on women's figures and bodies to spotlight variations from male figures and bodies. Most corporeal measurements come from military recruitment records that excluded or at least did not recognize women. The nineteenth-century sciences of anthropometry and anthropology measured far fewer women than men, and those women were mainly for comparison with "the male prototype."[1] Although these scientists had too few female subjects to make meaningful comparisons, they did so with these small samples and larger samples of men, usually to the detriment of women.

Because the pursuit of "accurate" data may distract us from establishing what French scientists, hygienists, and women knew about women's bodies, let us begin with the most reliable figures compiled in the Third Republic. In 1911, two morphologists, A. Marie and L. Mac-Auliffe of the Ecole des Hautes Etudes, made the by-then standard fourteen measurements of several hundred French people, including 255 women. Unlike most previous and many subsequent scientific or literary accounts, which reduced women's bodies to woman's body, Marie and MacAuliffe acknowledged the heterogeneity of women's physiques. Equally unusually, they reported how modest the average sex differences were. The biggest difference was two and three-quarters inches in height. The second biggest difference was less than an inch in the arm span. Their female subjects ranged in height from four feet six and a half inches to five feet eleven and a half inches[2]—a wider range than the four feet nine inches to five feet eight inches of the 140 Frenchwomen studied by Suzanne de Félice in the late 1940s.[3]

Other problems with the quest for accurate depictions of women's bodies stem from assumptions that statistics are neutral. Joshua Cole showed how standard fertility indexes, introduced in the 1860s and refined in the 1880s, gendered responsibility for reproduction. In the 1880s, preeminent French demographer Louis-August Bertillon (1821–83), adjusted the gross index of births over the female population into the net rate of births to women of childbearing age and the rate of births to married women of childbearing age. Aside from eliding men, all three ratios "effaced the individual woman's social and cultural context from the demographic equation by default." Historians must also correct the original researchers' gendered interpretations. In the 1890s, Bertillon's son Jacques (1851–1922) and other natalists used fertility indexes to "prove" that the declining birth rate was caused by women putting their well-being ahead of the national interest. Cole correlates acceptance of the asymmetrical assignment of responsibility for reproduction to nineteenth-century biological thinking.[4]

In Chapter 1 of this book I outline how sexual dichotomies took root in the natural sciences and how scientific dichotomies spread to the public. Philosophers of science have disclosed that scientists use metaphors not just as heuristic devices, but as "constituent elements of scientific theory."[5] In France, natural scientists employed "culturally endorsed metaphors" that made their measurements of women's bodies understandable to the public but also enmeshed their measurements in arbitrary interpretations about intelligence and reproductive functions. Physical anthropologists posited a resemblance between European women and "inferior" races as defined by a tiny minority of European men in the nineteenth century. Physical anthropologists also discerned similarities to animals and children in other supposedly "natural" hierarchies.

Starting with the eighteenth-century father of natural science, I identify how scientific reasoning about women's bodies reflected and reinforced prevailing beliefs about gender hierarchies. One way was casual borrowing from other privileged realms of knowledge about women's bodies, notably art. The social composition of the scientific and artistic communities also explains the distortions in scientific and artistic representations of women. Scientists and artists functioned in a milieu that included few women other than anonymous assistants and little-known models. Despite women's difficulties accessing scientific and artistic study, they encountered scientific and artistic popularizations, notably through health and beauty manuals and women's magazines.

In Chapter 2 I analyze biomedical perspectives on the body as biopolitical approaches to human bodies. David Le Breton defines the modern Western body as separate from other people and from the individual subject: even though the body is "the sign of the individual," the individual is often dissociated from his body. Le Breton contrasts this to African rural societies in which "the person is not limited by the contours of his body" but is "a knot of relationships." He links modern Western notions about the body to the status of biology and medicine as "a sort of official knowledge about the body" since the eighteenth century.[6] Although influenced by Foucault, Le Breton has not incorporated Foucault's thesis about the biomedical compulsion to classify. In *The History of Sexuality,* Foucault explores classification by sex "with the great series of binary oppositions (body/soul, flesh/spirit, instinct/reason, drives/consciousness) that seemed to require annexing sex to a field of rationality." He argues that one strategy to bring sex under the sway of science was the "saturation" of women's bodies with sexuality, putting them "in organic communication with the social body, the family space, and the life of children."[7] Defined this way, women's bodies were not separate from family and society, not individuals as defined in the West.

To understand this fusion of women's bodies with the species, in Chapter 2 I trace the acceptance of organic medicine and the emergence of endocrinology in the Third Republic. In the 1880s and 1890s, researchers were replacing centuries-old ideas about the uterus as the definitive female organ and nineteenth-century notions of the ovary as the "fundamental part of the female." The new theories posited the sex cells as the essential sex determinant. One challenge in studying contemporary medicine is the proliferation of medical specialties. Fortunately, for the study of women's bodies in the Third Republic, the critical development was the rise of endocrinology, which linked newly discovered hormones with sexuality. Finally, in this chapter I indicate how biomedical visions of women's bodies reached women. Because consultations with doctors were increasingly confidential, the major sources of information for this book are the burgeoning number of women's health manuals.

In Chapter 3 I chart the campaign to instill Pasteurian hygiene and its associated corporeal care to the nurses, mothers, and "future mothers" who would implement and inculcate domestic and personal cleanliness in the home. In addition to introducing hygiene into nursing and girls school curricula, hygienists published health and beauty manuals and columns in women's magazines. Together with the growing number of advertisements for household and personal hygiene products, these media created an impression that femininity implied cleanliness, comeliness, and the consumption of a wide variety of products. To persuade housewives and mothers to adopt new standards of cleanliness, they supplemented appeals about improving family health with pitches about enhancing individual beauty and status.

Chapter 1

Embodying Gender

SINCE the eighteenth century, the natural sciences and visual arts have been privileged fields for the observation of women's bodies and the production of knowledge about them. Both naturalists and artists have viewed women's bodies through a lens warped by gender assumptions and artistic ideals of feminine beauty. Because both fields were male dominated before and during the Third Republic, few women challenged scientific or artistic depictions of the female body. Most Frenchwomen learned scientific and artistic representations of the female body through scientific and artistic popularization. This chapter surveys the scientific and artistic representations of women's bodies disseminated, after some delay, to the French public between the 1880s and the 1930s.

Putting "Woman" in Her Place

Natural historians, who flourished in the late eighteenth century, collected and classified flora and fauna. Londa Schiebinger shows that they also sought sexual bipolarity throughout nature. In zoology, Carl Linnaeus (1707–78) introduced the term *mammalian,* in which a female characteristic (lactating mamma) linked humans to other mammals, whereas an allegedly male characteristic (reason) separated *Homo sapiens* from all animals. After Linnaeus classified plants by their pistils, stamens, and other parts that appeared to be analogous to human sex organs (1735), most botanists structured their taxonomies sexually. By employing sexual metaphors to describe plant reproduction, these botanists "imported notions about sexual hierarchy."[1] In turn, human biologists—and their popularizers—applied botanical terminology to female body parts and used floral metaphors to describe the female genitalia.

The pioneer French naturalist Georges-Louis Leclerc, Comte de Buffon (1707–88), found fault with aspects of Linnaean taxonomy such as the inclusion of humans (bipeds) in the quadruped category. Buffon was skeptical about arguments confusing sexual and gender traits and warned about masculine bias in scientific analysis. After a review of the protracted debate about the existence of a hymen, he concluded (incorrectly) that this tiny membrane did not exist and dismissed arguments that an intact hymen was physical proof of virginity: "Men, jealous of their primacy in everything, have always made a big deal about everything they believed they possessed first and exclusively: this sort of madness has made girls' virginity into a real thing." Buffon's interpretation of scientific intentions in studying these issues could be applied to much subsequent research on women's bodies: "men have wanted to find in nature what existed only in their imaginations."[2]

Despite his skepticism on some sexual subjects, Buffon expressed and therefore enforced prevailing beliefs about gender hierarchies in his influential book on human biology. Noticing that girls reached puberty sooner than boys did, he deduced that this was why women's bodies were shorter and softer than men's bodies. His comparisons of men's and women's bodies resembled contemporary art theorists' dicta on male and female nudes: "A well-made man's body should be squared; the muscles must be clearly visible. . . . In the woman everything is more rounded; the forms gentler; the traits finer. Man has strength and majesty; grace and beauty are the accessories of the other sex." Reasoning tautologically—apparently from nature to social institutions but actually from social institutions to nature—Buffon contended that "men's natural state after puberty is that of marriage." Retaining seminal liquids caused "irritations so violent, that reason and religion would hardly be sufficient to resist these impetuous passions."[3]

Generations of natural scientists who paid homage to Buffon abandoned his relatively dispassionate approach to sex differences. The next generation, called *moral physiologists,* sought sexual dichotomies throughout the body and deliberately confounded them with what they called *moral,* but what we call *gender,* attributes. In *Woman's Physical and Moral System* (1775), Pierre Roussel chided earlier anatomists for fixating on the reproductive organs. Citing recent findings that women have more soft tissue and a faster pulse rate than men, Roussel inferred that "a certain weakness contributes to the perfection of woman," making her tender, compassionate, imaginative, and capricious. Into the twentieth century, scientists quoted Roussel on women's fragile bodies and sensitive character.[4]

Another book that was cited into the twentieth century, *The Natural History of Women* (1803), identified a trait to distinguish women from female quadrupeds: the vaginal canal, which was horizontal in quadrupeds, was vertical in women (because they stood erect). According to the author, Dr. Moreau de la Sarthe, the vertical disposition of the vaginal canal accounted for women's difficulty giving birth.[5] Two decades later, a scientific popularizer, J. J. Virey, added that the upright position caused blood to flood women's sex organs, producing more intense activity than animals' sex organs.[6] These two propositions set off a biomedical discourse about women as problematic reproducers "saturated" with sexuality. Neither of these scientists, nor any of their successors, considered that they themselves might have problems with the combination of female sexuality and fertility.

If anatomical or physiological evidence of sexual dichotomies was not available, these physiologists and their followers shifted to stereotypes or inferences from history. Because anatomy had "not *yet* been able to discover obvious dissimilarities between the structure of men's and women's sense organs" [my italics], Moreau de la Sarthe extrapolated from stereotypes about women's love of perfume that women had a more refined sense of smell. Because brain differences were "too small or too hidden to find," he surmised from unspecified "history" that women had never made great scientific discoveries, and he attributed this to their physical constitution (although he admitted that their education, prejudice, and custom might be implicated).[7] Even in the twentieth century, when medical scientists conducted more rigorous investigations of corporeal differences, they casually introduced gender stereotypes and vague historical references into passages of careful calibrations as if the former had the same scientific weight as the latter. In *Gynecological Physiology* (1929), Dr. Henri Vignes inserted trite statements about feminine excitability and "natural disposition to modesty" into passages detailing sex differences in bone density and blood composition. In his contribution to a state-of-the-art text, *Sexual Physiology* (1931), Dr. Watrin evoked "history" in the abstract as proof that "feminism" had never "created a Pascal or a Descartes."[8]

Emulating Buffon, Roussel posited that women "differ less than man from the primitive constitution" and always retained "something of the child's temperament."[9] By the 1830s, biologists suggested that the term *evolution,* which to that point had been employed to describe the phases of embryonic development, be applied to the successive appearance of species on earth. Later biologists formulated recapitulation theories that individuals, like species, passed through stages of evolution, with some not reaching as high a stage.[10] Stephen Jay Gould found that French recapitulationists were fascinated with dubious signs of arrested development in non-Caucasian races, which they read as evidence of a racial hierarchy.[11] However, these theorists evinced almost as much interest in equally questionable signs of arrested development in European women, which they interpreted as indications of sexual hierarchy.

Virey stirred racial theories into the brew.[12] For his gross generalizations about black women, Virey drew upon Baron Georges Cuvier (1769–1832), known in France as the "legislator of science."[13] Cuvier, a comparative anatomist, conducted a public autopsy of Saartje Baartman, a Boschiman woman from the Kalahari Desert who had been exhibited throughout Europe for five years before she died in 1815. Cuvier's account of Baartman's autopsy accorded a lot of space to her long (four-inch) labia or genital lips. After he presented her excised genitals to the academy, they were displayed in the Museum of Man in Paris. As Sander Gilman showed, Baartman's parts became "the central image for the black female [in Europe] throughout the nineteenth century." This fixation on Baartman's extended labia reflected European construction of "primitive" sexual appetite and, more generally, their construction of female sexuality as pathological. Later French physiologists sought distended labia on the bodies of European prostitutes in hope of distinguishing prostitutes from respectable women. When they failed to find somatic differences, they sought the effects of "overstimulation" of the genitalia, although this quest was equally abortive.[14]

Illustrations of "normal" labia were commonplace in texts on obstetrics and gynecology. The detail in these drawings differentiates them from the proliferation of indistinct pornographic photos of the sexual triangle.[15] There were virtually no "artistic" representations of the external genitalia of European women. Even Degas's etchings of prostitutes which focus on the sexual triangle are vague about the genitalia, often because they are concealed by pubic hair. As Freud remarked in *Three Essays on Sexuality,* if [the European conception of feminine] beauty is related to sexual attraction, the genitals themselves are not judged to be beautiful. Rather, the artist diverts the viewers' gaze to the secondary sexual characteristics, notably the hips, buttocks, and breasts.[16] Presumably this tradition also diverted women's gaze from their own genitalia. Certainly the health, beauty, and sex manuals analyzed in subsequent chapters paid far more attention to internal reproductive organs than to external genitalia.

Cuvier's account of Baartman's autopsy also paid attention to her "protruding buttocks," which he dissected to discover "an elastic and quivering mass."[17] Baartman's steatopygia, which was an adaptation to the nutritional vagaries of nomadic life in the Kalahari Desert, was interpreted erotically and exotically. She was the original model for a series of statues and drawings which became known, collectively, as the Hottentot Venus. The ethnographic statues and photos of Boschiman women disclose little about them as representatives of their cultures but much about the racial stereotyping and sexual projections of European artists and viewers.[18]

French artists, scientists, and members of the general public had ambiguous views about body fat, especially that around the hips. With the exception of a Courbet painting, *The Source*, nineteenth-century French nudes were not pear shaped. When Degas looked "for a definitive syntax for the brothel prostitute's body," he had to invent a body that would match the occupation. Breaking with the conventions of the female nude, Degas devised an anatomy of thick, swollen bodies. The brothel monotypes are smudgy, the figures blurry.[19] In her study of the female nude, Linda Nead suggests that the fleshiness and fuzzy outlines of prostitute bodies reflect a fear of fat as excess, a false boundary, in the artistic esthetic.[20]

Conversely, Peter Stearns demonstrates that French medical researchers were not critical of fat per se (as opposed to obesity, which they condemned for medical, not esthetic, reasons). As Stearns also notes, some *fin-de-siècle* beauty advisors actually encouraged *enbonpoint*, or "a pleasing roundness."[21] However, Stearns fails to note that the same advisors called large, fleshy hips "disgraceful."[22] These authors hint at a changing ideal of female torsos, from a curvilinear to a smoother shape. Already a fervent cyclist and doctor, Mme. Gache-Sarraute had designed a more pliant corset. With the introduction of the tubular line in women's clothing before the Great War, stiff corsets fell out of fashion (see Fig. 2). Often forgotten in the celebration of their demise is their replacement by elastic foundation garments called *girdles*, which constricted the abdomen, hips, and buttocks.[23] Other, allegedly healthier, alternatives to the girdle included dieting to lose weight, a practice that certainly increased, and systematic exercise, which (we will see) did not thrive as much as the promoters of physical culture claimed. Ideally, diet and exercise were supposed to realize the new ideal: a slimmer, more androgynous body.[24]

Heads and Hips

Londa Schiebinger's study of eighteenth-century depictions of female skeletons uncovered significant distortions. Ironically, one of very few female anatomists, Marie Thiroux d'Arconville, drew the female skeleton that most

2. Photograph of Corset-fourreau Berthe Sauvigny,
23 avril 1905. *Archives de Paris, Cl. Françoise Rivière*

distorted the parts of the body which emerged "as sites of political debate: the skull as a mark of intelligence and the pelvis as a measure of womanliness." Thiroux d'Arconville inaccurately represented the female skull as smaller in relation to the thorax than the male skull. Perhaps because her model was a skeleton of a corseted woman, she depicted the thorax as a triangular cone, in which the tiny lower rib cage visually accentuated the breadth of the pelvis. By the early nineteenth century, anatomists preferred the drawings of German anatomist Samuel von Soemmerring, who represented the female cranium as larger in relation to the trunk and who did not reduce the size of the lower rib cage.[25] Nevertheless, subtler skeletal sexualization continued. A medical dictionary published in 1887 listed forty-three differences between the skeletons of men and women, not counting disparities that allegedly varied by race.[26]

One kind of distortion arose from privileging the "ideal" female skeleton. Von Soemmerring's model was the skeleton of a twenty-year-old woman whose skull did not satisfy him, so he drew in another skull. For the proportions of the skeleton, he checked the classical statues of the *Venus de Medici* and *Venus of Dresden,* with their moderately rounded hips and buttocks. Instead of using live female models, students in early nineteenth-century drawing classes sketched the female statues of Greek antiquity which were in the Louvre. From midcentury, the Ecole des Beaux-Arts and artists' studios used artistic photographs of nude female models to teach life drawing. Most of the models were professionals selected for their approximation to the classical female form.[27] Paul Gerdy of the Faculty of Medicine, author of the first text on female anatomy which was written for artists (published in 1829), waxed eloquent about the masterpieces in the Louvre but said little about the bodies of living women.[28] For ninety years, this was the only French-language text on female anatomy for artists.

In the nineteenth century, artistic canons that a well-proportioned male body was seven to nine times as long as the head (depending upon the theorist) and a vogue for phrenology, which mapped the contours of the skull to determine character, drew attention to the head and skull. Because women's head-to-height ratio did not fit any male canon, Gerdy calculated a feminine version by measuring the heads on ancient statues and in Renaissance portraits. He compared his measurements with phrenological maps of female skulls and deduced that the artists "captured" women's deeper eye sockets but not the bulges on their foreheads. After noting similarities between the brows of women and children, Gerdy made the freighted comment that women and children had "many physical and moral relations with one another."[29]

In 1920, Dr. Paul Richer, an instructor at the Ecole des Beaux-Arts and author of six texts on artistic anatomy, published the second French text on female anatomy for artists. In what was intended as an "exclusively scientific work," Richer compared "normal" women with "normal" men. Although Richer confirmed prominent parietal bones on women's skulls, he made no equation to bumps on the foreheads of children. He did note that the upper jawbone, or mandible, was larger that the lower jawbone in the skulls of women and children but eschewed the (by then usual) hierarchical assertion about women and children sharing prognotheism, or projecting jaws, with apes.[30]

By the end of the First World War, phrenology had fallen into disfavor, and (most) representational artists rejected artistic canons of harmonious proportions.[31] As Gunter Merken and Linda Nochlin show, the gradual disappearance of the skin as the natural boundary of the body, which began with the shaky and blurry lines of the female bathers in the works of Degas, was pushed to its limits in prewar Cubism. The fragmented female figures in the works of Manet and Degas became the bodily fragments, including mutilated dolls and "collapsible" women, of interwar surrealists.[32] High art no longer offered recognizable ideals of feminine beauty.

After a century and a half of calibrations, anatomists ceased to accentuate the other frequently measured skeletal site, the female pelvis. By the early twentieth century, biomedical objections to anatomical amplification of the pelvis reached the public in a mounting campaign against corsets. In his study of the corset, Dr. O'Fallowell presented x-rays of the female thorax to show that it did not form an acute angle terminating in a tiny lower rib cage, which in turn exaggerated the apparent swell of the pelvis.[33] This was one of a myriad of ways that the advent of radiography (available since 1895) changed European sensibilities about the body.[34] Of course, eliminating ladies' foundation garments would take more than x-rays.

In morphology, interest in women's hips and buttocks was constant. Beginning in the early 1800s, morphologists made typologies of human bodies based on the prominence of certain organs or tissues. Most believed that fat tissue was the distinctive female feature.[35] In 1902, for his doctoral thesis, Dr. Paul Clergeau did a meta-analysis of the scholarly literature on this subject. Clergeau identified as "distinctively feminine" the greater depth and wider distribution of subcutaneous fat, paler skin color, and greater localization of hair on women's bodies compared with men's bodies. He considered the fat deposits in the breasts, stomach, hips, and buttocks to be sexual adaptations that excited men's esthetic—by which he and many other scholars meant erotic—impulses. He explicitly rejected theories that women were childlike or incomplete men in favor of sexual dimorphism and the adage that "opposites attract."[36]

In 1918, an eminent endocrinologist and gynecologist, Félix Jayle, abandoned his attempt to compare the artistic canon with mathematically precise norms for the female body, explaining that most anthropological measurements were of men and that the best evidence about women came from cadavers. By correlating girth with height for both sexes in his *Morphological Anatomy of Woman*, Jayle disproved "received wisdom" that the pelvises of women are wider than those of men, as opposed to appearing wider because of their proximity to a smaller lower rib cage. Massaging anthropological data into an "index of robustness"—the dimensions of the shoulders over those of the hips—he inferred that men's "superior" shoulder dimensions were the result of greater height, not their sex. If Jayle disproved certain prejudices about hips, however, he was a natalist who believed human beings had a duty to reproduce.[37] He documented and recognized some feminine sexual traits. Because wide hips did not correlate with height, he labeled them a feminine sexual trait. He also discovered that women had an "accentuated" curve in the lumbar spine which explained why their buttocks projected more than men's did.[38]

Jayle classified European women's bodies by the distribution of subcutaneous fat tissue. In the regular type, evenly distributed fat rounded the body; in the slim type, the layer of fat was so thin that bone and muscle relief showed. The fat type was subdivided into a subtype with generalized fat and one with localized fat, the latter illustrated by a drawing of a female figure with a slender upper body and "padded hips and buttocks."[39] In 1935, another prominent endocrinologist and gynecologist, Dr. André Binet, published the *Medico-Artistic Morphology of Woman*, which described this padding as "an unsavory opulence." However, he added, "like all exaggerations of a feminine sexual trait, this deformation serves . . . to excite the male libido."[40] Although André Binet knew that fleshy hips and buttocks signified an accumulation of fat for reproductive purposes, he did not stress this in the sections on the hips and buttocks in his morphology. Yet like most gynecologists who wrote about women's bodies in the Third Republic, he was a natalist.[41] His contradictory position on women's hips and buttocks represents one of many paradoxes in the scientific vision of women's bodies.

Stature and Intellect

With the rise of statistical consciousness came a new science of anthropometry, or the study of body proportions. In the 1830s, Belgian statistician A. D. Quetelet calibrated the height and shape of several hundred Belgian men and women of different ages. Over the next forty years, he presented dozens of tables of average heights, girths, and dimensions of body parts, arranged by sex and age. His sex ratios (women's measurements over the paradigmatic measurements) confirmed some customary knowledge: on average, men were taller and broader across the shoulders, and women were proportionally broader around the hips. To explain the differences, Quetelet made convoluted and conservative inferences: "We can only admire these convenient proportions: the man, defender of women, in whom agility is necessary, seems to have the proportions best suited to the facility of movement. On the contrary, in the woman, who is the hope of the future of the family, the construction seems to guarantee solidity and stability."[42]

As early as 1876, Paul Topinard, a French anthropologist, revealed that Quetelet "simplified" his classification of data on height by assigning all data on tall subjects whose sex was not recorded to the tall-men category. Topinard also reported "discordant" findings that one group of colonial women was slightly taller, on average, than their menfolk were. He reassured readers that the reason for the "aberration" was that the researchers had gathered information on only twenty-nine women versus ninety-five men (an asymmetry that had gone unnoticed as long as the results validated gender stereotypes).[43] Nevertheless, biomedical studies of "woman" quoted Quetelet's sex ratios into the 1920s.[44]

By the 1880s, anthropologists applied formidable evolutionary theories to scanty evidence. Dr. Henri Thulié's *Woman: An Essay in Physiological Sociology* (1885) took a Darwinian approach. Given prehistoric man's struggle for existence, Thulié held, it was "impossible not to conclude that . . . the male, having physical superiority, alone would count in humanity." Thulié also argued that women were attracted to and selected strong men as sexual partners. As editor of the influential *Philanthropic Review,* Thulié was openly polemical. He insisted that sexual equality did not exist organically or functionally but that gender equivalence did. Women were made to be mothers, and maternity should be honored and protected. Thulié was concerned about high rates of infant mortality and about women's pursuit of "shameful and sterilizing pleasures" like careers and politics. "What," he asked rhetorically, "is a female citizen compared to a fecund woman?"[45]

Few French anthropologists embraced Darwin's theory of sexual selection, which implied that women were responsible for masculine strength by their choice to mate with strong men, finding it more comfortable to believe that "strength and agility are . . . primordial traits of masculine activity."[46] Conversely, many anthropologists adopted the transmission of acquired characteristics then identified as the central tenet of the early nineteenth-century biologist Jean Baptiste de Lamarck (1744–1829).[47] Neo-Lamarckians accepted biological adaptations or acquired characteristics, including what we call gender role behaviors. In 1903, Charles Letourneau contended that woman's "original constitution" was as capable of endurance as early man's had been. Once humans switched to a carnivorous diet, a sexual division of labor began. Hunting, incompatible with maternity and childrearing, developed "violent and ferocious instincts" in men. The fixed abode facilitated lengthy breast-feeding and domesticated women. The two sexes evolved in "diametrically opposed directions, the man becoming more accustomed to resorting to strength and the woman becoming less capable of defending herself."[48]

Late nineteenth-century French anthropology was much occupied with measuring skulls and estimating brain weight from these calibrations. Dr. Paul Broca, founder of the Anthropology Society in 1859 and of the Anthropology School in 1875, was an anatomist specializing in the brain. In addition to identifying the seat of articulate language in the left frontal lobe of the brain, Broca invented new instruments to calibrate skulls and accumulated 500 skulls and 180,000 measurements. Most of his students and colleagues were medical men and anatomists. Broca and his colleagues were notorious for using cranial calibrations as indexes of intelligence and claiming that they demonstrated the intellectual superiority of Europeans. Like the recapitulationists, these anthropologists gathered more information about the skulls of European men and women, made as many inferences about the brains of European men and women, and made equally invidious hierarchical comparisons.[49] According to Broca, the brain was bigger "in men than in women, in eminent men than in men of mediocre talent, in superior races than in inferior races." On the basis of thirteen prehistoric skulls, he suggested that the sexual gap in intelligence increased with the level of "civilization." A colleague, Gustave Le Bon, found that the difference in average cranial capacity between Parisian men and women was nearly double the difference between the [far less numerous] collected skulls of ancient Egypt.[50]

After Broca's death in 1880, one of his students revealed that Broca and Le Bon's comparisons were skewed. Lónce Manouvrier, by then a professor at the Anthropology School, demonstrated that Broca ascribed all craniums above a certain volume to men, much as Quetelet had put all measurements of tall but unidentified subjects into the masculine category. Le Bon used skulls from older female cadavers, ignoring a known atrophy of the brain after the age of sixty. By comparing skulls from male and female cadavers of the same height and age, Manouvrier lowered the estimated weight gap from Le Bon's 172 grams (and Poirier's 148 grams) to 109 grams. By calculating the ratio of brain weight to total body weight, he established the relative superiority of women's brain-to-body weight. "In virtue of her smaller organic mass," Manouvrier maintained, "woman needs less cerebral mass than man to display equal intelligence."[51] Nevertheless, a popular medical book on "woman's body" reported Broca's figures about women's brains (with the qualification that smaller brains did not signify intellectual inferiority) as late as 1905.[52]

One of Manouvrier's students, Madeleine Pelletier, conducted a study of Japanese skeletons and found that those of females had greater cranial capacity in proportion to their height and girth. Instead of arguing female superiority, this egalitarian feminist contended that the crucial variable was size, not sex. Differences between small and large skeletons were more significant than differences between the sexes or among the races. Pelletier rejected the whole exercise of relating intelligence, which she defined as a dynamic of perceptions, sensations, and energy, to an organic mass.[53] Her scholarly article attracted less attention than her cross-dressing lifestyle. A few years later, Paul de Regla, a scientific popularizer, taught that intelligence and imagination derived from the structure and harmony of the brain cells, and women's modest intellectual output was caused by religious and societal constraints. However, de Regla attributed feminine sensibility and suggestibility to fluctuations in blood circulating to the brain (an allusion to menstrual cycling) and pointedly distanced himself from "hysterical . . . women-men who want to be the equal of men."[54]

Once most anthropologists acknowledged that women's brains weighed proportionally more than men's brains, they restaked the claim to women's intellectual inferiority with assertions that women's lower brain was heavier and their spinal tissue more voluminous, making women, like children, "more spinal than cerebral beings."[55] Another response was to compare the two hemispheres of the brain. One study found that the left hemisphere (site of articulate language) weighed more in men, whereas the right hemisphere (site of perceptions) weighed more in women. Even after journalists began to satirize the brain sex school of feminine inferiority,[56] anthropologists discerned affinities between the skulls of women and children. As late as the 1930s, an anatomy text assigned in the Anthropology School included a section on "the sexual characteristics of the cranium." Starting from the seemingly indisputable proposition that the skull, "like nearly all organs, possesses secondary sex characteristics," the authors, Drs. Poirier and Charpy, held that women's skulls appeared more childlike than men's, which implied that some evolutionary processes ended earlier in women than in men.[57] In short, if the details changed, the principle of sexual hierarchy remained.

Representation in Absentia

The rules of admission into the scientific and artistic communities account for the uniformity and distortions of scientific and artistic representations of "woman's" body. Scientists and artists functioned in a masculine milieu that included few women other than anonymous assistants and little-known models. Londa Schiebinger summarizes the situation in eighteenth-century science:

> At a time when women were formally excluded from universities and informally excluded from scientific academies, the female body was consistently observed through the eyes of a socially homogeneous group. Elite European men (and, in the exceptional case of Madame Thiroux d'Arconville, women), sharing common interests and common backgrounds, saw the female body in similar light.[58]

In the following century, few women played any role in science other than social facilitator because of the professionalization of science and the declining status of amateur scientists.[59]

One exception was Clémence Royer (1830–1902), a self-educated philosopher and popularizer of science best known for the controversial preface to her translation of Darwin's *The Origin of Species* in 1862 and as the first Frenchwoman to be elected to a scientific society (the Anthropology Society) in 1870. As Joy Harvey shows, Royer's translation and public lectures introduced many French people to Darwin. Her translation used less aggressive and elitist terminology than the original—for example, "vital competition" for the struggle for existence and "natural election" for natural selection. Because Royer also expressed eugenic and feminist convictions, she was increasingly isolated. In 1873, during a debate with demographer Louis-Adolphe Bertillon, she asserted that women knew how to control their fertility and alluded to future matriarchal societies in which women would "engrave new customs on the solid rock of hereditary instinct." With two neat strokes, she undermined fundamental biosocial assumptions about the essentially reproductive purpose of the female body and a biological imperative of sexual hierarchy. The Anthropology Society, negotiating for funding for a school, refused to publish Royer's paper without revisions, and Royer adamantly refused to make them. By the 1880s, she found it difficult to publish in scientific journals. Instead, from 1897 until her death in 1902 she wrote about science in women's magazines and, notably, in the daily feminist newspaper *La Fronde*.[60]

Beginning in the 1850s, the life sciences relocated to research laboratories at French universities.[61] No woman enrolled in a science faculty until 1867. Admission to the university depended upon having a classical baccalaureate that was not offered by girls secondary schools until 1924. A few thousand French girls graduating from secondary schools (and, very occasionally, from the less academic senior primary schools) obtained dispensations allowing entry to most faculties. The percentage of female undergraduates at French universities rose from three in 1902 to twenty-seven in 1934. Although most co-eds enrolled in letters, surprisingly many enrolled in sciences: 1,778 or 20 percent of all science students in 1934.[62]

But fewer women pursued advanced degrees in science. In 1902, only eight women earned *licenses* (similar to bachelor's degrees) in science from the University of Paris (with half of the university students in France); to that point, the university had awarded four women doctoral degrees in science. Thereafter, the university conferred doctorates on women every year, reaching a total of eight in 1928-29. The provinces lagged far behind.[63]

Few women became professors in science faculties. By 1930, only two women had reached the rank of professor, whereas thirty-eight remained assistants. Although the majority of women with doctorates in science specialized in the natural sciences,[64] no biographies of these women exist. The case of physicist Marie Curie suggests that they encountered much resistance.

Curie was the first woman named to the faculty of the Sèvres Normal School (the elite normal school for women) in 1900 and of the Sorbonne in 1906. She was also the first woman to receive a Nobel Prize in 1903 and the only female laureate in the sciences until 1935. Before she was nominated to the French Academy of Science in 1910, Curie was a member of six foreign academies. Although supporters justified her nomination on strictly scientific grounds, the debate over her candidature focused on what it would mean for gender relations. Inside the academy, debate swirled around the assault to the tradition of masculine solidarity. As one engineer commented in revealingly defensive language: "Something will change at the institute when a woman invades it." Another objection was that Curie's work could not be separated from that of her husband, even though the Curies had always indicated what each partner contributed to a paper; Marie had published papers under her own name, and the students under her direction had been prolific.[65] She was not then elected to the academy.

Outside the academy women debated Marie Curie's nomination. The antifeminist novelist Mme. Regnier contended Mme. Curie was too special "to stoop" to membership in the academy: trying to make women the equal of man would destroy "all that makes for grace, charm, beauty, fantasy."[66] Equal-rights feminists such as Jeanne Deflou responded that the male monopoly of science contributed to "the domination of one sex over the other" and to the false hypothesis that women were incapable of doing science.[67] Generally, the public was averse to women in science. Julia Daudet, widow of novelist Alphonse Daudet, held that science was "useless to women, unless they are the exceptions who are inclined to a masculine career, and that is always too bad." Marius Decrespe, a theorist of the eternally feminine, had explained earlier that women are intuitive and inspirational but incapable of systematic reasoning. The "special functioning of women's sexual organs has a marked effect on her reason."[68]

Although some women had access to art instruction in the nineteenth century, they studied watercolors (not the more prestigious oils) as a "feminine accomplishment." Most of those who persisted, mainly as amateur artists, specialized in domestic subjects, which were disdained by high art until the Impressionists. Long prohibited from life classes, women artists avoided depicting the female nude and usually posed female models, fully clothed, with family members. One artist, Rosa Bonheur (1822–99), preferred to paint landscapes with large draft animals and outdoor work scenes.[69] Even Berthe Morisot, who exhibited at Impressionist and other avant-garde exhibitions in the 1880s, failed in her few attempts at female nudes or (like her contemporary, Mary Cassatt) subverted the genre by showing the nude image reflected from a mirror. According to Anne Higonnet, Morisot rarely identified her work as feminine,[70] nor did she join the Union of Women Painters and Sculptors founded by seventy women artists in 1881 because the Society of French Artists was "hostile" to feminine talent. The union had more than eight hundred members by 1920.[71]

Mediations

As Ludmilla Jordanova's work suggests, scientific and artistic representations of the female body are "mediations" that have implications far beyond their explicit content.[72] Although French girls learned little biological science or art in school, Frenchwomen were not scientifically or artistically illiterate, thanks to the popular science outreach and "pavement" art in an increasingly spectacularized urban culture of boulevards, shopping arcades, and department store display windows.[73]

Bourgeois girls received some formal instruction in science. The senior

primary, secondary, and normal schools established after the 1881 law on public instruction offered girls one to three hours of natural science instruction
per week. The curriculum covered zoology, including human organic systems
other than the reproductive system. Until the mid-1880s, when women began
to graduate from the normal schools for women which were set up after 1881,
most science instructors were men. Shortly after women began teaching
science, the Ministry of Public Instruction (temporarily) reduced hiring
science teachers for girls schools, partly because the subject was unpopular
with parents.[74] Required course materials included illustrations of plants, animals, and humans, as well as skeletons of animals and humans. Unfortunately, materials were not always provided in the prewar period.[75] Outside
scientific and medical circles, representations of the pelvis were less fixated on
sex difference. Only one hygiene text for girls had drawings of a male and a
female skeleton with obvious pelvic differences inserted to warn against "deformation" by corsets.[76] Schoolbooks also elided data on alleged sex differences in the skull or brain.

Scientific outreach, which flourished from 1880 through 1914, supplemented this very meager curriculum. "Amusing instruction" included public
lectures, magic lantern shows, demonstrations, popular science magazines,
and novels by best-selling authors such as Jules Verne.[77] Although most of the
outreach was directed to boys and men, there were efforts to interest girls and
women, at least in mathematics. For example, the magazine *Illustrated Science*
printed three articles on science in clothing, illustrating some practical applications of geometry.[78] Exhibits at the Museum of Man and the universal expo-
sitions held nearly every decade in the capital showcased women's bodies.
The natural history museums in the provinces, with their free Sunday, holi-
day, and class visits, doubled in number to twenty-four in 1900.[79] Museums of
anatomy which were open to the public displayed three-dimensional wax anatomical models of women. Dr. Spitzer's model *Venus* was attractive and supine; her flesh-toned covering could be pulled back to reveal internal organs.
Although her curvaceous hips and pelvis were displayed prominently, her external genitalia were discretely hidden. As Jordanova notes about eighteenth-
century wax models, this *Venus* was simultaneously realistic and evocative of
a [masculine] ideal of femininity.[80] Generally, popular images of women's
bodies reflected a masculine perspective on women's sexual features.

During this time, anthropological theories spilled over to the educated
public. In the 1890s, Henri Marion taught women's psychology at the Sorbonne, and in 1900, a professor at Sèvres Normal School published Marion's

revised lecture notes. What future female teachers encountered was a hodge-podge of anthropological theories. Quoting social Darwinist Herbert Spencer, Marion postulated that women select sexual partners on the basis of strength. On a neo-Lamarckian track, he posited that the higher the division of labor, the greater the differentiation of the sexes. Despite disagreements among anthropologists, he insisted that "all are unanimous in declaring that woman is less well organized, less resistant, less vigorous than man."[81]

Feminists, too, appropriated some anthropological theories. Radical feminist Nelly Roussel (1878-1922) defined feminism as "the doctrine of natural equivalence and social equality of the sexes" and quoted Charles Letourneau's opinion that social progress was possible only if woman participated in it.[82] Conservative feminist Anna Lampérière, who criticized equal-rights feminists for ignoring "biological laws," also quoted Letourneau but chose his opinion that maternity was such a heavy burden in "superior species" that women's survival required "absolute interdependence" with men. Happily, she reasoned, nature has arranged for "selection—love—and union of the two portions of humanity."[83]

Few women viewed the statues at the Louvre or the canvases mounted in annual salons; few could afford to read art criticism on the "image of woman" in art. (Book titles used image and woman in the singular, although the authors made fine distinctions among painters.)[84] A few more women encountered classical standards and artistic definitions of beauty in expensive beauty books published in the Belle Epoque. In *The Woman's Breviary* (1903), the Countess de Tramar reprinted a classical formula for [male] bodily proportions (nine head lengths from head to toe). In *All Woman's Secrets* (1907), the Baronne d'Orchamps praised figures with "harmonious" but "not strictly symmetrical" curves, phrases art critics used to describe the torsos of the statues of classical antiquity. In *An Honest Woman's Dressing Room* (1909), the Countess de Gencé compared applying makeup with "making a work of art."[85] The "beauty countesses" of the Belle Epoque invoked the *style moderne*, which involved representing aristocratic women as works of classical art. More girls and women learned a little about artistic principles in school texts and less expensive advice literature. Home economics texts, women's health guides, and feminist dress reformers all contrasted corseted women with their tiny waists and accentuated busts and hips with the smoother shape of the *Venus de Milo*.[86]

In the Belle Epoque, many women saw the sinuous female figures in organic settings which were recurring motifs in Art Nouveau wallpapers, rugs, fabrics, stained-glass windows, and jewelry.[87] These products were displayed in department store window and counter displays and on magazine covers and posters.[88] Increasing numbers of women acquired their body ideals from popular art and advertising. In the 1880s and 1890s, technical improvements permitted cheaper reproduction of color images and revolutionized advertising. New laws eased state control of the media, and city councils allowed rental of the walls of city properties. Before long, Morris columns to which posters could be affixed dotted urban space. Art Nouveau posters took to a new height the public display of images of feminine desirability for commercial purposes. Many of the posters with inviting, curvaceous, female figures were intended as lures for dance halls, which were not respectable, and products such as cigarette paper, which were used primarily by men. Other posters with seductive, smiling female figures touted cosmetics for women.[89] In addition to the well-known representations of actresses, dancers, and demimondaines, Art Nouveau posters included images of elegant, respectable women.[90] The Goncourt brothers, who revived the *style moderne,* inspired many poster artists.[91] These posters were displayed for a "pavement public" that included respectable women.[92]

By the 1920s, beauty counselors rejected classical ideals of pale, passive facial beauty,[93] but advocates of physical culture continued to promote the classical figure. The most progressive postwar advocate, Georges Hébert, argued that his program of outdoor activities enhanced true beauty, meaning harmonious proportions and graceful movements. To illustrate true beauty in *Feminine Physical Education* (1921), Hébert selected a photo of an ancient statue with a torso similar to those of the Venuses and Dianas in the Louvre. Into the 1930s, purveyors of physical culture promised to sculpt women's bodies to classical proportions.[94]

In the late 1920s and early 1930s, Miss France beauty pageants also publicized classical ideals. The organizer, Maurice de Waleffe, filled the jury with painters and photographers, plus a few couturiers and cinematographers. In 1927, the jury selected "a tall, slender, admirably proportioned" model, whose face was "a perfect oval, . . . evoking those pure beauties displayed in the Louvre." When this woman did not win the Miss World title in Galveston, Texas, Waleffe blamed the large number of "cute," young, blond American contestants. The next Miss France was only sixteen years old (though she was not a blond); she came in second at the Miss World pageant. Although journalists noted that international beauty queens rarely corresponded to the classical canon, French jurors continued to prefer "the classic face and adolescent body."[95]

Finally, although the "normal" models of the artistic anatomist Paul Richer had little artistic impact, his "normal" female model survived in home economics courses. A 1922 text admitted that there were deviations but alleged that seamstresses ought to know "normal proportions."[96] There certainly were deviations: prewar manufacturers of dressmakers' wooden or wax mannequins produced up to twenty series of mannequins in dozens of sizes. Some dressmakers had fifty to one hundred of these mannequins. In the 1920s, most dress shop display models had faces of famous beauties and came in many sizes. They continued to be manufactured through a haute couture vogue for stylized, slim Art Deco display models. The major manufacturers, Siegal, had sixty-seven factories in 1927.[97]

Conclusions

In the 1930s, endocrinologist René Biot compared early nineteenth-century biology texts with contemporary biology texts and found that the latter put more emphasis on sexual dichotomies. To a much longer list of anatomical and morphological sex differences than have been mentioned in this chapter, Biot added data on sex differences in basal metabolism and other physical processes which had been compiled by physiologists. An experimental biologist who had left the laboratory for the Lyonnais Institute of Endocrinology and Psychology, Biot concluded that "we are masculine and feminine in each of our organic processes."[98] If biologists critiqued their predecessors' methods of measuring sexual bipolarity, they replaced them with more refined methods. Documenting sexual dichotomy was far more important to these scientists than investigating the diversity of women's bodies. If anatomy failed to find sufficient differences, physiology could bear witness.

Chapter 2

Biomedicine and
Femininity

URING THE Third Republic, physiologists and physicians moved from an organic to a hormonal conception of human sexuality. Whatever the theoretical lens, physiology and medicine envisioned a female body linked to the entire species, and specialists in women's diseases, who became known as gynecologists in the 1890s, transmitted this vision to women patients. Because the medical profession included some women and interacted with women as patients, it disseminated more biological ideas to women than scientists did, but physicians' increasing respect for patient confidentiality limits our knowledge about doctor-patient consultations. Fortunately, between 1880 and 1940 several dozen physicians wrote women's health and beauty manuals or columns in women's magazines. These hygiene manuals and columns relayed the progress of medicine, after a delay of ten to twenty years, to tens of thousands of women. At least eight of the authors were women, who spoke with special authority about women's health and sexuality.

Throughout the Third Republic, doctors had to counter or cope with traditional ways of understanding human bodies. The best information on the persistence of these ways of understanding comes from Françoise Loux's study of five thousand proverbs about the body which were collected in late nineteenth-century rural France and of corporeal advice in almanacs circulated in the countryside at that time. Her study found that these adages posited similarities between the external body and its inner nature—for instance, "The face is the mirror of the heart."[1] This kind of analogical thinking, which derives from the medieval "medicine of signatures," was not confined to peasants. Between 1880 and 1940, many of the health and beauty manuals addressed to bourgeois urban women contended that external appearance reflected internal physical and later psychological conditions. These guides updated the maxim that "The complexion is the mirror that reflects the incidents of our physical life" to say that the face is "the screen on which our interior life projects its incessant film."[2]

Loux insists upon the flexibility and adaptability of peasants, who resorted to physicians as well as popular healers (often women) and to several medical traditions. Rural proverbs indicate that peasants had recourse to doctors but criticized them for arriving late, charging too much, and being unreliable. Peasants also tried herbal remedies and had faith in the healing powers of various stones, religious objects, fountains, and springs.[3] Although the medical profession grew rapidly in the twentieth century, Claude and Jacques Seignolle, who traveled through 170 rural communes near the capital in the 1930s, found two hundred healers using prayers, plants, and manual skills.[4]

Women's beauty guides exhibited some of the same qualities. By the 1880s, most guides encouraged women to purchase herbal ingredients and either blend and steep them at home or have their herbalist or pharmacist prepare them according to the author's recipes. By the turn of the century, one guide appended a sales catalog listing dozens of manufactured beauty products made (or so the author and manufacturer claimed) of plant material.[5] Many subsequent guides included two appendices: one for recipes, the other for prepared products. The beauty countesses were also eclectic: Countess de Gencé referred to the dressing room as both the confessional and the laboratory of beauty. Even beauty institutes promising to deliver the "science" of beauty, referred to beauty as a "religion" and beauty routines as "acts of devotion."[6] Finally, a minority of beauty counselors in the 1890s and the 1930s believed in the "language of flowers" and the "language of [precious and semiprecious] stones."[7]

Humors and Organs

Despite the emergence of organic medicine in the eighteenth century, the Aristotelian tradition did not disappear. Although anatomists had overturned Aristotle's vision of women as imperfect men, vestiges remained in popular medical literature. In 1904, Dr. Caufeynon (nom de plume for Dr. Jean Fauconney) quoted Diderot on the uterus as an "unruly animal." Of course Caufeynon's "history of man's companion" was propaganda written to discourage lesbianism and encourage women to reproduce: "To bring children into the world is her special destiny. . . . Everything conspires toward this goal, while in men it is only secondary, as the anatomical disposition of the organs demonstrates." By *anatomical disposition,* Caufeynon (as Aristotle interpreted by Galen) meant that women's reproductive organs are internal whereas men's are external.[8]

Galenic medical theories also had proponents.[9] Galenic bodies were composed of four humors or fluids that corresponded to the elements in the macrocosm. These fungible fluids could be combined in a variety ways to form the material body and its "temperament" or, in modern parlance, personality. Organs were mere channels for humors. Differences between the sexes derived from different combinations of humors, not organs.[10] In 1893, Alfred Fouillée urged modern scientists, who no longer believed in humors, to connect cell biology to personality. He linked recent advances in the analysis of cells, the new building blocks of life, to personality traits. Drawing analogies between "immobile" eggs and feminine personalities and between mobile sperm and masculine personalities, he further characterized feminine and masculine personalities as conserving versus expending personalities.[11] The classical economic metaphor merely reformulated the hoary dichotomy between active and passive sexes and genders.

In spite of continuities, the "genital landscape"—but not the gender landscape—changed in the nineteenth century. First, the notion of a uterus richly endowed with nerves and connected to the rest of the organism through sympathetic nerves replaced the old notion of the uterus as mobile. On the basis of connections between the uterus and the nervous system, Moreau de la Sarthe claimed that the female is female all her life, unlike the male, who is only male on certain occasions.[12] In this way, Moreau de la Sarthe refurbished the old saw about the wandering womb making women unstable. Eighty years later, in 1883, a homeopathic doctor and his female coauthor (a common combination) described the uterus as continuously active under the influence of nerve ganglia and (in a more contemporary vein) ovular releases.[13] About the same time, the senior lecturer on "women's diseases" at the Paris Medical School, Prof. Bernutz, taught that the uterus, where incubation occurred, was "the essential organ of gestation" or maternity. And, he avowed in his lectures, "Woman is maternity."[14] As late as 1929, Henri Vignes's textbook on gynecological physiology still called the "tyranny of the nervous over the utero-ovarian system" the distinctive feature of "the female of our species."[15]

The ovary acquired new respect. In the 1840s, a professor of zoology, F. A. Pouchet, demonstrated that female mammals ovulated spontaneously and hypothesized that women must ovulate spontaneously. In the following three decades, German physiologists deduced, from a new operation to remove ovaries, that their removal stopped the menstrual cycle. At this point, physiologists still believed that the ovaries activated menstruation through nerve impulses. By 1882, the physiology course at the Paris Medical Faculty taught medical students that "the fundamental part of the female is the ovary." Thomas Laqueur drew attention to contemporaneous medical assumptions of a synecdochal relation between the ovary and feminine character.[16] This reduction of femininity to one of the internal sex organs continued to have purchase beyond the Third Republic. The first chapter of *The Second Sex* (1949) begins: "Woman? Very simple, say the fanciers of simple formulas: she is a womb, an ovary; she is female—this word is sufficient to define her." Simone de Beauvoir goes on to make a distinction important to her personally and intellectually: "The term 'female' is derogatory not because it emphasizes woman's animality, but because it imprisons her in her sex."[17]

How common was the new language of organs? According to Mikhail Bakhtin, colloquial language and literature had long represented the body as grotesque, as "the body that fecundates and is fecundated, that gives birth and is born, devours and is devoured, drinks, defecates, is sick and dying." Thomas Laqueur noted that this grotesque body, with its seeping orifices, seems more female than male. Beginning in the sixteenth century, a new "bodily canon" in literature and polite conversation privileged a closed (and clothed) body without obvious leaky orifices. This impenetrable, strictly delimited individual entity did not merge with the world. The genital organs and buttocks were discretely covered; no fluids oozed from this body.[18] This isolated, individual body seems very masculine.

This largely literary canon had less effect upon colloquial language. In the 1880s, Dr. Edouard Brissaud prepared a lexicon of popular expressions for body parts to help doctors who were starting practices. Although people still referred to orifices and humors, Brissaud felt that *organicism* was replacing *humoralism*. There were many popular terms for bodily orifices, particularly the anus, but few for tissues, including specific muscles, which were usually called, generically, *flesh*. Most patients knew the names of only six bones, including the skull and jawbone. Whereas erotic dictionaries had "a prodigiously rich vocabulary" for women's sex organs, including the genitalia, everyday parlance had few such terms, such as *nature, lower parts, womb,* and *mother,* and these terms referred primarily to internal organs. As a female physician noted in 1909, patients often used terms such as *matrice,* which meant uterus to physicians, to refer to their entire genital system.[19]

By the turn of the century, natural science and hygiene classes taught twelve- and thirteen-year-old girls a little anatomy but almost no physiology—and then only if their teachers, who received no physiological training, had studied the subject independently.[20] By 1910, scientific and pedagogical criticism led to the introduction of units on organic systems.[21] After the introduction of some anatomy, one interwar physician, Hélina Gaboriau, felt that women's knowledge of their tissues and organs, including their internal sex organs, had improved.[22] Catherine Pozzi's journal illustrates the change. In 1913, as a thirty-one-year-old woman, she called her sexual fantasies a psychouterine crisis and chided herself: "Alas! What does this shameful sex want from me, and to what do these nerves aspire"? Fourteen years later, as she pursued advanced studies in physiology, she focused on and dissected ovaries until she grew so bored she took up philosophy as a distraction.[23]

Cells and Hormones

Although European biological thought can be traced back to Greek antiquity, the term *biology* was not coined until 1802, by Lamarck in France and Treviranus in Germany. Naming reflected changes in the methods and objectives of the undertaking. Neither Lamarck nor Treviranus put much stock in the collecting and classifying missions of natural history. Biologists studied life itself in the forms and functions of increasingly small parts of the organism. Physiologists investigated functions such as respiration, digestion, and reproduction.[24] By the 1880s, cell theory and the optical microscope were fully developed, and most scientists agreed that the cell was a recognizable entity. Although many still believed that the cell's interior was homogeneous protoplasm,[25] researchers had discovered a nucleus with further specialized structures. Cell theory influenced all fields of biology, including sex determination. The entry on sex in an 1880s medical dictionary stated that "The existence of one or several ova characterizes the female sex."[26] The author, Dr. Charles Robin, was the first incumbent of the chair in histology at the Paris Medical School and one of the founders of the Biology Society. His definition of the female sex reflected a fundamental shift in biomedicine, from organs to cells and from anatomy to physiology.

In the second half of the nineteenth century, French physiologists found that chemical agents called *internal secretions* cooperated with the nervous system in regulating the organism. In the 1840s, Claude Bernard (1813–78) worked on the roles of the gastric and pancreatic juices in digestion and elucidated the glycogenic function of the liver. Bernard offered a "bold delineation of the organism as a functional whole, a whole whose integral behavior depended on the dynamic interaction of the cell and the body fluids in which it bathed." He introduced the important idea of internal milieu, or the physiological environment in each living being regulated by the nervous system and internal secretions, later called *hormones*.[27] Bernard was very influential. In 1854, the Sorbonne created a chair in physiology for him, and in 1858, he assumed the chair of medicine at the College de France. He wrote books to disseminate his views, notably the frequently reprinted *Introduction to the Study of Experimental Medicine*. Together with the father of sociology, August Comte, Bernard popularized the idea that pathological states were like normal states except for quantitative variations. Unlike Comte, Bernard supported his pathology with verifiable evidence, experimental protocols, and quantitative methods. Bernard had a profound impact on physicians and on literature in the heyday of naturalism. He established the experimental method and the dissection of live animals in physiology—in opposition to his wife and daughters, who were committed antivivisectionists.[28] Even before Pasteur's germ theory introduced laboratory testing of animal tissues, Bernard added laboratory research on animals to clinical medicine. After Bernard, it was necessary to train in chemistry and zoology to run a physiology laboratory.[29]

Prominent physiologists encouraged the teaching of physiology, even to girls. After the Prussian victory over France in 1870 and during the Paris Commune of 1871, Bernard's successor at the Sorbonne, Paul Bert, made a stirring speech about physiology as a way to address the urgent national agenda of revenge and regeneration. When Bert entered parliament a few years later, he published the speech. Bert also taught a zoology course for the Association for the Secondary Instruction of Young Girls. His published lectures explained that they avoided "indelicate" subjects that offended the sensibilities of sixteen- to eighteen-year-old girls. Although he included units on embryology and evolution, he (and virtually every educator who followed) avoided the topic of sexual reproduction and limited the number of experiments girls were allowed to do.[30] As minister of education for one crucial year in the early 1880s, Bert influenced the girls' school science curriculum by introducing hygiene classes, which were later integrated into natural science classes.[31] Girls' hygiene and natural science classes also eschewed sexual reproduction and only integrated more experiments in the 1930s.[32]

Physiology did not make converts of many women. In the 1880s, when antivivisectionist societies were fashionable, the Antivivisectionist League included prominent feminists who linked vivisection to women's concerns. One of the most prominent, Marie Deraismes, criticized the devaluation of feeling: "One of the most striking characteristics of the man who calls himself a scientist is his disdain for feeling." She foresaw the possibility of eugenic proposals to dispose of "misfits, crazies, and criminals. . . . Nothing, really, differentiates them from animals." Claude Bernard's daughter and many other women took up animal rescue. Generally well educated, these women may have perceived that the *Introduction to the Study of Experimental Medicine* "described nature as a woman who must be forced to unveil herself when she is attacked by the experimenter."[33] For decades, some feminist journals condemned vivisections in physiology laboratories.[34]

In the prewar decade, a generation of science popularizers retired, and most popular science journals ceased publication. In most cases, they were not replaced. A notable exception was Prof. Charles Richet, who held the chair of physiology in the Paris Medical Faculty and devoted some of his many talents to popularizing physiology. A Nobel laureate for his work on anaphylaxis, Richet wrote novels, dramas, pacifist propaganda, and apologies for the "occult," or paranormal, sciences. He directed the *Review of Science Courses* and the *Scientific Review,* which he ran as a "journal of popularization for savants." For general interest periodicals, he wrote articles to give educated men "an abridged, but clear, notion of present-day physiology."[35] Yet when he wrote a guide for volunteer nurses, he stressed antisepsis, routine, and docility, not physiology.[36] Another exception was the newspaper *Figaro,* which hired graduate students to introduce its bourgeois readers to new physiological and medical concepts. One contributor was Catherine Pozzi, who was then pursuing advanced studies in physiology.[37]

Although physiological research was highly specialized, it did attract intellectuals and socialites. In 1928–29, the Duchess Edmée de la Rochefoucauld visited Prof. Gley's physiology laboratory and borrowed books on the subject. Catherine Pozzi was more dedicated to her studies but did not complete her *license* because of intermittent ill health and slights from professors and laboratory assistants, who treated her like a wealthy dilettante. She was even less impressed with her professors. The insensitive way vivisections were conducted horrified her. At a low moment, she wrote "I have seen hell. . . . The demons there do not have black bodies and flaming tongues; they are men full of wisdom, cold as their knives."[38]

Sex Determination

In the nineteenth century, there were two approaches to determining the origin of sex: externalist, which emphasized the role of the environment, and internalist, which focused on the sex cells or fertilized eggs.[39] Externalists prevailed in France. By midcentury, embryologists had discovered that the Wolffian ducts, destined to become the male genital tract, and the Müllerian ducts, destined to become the Fallopian tubes, coexisted for eight weeks after conception. A theory that complicated organs arose from simpler ones—or epigenesis—undermined ideas of primary sex differences and opened the door to environmental explanations of sex.[40] In the 1880s, Dr. Augustin Cleisz wrote *Research into the Laws Presiding over the Creation of the Sexes*, which began with the assertion that the fetus was sexually "indifferent" until the twenty-seventh day, when one of the ducts began to develop into ovaries or testicles. "External" factors such as parental age and maternal nutrition could determine the sex of the infant. Without providing any evidence, Cleisz claimed that mothers younger than twenty-five or older than thirty-five years were more likely to have girls. Cleisz also cited neonatal sex ratios in different populations which showed, for instance, that peasants had more boys than girls (which he claimed was because of the sexual vigor of peasant men).[41] Within two decades, scientific research relegated speculation about the effects of parental age and sexual vigor to the dust heap. But popular medical guides repeated this kind of assertion into the 1930s. As one scientist noted dryly, people wanted to be able to affect the outcome.[42]

From the mid-1880s, internalists gained ground. Drawing on German embryology and histology, scientists traced sexual identity back to the sex cell or fertilized egg. In a collection of French essays on the nature of sexuality, one essay outlined Nussbaum's theory of sex difference. This theory postulated that the essential "polarity" was between the preponderance of centrifugal elements in the small, mobile male sex cell and of concentrating elements in the big, immobile ova. The author, Dr. Armand Sabatier, took "a short excursion on the moral terrain of sexual differentiation." He related the "mobile and seeking element in the sperm" to "the general tendency of the male to have an active, travelling, outdoor life," and the "relative immobility" and integrating role of the ova to the needs for intimacy, domesticity, and union which are "appropriate to the female."[43] Even before the war, some biologists objected to this facile projection of sex cell "dimorphism" into sexual personalities.[44] In the 1930s, Adrienne Sahuqué traced the tendency to oppose spermatic dynamism to ovular dormancy back to the Aristotelian traditions of conceptualizing masculinity and femininity as bipolar and of representing femininity as "lack of energy, intelligence, will, dignity, rights." By the 1930s, scientists were aware that ovular volume did not denote "dormancy," and ovular stability did not signify "torpor, . . . but tension, . . . because the ovular protoplasm is the seat of continuous internal movement."[45]

In the early twentieth century, specialists had three theories about sex determination: that it happened before fertilization, at fertilization, or after fertilization.[46] Discovery of a chromosome that bore sex and was carried by sperm was pivotal to the hereditary approach. French biologists did little groundbreaking genetic research during the Third Republic because few of the two dozen physiology laboratories were equipped to do genetic research and because two of the three major laboratories were pursuing another line of inquiry.[47] By 1910, one French physiology text declared that the union of chromosomes from ovular and spermatic cells was "the fundamental biogenetic law." But symptomatically, the author, Prof. Gley, was more interested in recent French observations that the gonads released "internal secretions" with sexual implications.[48] Even in the interwar, Prof. Champy had to bolster his exposition of chromosomal sex determination with criticism of more popular theories that sex hormones induced sexual characteristics.[49] As late as the mid-1930s, foreigners lecturing in France made the most definite statements about chromosomal sex determination.[50]

In France, the developmental approach to sex determination predominated because it was associated with promising medical treatments and the interests of a new medical specialty. In 1889–90, Bernard's successor at the College de France, Charles Brown-Séquard (1817–94), publicized his hypothesis that the gonads produced internal secretions that helped keep the organism healthy. On the basis of very few trials, Brown-Séquard claimed that extracts of animal testes could "regenerate" older men.[51] For a decade, medical practitioners injected extracts of or transplanted tissues from monkey testes as antidotes to male aging or male menopause. In the absence of any verifiable results, organotherapy lost favor in the early twentieth century, to be revived, amid controversy, twenty years later.[52] No doubt exploiting anxieties about virility after the First World War, Dr. Dartigues performed thyroid and gonad grafts to correct arrested genital development, impotence, sterility, male (and female) menopause, and premature senility in the 1920s.[53]

In the 1890s, Dr. Félix Jayle (author of the morphology text analyzed in Chap. 1) experimented with administering extracts of animal ovaries to women. After reviewing a hundred cases of women suffering from hot flashes, night sweats, and headaches after bilateral ovariotomies, he administered ovarian extract to six postoperative and three preoperative patients. Everyone in the postoperative group and one woman in the preoperative group reported some alleviation. Jayle recommended preserving the ovaries, interviewing patients to diagnose ovarian problems, and—despite equivocal results in preoperative patients—ordering organotherapy before trying surgical intervention. By 1900, he had defined female menopause as "ovarian deficiency" to be treated with opotherapy (ovarian organotherapy).[54] Over the next two decades, French physicians pioneered the study of menopause as an endocrinological crisis and opotherapy as the treatment of choice.[55] Endocrinologists also became specialists on puberty and fertility.

Opotherapy did not prevail over surgical or radiation treatments for gynecological problems because it offered better treatment, but because "preserving" ovaries was compatible with the hegemonic vision of women's bodies. Effective oral estrogen and progesterone preparations were not available until the 1940s.[56] By the 1930s, medical researchers questioned the efficacy of opotherapy because of uncertainties raised by the identification of two ovarian hormones and new theories about a synergy among all hormones.[57] But these researchers had little impact in a climate in which physicians spoke of the normal functioning of the sex glands "assuring virility in men and the maternal sentiment in women," and gynecologists wrote columns in women's magazines cautioning against "surgical menopause." Even gynecological surgeons condemned "castration" for inducing and intensifying the symptoms of menopause. Although prepared to remove the uterus for a variety of uterine problems, they accepted opotherapy for most ovarian problems.[58]

In 1900, a Viennese gynecologist demonstrated that ovaries release a secretion that stimulates the other genital and mammary glands.[59] Within a decade, an English researcher coined the term *hormone* to replace *secretion*, and the ovarian hormone was shown to induce menstruation. Researchers attached the label *female* to this hormone. In 1910, a researcher postulated that sex hormones stimulated homologous or sex-appropriate characteristics and suppressed heterologous or opposite-sex characteristics. According to Nelly Oudshoorn, the idea of "gonads as agents of sex difference had been transformed into the concept of sex hormones as chemical messengers of masculinity and femininity."[60]

In the early decades of the twentieth century, laboratory scientists played a dominant role among endocrinologists. Initially they conducted more research on men than on women, but with increasing dependence upon commercially produced hormones, the pendulum swung to research on women. Pharmaceutical companies such as Roussel in France and Zondek in Amsterdam realized that they could distill hormones from pregnant women's urine, which was readily available from gynecological clinics.[61] Only when male sex hormones could be produced synthetically in the mid-1930s was equally extensive research on male hormones feasible. Biochemical research raised disturbing issues about sexual identity. In the 1920s, biochemists identified estrogen and progesterone, discovered that these "female" hormones were present in the testes of "normal, healthy men," and decided that male and female hormones were closely related chemically. As Oudshoorn remarks, "In this manner they broke with the dualistic concept of male and female as mutually exclusive categories."[62]

Glandular secretions had been correlated with the growth process. As one French researcher put it, rather alarmingly, "glandular products . . . can make an individual a giant or a dwarf, a male or a eunuch."[63] Soon researchers linked sex hormones to the appearance of secondary sexual traits such as pubic hair and breasts at puberty.[64] Then, in 1929, a Spanish endocrinologist introduced the unsettling idea of normal intersexuality. Gregario Maranon posited that masculine sexual characteristics are similar to, but more highly evolved than, feminine sexual characteristics. The exceptions were highly developed maternal characteristics such as the uterus, pelvis, nipples, and more fat tissue. Maranon hypothesized that a sexually ambiguous phase was normal in pubescent boys and menopausal women. He claimed to have replaced the classic notion of two sexes with the notion of a single sexuality, with two distinct phases: one feminine and the other masculine. "In men, the feminine phase evolves rapidly and with little intensity during sexual dormancy, then at puberty, the principal sex, the masculine one, dominates until the menopause. In women, the sexual awakening of puberty lasts until menopause, when a virile phase, of a rapid and superficial kind, takes over."[65] Maranon's hypothesis, which originally generated antagonism, acquired some French adherents after his *Sexuality and the Intersexual State* was translated in 1931.

French researchers were already speculating about *sexual inversion,* a term used for (male) homosexuality. One hypothesis was that inversion was the result of *androgenation,* defined as the dilution of sex-appropriate traits caused by the endocrinological state during the maturing of the sex cells.[66] By 1935, sophisticated researchers such as Etienne Wolff at Strasbourg were changing the primary sexual traits (genital ducts) of male eggs by injecting "female" hormones into chicken eggs. Vera Dantchakoff's experiments with the somatic plasticity of fertilized eggs in mammals were publicized. Even those who accepted chromosomal sex determination were interested in sexual inversion. But interest was confined to scientific circles until the research was popularized after 1940.[67] By 1948, Simone de Beauvoir contended, "It is well known that the sex of offspring is determined by the chromosome constitution established at the time of fertilization." Yet "numerous experiments show that by varying the hormonal (endocrine) situation, sex can be profoundly affected." In particular, "intersexuality may result when the hormones are abnormal."[68]

Although much of the anxiety aroused by less stable notions about sexuality focused on virility, some of it was directed toward femininity or more precisely, fertility. Nicolas Pende, director of the Institute of Biotypology at the University of Rome, sought "the sexual value of an individual." In a work translated into French, Pende and his assistant, Miss Gualco, posited three biometrical indexes of femininity. One was an index of robustness, interpreted to mean that the more fertile the woman, the broader the hip relative to the chest. The second compared the length of the calves with that of the thighs and construed the results to mean that women with active ovaries had longer thighs than calves. The third hypothesis was that the more active the ovary, the wider and longer the cranium.[69] These hypotheses, which today seem bizarre (except perhaps to some sociobiologists), fed into gender uncertainties in the interwar. In a speech to the 1934 Congress on Gynecology, André Binet (discussed in Chap. 1) reassured all those worried about sportswomen acquiring a "masculine morphology" or young women adopting the "garçonne look" that there was a "renaissance of femininity." As evidence, he pointed to the popularity of beauty contests and film stars. However, vigilance about femininity and fertility was still necessary. Women who actively pursued physical attractiveness sought to please themselves, not men, and lost "their maternal vocation."[70]

Doctoring Women

Medicine was slightly more open to women than science was. In the mid-1890s, when 16 percent of the 343 women enrolled at the University of Paris were in science, 45 percent were in medicine. By 1914, four hundred women attended medical school. But far fewer women graduated,[71] and still fewer completed their education with a residency and internship at a teaching hospital. To enter a teaching hospital, a nomination was necessary, and for that, the patronage of a faculty member was indispensable. Female physicians petitioned several years before they were allowed to take the residency examinations and two more years before they could take the intern exams. Famous scientists such as Paul Bert and Charles Richet supported women's admission to hospital training; prominent physicians such as Samuel Pozzi (first chair of gynecology at the Faculty of Medicine and father of Catherine Pozzi) and the Society of Hospital Doctors vocally opposed it. Throughout the struggle, male interns led a campaign against admitting women on the grounds that women lacked the necessary "masculine" qualities of strength, courage, independence, and judgment, whereas their feminine delicacy and modesty would be revolted by contact with cadavers and deformed patients. In the mid-1880s, the Paris City Council authorized women's admission to the hospitals.[72] Although three women were admitted between 1886 and 1888, eleven years elapsed before another woman became an intern. The first Frenchwoman, Marthe Francillon, was nominated in 1905. (We will consider her doctoral thesis on puberty and her women's health guide in Part Two.)

Beginning with Dr. Blanche Edwards-Pillet, who was appointed to a nursing school in 1891, teaching positions at nursing schools opened up for women. Upon the death of her husband, whom she had assisted for two years, Edwards-Pillet achieved another first: appointment to his chair in physiology at Lariboisière Hospital. During the war, women entered the ranks of heads of hospital laboratories and heads of clinics. Promotion to the lower ranks of the professorate came last, with one in the 1920s and two in the 1930s.[73]

By 1903, ninety-five women practiced medicine in France. It was an inauspicious time for anyone to enter the profession. The country had one physician per two thousand inhabitants, a ratio that many physicians considered too high. Doctors still fought to establish professional boundaries by differentiating themselves from empirics, pharmacists, charlatans, dentists, and midwives. Some denounced women entering "our rude profession," which required qualities more common in men: "strength, activity, courage, energy."[74] Professional organizations were legalized in 1892; the first congress to create a single code of medical ethics met in 1900 (although the first unified code was not published until 1936). As Robert Nye demonstrates, the profession was imbued with an older, aristocratic code of male honor which operated informally to exclude women.[75]

Not surprisingly, the women pioneers in the medical profession experienced difficulties building their practices, including attracting patients and coping with patient expectations that women would charge lower fees. In addition, women doctors had a negative public image. Plays and novels used cross-dressing *doctoresses* in the old Marivaux theme of a feminine plot to assume the masculine role and to emasculate men. Usually the denouement reconfirmed conventional gender expectations, with humiliated doctors closing their practices to assume customary and comforting wifely roles. Yet the only notorious example of a cross-dresser was Madeleine Pelletier, the first woman to take the exams for a psychiatric internship in 1903.

Ordinarily, women physicians tried to assert their femininity without threatening the masculinity of the profession. One early strategy was marriage within the profession. Another strategy, developed by Dr. Brés, the first Frenchwoman to become a doctor, was specializing in medicine for women and children.[76] In an interview with the *Medical Chronicle*, Brés reminded her largely male colleagues that she never saw male patients and taught hygiene rather than chemistry, although she could not forbear mentioning that she was qualified to teach both. By 1890, Drs. Hélina Gaboriau and Mathilde Pokitonoff worked in charitable clinics for women. Three years later, Pokitonoff published a manual, *Mothers and Children's Health*. In the late 1890s, Gaboriau edited a journal entitled *Happiness in the Home: Review for Wives and Mothers of Families*.[77]

Many female physicians had maternal feminist connections. At the International Congress on the Condition and Rights of Women in 1900, Edwards-Pillet proclaimed, "The time will come when woman will be considered a veritable social functionary during her gestation and nursing period. At this time, she is in the debt of society, which in exchange for the enormous effort of maternity, owes her nourishment, lodging, and rest."[78] At the Congress of Feminine Charities that same year, maternal feminists resolved that women should "rid themselves of the prejudice that women doctors lacked decision and sang-froid in serious cases" and patronize women doctors for their health problems.[79] After the First World War, five French women attended the Young Women's Christian Association conference that inspired the International Association of Women Doctors.[80] The next year, these five women helped form a national branch of the association with professional objectives such as exchanging information and offering mutual assistance as well as maternal feminist goals. The national branch formed an alliance with the national branch of the Federation of University Women, which passed resolutions against "exceptional" measures removing married women doctors from official posts.[81]

Analysis of the 275 members of the French Association of Women Doctors in 1931—about half of the women doctors in France at that time—suggests that the pattern of concentration in medicine for women and children continued. The largest number (45) of the 114 members who were specialists practiced gynecology, and the next largest number (31) practiced pediatrics.

One quarter held official positions in hospitals, shelters, schools, and the like. Official positions were attractive because they did not require start-up funds and because they came with a ready-made clientele.[82]

Between 1903 and 1933, eight women doctors published women's health manuals in French. Few of these hygienists questioned the existence of physical and psychological dissimilarities between the sexes because questioning dissimilarities would have undermined the authors' claims to be both medically competent and specially qualified to pronounce upon women's health. Nevertheless, women hygienists diverged from their more numerous competitors, whether they were male doctors or laywomen. Women hygienists were more skeptical about the social conclusions to be drawn from the physical and psychological differences between the sexes. Most of them were more interested in elevating the status of motherhood than their male competitors were. Feminist magazines recommended these manuals.[83]

Three of these women—and one who wrote a sex guide for girls—expressed distinctive opinions on feminine sexuality. All were in some way outsiders. Two of them were associated with Theosophists, spiritualists influenced by Hinduism with a positive attitude toward feminine sexuality, which had a following in Paris at the turn of the century.[84] One Theosophist, Marie Schultz, authored the first women's health manual written by a woman doctor and the first and only manual on "genital" hygiene intended for women (as opposed to doctors) published in the Third Republic.[85] The other Theosophist was Dr. Hélina Gaboriau, who wrote articles on feminist philanthropy in her journal, *Happiness in the Home*, and in 1923 and 1924 published a manual that was unusually positive about female sexuality (within marriage).[86] The other two women doctors with unusual views on feminine sexuality were foreigners. In the first translated edition of *Woman, Family Doctor* (1905), Anna Fischer, a Swiss feminist, included the only illustrations of women's external genitalia to appear in Frenchwomen's health literature before the Great War. The illustrations were so controversial that the publishers had to eliminate them before reprinting the book several times between 1905 and 1924. Her manual was almost alone in openly promoting women-controlled contraception before or after the First World War.[87] Finally, Dr. Nelfrand, author of the only sexual and genital hygiene guide for French girls, published in 1932, was an American eugenist.[88]

In 1930, Dr. Marie Houdré-Boursin published *My Doctoresse*. Despite the anachronistic title (by then most women doctors eschewed the diminutive title), her manual was subtly supportive of contraception and openly supportive of the almost-as-controversial subject of women's sports. She had been head of a hospital laboratory during the Great War and, as such, had been one of the few female physicians able to mentor women doctoral candidates. In the 1920s, she presided over the Femina-Sports club for six years. With several other women physicians, she gathered and publicized information on the viability of sports for women.[89]

Conclusions

Nineteenth- and early twentieth-century biologists and physicians who made pronouncements about women followed the natural science tradition of projecting bipolarity onto bodies and a medical tradition of linking humors with temperaments. These scientists and doctors progressed from linking sex organs to sexual character, to linking sex cells to gendered personalities, and finally to linking sex hormones to gendered identities. Much of this biomedical information was charged with gender implications, and some of it was transmitted to girls and women through contact with physicians. Far more biomedical information on women's bodies was acquired from school hygiene courses, health and beauty manuals and magazines, and sexual advice literature, which are analyzed in the rest of the book.

Chapter 3

Hygiene and
Housewifery

*A*FTER DEFEAT in the Franco-Prussian War and the consoli-
dation of the Third Republic, French politicians added health to
the political agenda. As Jean-Pierre Goubert comments, "A bio-
politics of pious wishes, between 1750 and 1880, gave way to the construction
of a vast sanitary domain from 1880 to 1940."[1] Hygienists realized that expenditure on public hygiene entailed education about private hygiene because
sewer lines and sanitary regulations accomplished less if people did not practice personal cleanliness. Scientists and doctors might direct programs of private hygiene, but teachers, nurses, housewives, and mothers had to inculcate
the practice of personal cleanliness. The first section of this chapter describes
official and professional hygiene efforts; the next three sections examine how
girls and women were socialized to execute the new hygienic practices.

Françoise Loux's study of rural French proverbs confirms that vestiges of
what Vigarello calls the *prescientific code* about the body and corporeal care
lingered in the late nineteenth century.[2] Before the eighteenth century, Europeans imagined the body as a house vulnerable to external attack because its
covering, the skin, was open to penetration by threatening substances. Water,
which removed a protective crust of dirt, became problematic after the epidemics of the late Middle Ages had replaced ancient associations of water
with festivity and eroticism with a reputation as a means of transmitting diseases. Eighteenth-century physicians and hygienists redefined pores as exits
for the necessary excretion of humors (and later perspiration) and maintained
that dirt and sweat on the skin blocked the exit of harmful substances. By the
late eighteenth century, hydrotherapists were prescribing hot water to calm
nerves and cold water to fortify muscles and morality.[3]

One century later, French peasants still considered a strong body odor a sign of sexual prowess. Rural bathing schedules varied from a weekly sponge bath in one district to never in the Morvan. Most rural people bathed two or three times a year in streams, outdoor pools, or public bathhouses. Women bathed as infrequently as men did. Few French peasants installed indoor plumbing before the 1950s, and as late as 1985 only half of the agricultural population deemed daily washing necessary. No doubt this is why Goubert calls the rural exodus to cities the "entry into the civilization of water."[4] However, in the Belle Epoque, most city dwellers also took two or three baths a year, in either portable tubs or public baths.[5] Although many republican city councils procrastinated about funding bathhouses out of concern about promiscuity, municipal socialists and enlightened industrialists built bathing facilities. By 1898, a group of prominent hygienists and republican politicians formed the Parisian Charity for Cheap Baths and Showers. In 1901, Parisian women made up one fifth of all public bathers.[6] We will see that they made up a majority of private bathers.

Public and Private Hygiene

In the 1880s and 1890s, the germ theory of disease changed hygienic practice. Hygiene, which had meant a set of rules to maintain good health, was transformed into the modern notion of cleanliness, with dirt as "the visible manifestation of the invisible, or the hidden bacterial agents of disease."[7] Louis Pasteur (1822–95) was pivotal in these developments. From 1851 to 1881, his research on fermentation, pathogenic microbes as agents of animal diseases, and prophylaxis by vaccination had tangible results in agriculture and industry. Between 1882 and 1886, Pasteur, Chamberland, and Roux attacked and resolved the problem of rabies. A subscription destined for the creation of a rabies institute raised enough money to set up a research and teaching institute. However, medical faculties were slow to adopt germ theory until 1894, when Pasteur's associate, Roux, announced a vaccine against diphtheria, a bacterial infection of the mucous tissues which decimated children in the early 1890s.[8] Lacking instruction in hygiene, most medical practitioners learned of new hygienic products and practices through journals such as *Health*.[9] This route to knowledge was only supplemented in the mid-1880s, when Etienne Layet first taught hygiene at the Bordeaux Medical Faculty. Two decades later, the Institute of Practical Hygiene opened in Lyon, but the Paris Medical Faculty did not offer a diploma in hygiene until 1921, at the instigation of a professor inspired by the League of Nations Hygiene Committee.[10]

Nursing schools incorporated hygiene into their curriculum sooner than medical schools did as a result of coinciding campaigns by Pasteurian doctors and republican municipalities (which subsidized and supervised most hospitals) to dismiss the 225 religious orders that dominated French nursing. Anticlericals disliked the Church hierarchy's authority over the sisters; Pasteurians complained that the sisters resisted new medical routines. (Certainly, the sisters' dark, heavy, complicated habits and veils made asepsis difficult.) For several decades, hospital authorities could not replace the sisters with the existing lay nurses, who had a reputation for being ignorant and immoral, and, in any case, were not numerous enough to staff all of the hospitals. Beginning in 1878, large cities sponsored public nursing courses and subsidized private nursing schools. After 1902, the government required nursing schools in every department.[11] These schools instilled strict rules about personal hygiene along with some principles of anatomy and physiology in tens of thousands of women.

Two of the new nursing schools were in Bordeaux. The Saint André School was dedicated to ensuring the personal cleanliness of caregivers and to enforcing the sexual virtue of students through strict supervision of their free time and living arrangements. In this era, purity had moral as well as physical connotations. Next in importance in the curriculum were asepsis and antiseptic procedures. The Florence Nightingale School had a more demanding program of studies in asepsis and antisepsis, but the director, Dr. Anna Hamilton, was equally devoted to ensuring the immaculate appearance and irreproachable behavior of her students in order to offset lingering doubts about the respectability of lay nurses.[12] The Florence Nightingale School served as a model for nursing schools throughout France, and its graduates reorganized nursing in hospitals throughout southwestern France.[13]

For most of the nineteenth century, hygienists stressed public health measures. In response to a series of cholera epidemics, governments paved and drained streets, put in sewer lines, and cleared overcrowded neighborhoods. Yet a century later, public places still reeked of garbage, urine, and excrement. Paris had eighty thousand cesspools serving 70 percent of the population. Sewers were unknown in villages. In Lisieux, Mlle. Lucie took chamber pots "whose contents would soon be fertilizing the Norman fields" to the door to be collected—and profited from the occasion to greet neighbors or flirt with passing soldiers.[14]

Between 1880 and 1914, hygienists intensified their sanitary efforts. Most progress was made in the provision of potable water. In 1880, Pasteurians identified the typhoid bacillus, and in the early 1890s, the Pasteur Institute conducted bacteriological analyses of the capital's water supplies. After the release of their disturbing findings, city councils improved the quality of the drinking water and more than halved the typhoid mortality rate—to 2.4 per 10,000 people. In one of the earliest hygienic campaigns directed to women, homemakers' magazines informed readers about bacteriological counts and safe sources of water.[15] A 1902 law on public health completed a century of piecemeal state regulation of water supplies. For a quarter of a century thereafter, there was a tide of publicity about clean water. Publicity was necessary because implementation of the law was impeded by popular belief in the purifying, regenerating, and fecundating powers of source water.[16]

Such massive public intervention required political will. Dismayed about degeneration and depopulation, the republican elite was determined to lower mortality rates. Hygienists and politicians alike argued that France needed a healthier population in order to avenge its defeat in the Franco-Prussian War and to restore national prestige.[17] Solidarist republicans supported public health measures to prevent the epidemic diseases that infected entire urban neighborhoods.[18] The First World War revitalized demographic and public health rationales. *Hygiene Handbook,* reissued several times in the late 1920s and early 1930s, reported that the German population had increased by twenty-five million since the Franco-Prussian War, whereas the French population had only risen by three million. According to the authors, Drs. Courmont and Rochaix, much of this difference was the result of a higher proportion of French deaths from preventable diseases such as infant gastroenteritis, pulmonary tuberculosis, and chronic bronchitis. Like other hygienists, Courmont and Rochaix implicated maternal care because mothers cared for the infants, children, and adolescent girls who accounted for most of the mortality from these diseases.[19]

If microbiology transformed the meaning of washing from an act of propriety into one of eliminating germs, the habit of regular washing issued from a revised code of respectability.[20] Pasteurian hygiene relied heavily upon women implementing hygienic principles and inculcating them in the next generation. Before the Third Republic, physicians were pessimistic about teaching hygiene, even to "worldly people."[21] During the Republic, hygienists accepted that public hygiene required private hygiene and would involve public education for adults as well as children. Initially, public hygiene courses open to the educated public added lectures on housing, clothing, food, and bathing. By the turn of the century, most hygiene lectures emphasized the prevention of infectious disease.[22] Specialized periodicals on private hygiene appeared. *Be Healthy* warned readers about claims that absinthe was an elixir, informed readers about new diagnostic and therapeutic techniques such as x-rays, promoted the editor's sanatorium, and ran advertisements for an assortment of antiseptics, over-the-counter drugs, soaps, dental powders, hair pomades, and skin creams.[23] However, earnest periodicals that tried to interest the public in private hygiene rarely survived long.[24]

Mass circulation magazines reached a wider reading public. Goubert analyzed the hygienic messages in *L'Illustration*, a lavishly illustrated magazine with press runs of 200,000 in 1910 and 400,000 in 1931, and in *Le Petit Journal*, a modest magazine with four times as many readers. The former was addressed to the bourgeoisie, the latter to the petty bourgeoisie and workers. *L'Illustration* ran articles and advertisements for skin and hair care products and, after 1920, for tooth powders. Both the articles and the advertisements promoted cleanliness for individual health and social distinction. With the exception of tooth powders, most of the hygiene products showcased in *Le Petit Journal* differed from those publicized in *L'Illustration*. The pitch to petty bourgeois readers also varied: cleanliness would alleviate the wear and tear of life. Interestingly, the popular magazine appealed more to faith in science than did the bourgeois magazine.[25]

By comparison, women's magazines contained far more advertisements for household cleansing agents, bath soaps, and, after 1920, the deodorant Odorono, as well as for clinics for women and children and an assortment of tonics for anemia, constipation, migraines, and other common "feminine complaints."[26] The early advertisements for cleansers and prophylactic products were informative and intimidating; they told consumers about the ubiquity of germs and therefore the potential for infections. In the course of the 1890s, French advertisements (like those in America) became more positive and persuasive in the sense of promising that cleanliness meant comeliness.[27] If the advertising business abandoned scare tactics four decades before official hygienic propaganda did,[28] it also correlated cleanliness, comeliness, and ultimately femininity with the consumption of health and beauty products.

After the First World War, hygienists criticized the dry factual approach of their predecessors. According to Dr. Chavigny, hygiene should not be "the art of boring people like themselves, wrapping it in prescriptions so rigid, impractical, and revolting that it becomes a virtue accessible only to members of an elite resolved to mortify themselves." Evidently Chavigny had not perused beauty magazines and manuals! He called for an army led by physician-hygienists and troops of teachers and administrators[29] but ignored visiting nurses and mothers. Unlike Chavigny, most hygienists considered nurses, housewives, and mothers important allies in instilling habits of cleanliness. Changes in their advice to nurses and mothers between the 1880s and 1930s indicate that hygienists made some progress.[30]

According to Goubert, historians have too long accepted hygienists' representation of women as traditionalists hindering their campaigns for cleanliness.[31] Although most nineteenth-century charities serving the sick involved hospital volunteers, hundreds of maternal charities sent lady visitors to distribute assistance to married mothers and to offer them child and house care advice. Even before state subsidies were available in 1886, secular charities such as the Ladies of Republican Assistance stressed hygienic counsel. With the exception of the Evangelical Church deaconesses, who received some training, lady visitors were expected to know basic hygiene and bedside nursing as feminine attributes. In reality, they learned some skills in the home and the rest while volunteering.[32]

In the 1880s and 1890s, volunteers sought formal training through the women's auxiliaries of the Red Cross. Dr. Duchaussoy, who had established a school for ambulance attendants in 1877, founded the Society of French Ladies in 1879. Two years later, the rival Union of French Women formed to care for soldiers and civilians wounded in war or natural disasters. From the beginning, the union offered free courses to train hospital nurses and "spread indispensable ideas about hygiene." By 1900, the two associations offered courses in seventy cities. Cities and departments subsidized clinics with two-year courses on volunteer nursing.[33]

In 1913, a law recognized trained Red Cross volunteers by placing them under the authority of the military medical service but prohibited them from hospital service on the front lines. For a few months after the outbreak of war, these volunteers ran an ambulance service transporting wounded soldiers to convalescent hospitals and staffed the hospitals, many of them located in members' homes. But by 1915, Red Cross nurses were serving in front-line hospitals. All of the approximately 500,000 women who served as nurses during the war learned something about anatomy, physiology, and hygiene. Most wartime art, literature, and propaganda represent nurses as white-robed angels of mercy or as society ladies seeking intimate contact with men. Margaret Darrow argues that the latter image prevailed because it reflected fears of feminine intrusion into the preeminently masculine sphere of war.[34] The negative image also obscured the impact of hundreds of thousands of women acquiring some medical knowledge of the human body.

After a 1893 law on free medical assistance, there were schemes to train professionals based on the model of English district nurses, whose primary duty was teaching household and personal hygiene during home and school visits. A maternal charity began training home nurses, and the Association for Assistance to the Sick opened a school with anatomy, physiology, hygiene, first aid, and medical and surgical nursing classes for home nurses. In the second year of training, one of the two practicums involved visiting homes and schools. Under the direction of Dr. Germaine Montreuil-Strauss, the school attracted some of the country's most distinguished medical professors.[35] Yet the real impetus came after the war, when the Rockefeller Mission encouraged public nursing, provided equipment, and funded seventy scholarships at five French nursing schools. In 1922, the new Ministry of Health, Welfare, and Social Insurance created two diplomas in visiting nursing, one specializing in tuberculosis care, the other in infant care. By 1929, there were twenty-nine schools training public health nurses, and they had awarded 25,000 diplomas in public health nursing.[36] These women carried their knowledge into hundreds of thousands of homes.

As early as 1883, Dr. Monin, winner of a contest on the subject of household and individual hygiene, made the connection between public and private hygiene. Monin held that "House care is an indispensable factor in urban hygiene; making cleanliness habitual is the only way of attenuating the causes of infection in populous cities." Most of the house care chapter informed "the master of the house" of police ordinances on ventilating the lavatory, disposing of organic waste, and other "masculine" tasks. Although the rest of that chapter did not address housewives directly, it advised daily damp mopping and beating of rugs and drapery to avoid accumulating dust and spreading contagion.[37] With the diffusion of Pasteurian principles and the mounting crusade against tuberculosis in the 1890s, the link between antiseptic hygiene and housewifery was forged.[38] Housewifery manuals and magazines provided instructions about the use of antiseptic cleansers to eliminate germs.[39] Women's and feminist magazines ran columns by women doctors whose topics alternated between personal hygiene and beauty one month and hints for disinfecting homes the next month. In the 1920s, these magazines distributed throughout each issue advertisements for soaps, lotions, bleaches, and other household cleansers, locating them conveniently close to articles advocating their use instead of confining them to the last four pages of each issue.[40]

As bourgeois standards rose to weekly laundering, there was a trend to home laundering and the purchase of washing machines. Household manuals endorsed vacuum cleaners around 1900, but the French adopted them slowly.[41] Unlike the Fourth Republic,[42] the Third Republic did not witness a rush to acquire household appliances. After the First World War, mass merchandising of household appliances began. In 1923, more than 100,000 visitors attended the first Salon of Household Arts, which exhibited two hundred appliances. Many visitors to the annual salons had their first glimpse of washing machines, vacuum cleaners, electric stoves, and refrigerators, but most bought only small items such as graters. In the late 1920s, manufacturers financed a magazine, *Household Art*, in which medical professionals promoted appliances such as refrigerators, which they said would prevent the multiplication of germs in foods. Pauline Befnage, the magazine editor, was a proponent of the American domestic science movement. She urged bourgeois women to solve the postwar servant crisis and family financial crises by purchasing "time-saving" devices that would allow women to have a career and raise their children. However, French housewives were not as inclined to define their status by appliances as American housewives were. Even with new credit opportunities, few French households could afford these appliances.[43]

According to Social Catholics, France lagged behind other European countries in "scientific" home economics.[44] At the turn of the century, girls in boarding and normal schools did household tasks, which were justified as "instructive of good order and economy, and a way of occupying both their body and their spirit." At that time, girls took one hour a week of domestic economy for two years at senior primary school or studied "domestic duties" in the third year of secondary school.[45] After changes in 1908, the domestic economy course still emphasized "administration of the house, . . . order, foresight, economy, upkeep, sewing, general cooking principles, and household accounts." Social feminists such as Lydia Martial, who believed that home economics could lead to female enfranchisement, put as much emphasis on economy as she did on cleanliness.[46] The home economics curriculum did not significantly increase its natural science content until the mid-1930s.[47]

Expectations of housewives rose after the three feminist congresses held during the 1900 Universal Exposition in Paris. These congresses expanded the definition of housewifery to include charitable work, careers, and even political involvement. Social Catholics mobilizing against the anticlerical Combes cabinet (1902–5) were especially active. By the elections of 1902, the League of French Women had seventy-three local committees, many of which opened institutes on housewifery to teach ladies how to pass on their knowledge to working women. Charities such as the Trousseau made gifts of household necessities upon marriage conditional on household training: "to form a generation of women and mothers which we hope will bring France more stable and fecund homes." By 1933, when two Catholic feminist leagues merged, the new league had one and a half million members.[48]

Hygienists also advocated a broader definition of housewifery. In 1908, Dr. Héricourt contended that a housewife could work part time to "supplement" her husband's salary without neglecting her house and children. The following year, Dr. Marthe Francillon-Lobre claimed that "moral hygiene" required intellectual endeavor and foresaw a future "when, with full consciousness of her duty as a woman, she will have . . . a more general social role."[49] Concurrently, hygienists expanded the maternal and domestic role. The new science of nutrition introduced notions such as the caloric intake needed for body heat. Housewives were urged to learn about carbohydrates, proteins, and combinations suitable for men, women, children, and different physical conditions. One manual printed twelve diets, which were divided about evenly among regimes for gaining weight, for losing weight, and for various occupations.[50] In addition to preparing home remedies and stocking "family pharmacies," housewives were supposed to learn about germs and common diseases, keep sick rooms antiseptically clean, and carry out doctors' orders.[51]

Although criticism of housewives peaked with expectations, at least feminists were constructive. In 1897, the moderate feminist Augusta Moll-Weiss (1863–1957) established a mothers' school in Bordeaux with separate classes and fee schedules for bourgeois and working-class women. In 1904, a similar school opened in Paris. Moll-Weiss was an advocate of domestic economy in twenty texts over the next twenty-five years.[52] Soon a Society for Modern Instruction offered adult education courses in family medication; normal schools for women mounted similar courses. To allay medical opposition, Mlle. Munié, the course designer for the normal schools, reassured doctors that it would make mothers their handmaids. Certainly the units on asepsis and antisepsis resemble the same units in practical nursing texts.[53] However, family medication courses did not thrive, largely because the Ministry of Public Education, swayed by the opposition of the medical men on their advisory council, rejected public school courses. Instead, the ministry increased the rudimentary medical content in the girls' hygiene and home economics curricula.[54]

Bathing Beauties

New standards of cleanliness increased the workload of housewives and mothers. Women were persuaded to undertake these new responsibilities not solely by altruistic appeals to foster familial health, but also by more self-serving appeals about enhancing personal beauty and status. For instance, a "feminist university" with courses on childcare, cooking, and mending mounted courses on "beauty, happiness and health by hygiene."[55] The hygienic promotion of bathing best illustrates the process of "seduction."[56]

In Dr. Monin's 1884 book on household and individual hygiene, the chapter on personal cleanliness described the skin as an organ of respiration, secretion, excretion, and absorption and declared that keeping pores free of dirt and sweat was the foundation for health.[57] Earlier health and beauty guides had stressed cleansing facial skin to achieve a clear complexion;[58] after 1884, health and beauty guides put more emphasis on washing the whole body with soap and water to remove dirt, sweat, and, after the 1890s, germs.[59] As early as 1886, in *The Hygiene of Beauty*, Monin coupled corporeal cleanliness with comeliness. Similarly titled books, with identical messages, soon followed.[60] By the mid-1890s, a journalist reported that bathing was a "fad" among "refined" women, a sign of self-respect and "a demi-virtue." One hygienist felt that he had to remind his female readers that bathing was not an act of coquetry but of cleansing.[61]

At this time, whole-body bathing was a very complicated affair. There were several kinds of baths depending on the temperature of the water, the products added to the water, and the purpose of the bath. Hygienists did not prescribe hot baths, which they believed made the skin flabby and the bather lethargic; they preferred cold baths to accelerate blood circulation and tone the skin. Cold baths subdued nervous or hysterical people, who, in their opinion, were mainly girls and women. Fortunately, most beauty books counseled splashing cold water on the breasts alone, to prevent them from sagging. Tepid water, with a dash of lemon juice or ammonia, would prevent "the birth of microbes."[62] Although most hygienists dismissed the milk, berry, or champagne baths linked to the names of royal mistresses and courtesans as frauds, expensive beauty manuals reprinted recipes for Diane de Poitier's milk bath and endorsed expensive additives for beauty baths. Modestly priced beauty guides promoted cheaper alternatives. Both hygienists and beauty counselors approved of adding plants and chemicals to the bath water for health or beauty purposes—for example, bran for oily skin. In 1912, Dr. Mestadier's *Beauty: Feminine Hygiene* included fifteen recipes for herbal and chemical baths.[63]

Lack of bathing facilities limited who could bathe and how often anyone could bathe. Around 1900, one million Parisians were without running water in their residences and had to get their water from wells or fountains; only 4 percent of homes had installed bathtubs; even fewer had hot-water heaters.[64] In many bourgeois households, a full bath required maids to take as many as thirty trips to a fountain and then heat much of the water. Other bourgeois families hired a bathtub from agencies whose porters carried the tub and hot water up the stairs (where most bourgeois had their private quarters).[65] Bathrooms were a novelty. Introduced as an aristocratic luxury in the eighteenth century, they barely figured in domestic architecture texts until the 1890s and did not become a standard feature in Art Nouveau apartments until 1900. At that time, only five out of eight Parisian bathtubs were located in bathrooms.[66]

In this context, publishers put out two books devoted to bathrooms and two beauty books with long sections on bathrooms.[67] All four recommended white tile walls and floors and white porcelain fixtures for easy disinfecting and vents to evacuate steam, gas fumes from water heaters, and odors. Like advertisements in magazines and on posters, these books described and depicted various sizes and shapes of bathtubs, showers that sprayed the body from different angles, and sinks affixed to commodes instead of the conventional basins and jugs. The illustrations signal a purified but luxurious space. Like the advertisements, beauty books listed manufacturers' addresses. Together, books, magazines, and posters publicized marble dressing tables and chaise lounges, soap dishes, towel racks, and a staggering array of bath salts, creams, and lotions.[68] They also decisively associated women with bathing and feminine beauty with bath products (see Figs. 3 and 4).

Despite the real lack of privacy for bathing, beauty counselors were obsessed with privacy in the bathroom. They were determined to dissociate bathing from the voyeuristic paintings and prints of bathing women which had been in vogue in the last three decades of the nineteenth century. Respectable women associated the figures of women bathing in the presence of men (and models posing for male artists) with prostitutes and demimondaines.[69] The beauty countesses also instructed their readers not to allow their husbands to watch them bathing as a form of marital titillation[70] (see Fig. 5). These canny authors appreciated that the halving of the birth rate among bourgeois women freed them from perpetual childrearing and allowed them

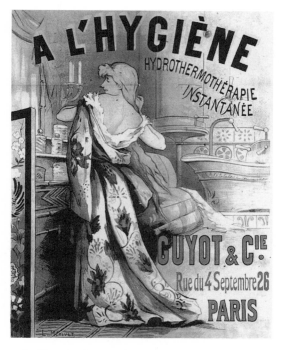

3. "A l'hygiène" poster by Lucien Metivet, about 1897.
Bibliothèque Forney

some time to cater to their bodies. They called bathrooms *sanctuaries* and *asylums* to underscore that bathing and beauty routines were times that were free from responsibilities to others. The waning of arranged marriages put a high premium on acquiring husbands through physical attraction and heightened women's aspiration to be attractive. So, too, did the burgeoning number of beauty books with their refrain about the "innate" desire of women to be beautiful and the need to "work at beauty" in order to be loved.[71] A few hygienists used similar rhetoric. Dr. Jean d'Auteuil, who critiqued "scientific theories" of feminine inferiority, was nevertheless confident that woman's "mission" was "to please, charm, love and be loved."[72]

Into the 1930s, health and beauty books described model bathrooms, although the new ones included fewer fixtures and did not assume built-in tubs or running water. The model room remained a sterile white, but washable oil paint or wallpaper covered the walls, and linoleum or flagstone covered the floors.[73] Installation of simpler bathrooms proceeded slowly until the 1960s.

4. "Savon Cadum" poster by Georges Villa, 1930s.
Bibliothèque Forney

Between the early 1960s and the mid-1970s, the percentage of French homes with a bath or shower rose from 29 to 70. Behavior also evolved; in the 1970s, one quarter of the populace bathed or showered daily, and half bathed or showered two or three times weekly. Women were nearly twice as likely to bathe daily. A majority of women considered washing "a question of physical well-being and pleasure."[74]

Incidentally, the 1930s bathroom had a new fixture. In the late nineteenth century, only 5 percent of Parisians owned bidets. In the popular imagination, bidets were located in bordellos and used for birth control.[75] Dr. René Martial and Mme. Léontine Doresse's hygiene textbook, *Popular Feminine Hygiene*, which told how to use a bidet, was hastily removed from school libraries.[76] Most boarding schools for girls did not have bidets until the 1930s. Very few girls' schools taught "intimate hygiene" until the late 1930s.[77]

5. Caricature, "Secret professionnel," 1890s.

Bibliothèque Nationale de France

Schooling "Future Mothers"

Another way to inculcate cleanliness—and corporeal awareness—was to educate girls in hygiene. Even before the Third Republic, some hygienists advocated "setting aside natural feminine modesty" and instituting hygiene courses for girls on the grounds that certain health precepts differed by sex and that "their families will be the first to benefit."[78] As dread about tuberculosis and syphilis mounted in the early twentieth century, another rationale for girls' hygiene courses was to prepare "the first rank of combatants against the plagues menacing our times."[79]

Before the official hygiene programs of 1897–1902, textbooks defined hygiene as the art of conserving health or of ensuring that "every system functions freely, easily, and regularly." In this enduring formulation, health required sobriety, temperance, exercise, and serenity.[80] After public criticism about neglecting modern scientific principles, educators redefined health as cleanliness based upon physiology and bacteriology. In 1902, rudimentary germ theory made its appearance in school hygiene texts, mainly in warnings that clothing was "a vehicle for germs."[81] Long after commercial advertisers and health guides discarded the informative but frightening approach, school texts illustrated the importance of cleanliness in disquieting ways. For instance, a 1932 text reported that the skin had so many microbes, it left more than 500 million behind in the bath water.[82]

After the First World War, hygienists condemned primary school teachers for "dogmatic pedagogy" and secondary school teachers for disdaining hygiene as a practical subject.[83] The 1923 hygiene program specified three pedagogical principles: teach good habits, promote health precepts, and include physical exercises. Rejecting rote learning, the program mandated practical experience. But this was not done easily. A village teacher, Emilie Carles, described her efforts: "Whether it was hygiene or morals, I did my best to go beyond words and sentimental platitudes and to offer them direct contact with reality. When I talked to them about cleanliness and personal hygiene, I took them to Les Arcades [her family hotel], showed them a bathroom, lavatory, washing machine. . . . I was lucky to have all that at hand."[84]

In school hygiene texts, as in commercial health manuals, class and gender set the parameters. Whereas primary school textbooks for children from humble circumstances emphasized scrubbing hands and nails, secondary school texts for bourgeois children dictated weekly baths.[85] Primary school texts made few changes in precepts, suggesting a very slow acculturation in the new practices. Twice-daily face and hand washing remained the core of the repetitive primary school curriculum because these simple routines might actually be performed in most homes and because teachers could enforce them by inspecting students' faces and hands. (Texts did change rationales. Early republican texts presented a monthly tub bath and a weekly sponge bath as moral duties.[86] After 1902, primary school texts kept the same schedule but reinforced it with social stigmas such as the warning about how shameful it would be to be found with soiled underwear after an accident.[87])

At the senior primary and secondary schools, twelve hours of hygiene lessons covered potable water, ventilation, and infectious diseases plus four hours of antialcohol education. At twelve or thirteen, boys studied cesspool management and animal husbandry; girls studied safe cosmetics, clothing, and childcare.[88] Aside from the obvious assumptions about future gender roles, there were disturbing omissions. Despite statistics showing that adolescent girls were more susceptible to pulmonary and bronchial infections than adolescent boys, girls learned less than boys did about infectious diseases. However, shortly after the introduction of this curriculum, private courses in family medicine, with units on preventing infectious diseases, began.

Age and gender differences recurred in units on hair care. Primary school texts instilled the idea that children should wash their hair to cleanse the scalp and get rid of parasites. As Mme. Lucie makes clear, "people didn't wash their hair all the time, and more or less everyone had little bugs—not lice—or scales in their hair." Children joked about the bugs. In vain, school texts discouraged the use of pomades, oils, and dyes, all of which were advertised in magazines for girls.[89] Health guides for women were more exigent about washing hair but more indulgent about pomades. Until the 1930s, most guides instructed women to wash their hair once a fortnight; in the 1930s, guides switched to a weekly schedule. The stated purposes were the very bourgeois goals of cleanliness, propriety, and appearance; no one mentioned comfort or removing parasites from the hair. Hygienists disapproved of dyes and bleaches because they damaged hair follicles, but they were fighting a losing battle. Even *La Fronde* advertised dyes to eliminate gray hair and "a gentle, progressive bleaching agent." After salons introduced hair dryers in the first decade of the new century, hygienists found themselves promoting hair oil to combat dryness and split ends.[90]

Hair length caused concerns other than the gender anxiety and cultural commotion provoked by the bob in the 1920s. One prewar text explained that boys could wash their hair weekly but that girls should only wash their longer

hair monthly because it took longer to dry. A women's health guide recommended dividing long hair into sections, rubbing soap into each section,
and rinsing each section with a wet cloth. Another insisted that blonds should
comb in rice powder, leave it overnight, and then brush it out. Postwar hygienists did not mention such complicated procedures because they were less
anxious about immersing long hair and because women wore their hair
shorter.

Protecting the Female Body

If the core of the school hygiene curriculum was washing the body, classes for
girls also included clothing. Although most of the clothing rules differed
from those in health and beauty manuals for women, one common theme was
protection of the female body because of pervasive anxieties about feminine
frailty and sexual allure.

Hygiene texts for girls taught that clothes should be clean, warm, modest,
and loose. The most common precept was to change underwear every two or
three days—a precept that reflected the fact that few households did weekly
washes or had several sets of underwear per person. Before the Third Republic, hygienists had dictated warmer underwear for girls, who were allegedly
weaker and less active than boys were.[91] As new knowledge about maintaining
body heat by physical activity filtered into textbooks, concern about preventing heat loss dissipated. Most republican texts recommended cotton flannel
underwear, which was washed more easily and was less easily "impregnated
with odor" than woolen underwear. Around 1900, modesty meant dresses of
white or pale-colored material with long skirts and high necklines. After the
war, only the dictum about high necklines remained in textbooks. The final
rule was that clothing should not constrict growth, circulation, or respiration.
In the 1890s, texts blamed garters for varicose veins and endorsed garter belts.
Within a decade, garter belts replaced garters.[92] By 1900, texts targeted rigid,
tight, laced corsets.

In the 1880s and early 1890s, laywomen who wrote commercial health
guides accepted the custom of adolescent girls wearing corsets to support
their spinal columns, which were supposedly weak because of soft bones.
These writers publicized the new flexible corsets with front laces and pliable
whalebones, saying that they would not obstruct circulation as much as back-
laced corsets with rigid metal stays did.[93] Early republican school texts agreed
that adolescent girls needed corsets to support their spinal column. Concerned
about compression of internal organs and possible asphyxiation, these texts

championed corsets made of expandable fabrics with no mention of stays.[94] By the turn of the century, hygienists launched a campaign against corsets for adolescent girls (except for prophylactic, mainly orthopedic purposes), arguing that corsets hampered development of the thorax and lungs. Dr. O'Fallowell (mentioned in Chap. 1) endorsed the new, full-length brassiere held up by shoulder straps but laced at the bottom because this foundation garment left the upper thorax free to expand and the lungs room to breathe while bolstering the lower vertebrae.[95] The dissemination of information that girls breathed from their chest (unlike boys, who breathed from their diaphragm) contributed to the precipitous drop in the number of adolescent girls wearing corsets in the prewar decade.

Health guides for women had less rigid rules about clothing. They did discourage low necklines on the grounds that bare necks and shoulders were vulnerable to colds and influenzas. Although they rarely mentioned modesty, they suggested that too much *décolleté* was indecent, indeed *déclassé*. Only Dr. Marie Schultz (the Theosophist) proclaimed that light clothing "hardens the body against the cold."

Health manuals were more fashion conscious than girls' hygiene texts were. At the beginning of the transition to looser dresses (in the first decade of the twentieth century), Schultz approved the new tubular line dress style because it did not constrict the thorax and lungs. Like many authors of health books for women, she welcomed the disappearance of trains because they accumulated dust and germs.[96] Later women doctors joined dress reformers in support of shorter skirts for greater freedom of movement but drew the line at trousers. In the early 1930s, one author of a health guide (who wrote a column for a fashion magazine) joined in the fashion industry's celebration of shorter skirts for women's more active life. "The active, difficult life of women no longer allows us to be hampered by trains and heavy materials. Using the automobile, metro, and bus demanded an agility paralyzed by long, heavy dresses."[97]

The battle about corsets for adult women was contested bitterly. Writing at the end of wasp-waist fashions, the beauty countesses of the Belle Epoque acknowledged that acute angles and rigid posture were no longer chic, but they advised changing from corsets with steel stays to corsets with whalebone stays for smoother lines and more graceful movements.[98] *La Fronde* published articles on how women could measure themselves for corsets and promoted an expandable corset for freer movement. Physicians made serious (although undocumented) allegations that laced corsets squeezed the lower ribs together, squashed breasts and nipples, and thereby jeopardized pregnancies and breast-feeding. Lay women forcefully defended corsets for women with full figures or distended abdominal muscles after several pregnancies.[99]

In the first decade of the twentieth century, accord developed on the dangers of corsets for pregnant and lactating women. Typically, hygienists decried their effect on fetuses and nurslings, and beauty counselors and feminists spoke about the pregnant and lactating woman's comfort. Hygienists recommended smaller elastic belts to support the distended abdomen; these "pregnancy belts" were still sold in the 1930s.[100] By then, hygienists declared the corset "*passé*" either because looser dress styles did not require corsets or because women's employment and sports made them impractical.[101] In actuality, many women wore longer, elasticized corsets (girdles) that reduced the hips to attain the newly fashionable straight, slender silhouette.[102] However, public attention focused more on exercising for a more androgynous and adolescent body. We will return to the subject of exercise in Chapter 8.

Conclusions

Instilling the practice of private hygiene was political in many senses of the word. In the public arena, politicians concerned about revenge, degeneration, and depopulation instituted and influenced school hygiene programs, and educational bureaucrats structured programs around gendered assumptions about feminine responsibility for household and family hygiene. In marketing, there were also gendered appeals to women's duties toward their families and, more seductively, to their right to take care of their bodies. Despite some tension between the utilitarian advice in the manuals and the more self-indulgent appeals in the advertisements, together they had considerable effect.

PART 2

Reproductive Rhythms

—◦❧ • ❧◦—

CAROLL SMITH-ROSENBERG says that puberty and menopause in
nineteenth-century America were socially defined "points of entrance
into new social roles and responsibilities" and that physiological tran-
sitions heralded by the appearance of menstrual blood and hot flashes,
for example, were signposts that "even the most sexually repressed"
culture had to acknowledge. She finds that the physiological changes
and rites of passage of adolescence and old age were not solely feminine but had a more exclusively sexual meaning for women because
of medical and popular assumptions about the sway of the reproductive organs over the female body and the feminine personality. Wom-
en's attitudes toward these turning points were ambivalent.[1] In Third
Republic France, similarly sexualized and ambivalent attitudes concerning feminine puberty and menopause and about sexual initiation
and maternity prevailed. By the end of the nineteenth century, competing medical etiologies and, in France, a hegemonic discourse about
natality, further complicated representations of puberty, sexuality,
maternity, and menopause.

In many cultures, menarche is a biological event "fraught with
cultural implications," symbolizing adult womanhood and accelerat-
ing socialization in heterosexuality.[2] In Third Republic France, parents, educators, and moralists preferred to postpone the acknowledgment of adulthood and sexuality. Because the first period presaged
sexual activity, they worried about the virtue of young girls. As Chapter 4 reveals, French parents and experts responded by trying to protect girls' "purity," meaning naiveté about their bodies and sexual relations. In one of many ironic twists in the discourse on women's
bodies, a society obsessed with natality offered young women little in-

formation about sex organs and only vague allusions to sexual desire. One consequence was that adolescent girls felt alienated from their sexuality—which may have been adaptive, given the convoluted attitudes toward adult women's sexuality. Although the medical profession denied that puberty, maternity, and menopause were "morbid states," they defined them as periods of vulnerability to morbidity and mortality. Endocrinologists and psychiatrists defined the psychology of puberty much as they defined the psychology of adult women: irrational, modest, and coquettish.

Since Foucault, many scholars have argued that modern sexuality—as the "matrix through which other factors . . . worked to produce an individual"—emerged in the *fin de siècle*.[3] As Angus McLaren demonstrated, defining masculine sexuality by the sex of their partners was not sufficient. Psychologists, criminologists, and judges set and policed boundaries to male heterosexual "excess" by identifying certain heterosexual practices as perversions. By 1900, Octave Uzanne observed that sadism, fashionable among the literati fifteen years before, had become a "perversion."[4] To explain literary and biomedical interest in masculine reproductive heterosexuality, historians refer to the "sexual anarchy" or "crisis of masculinity" in the *fin de siècle*.[5] After the Great War, another gender "crisis" occurred in which literary and journalistic criticism of independent and childless women was juxtaposed with praise for married mothers of large families.[6] In the context of *ongoing* gender debates—not periodic gender crises—sexual advice literature proliferated.

The new expertise created dilemmas about sexuality. Newly identified deviancies destabilized the notion of anatomically determined sexuality. Once sexual deviation could not be linked to pathological anatomy, scientists sought psychological explanations. In addition to their recourse to the all-purpose diagnosis of degeneration, psychologists "discovered" a sexual instinct.[7] But French psychologists resisted a complete severing of a sex drive from a physical site as well as the implications of Freudian notions that a sexual instinct was separate from a reproductive outcome.[8] Sexual advice books, which lagged behind sexual research, mirrored researchers' uncertainty about sexual identity. Long after researchers denied that sex organs were the determinants of sexual identity, sexual advice books privileged (some, primarily male) genital measurements. Eclectically if inconsistently, they postulated a sexual instinct in men[9] and later, and begrudgingly, in women.

In Chapter 5 I analyze the maternal supervision of courtship and its breakdown as young women acquired more freedom to choose husbands after the First World War. A new genre of premarital sexual advice, designed to help mothers teach their daughters about sex, flourished. Compared with contemporary sex guides for girls in the United States, more of these guides were written by medical men, and almost all were preoccupied with natality. To establish their authority on the subject of sex, secular authors appealed successfully to the authority of medical science. This appeal was part of a larger trend to privilege scientific ways of knowing, a trend that tended to stifle alternative ways of knowing about sexuality.[10] These guides were pessimistic about the pleasures of early conjugal relations, even as they and their counterparts, marital sex guides, tried to persuade young wives to reproduce as often as possible. Not surprisingly, young women resisted their mixed message.

In Chapter 5 I also compare these sex guides with the companion form of prescriptive literature, guides for grooms. Many cultures single out "first sex" as a "key act" in establishing sexual identity. Some anthropologists believe that first sex is especially important for young men because they have not experienced menarche and a socially recognized puberty, other "constitutive moments" in the establishment of sexual identity. The implication is that young men do not achieve sexuality as naturally and passively as young women do but rather must learn and express it actively, even aggressively.[11] In Third Republic France, there was as much if not more interest in the sexual initiation of brides. Experts were concerned because so many brides entered marriage ignorant of the details of sexual intercourse. They were also uncertain that young women had acquired an appropriately reproductive sexual identity naturally.

In Chapter 6 I explore the motif of the necessary correlation among marriage, sex, and maternity in women's sex and health advice literature throughout the Third Republic. In this chapter I also identify a growing number of sexual experts who espoused the desirability of feminine sexual pleasure, even in marriage, and a tiny minority of experts who cautiously endorsed new female-controlled forms of contraception. One consequence of the contrast between the mainstream stark and deterministic message and a more optimistic and self-determining alternative vision was the complete failure of the conservatives to achieve their goal of raising the marital birth rate. In addition, the ambivalence of medical experts about maternity and their perversity about the necessity of labor pains countered their appeals to have more babies.

At the other end of the spectrum, European historians have virtually ignored menopause, perhaps because of European antipathy toward aging in general and aging women in particular.[12] Another explanation for the omission in pronatalist countries such as France may be that cultural representations of "woman" as a reproductive being implied that menopause meant a loss of femininity and fertility.[13] In Chapter 7 I show that this negative conception of menopause threatened many women's sense of self and encouraged denial in the historical record. Conversely, negative expectations boosted women's demand for medical services to alleviate any possible pain. A new specialty, endocrinology, redefined menopause as an ovarian deficiency entailing a loss of fertility and femininity and offered an antidote in the form of ovarian therapies.

Women who lacked knowledge of their organic processes but knew the negative image of menopause may well have remained silent about their menopause, at least in their journals and memoirs. However, autobiographical silence may have another meaning. Certainly reports that many nineteenth-century practitioners never treated symptoms identified as menopausal dovetail with recent surveys showing that most women do not report enough suffering to disrupt their lives or to consult doctors.[14] For some insight into women's experience of menopause, we turn to the few medical writers who discussed social factors and to women's fiction. Both suggest that women who had defined themselves by their physical charms were most apprehensive about loss of sex appeal.

Chapter 4

Puberty and Purity

D̶ESPITE negative interpretations in the Greek medical and Judeo-Christian traditions, Europeans in the nineteenth century had ambivalent attitudes toward menstruation, the stage of life initiated by its appearance, and, by extension, sexually mature women. During the Third Republic, popular attitudes about menstruation combined disgust about pollution—material or symbolic contamination—and more positive beliefs. Although anthropologists remind us that the word *taboo* fuses the notions of holy and forbidden, it also conjures up supernatural beliefs, which are so often disdained. Accordingly, this chapter deals with the medico-social rules about menstruation described below as menstrual etiquette enforced by ridicule and ostracism, not fear of magical reprisals.[1]

Pollution and Power

In the late nineteenth and early twentieth centuries, French terms for menstruation included *period, menses, monthlies, moons, the business, the usuals, the red loss, the curse, indisposed,* and *illness.* The last two terms derived from Jules Michelet's mid-nineteenth-century study of women as "eternally wounded."[2] Whatever the term used, it had disparate connotations. Many French people associated menstruation with evil powers—for example, a capacity to spoil preserved foods that had been prepared by men and were understood to be strong or virile foods. In some rural areas, menstruating women were forbidden to salt or preserve foods. In the north of France, where many women worked in sugar refineries, menstruating women were not supposed to enter refineries for fear that they would "blacken" the sugar.[3] Although these exclusionary practices had negative implications, they may have provided welcome relief for overworked women. Balancing these exclusionary practices were positive feminine traditions, such as the conviction that menstruating women could predict the kind of month to come by the day their period began.[4]

In popular opinion, menstrual blood was toxic, including menotoxic, meaning that it irritated the genitals of women and their sexual partners. This belief was the cause and consequence of customary rules about not changing underwear, washing the pubic region, or engaging in sexual intercourse during the flow. Throughout the Republic, hygienists campaigned against the first two rules. (In Chap. 6 I discuss hygienists' more diffident approach to intercourse during the flow.) Most girls and women wore folded rags or old skirts to absorb menstrual blood. Doctors argued that the rags were not washed often enough and that the skirts were "disgusting." In their estimation, menstrual blood was not to be seen or smelled.[5] The near silence about menstrual periods in Frenchwomen's autobiographical writing testifies to their authors' internalization of this opinion.

In contrast to menstruation, there were few popular terms for puberty. Some people used the generic phrase *critical age*, which was also applied to menopause. A more specific phrase was *the unattractive age*, meaning the gangly, awkward phase of development. Not surprisingly, there was little positive recognition of an important stage in the lives of girls. At best, some families acknowledged "the change" by beginning to call their newly menstruating daughters "big girls."[6] Generally, society surrounded the word *puberty* with "a halo of mystery, an unhealthy, dangerous halo."[7]

In popular and learned opinion, mothers were expected to teach girls about their private parts and pubic hygiene. According to lay and medical manuals on women's and family health, mothers were to wash the genital region of their prepubescent daughters because it was vulnerable to infections and because scratching these infections could lead to masturbation.[8] (Otherwise, concern about girls practicing "the solitary vice" concentrated on boarding schools.)[9] Medical manuals were especially exigent about mothers watching for signs such as lethargy and a white vaginal discharge to alert them to the approach of menarche. When their daughters reached puberty, mothers were supposed to supervise their twice-daily pubic ablutions. Hygienists were not satisfied with maternal observance of these strictures because they constantly admonished mothers not to be embarrassed about overseeing their daughters' pubic care.[10] Maternal reticence no doubt reflected ignorance and shame about "private parts." Texts on natural science and hygiene did not describe the pubic region. Even maternal feminists such as Augusta Moll-Weiss, who designed a course to educate future mothers "according to their physiology," omitted reproduction and the sexual organs.[11]

The significant minority of French girls who were taught by nuns (38 percent of schoolgirls in 1886 and one quarter in 1911) encountered mistrust of their sexual parts in convent and boarding school proscriptions against bathing naked and washing above the knees in footbaths.[12] Sometimes parents had to insist on their daughter having a full-body bath, which, in the case of Judith Gautier, meant that the mortified sisters left the confused young girl alone with a tub of water and orders not to remove her chemise. This kind of prudery, which was called *modesty*, persisted outside the convent and boarding school. The mother of courtesan-turned-princess Liane de Pougy made her wear a chemise when she bathed "for the sake of modesty and good breeding." When Pougy "deliberately left off the chemise" after she married her prince, it "caused a scandal in the house, scolding, predictions of disaster. Modesty, even if only in her own eyes, was a woman's loveliest quality; losing modesty, she lost everything, even her husband's respect."[13]

One need not be a Freudian to recognize that silence about and concealment of female genitalia might impair girls' and women's body images and sexual imagination.[14] Note what fifteen-year-old Catherine Pozzi elided in the otherwise comprehensive (and disturbingly judgmental) inventory of her body parts in her private journal. "My arms are thin, my entire body is long and thin. . . . My legs are long, my ankles slim, and my feet very big. My hands are long and slender; they would be pretty if they were not so brown. Together this forms a rather unsatisfying whole."[15] Although autobiographies written for publication are less candid, they confirm embarrassment about exposed genitalia. Louise Weiss records that when she opened a temporary hospital in her home during the First World War, she was too dismayed to assist a doctor treating an elderly woman with a prolapsed uterus. Emilie Carles tells of another peasant woman who had never seen another adult woman naked. She "could not imagine exposing her nakedness [pubic region] to anyone," even to a midwife, with the result that the peasant died during a difficult delivery.[16] Other factors such as sexual abuse may explain this unusual degree of inhibition. Whatever the reason, Anne-Marie Sohn found that most Frenchwomen in this period preferred marital relations in dark rooms.[17]

Consider how two feminists learned about menstruation. When Madeleine Pelletier's autobiographical heroine noticed blood on her skirt, she asked a teaching sister about it; the sister called her "a dirty little girl" and sent her home, where her father explained menstruation in a way that disgusted her. As a doctor, a militant feminist, and an advocate of birth control in her adult life, Pelletier fought the idea of sexual shame yet often herself expressed disgust about the body. A female cousin had told a prepubescent Simone de Beauvoir about "the whites and the reds," but Beauvoir repressed the information. When she began to flow, her mother explained that she had become "a big girl" and "bundled" her up. Relieved that she was not to blame for the hemorrhage, Simone was nevertheless ashamed when her father referred to her condition and horrified that "he suddenly considered me to be a mere organism." In *The Second Sex,* she represents menstruation, like pregnancy, as a source of female alienation, a time when the species "invades the individual." If the philosophical framework is existentialist, the language might have been borrowed from contemporary medical and hygiene texts. (Beauvoir was less disdainful later in life. In response to feminist critics, she agreed "that a woman should not be made to feel degraded by, let's say, her monthly periods.")[18]

Even girls living in homes with little privacy remained ignorant about and therefore fearful of menstruation. While living in a row house with her parents and two sisters, Marie-Catherine Gardez asked why her father slept on the floor a few days every month and was told that it was good for his rheumatism. When Gardez awoke one morning covered with blood, she thought that she had a hernia from stoking grain. Her mother had some difficulty reassuring her that this kind of bleeding happened to all women.[19] Medical guides corroborate that uninformed girls were frightened by their first period. Some sat in cold water to staunch the flow, a practice that outraged doctors, who wanted no impediments to the discharge of menstrual blood. In *The Four Ages of Women from the Physiological Point of View* (1899), Mme. Gensse urged menstruating girls not to go out in cold, rainy, or inclement weather and not to do laundry, bathe, or touch cold water. Making an admission rare in hygienic literature, Gensse acknowledged that this advice was only practical for the wealthy classes and advised working-class girls to avoid heavy labor, night work, and spending the entire workday damp or cold.[20] Aside from a few case studies showing that working women took more sick days than working men,[21] there is no evidence that working-class women slacked off when menstruating. Laundresses, who worked soaking wet and were prone to gynecological infections, did not request special dispensation.[22]

During the flow, mothers told girls never to speak of their condition but also tried to keep them warm and subdued. Most girls simply moderated their normal routine.[23] If they had abdominal pain, they might rest for a day or two, drink herbal teas, and eat hot food. Some mothers administered saffron or absinthe to alleviate debilitating cramps and migraines (possibly intensifying the pain in the case of migraines). Herbalists prescribed extracts of viburnum to stop painful contractions. Women's magazines advertised medications to "regulate feminine troubles" (which sometimes were abortifacients). Although practitioners published recipes for potions to hasten or retard menstruation, most refused to prescribe pills to suppress a period for frivolous reasons such as attending a party.[24]

During the one to three years until regular menstrual cycles were established, girls were often highly sensitive, irritable, and changeable; some had temper tantrums, crying spells, and giggling fits. Some parents chastised "moody" girls; others threw cold water on distraught girls, and those who could afford it arranged for tepid (calming) baths. If girls were seriously depressed, parents took them to general practitioners who prescribed tranquilizers made of ingredients such as cannabis.[25] In the 1920s, Dr. Germaine Montreuil-Strauss stressed that "crises of the soul, sadness without any cause, fantastic ideas" should be treated firmly but with "tact and affection."[26] This advice was part of a midcentury trend to adopt more psychological approaches toward puberty.

Menstruation and Maturation

The French medical profession had a twofold definition of puberty, comprising the onset of menstruation and a stage of corporeal development. For most specialists, puberty encompassed the inception of fertility—without mention of sexuality—and a new vulnerability to morbidity and mortality. This mélange is a prime example of biomedical contradictions on feminine sexuality, fertility, and ultimately, identity.

In the 1880s and 1890s, specialists in women's diseases called puberty the *nubile age,* when girls ceased to be "neutral" beings and began their "real" life as women. This "capital epoch of feminine life" was susceptible to latent organic defects or pathological microbes. The eclectic resolution of this troublesome combination of sexual maturation and pathology was to define puberty as a time of transition, which left the "terrain" vulnerable to "morbid entities." Although most specialists formally rejected the old notion of menstruation as the elimination of bad humors, many believed that blocked menstrual blood "detoured" and escaped from ulcers, the navel, ears, and the nose.[27] The next generation of gynecologists quoted Prof. Samuel Pozzi on "vicarious" menstruation and repeated his metaphor about menstruation as a safety valve that expelled bodily "resources" not needed for "the reproduction of the species."[28]

Until 1930, gynecologists and hygienists cited Adam Raciborski, who had adopted Pauchet's discoveries about spontaneous ovulation and posited a relationship between human ovulation and menstruation in the mid-nineteenth century. Raciborski cited recent European studies reporting average ages of onset of fourteen and a half and fifteen years and European travelers' accounts of an earlier menarche in Indian girls. In an Aristotelian manner, he explained that Indian girls started flowing earlier because heat hastened the maturing of the ovaries. On a more modern note, he blamed poor nutrition for late menarche among poor European girls and among bourgeois girls at boarding schools.[29]

Casual correlations of race, class, and living conditions with menstrual patterns remained in the medical literature. An 1897 study of puberty speculated that working-class girls had irregular cycles because "bad examples, pernicious contacts," incest, and pedaling treadle sewing machines overstimulated their "carnal instincts." Spa doctors Barbaud and Lefevre treated bourgeois girls, who, they claimed with some self-interest, were subject to "excitable ovarian systems" from urban distractions.[30] Although subsequent studies of the age of menarche in Europe recorded a drop to thirteen years in the 1930s, so little research was done on social variations in menstrual patterns that the major study published in the 1930s made similar suppositions about social conditions.[31]

Inconsistent information was one reason for continued supposition. Doctors saw bourgeois girls in private consultations; they treated some working-class girls (but few peasant girls) in urban hospitals and clinics. Social and moral constraints also encouraged conjecture. Dr. Arnould, one of the very few industrial hygienists who interviewed working girls, complained that they could not or would not answer detailed questions about menstruation. Establishing patterns was also difficult. When Charles Mannheim, a physician at a state-owned tobacco plant, documented menstrual irregularities among tobacco workers, physicians at nineteen other state-owned tobacco plants could not replicate his findings.[32]

In the Third Republic, hospital-based researchers investigated the length of the menstrual cycle, the duration of the flow, and the quantity of the discharge. Despite evidence of variability, researchers calculated averages and discovered a putative "normal" cycle of twenty-eight days and a putative "normal" period of four days. In the early twentieth century, researchers spoke of "abnormal" cycles of less than four weeks or more than five weeks. Hospital studies, which covered only women with menstrual or other medical difficulties, measured the amount of blood lost, reporting from 100 to 150 grams in the late nineteenth century and 150 to 500 grams (more than a pound) in the 1930s. Lacking definitive data, practitioners told patients that no healthy woman should need more than three or four sanitary napkins a day.[33]

French specialists in women's diseases deduced that folklore ascribed evil powers to menstrual blood because of its distinctive—usually described as "rank"—odor and consistency. In the 1880s, Dr. Goupil, who operated the largest gynecological clinic in Paris, insisted that menstrual blood was "the same as normal blood except it was mixed with mucous" expelled from the uterus, and this accounted for its smell and viscosity. He added that washing the pubic area during the period would reduce the smell and the incidence of genital inflammations.[34] Goupil and other specialists convinced hygienists, but not the public. Whereas foreign scientists continued to formulate theories about the menotoxic qualities of menstrual blood into (and beyond) the 1930s,[35] French researchers steadfastly denounced "popular fantasies" about the evil properties of menstrual blood, and French hygienists assured lay readers that menstrual blood was vascular blood with "no mysterious properties."[36]

Specialists also described physical and psychological manifestations of puberty. Raciborski described the enlargement of the uterus, ovaries, and pelvis and the appearance of external genitalia "that Linneaus so ingeniously compared to the petals of a flower." During the flow, Raciborski contended, the congested ovarian system caused abdominal and lower-back pain and vascular troubles, including migraines. Writing before Brown-Séquard speculated about the genitals as glands, Raciborski held that modifications in the ovarian system "excited" the nervous system. This excitement expressed itself normally in excessive friendships with other girls, coquetry and melancholy, and pathologically in cataleptic fits, hysteria, and nymphomania.[37] Aside from this kind of remark, few specialists acknowledged any awakening of sexual desire.

In the early twentieth century, pediatricians and endocrinologists became the experts on puberty and menstruation. Pediatrician, professor, and politician Adolphe Pinard (1844–1934) focused on the ova and introduced the disturbing notion that menstruation was "ovular abortion."[38] Somatically, the emphasis switched from alterations in the genital organs to the appearance of secondary sexual characteristics. In 1906, Dr. Marthe Francillon's inventory of secondary sexual characteristics in the skeleton added chemical differences in bones to the structural features described in Chapter 1, documenting the effects of ovarian secretions on calcium uptake and hence bone density. She also measured rapid growth in forty-three girls from the ages of ten to fifteen. Three years later, Francillon (now Francillon-Lobre) showed that girls accounted for three-quarters of all cases of scoliosis (deviations of the spinal column) among preadolescents and early adolescents. Her contemporary, Paul Dalché, studied and described changes in the pigmentation of adolescent girls' secondary sex organs, notably darkening around the nipples.[39]

Until the late 1930s, endocrinologists dominated puberty studies. In that decade, the major study of puberty defined it as "a natural, necessary, normal, and essentially physiological phenomenon." Dr. Derville refused to label puberty *morbid* but did use the term *puberal crisis*. Late in the decade, a few critics raised objections to the endocrinological approach to puberty. Dr. Madeleine Hirsch accused endocrinologists of having "two simplistic notions: more or less (hyper- or hypofunctioning), and synergy or antagonism." She ascribed most adolescent menstrual complications to developmental problems, rather than the reverse. Other specialists pointed to data on sex differences before puberty, and a few diffidently mentioned Freud's notion of childhood sexuality.[40] These criticisms and alternatives were not disseminated widely until after the Second World War.

Less research was conducted on masculine puberty. Experts and hygienists who dealt with masculine puberty defined it physically, as changes in the sex organs and the appearance of secondary sexual characteristics such as beards, and psychosexually, as a time of embarrassment around and contempt for the opposite sex. Unlike sexual advice guides for girls, guides for boys warned about the first "purely sensual" impulses and cautioned that "seminal losses" through "night emissions" weakened the developing organism by depleting it of "precious material."[41]

Comparative studies confirmed that boys entered puberty one to two years later than girls did and completed their sexual development two to three years later, at seventeen or eighteen. Developmental studies discovered that skeletal growth continued until the age of twenty-one for young women and twenty-five for young men.[42] Medical manuals warned that people who married before sexual maturity risked premature sterility and insisted that the age of sexual maturity should supersede the legal age for marriage, which was fifteen for girls.[43] Dr. Anna Fischer's medical manual, published in 1905, recommended that women postpone marrying until skeletal growth was finished at twenty-one. Writing two decades later, after researchers learned that some joints did not knit until women reached twenty-five, Dr. Marie Houdré-Boursin recommended that women wait until twenty-five.[44] In most cases, the advice was unnecessary. On average, women first wed between twenty-three and a half and twenty-five years of age and even later during and after the Great War and again in the depression of the 1930s.[45]

By the 1920s, developmentalists defined puberty as a series of physical, physiological, and psychic changes which transformed the organism of a child into that of an adolescent. Influenced by North American studies of adolescence as a distinct stage of life,[46] developmentalists distinguished a prepubescent phase from seven to eleven years of age, a pubescent phase of about two years, and a postpubescent phase once adolescents reached full development. Anthropometrists documented rapid gains in the height, weight, and hip measurements of girls between the ages of eleven and sixteen years.[47]

Irregularities and Illnesses

In the late nineteenth century, specialists in women's diseases denied Michelet's thesis that menstruation was an illness, yet they affirmed that this "physiological hemorrhage" had more "irregularities" than any other organic function. Thirty years later, clinicians contended that one fifth to one third of women, and higher proportions of girls, experienced difficulties.[48]

Most girls tolerated the white discharge that often preceded or accompanied a period and which the public called *white flowers*. If girls found that the discharge caused discomfort, their mothers purchased empiric remedies such as balsamic vinegar to relieve itching.[49] Conversely, late nineteenth-century specialists expressed great concern about a heavy discharge, which they knew as leukorrhea. The most popular Parisian specialist, Dr. Goupil, diagnosed leukorrhea as pus from internal infections and treated it with astringent pads and douches. Goupil based his diagnoses only on inspection of the discharge because he, like many practitioners, believed he had no right to do a "direct examination of a virgin" for diagnostic purposes.[50] (Regrettably, this respect for feminine modesty—and insurance against accusations of licentiousness—resulted in misdiagnoses.[51])

Many women who complained about leukorrhea and other vaginal irritations tried hydrotherapy. They bathed in the mineral springs and douched with the mineral waters at Vichy or Bagnères-de-Bigorre, where one third of the clientele had "women's diseases." Sufferers who could not afford a stay at a spa purchased bottled mineral water for douching. Because of the long association of water with eroticism and because spa doctors administered vaginal douches, critics accused them of running "sanctuaries dedicated to Venus." A consultant at Vichy, Dr. Alquier, admitted that some spa doctors had sexual relations with patients, but he assured the public that most spa doctors "erected a sanitary barrier" by marrying. He did not take extramarital affairs with patients into account.[52] Although the French state employed prominent physicians to monitor spas, physicians influenced by germ theory raised an alarm at the turn of the century about hydrology spreading infection.[53] Spas lost business but remained a therapeutic option, thanks to more rigorous sanitary controls and the many distractions they offered.[54] Endocrinologists, who supported an internal theory of gynecological disorders, rescued the practice of vaginal douching.[55] By the 1930s, leukorrhea was less common because of improved genital hygiene and less uncomfortable because of treatment by over-the-counter antiseptic douches.[56]

Irregularities in the quantity of menstrual discharge attracted medical attention, although the number and variety of treatments suggest that none was very effective. Consider only prewar treatments for dysmenorrhea or excessive flow. Paul Dalché, a leading endocrinologist, ordered light exercise between periods and very hot "vaginal irrigations" during periods. Mothers who were supposed to administer the hot douches balked, fearing that they would tear their daughters' hymens (proof of their virginity) or scald their genitals. If these home-based remedies did not work, Dalché injected ergotine to reduce the flow. Another doctor, Natalie Sirbitzow, reported that doctors prescribed seventeen different antispasmodics and opiates and performed seven operations, including "ovarian and uterine castration," to cure dysmenorrhea. Noting the "disproportion between means and ends," Sirbitzow advocated gynecological kinesiology, which involved patients exercising their abdominal and pelvic muscles and doctors performing abdominal and pubic massages to relieve congestion in the pelvic system. Sirbitzow only referred to manual massages or masturbation, but other doctors promoted electric vibrators.[57] Medical masturbation had been tried on hysterics, but even for these unfortunate patients, it was deemed to be a dubious therapy.[58] Later advocates of gynecological kinesiology concentrated on abdominal and pelvic exercises.

Specialists did learn how to cure chlorosis, an aggravated form of anemia associated with menstrual problems and delayed development. The public was sympathetic toward chlorotics because the disease was disturbingly visible in their pale greenish complexions and the dark circles under the eyes. Symptoms included breathlessness, palpitations, poor appetite, nausea, and constipation. In the 1880s, specialists attributed chlorosis (and many other conditions) to nervous problems and environmental conditions such as overwork, inadequate ventilation, and sexual perversion. Magazines for girls advertised fortified "vinegars" to cure or alleviate anemia, chlorosis, and "poor blood."[59] By the late 1890s, medical science linked chlorosis with a low hemoglobin count. As blood tests became more available in the next decade, physicians realized that chlorotics had low red blood cell counts. Their new prescription, a diet rich in iron, greatly reduced the incidence of this disease.[60]

Chronic pulmonary infections, especially consumption, afflicted many pubescent girls. Although elderly men also had high rates of tubercular mortality, the popular image of tuberculosis was as a young woman's disease associated with "a kind of suffering that was morally and spiritually redeeming." David Barnes points to the popularity of Verdi's opera *La Traviata*, of Sarah Bernhardt in *La Dame aux Camelias*, and Saint Thérèse of Lisieux's autobiography, *Story of a Soul*.[61] Susan Griffin suggests that the opera and novel about a passionate but dying courtesan may have offered some solace to sufferers, insofar as these heroines did not "give in" to their affliction.[62]

In addition, many maternal accounts of daughters defying but finally dying from unnamed but clearly tubercular diseases were published, and often reprinted, between 1880 and 1914. Although maudlin to our sensibilities, their depictions of symptoms, futile treatments, and the ultimate resignation of young girls to early death qualify the hegemonic image of pubescent girls as immature and mercurial. In 1895, Jeanne Angèle Dupasquier published a short biography of her daughter, who had fallen ill at the age of twelve in 1879 and tried mountain, sun, and spa "cures" for the next twelve years. When the daughter could hardly stand and had little appetite, she was visited and comforted by the "Good Shepherd." As Dupasquier records it, at first her daughter asked how much more pain God had in store for her; toward the end of her life, she made peace with approaching death and prayed to achieve the "Christian life . . . a continual death of self-love, pride, sensibility, self-seeking."[63]

Because mainstream medical and public opinion considered tuberculosis hereditary, families never referred to this "shameful" disease by name.[64] At the turn of the century, the League Against Tuberculosis disseminated posters, postal cards, and a journal (with a circulation of four thousand readers) addressing teachers, mothers, and nurses as well as doctors. Under pressure, governments instituted the Permanent Commission on Tuberculosis. Statistical studies showed a rising tubercular mortality rate in large cities, especially in impoverished urban quarters. Tuberculosis became a social issue. As the propaganda and statistics mounted, it was linked with alcoholism and syphilis in a "triad of modern plagues."

The French medical corps opposed sanitariums, which were German in origin. Nationalists believed that the French would not accept the quasi-military discipline; more pragmatic doctors pointed out that the Republic lacked the public medical insurance that made a network of sanatoriums possible in the Reich. Because pulmonary specialists objected to sanitariums, the Permanent Commission opted for a policy of dispensaries and decontamination of insalubrious sites, both of which accomplished very little until the 1920s. The Academy of Medicine resisted making declaration of tuberculosis compulsory, explicitly to protect medical confidentiality but implicitly to protect the privacy of their bourgeois clientele.[65] After the war, the number of antitubercular clinics rose to 640, employing about 1,200 visiting nurses, who tracked down the afflicted, sent them to hospitals or sanatoriums (if beds were available), tried to limit contagion, and dispensed an ineffective vaccination invented by the Pasteur Institute.[66]

Some progress was made. Although consumption remained the major cause of death for adolescent girls, the mortality rate dropped in the late 1920s and 1930s.[67] Specialists learned that certain forms of tuberculosis, such as scrofula, sometimes went into remission or disappeared during adolescence.[68] By the 1930s, gynecologists recognized that puberty was a period of "general vitality" with fewer deaths than other ages. If girls were more susceptible to chronic diseases, they also put up more resistance to them. Endocrinologists remained vigilant, however, because latent pulmonary tuberculosis delayed the appearance of secondary sexual traits.[69] In 1909, Dr. Mery, who had monitored student health in seven schools, reported that 16 to 25 percent of the girls presented symptoms of latent pulmonary tuberculosis.[70]

Even privileged adolescents such as Catherine Pozzi, who had tutors because of her ill health, suffered the consequences of undiagnosed tuberculosis. After she was treated for pleurisy, she continued to experience episodes of coughing up blood and sputum, labored breathing, and fatigue. As an adult, she consulted up to eight physicians at a time, tried the ineffective Pasteur Institute vaccine, resorted to clinics, sanitariums, and surgery, and self-administered laudanum, morphine, and cocaine (sequentially) to alleviate her pain. Always dubious about conventional medicine, as she approached her death from tuberculosis Pozzi tried a psychic healer and unconventional treatments including massages with medicinal oils.[71]

Physiology and Psychology

Interwar gynecologists defined the *psychology of puberty*. Many talked about individuation; girls were detaching themselves from their families. Vignes depicted the adolescent girl's personality as both reserved and flirtatious, the first caused by "a natural disposition to modesty," the second by "an instinctive need to seduce, to please."[72] He was not the only physician to devote space to coquettish or flirtatious behavior; anxiety about female sexuality marked much of the physiology and psychology of women.

Generally, psychological interpretations were not positive. In 1890, Dr. Icard reviewed the research on connections between menstrual and psychic functions. His interpretation of menstruation drew on the century-old view that there was a "sympathy" between the uterus and the nervous system. Because of the abundance of ganglia emanating from the uterus, women were "the nervous part of humanity." Stringing together clinical studies of premenstrual syndrome and of institutionalized women with menstrual irregularities, Icard declared menstruation "a veritable psychic crisis." He concluded that women should not enter public life, "distressed" premenstrual and menstrual women should not act as witnesses or defendants in court, and girls should not attend boarding or coeducational schools.[73]

In the early 1900s, Dr. Marthe Francillon pointed out faults in Icard's use of medical statistics, notably the lack of medical data on healthy menstruating women. She suggested more attention to social conditions: "hysteria is two times more frequent in the poor than in the rich classes."[74] Despite scientific criticism, Icard's depiction of puberal girls and menstrual women reflected medical and popular prejudices and lingered in popular medical literature. A 1911 book on women's health written by a homeopathic doctor opened with a husband asking, "My wife is insupportable, what is wrong?" The author, Abbé Chaupitre, answered that she was having her period, a curse that "has deformed her entire being." According to Chaupitre, a badly regulated period caused 80 percent of female madness; a well-regulated period meant a healthy woman and a happy family.[75]

In the *fin de siècle*, hysteria in adolescent girls also attracted much medical and media attention. In 1891, Dr. Emile Laurent speculated that hysterical girls engaged in "morbid love," defined as affairs with servants or upstarts. He presented one case study of a sixteen-year-old girl from an alcoholic and abusive family. After being sexually assaulted by her first employer, she had lived with a student who mistreated her; she posed for well-known painters and danced professionally at a café and finally fell into prostitution.[76] In his account, Laurent did not consider the effects of dysfunctional family life or sexual harassment.

At the turn of the century, hysteria drew less psychiatric but more public attention. Marthe Noel Evans shows that Charcot's students "dismembered" hysteria by stressing mental states or socialization. Dr. Georgette Dega described hysterical behaviors as exaggerations of the emotions adolescent girls were supposed to exhibit and contended that "nerve crises" were the only way some of them could get attention. Given the strictures on adolescent girls' behavior, Dega's social diagnoses seem sensible. Unfortunately, the publication of the *Iconography of the Salpetrière*, with its shocking photographs of the "characteristic" arched body of hysterical women, imprinted on public memory the images of irrational women.[77]

After the First World War, neurologists attributed hysteria to cortical damage, an interpretation that threatened to break the links forged among puberty, femininity, and hysteria. Psychologists promptly distinguished war traumas from effeminate character-disorder diagnoses rooted in stereotypes of women as irrational, emotive, and deceptive.[78]

Clean and Chaste

Long after the Third Republic had introduced free primary education for girls, maternal education—which the French distinguished from instruction in academic subjects—remained the ideal.[79] Clerics and physicians published manuals in maternal science, assigning mothers special responsibility for the physical and moral education of girls, sometimes from the age of six or seven, when some claimed that sex differences began to emerge, but more often from the age of puberty.[80] These manuals urged mothers to stress their daughters' future motherhood "from the crib" and to protect them against conditions that would "compromise" their future reproductive health.[81] In the interwar, endocrinologists such as René Biot told mothers that "the young girl accumulates in the mystery of her flesh, biological qualities or defects" and that these could be transmitted to the next generation. To maintain their "biological value," girls must be protected from overwork and debauchery.[82]

At no stage in a girl's life would she require more surveillance, the manuals declared. They instructed mothers to explain "white flowers" and to ensure that their daughters washed daily to avoid "vicious practices with incalculable consequences."[83] By the interwar, the approach was more positive. In 1924, an English nurse's advice about warm baths and normal physical activity (except bicycling) during the menstrual flow was translated and published in a journal for visiting nurses. In the following decade, Drs. Montreuil-Strauss and Houdré-Boursin explained that the purpose of twice-daily topical washing was not only to avoid offensive odor but also to ensure comfort. Houdré-Boursin proposed commercial solutions such as sanitary belts and napkins and the use of bidets.[84]

So that mothers could monitor conduct, companions, and occupations, hygienists advised keeping pubescent girls in a family setting. Their operating assumption was that idleness left impressionable girls prey to melancholy, irritability, romantic fantasies, and religious enthusiasms. Even after the First World War, hygienists forbade romantic literature, attending "lascivious plays," and looking at "obscene" paintings (which included "artistic" nudes). Many French people believed that even reading a book could have dangerous effects.[85] A few hygienists remarked that reading was only a problem for bourgeois girls. For working-class girls, the problem about sexuality was their crowded living conditions and "forced contact with amoral and evil people."[86]

Believing that girls needed all of their energy for development, hygienists cautioned against tiring pubescent girls and advised eight to eleven hours of sleep each night. Hygienists also proclaimed that prolonged sewing or reading in dim light encouraged poor posture, curvature of the spine, and myopia. Although the egregious examples were surely workshops, where many young women worked, this relentlessly bourgeois literature indicted classrooms.[87] Hygienists such as Dr. Monin (mentioned in the previous chapter) railed against "this idiotic and claustrophobic school regime and intellectual overexertion imposed on future mothers of families by the enlightened barbarity of electricity."[88] By the 1930s, such rhetoric diminished, but a gynecologist, Dr. Derville, still remarked that he regretted girls cramming for examinations because girls were "more sensitive to overwork than boys."[89]

Some of these medical opponents of higher education for girls argued that it would distract girls from their reproductive role; none made the notorious Anglo-American argument that higher education would literally render them unfit for motherhood. Most expressed realistic apprehension about the unhealthy condition of French schools. Surveys conducted in the 1880s reported regions in which half of the schools had only three toilets per hundred students (with one third of these toilets being holes in the floor). One third to one half of these schools had no covered entryway where children might wait for school to open.[90] In the same decade, physicians raised legitimate concerns about the health consequences of poorly designed desks, inadequate lighting and ventilation, and crowding. When the government instituted free secular education, Minister of Education Jules Ferry appointed a commission to study the effect of school design and furnishings. The commission blamed dim lighting for myopia and desks that did not conform to children's bodies for scoliosis.[91] Over the next two decades, many doctors criticized the six- to eleven-hour school days (depending upon the grade) and linked sitting still with indigestion. Headaches and tuberculosis were attributed to breathing confined air. If a few doctors remained distraught about young women's "mania for diplomas," most noted reasonably that schools for girls had fewer recesses than schools for boys and less physical education to break the sedentary routine.[92]

Efforts to improve conditions in the schools proceeded slowly.[93] The 1902 Public Health Act mandated building permits in cities with a population greater than twenty thousand, demolition of egregiously unsanitary buildings, and temporary closure of institutions wracked by epidemics. Unfortunately, enforcement was the responsibility of elected mayors who were caught between powerful and fiscally conservative political and financial interests[94] and medical and educational lobbies such as the Alliance for School Hygiene.[95]

Conclusions

After receiving many mixed messages about puberty, some pubescent girls were ashamed of their bodies and feared sexual maturity. As early as 1873, Dr. Charles Lasègue, often credited with identifying anorexia as a syndrome,[96] reported that anorexic girls spoke about emotional triggers such as marriage proposals and suggested that these triggers indicated that patients were having difficulties breaking away from their close-knit families. He did not mention, but we might discern in his data, a pattern of patients avoiding sexual maturity or maybe just marriage. Thirty years later, Dr. Pierre Janet recorded verbatim conversations with anorexic patients embarrassed about their body and bodily functions. Menarche or other manifestations of sexual maturity apparently precipitated all of Janet's extreme case histories.[97] By 1930, Prof. Marcel Labbé of the Paris Medical Faculty diagnosed "mental anorexia" in young women who feared being fat or had other "obsessions" associated with the vogue for slender bodies. He prescribed psychological and physiological re-education, including isolation in a nursing home and prolonged persuasion to get them to eat. He had doubts about overfeeding techniques because the problem was to get patients to eat without vomiting. Obviously, he had also encountered bulimia.[98]

Chapter 5

Sexual Initiation and
Sex Education

NEW GENRE of premarital sex manuals appeared in France in the 1880s, a decade before sex education guides for young adults emerged in England and the United States.[1] Although much French erotica was didactic fiction detailing sexual techniques for men who aspired to be skilled lovers,[2] none of the French handbooks for fiancées and fiancés qualified as erotica. Similarly, none of the premarital manuals was pornographic, although some of their chapters criticizing brutal sexual initiations may have titillated sadists. The authors certainly tried to ameliorate the abuses of an aggressive male-defined heterosexuality,[3] but their primary motivation was to raise marital natality. Neither the physicians who claimed scientific expertise on sexuality nor the clerics who claimed ethical competence on sexual matters investigated the attitudes of young women toward premarital sex. Despite systematic criticism of maternal preparation of daughters for conjugal relations, most experts did not reject the convention of maternal sex instruction. The few efforts to introduce sex education into the public school system failed, which illuminates another paradox about sexuality and fertility: a public school system resistant to sex education in a polity interested in promoting natality.

Courtship and Coquetry

Before the First World War, mothers prepared their daughters more for courtship than for conjugal relations. For bourgeois mothers, this assignment involved instilling an ambiguous mix of sexual innocence and coquetry, a set of subtle signals that the innocent was available for marriage. Even before the war, courtship customs were changing, but it was the loss of a generation of young men in the war and the flu epidemic of 1918 which undermined, without completely overturning, parental control over courtship. Given more freedom of conduct in relations with the other sex after the war, single women contrived a new and more complex message about both their innocence and their interest in dating and marriage. Clerical and medical critics decried their new liberty.

Mothers began by imposing a strict code of appearances. In the 1880s and early 1890s, young single women were not allowed to use powder or rouge, although they could apply flowery perfumes, which were considered to be fresh and virginal. For a chaste look, young women were expected to wear white or pale-colored dresses with high necklines, but no jewelry. Of course, young women subverted cosmetic restrictions by rubbing their cheeks until they were rosy or applying solutions made by soaking red ribbons in water.[4] Some, like Elizabeth de Gramont, rearranged their necklines to show some shoulder, if not cleavage.[5] By the turn of the century, Catherine Pozzi and other respectable young ladies applied powder, donned evening gowns with some *décolleté*, and adorned themselves with jewelry, all signals that they were "grown up" and available.[6]

In the *fin de siècle*, mothers or aunts escorted single women aged eighteen to twenty-five to balls, parties, theaters, resorts, and casinos to meet eligible men. Ideally, single women were not supposed to dance or talk with unknown men or to stay with any dance partner unless they and preferably their families had an arrangement, or at least an understanding, about marriage. In actuality, "flirts" or more intimate conversations were permissible.[7]

In those decades, single bourgeois women had little physical contact of any kind with men outside their families, with the predictable result that the slightest touch could provoke or please these young women far more than the same gesture would today. At nineteen, Julie Manet (daughter of Berthe Morisot) recorded in her diary how much she had enjoyed her bicycle instructor's hand on her shoulder to steady her. At the turn of the century, new kinds of social dancing increased the opportunities for physical contact. As a teenager, Clara Malraux reveled in the "swing of my body in a boy's arm during a tango, an expected or unexpected kiss." She recorded that her first kiss "filled me with disgust and . . . longing to experience it again." When her brother "darted his tongue into" her friend's mouth, the "half-rape filled her with disgust." Upon reflection, Malraux decided that "this invasion might give rise to sensual delight."[8]

The First World War intensified interest in sex without simplifying the situation of young women. Clara Malraux is a good witness:

The conditions under which girls lived in those days were perfectly ludicrous, and although the war had brought a certain freedom, it had also made them worse. There was a continual obsession with sex, even for those whose reading was supervised; it was splashed on the walls and on the Morris pillars with their film and theater posters; it ran through the songs . . . in our recently shortened skirts, in our more and more exaggerated make-up. In the midst of all this girls were supposed to be chaste, though not in the least ignorant; since they were freer, so they were also more threatened.

Although it may have been acceptable behavior for young shop girls to run after departing troops, waving and blowing kisses, for young bourgeois women it was not. Yet these same bourgeois women worked as nurses in ambulance services and temporary hospitals, where they had contact with wounded soldiers. When the fashion industry revived in 1915, young *Parisiennes* adopted the new, practical, but more revealing short, swingy skirts. As the war wound down in 1917-18, many danced with English and American soldiers passing through Paris.[9]

After the war, single women were less docile. Parents financially ruined by the war found themselves unable to afford dowries and thus to arrange marriages, which reduced their control over the conduct of their daughters and over courtship rituals.[10] Aware that there were more than one million more marriageable women than men, but not foreseeing high rates of remarriage, social commentators magnified the predicament of young women. Nor did commentators consider that poor prospects for marriage provided some young bourgeois women with an excuse to avoid unwanted alliances or, like Simone de Beauvoir, marriage itself.[11] Conversely, greater personal liberty gave some young women permission to make up, dress up, date, and flirt. Moralists bemoaned the way the more fluid situation encouraged women to engage in this kind of behavior.

To the delight of young women and the dismay of moralists, there were new and more affordable cosmetics, such as lipstick, which daring women even applied in public.[12] Looser dresses with shorter hemlines, promoted as simple, sporty, and youthful,[13] were popular with young women but censured by moralists. Roberts suggests that the waistless "tube look" signified youthfulness and mobility to young women, although it drew moral condemnation because it de-emphasized breasts and hips, signs of a womanly body. According to Roberts, Catholic moralists led the 1920s crusade against the tube look because it blurred the boundaries of sex differences.[14] However, Brother Philippe de Jésus also targeted "immodest" apparel—tight or clingy dresses with plunging necklines—for revealing the female body.[15] Even after the return of the natural waistline and fuller skirts in the 1930s, sporty versions of this "new look" were advertised as youthful,[16] and Catholic moralists continued to chastise women for wearing seductive attire. Emmanuel Viau accused modern girls of wearing "indecent ball gowns" to do "dances imported from Negro countries that required troubling postures and contacts."[17]

In the mid-1930s, Canon Cordonnier took on flirting. Accepting the cultural consensus that coquetry was part of feminine nature, he called flirtation cruel to a (male) partner because sexual attraction was "very violent and imperious in young men." He faulted young women for arousing men "by naked arms and legs, too much cleavage, too tight or too short dresses in light or transparent fabrics." He also blamed mothers who failed to curb their daughters,[18] adding one more note to the veritable chorus of criticism about mothers. The same year, a lay Catholic, Monique Levallet-Montal, conceded that slightly more physical contact would be proper, although only between engaged women and men; she allowed women to kiss their fiancés on the lips if the kisses "did not provoke carnal excitement." She was indecisive about caresses because men reacted differently.[19]

The more public and permissive courtship customs of peasant and working-class youth affronted bourgeois sensibilities. In some rural regions, groups of unmarried couples engaged in very public displays of affection, including deep kissing. *Veillées* (evenings young single people spent working, talking, singing, and socializing, usually under maternal supervision) had some kinship with bourgeois events. But in many rural areas, the community tolerated premarital sexual relations once the couple had agreed to marry. The urban-worker custom of "walking out" also evoked bourgeois consternation because the couples fondled one another in doorways and other semipublic places. Many working-class communities also sanctioned consensual unions, given the high cost of marital paperwork and suitable wedding clothes. An inevitable consequence was premarital conceptions, which occurred in about one-fifth of all legal unions during the interwar.[20]

Innocence and Initiation

In the Third Republic, sex experts drew attention to maternal education of daughters for the wedding night because they were concerned about the implications of bridal innocence for sexual initiations and ultimately for the birth rate. Mothers reluctant to talk to their daughters about sexual initiation asked their confessors "Why scandalize them, possibly filling them with disgust for marriage?" These mothers held the popular belief that speaking to a young girl of sexuality stripped her of "innocence"[21]—an ignorance of intercourse valued by most potential husbands in the 1890s but by fewer men in the 1930s.[22] These mothers were imbued with the Catholic concept that sex was shameful, a notion imbedded in the Christian belief in an opposition between body and soul and reinforced by clerical warnings against "the seductive aspects of pleasure."[23]

In 1884, Dr. Coriveaud reported that mothers (and aunts) waited until the night before the wedding to whisper confusing and not very comforting words to the new bride: "Don't be afraid . . . love has its duties." Such an approach may have reflected bad memories and accordingly low expectations. Although Coriveaud assured his readers that their husbands would use tender caresses, he worried about husbands who considered the wedding night "a sort of savage rutting" and committed "veritable rapes" that hurt and permanently scarred brides.[24] Most gynecologists were familiar with these "ballistic uterine inflammations" and into the 1920s reported stories of brutal wedding nights, although few other than sexual radicals such as Madeleine Pelletier repeated the term *rape*.[25] Some nonexperts were almost as frank. In the chapter of *Eroticism* on transgression in marriage and in orgy, Georges Bataille called "the initial sexual act constituting marriage . . . a permitted violation."[26]

It also happened that daughters cut short their mothers' embarrassed efforts to introduce the subject of sex. Sixteen-year-old Simone de Beauvoir told her relieved mother, "I know all about that!" In fact, Beauvoir knew nothing except what she had read in novels; she did not even understand what was happening when a strange man publicly fondled her. She did flee when another man exposed himself to her and interpreted her reaction as an expression of her family's confusion of nudity with indecency. But she also believed that adult male bodies inspired terror in virgins.[27] Although terror seems an extreme reaction, disgust may have been common. Certainly most girls who learned anything about male organs heard dismissive terms for the penis, such as *piece of meat* or *the thing*.[28] After the First World War a proposal to teach fiancées about the male reproductive system was dismissed out of hand by most sex experts and educators.

Notwithstanding higher rates of premarital relations, many peasant and working-class women knew little about sex before marriage. Emilie Carles wrote of a newly wed woman who resisted her husband's advances every night for weeks by yelling for her father, who shared his tiny cottage with them. The husband finally contrived to make love in a secluded location, apparently with satisfactory results. Mme. Lucie, who also spent her wedding night in her parents' home, found intercourse shocking "because, except for my few months as an apprentice, I had never heard much about sex." Happily, family and friends sang a humorous Norman song that relaxed her:

> Said the mattress to the sheets
> I have never seen such feats.
> Said the pillow to the case
> We've been shaken to the base.

Hers was a happy initiation and a happy union.[29]

Inspired by a mother "terrified by the ravages caused by this disastrous ignorance," Parisian gynecologist E. A. Goupil wrote a general book on women's reproductive functions which mothers could give to their daughters before the wedding night.[30] More than a dozen specifically premarital sex guides were published during the next fifty years. All of them advocated virginity before the wedding and sexual initiation on the wedding night. Although several guides noted the logical contradiction between keeping girls ignorant of intercourse and then expecting them to perform conjugal duties, few proposed any solution other than maternal sex education. None identified the young women's conundrum as frankly as the actress Emilie Lerou in her memoirs: "How can an act called holy, sacred, natural, and compulsory in the state of marriage become filthy, infamous, the final outrage, outside that state?"[31] Actresses and artists' models were the only Frenchwomen, other than Beauvoir, who admitted in their memoirs or diaries of having had extramarital heterosexual relations.[32]

Despite their professions of concern about the predicament of individual women, experts were actually dedicated to reinforcing marriage as a "bulwark against sexual decadence." In addition to the well-known literary decadents of the *fin de siècle*,[33] Joseph Peladin's novels about androgynous, sexually active, and lesbian adolescents and Pierre Louys's books extolling Greek—bisexual and lesbian—love without the Judeo-Christian "concept of shamefulness and immodesty" were popular at the turn of the century. One of Louys's novels about a young courtesan was adapted for the stage, and a company put out a line of beauty products named after the heroine, Chrysis.[34]

Premarital sex manuals reinforced marital sexuality in different ways for young women and for young men. Prewar manuals for young men warned them about "wasting" their reproductive potential in homosexual relations, and contemporary guides for young women were taciturn about homosexuality.[35] Most experts worried about young women's vulnerability to men's sexual advances. Dr. Mathé, who despaired of maternal education and favored teaching sexual hygiene at school, cautioned that young women "walk on a precipice, the path of duty and virtue is narrow, the road of vice is wide and full of attractions." Mathé felt that young women had to arm themselves against sexual assault and temptation.[36] His language expressed rarely articulated anxieties about female sexual desire and frequently articulated assumptions that young men could not contain their sex drive.

In the 1890s, the campaign against venereal diseases also put the issue of sexual initiation on the public agenda. A specialist in venereal diseases, Dr. Albert Fournier, introduced the notion of "syphilis of the innocents," defined as the chaste bride and the nursling, and warned of the frightening prospect of hereditary syphilis. Fournier reported that 14 percent of the 572 syphilitic women in his practice had contracted the disease from their husbands when they first married. Addressing men, he proclaimed that a medical examination, treatment of venereal symptoms if necessary, and certification of no symptoms for an unspecified period of time should be "preconditions" for marriage.[37] In 1901, the Society for Sanitary and Moral Protection formed with the sole purpose of fighting venereal diseases. Over the next two decades, the society campaigned for prenuptial medical examinations and information for future spouses. It encouraged Hélina Gaboriau and later other female physicians to write premarital sex guides to alert mothers about the need for vigilance in detecting infection in potential fiancés.[38]

In 1907, Léon Blum, then a socialist lawyer and journalist (and in the 1930s, a premier of France), raised many hackles with a critique of premarital chastity. *On Marriage* declared that the essence of contemporary marriage was wedding a virgin girl to an experienced man, leaving her sex education to him. Instead of girls fighting their instincts, Blum proposed that they "give in to all instinctual demands" for ten to fifteen years before marriage. *Planned* and *voluntary procreation*—code words for contraception—would prevent pregnancies. An experienced woman would have a better introduction to marriage and, therefore, a better marriage.[39] Blum's critique does not seem to have persuaded respectable young women to abandon their chastity before marriage. Marie Lenéru, who read Darwin's *The Origin of Species* without recording any qualms in her diary, remarked after reading Blum that she could not imagine love outside marriage.[40] But publication of Blum's views galvanized moralists.

In 1908, the Catholic Church chimed in with changes in canon law on engagement and marriage. To discourage "lightly entered clandestine unions," Pope Pius X required written engagement contracts signed by the two parties, the parish priest, and two witnesses and weddings before the couple's parish priest or a designated priest and two witnesses. The commentary accompanying the decree deplored promises of marriage made "under the empire of fleeting passion" as "incitements to sin and causes of inexperienced young girls' deception." To deter divorce, parish priests were ordered to give affianced and newly wed couples brochures on marital and parental duties.[41]

Written by clerics, these brochures counseled chastity before marriage and continence in marriage. Although they seem curiously unappealing today, they were distributed widely and may have had some, likely negative, impact on Catholic women. Most stories in a collection subtitled *Toward Marriage* extolled the celibate life. In the pivotal story, a wise virgin decides to marry because "she had been called to sacrifice herself." Hoppenot's *Little Catechism on Marriage* recommended chaste marital sex for the purpose God prescribed— procreation, not voluptuousness. His catechism was reprinted nineteen times between 1908 and 1930, and 170,000 copies circulated in the early 1920s.[42]

Anticlerical and feminist critiques of the Church's position on chastity and sexual initiation inevitably appeared. In 1910, Paul de Régla, a philosopher and popularizer, accused the Church of fostering prostitution with its advocacy of chastity over sexual congress. He further charged that the Church drove some wives to lesbianism by recognizing marriages only after consummation or after husbands "possessed" their wives, often painfully.[43] A survey of prominent feminists indicated general agreement that mothers should instruct their daughters, with a minority adding that society also had a responsibility to protect young girls against immorality. Every feminist surveyed preferred a scientific to a religious sex education. Although none of the respondents criticized marriage, Arria Ly of Feminist Combat railed against the "unclean acts that husbands believe they have the right to impose on their wives for their entire lives." Nelly Roussel blamed the Church for the bride's suffering during initiation as well as for the pain of repeated childbirth.[44] Monsignor Bolo, who had written on girlhood and divorce, reacted polemically, by describing feminists as unwomanly and unattractive. In a series of speeches to Catholic schoolgirls, Bolo disavowed "this odious feminism that, under the pretext of emancipating woman, denatures and makes her ugly."[45]

The dialogue evolved. A more radical critique of premarital chastity circulated shortly before and during the Great War. One anarchist, Jean Marestan (nom de plume of Gaston Harvard), published an inexpensive pamphlet that accused cultural "disdain for the body" and "horror of everything to do with sex" of making human beings seem ugly and dirty. He attributed this hatred of the body and sexuality to capitalists' need to ensure that their property went to their legitimate heirs. "[A] false sense of honor furnished convenient pretexts for the male's instinct for jealous domination."[46]

After the war, Abbé Viollet and priests active in Social Catholic outreach founded the Association for Christian Marriage (ACM), which attracted Catholic physicians and educators. The ACM published a newspaper with up to thirty thousand subscribers and produced more positive pamphlets than prewar clerics had. Although ACM pamphlets agreed with the clerical position on marriage as self-sacrifice, they assured girls that love "embellishes and transforms the sacrifice" and claimed that "suppressing carnal pleasure under the pretext of purity would distort the divine plan." Of course, young people of both sexes were supposed to enter into the marriage "intact in body and soul."[47]

Respectable Scientific Advice

Around the turn of the century, North American sex guides for girls also responded to anxieties about the new advocates of sexual pleasure and the apparent disintegration of the social order. Some volumes of the famous Self and Sex series were translated into French.[48] However, most sexual advice given by French experts differed from sexual advice given by American experts in four respects.

First, French advice addressed only young bourgeois women on the verge of marriage. If working-class girls figured in these guides, they did so as the shady women of "easy virtue." Some manuals explicitly excluded peasants on the grounds that they knew about sexuality because they had observed farm animals coupling. The logic of the manuals was doubly misleading. On the one hand, peasants did not connect animal coupling with human copulation, perhaps because of rural repugnance about bestiality.[49] On the other hand, none of these manuals actually depicted or described copulation. In addition to publishers' calculations about who could afford to buy books, authors were aware that rural folklore regarded the body as an agent of sexual pleasure and that many popular terms for agricultural tools and gestures had sexual overtones. Some authors knew that at the banquets associated with festive rural events, adults told stories about sexual transgression in front of children.[50] Some sexual advisors quoted medical studies that claimed that peasants copulated "in a bestial manner . . . without any fuss."[51]

As Carles makes clear, more openness about sex did not necessarily mean more comfort for women. She describes one "brutish" relationship: "When he was in heat he went after her in the woods, pursuing her insistently until she yielded to his superior strength; just about anywhere would do, he'd pull up her skirt and then leave her there when he was finished."[52] In short, inexpensive sexual advice for working-class and peasant women might have been helpful.

Second, French guides actually targeted bourgeois mothers, to coach them on how to answer their daughters' questions or, if the mother or daughter was uncomfortable talking about sex, to give to their daughters. The few sex manuals that directly addressed mothers promoted pre- or early adolescent, not immediately premarital, sex education. A 1908 booklet by Frédéric Passy (better known for popularizing political economy) used the format of a preteen girl questioning her mother about human reproduction and her mother answering with plant and animal analogies. Twenty-two years later, a strict Catholic, Jeanne Leroy-Allais, adopted the dialogical and analogical approach for early teens. Even though the Vatican had approved "the family teaching strategy," Leroy-Allais felt compelled to explain that her husband insisted on their daughters' sex education to avoid unhappy sexual initiations, and her brother-in-law, a doctor, had persuaded her that learning about nature never corrupts.[53]

Third, French sexual advisors were more preoccupied with natality than their North American counterparts because most of the French advisors were natalists, more of them were medical men, and many of these medical men worried about degeneration. Especially after researchers discovered that microbes infiltrated the uterus and that this had serious repercussions on fertility, sexual advisors expressed concern about genital complications from rough sexual initiations.[54] Specialists in "frigidity," female physicians, and novelists explained that painful initiations made young women resist intercourse and that, even if their resistance was ineffective, it lowered the prospects for conception.[55] Although it is difficult to substantiate these claims, of the eighty women who wrote to a priest who counseled married couples, five blamed wedding night initiations for their revulsion toward sex.[56]

Fourth, competition among experts characterized French sexual advice. Since the eighteenth century, hygienists had competed with clerics as moral and sexual counselors. Whatever Frenchwomen thought about practical sexual advice from (theoretically) celibate male clerics, many accepted their authority. One reason for the "feminization" of Catholic observance in the nineteenth century was the Church's attitude toward sexuality. The Tridentate

Church reforms had imposed a new sexual ethic that provided some protection for women and girls from sexual assault by rowdy gangs of young men.[57] The Church also accorded the responsibility for sex instruction to mothers, albeit under clerical guidance. Finally, the Church's campaign against the pornography that proliferated after 1890 appealed to mothers. The Church protested because it felt that this pornography was sacrilegious and selfish (signifying nonreproductive). The sacrilegious and nonreproductive aspects may not have worried mothers as much as the motif of adult men thoughtlessly "seducing" young virgins.[58] Despite the literary "redemption" of pornography in the postwar period,[59] the Church continued to place offensive works on the Index, the list of books forbidden to Catholics, and from 1900 to 1930 distributed antipornography propaganda emanating from M. Pouresey, a moral crusader.[60]

To establish their authority on the subject of sex, to cater to feminine modesty, and to distance their manuals from erotica, these French secular authors appealed to medical science. In the 1880s, Alexis Clerc assured his readers that "Science is always chaste. Do not blush, Madame, your modesty has nothing to fear." In the 1910s, G. M. Bessède reiterated this assurance.[61] However skeptical feminists might be about the life sciences, scientific appeals were quite persuasive. Even doctors writing manuals for the ACM began to refer to the authority of science.[62]

Secular authors also avoided charges of prurience by using Latin terminology for sex parts and by omitting sexual performance. Swiss psychologist August Forel complained about the distaste among the French public for "calling things by their proper names," which, he thought, merely "excites curiosity."[63] Silence on performance clearly reflected a cultural consensus against young women knowing about intercourse. This consensus existed in tandem with pronatalism, although the two positions might be considered contradictory.

French books for fiancées did not mention foreplay or how to prepare for intercourse beyond relaxing and trusting their husbands. Many warned young women against expecting romance in the marital bed, as they might have learned in romantic novels. These warnings add a layer of meaning to the strictures on girls reading romantic novels: such reading material might raise expectations about marital sex.[64] Premarital guides implicitly offered negative prognoses for early conjugal relations. Only one prewar women's health manual admitted that women had a sexual instinct, and the author, Swiss doctor Anna Fischer, also felt obliged to insist that women had no reason to be ashamed of their desire.[65] Similarly, only one postwar health manual for women waxed enthusiastic about early marital sex. Another woman doctor, Hélina Gaboriau, claimed that women "bloomed" after a few weeks of married life: the sexually awakened body rounded out, and the newly "animated" face became more attractive.[66]

In the mid-1930s, more practical and attractive guides for young women appeared—one of many signs of expanding possibilities, not regression, for young women after the *années folles* (1920s).[67] A bilingual woman doctor, Dr. Nelly Nelfrand of the University of Chicago, wrote the most permissive guide, *What Every Young Girl Should Know at Puberty,* and addressed it to "young French working women and their mothers." The guide was written at the suggestion of the Society for Sanitary and Moral Protection. Nelfrand quoted Alphonse Paré, a seventeenth-century French writer, on the necessity of flattery, titillation, and caresses to arouse women. In detail comparable to erotica, she divulged arousal techniques that her readers would otherwise have learned only by clandestine reading or from experienced lovers. Most provocatively, she called any wife "who serves passively as the instrument of her husband a saint and a martyr," and her husband "an egotist or a sot."[68] Although she sanctioned masturbation if husbands did not bring wives to orgasm, she did not authorize women to take more sexual initiative with their husbands. The notion of wives making advances or stating their preferences was simply not part of premarital (or most marital) sexual advice. Even suggestions about arousing husbands by wearing sexy lingerie were confined to worldly beauty guides written for women of a certain age.

Modifying Masculine Heterosexuality

French publishers began issuing sex manuals for fiancés about 1900, nearly two decades after they put out the first sex manuals for fiancées. Like contemporary Anglo-American manuals for young men, French manuals depicted a rapacious and possessive masculine heterosexuality; but compared with their counterparts, French manuals expressed far greater fear about "squandering" masculine procreative potential.[69] With the notable exception of clerics, French sex experts were less repressive of male heterosexuality. As Dr. Stérian explained in 1910, youths found abstinence difficult, and, in any case, abstinence was bad for "youths full of energy." To prevent "pollution" such as wet dreams, masturbation, and homosexual contacts, Stérian recommended early marriage. Although pronatalist propaganda encouraged young men to postpone coitus until marriage so that they would have a high sperm count when they wed, most secular sexual advisors expected that grooms would be familiar with "easy love."[70] These advisors believed that the groom needed experience to take charge of the bride's sexual initiation. In addition, some fiction writers offered cautionary tales about inexperienced grooms "straying" after marriage.[71] A few experts recognized that it might be problematic to entrust the initiation of a virgin to young men whose experience consisted of sex with "easy women."

Only advocates of public sex education such as Dr. Jeanne Stephani-Cherbuliz criticized negative attitudes toward single women with sexual experience, notably single mothers. Only Dr. Marie Houdré-Boursin, in her women's health manual, raised the conjoined problem of a double sexual standard: "While we shame the young girls, we laughingly compliment the gay blade who knows how to 'confirm' girls."[72]

Prewar guides for fiancés devoted considerable space to penile penetration of the hymen, described as *defloration*. Dr. Surbled stated baldly that the hymen had to be ruptured, ensuring that "entrance into marriage is normally bloody." For several experts, the hymen remained "the best proof of feminine virginity." Even Dr. Stérian, who counseled "a slow, progressive initiation," told grooms to check for fraudulent virgins by taking the bloody linens to a laboratory to be tested.[73] By iterating the myth of a necessarily traumatic initiation, the guides probably induced some men to be rough and insensitive to their partners' discomfort and possibly legitimated sadists' pleasure in brutal initiations.[74] Yet the guides themselves do not suggest masculine indifference to bridal comfort or pleasure in their partners' pain so much as performance of a duty. If numerous metaphors reflect a lingering conception of masculine honor as the sole possession of a wife's body and fertility, the reiteration suggests a certain lack of confidence in the outcome.

Unfortunately, prewar guides did not describe foreplay beyond the need for kisses and "caresses" to prepare the brides, with little indication that there might be such a thing as "fore-pleasure."[75] The only suggestion about alternative sexual comportment came in the form of an aside about "supplementary satisfactions" from "agile hands and tongue," followed by a disingenuous denial that the author recommended these "improper" practices. Only radical advocates of sex education and authors of erotic manuals described the preliminaries and positions for copulation. Although these advocates and authors favored the missionary position, they indicated other positions if the "normal" one was impossible—for instance, in late pregnancy.[76]

At least some advisors urged grooms to conduct the initiation slowly and as gently as possible. A 1913 manual told grooms to explain the sex act—

clearly articulating who the teacher would be, if the mother had failed in her duty. Dr. Bourgogne advised the groom to hide his impatience if the bride remained fearful, because her "expressed or tacit" consent was required. Few shared Bourgogne's confidence in the bridegroom's restraint. According to Dr. Anna Fischer, "The delights of the first possession without obstacle make the most self-contained man lose control." Others noted that insecure men would consider waiting a sign of impotence. Another problem must have been confusion about tacit consent, given assumptions about women being "the passive agent of the common operation."[77] Recommending restraint without explaining techniques to alleviate sexual tension must have contributed to frustration and performance anxiety.

After the Great War, guides were less fixated on rupturing the hymen. Possibly fewer young men valued "innocence" over other considerations, given the sexual disruption of the war and the phenomenon of "modern women" in the 1920s. Another possibility is that the mounting number of publications by sexual radicals such as the Surrealists, who publicly discussed the pleasures of "first sex" with experienced women, had some influence.[78] Other contributing factors were medical publicity that hymens could break before initiation and medical promotion of "defloration by dilation," either by husbands or by gynecologists.[79] We consider the postwar trend toward more considerate marital sex in the next chapter.

Both before and after the war, bridal passivity was apparent in a popular metaphor about the groom mastering a musical instrument. Dr. Mayoux felt it took "an adroit and supple hand to make this delicate instrument vibrate." At least a musical instrument is not as easily manipulated as the robotic or doll-women popular in risqué novels of the Belle Epoque were.[80] Other analogies were commercial or diplomatic: "Instead of considering the marriage act an immediately negotiable letter of exchange, the husband should bring to the first relations a bit more tact and diplomacy."[81] References to diplomatic relations also appeared in manuals for brides, which may have alerted brides that they could demand some consideration. If so, it was one of very few departures from the tendency to accept a predatory and possessive male heterosexuality in the literature for brides-to-be.

Public (Mis)Education

Despite the mounting interest of the Third Republic in natality, the official approach to sex education for boys and girls changed little. At the turn of the century, many girls still attended convent schools. Although these schools disciplined the body by regulating it, sex education consisted essentially of "surveillance and silence." To discourage masturbation and youthful exploration of one another's bodies, students had to sleep one to a bed, with a sister in every dormitory room. Sex was not on the curriculum, but this did not discourage girls from talking about it (even though their sources of information must have been limited). Progressive Catholic schools introduced physical education to develop the muscular and circulatory systems, which they claimed would counteract the girls' sensibility, often associated with their sexuality, and strengthen their bodies for healthy pregnancies and babies.[82] After the war, the ACM published pedagogical works that criticized teaching sisters who, "under the pretext of guarding the purity of the young girl, awaken feelings of disgust and revolt."[83] The association advised progressive maternal sex instruction—when a child asked, the mother should offer no more information than necessary to satisfy the child's curiosity; she should tell stories about pollen and eggs, but also about Adam, Eve, and original sin. At puberty, mothers should tell daughters about maternity. The purpose was preventive and prophylactic: mothers were to dissuade children from masturbation and instill the idea that chastity was "the only protection against the plague of venereal diseases."[84]

The secular school system was almost as conservative about sex education. As early as 1900, Dr. Georges Stodel linked the lack of sex education in girls schooling to ignorance about reproduction and hence to low natality.[85] Proponents of sex education for boys tried to sanitize the subject by calling it *sexual hygiene* that would teach genital cleanliness, continence until marriage, and respect for women. These proponents promised that sexual hygiene would make boys aware of venereal diseases and encourage them to avoid contact with "impure women" who could infect "innocent victims" such as future wives and children. At the Third International Congress on School Hygiene in 1910, prominent French physicians endorsed proposals to "prepare" adolescent boys for sexual life.[86] Their endorsement and postwar alarm about venereal disease persuaded educators to revise the hygiene curriculum, adding sections on venereal diseases for adolescent boys and on infant care for adolescent girls.[87] The additions reflected gendered assumptions about the emerging sexuality of boys and the future maternity of girls.

After the war, medical and educational advocates claimed that public school courses on sex were more necessary because the war had brought a decline in moral standards, indifference about reproductive outcomes, and a resort to "egotistical"—meaning nonreproductive—sexual passion.[88] Feminists became more vocal about public sex education. Mme. Avril de Sainte-Croix gave a pronatalist rationale: public education would serve the "future of the race." She recommended teaching the natural sciences and progressing from vegetable to animal reproduction. In contrast to Catholic sex educators, Avril de Sainte-Croix favored a positive introduction to sex as "an initiation in the good, healthy life."[89] Because the public associated her proposals with opposition to the recent antiabortion bill, her rather modest proposals had little chance of success.[90]

In the postwar climate of anxiety about gender and natality, any proposal for public sex education aroused heated debate. Accordingly, one proponent, Dr. Vaucaire, reverted to the traditional panacea of maternal "tact," supplemented by the new notion of "psychological finesse," to enlighten a girl without "wounding or destroying her modesty." Vaucaire took a eugenic approach: he listed the symptoms of venereal diseases, urged premarital medical exams, and proscribed marrying anyone with hereditary or degenerative diseases.[91] Although the French Eugenics Society (formed two years before the war) was always marginal, it was in tune with a wider discourse about syphilis which gave rise to claims that four million people, or 10 percent of the population, were infected.[92]

In the 1920s, ministry officials considered sex education, but the concept remained controversial. When the Paris Medical Faculty endorsed a proposal that sexual hygiene should be a branch of public education, the Congress of Christian Marriage rejected it decisively. The assembly of French cardinals and archbishops rejected "scientific initiation" because courses would be morally neutral: "Even worse, they may promulgate . . . physiological laws (such as the impossibility or dangers of continence) contrary to truth as much as the moral order."[93] By the mid-1930s, many teachers thought that children should learn about sexual life at school, but parental convictions that the subject was "dirty" prevented teachers from offering this kind of instruction. Proponents who associated public sex education with Freudian notions of childhood sexuality did not enhance its respectability.[94] Even when the Ministry of Public Instruction finally accepted sex information in the curriculum in 1973, it provided few instructional resources. The Planned Parenthood Federation attributed this procrastination to the conservative Catholic tradition.[95]

Alternative teaching reached some young women. In the early 1920s, Dr. Germaine Montreuil-Strauss of the French Association of Women Doctors and the National Council of French Women joined with the French League Against the Venereal Peril to organize all-women meetings. By 1925, the Association of Women Doctors constituted a Feminine Education Committee of the Society of Sanitary and Moral Protection with Montreuil-Strauss as president. Over the next decade, the committee gained the support of the French Union for Women's Suffrage, the League for the Rights of Women, Red Cross societies, and 175 other organizations, including student, nurse, and Catholic youth groups. With subsidies from the Ministry of Health, Welfare, and Social Insurance, the committee held 644 conferences, often with films, on subjects such as maternity and venereal diseases. The conferences attracted 140,000 people. The committee also distributed 83,000 brochures to about one third of all female public school teachers.[96] In talks sponsored by the Ministry of Public Health, Montreuil-Strauss favored "biological education for maternity," warned about hereditary and venereal diseases, and occasionally gave directions for douches to prevent syphilis and gonorrhea. (The last topic was so controversial that distribution of posters with recipes for antivenereal douches was delayed until the American Embassy made an "energetic intervention.")[97] Gynecologists recommended the brochures and conferences of the Feminine Education Committee. Even the ACM printed Montreuil-Strauss's report on a survey that showed, not surprisingly, that young women were not shocked, but reassured, by sex education.[98]

Conclusions

It is estimated that the proportion of young French wives who had had premarital relations rose from about one-fifth in the Belle Epoque, to more than one-third in the interwar. For most of these women, premarital relations were strictly prenuptial—that is, they followed promises of marriage. Of course this varied by class, region, and religious observance.[99] The first French survey of sexual comportment before marriage was carried out in the mid-1960s and found that two-thirds of the 142 respondents had had their first sexual intercourse on their wedding night. More than 60 percent of both sexes agreed that the first encounter was less satisfying for the woman. Thirty-five percent of the women enjoyed sex the first time, 44 percent took pleasure after a few months, and 17 percent had no satisfaction for longer than a year.[100] Although it is impossible to generalize from this largely professional and administrative group, the results suggest that the phenomenon of bourgeois girls' chastity until marriage persisted.

Chapter 6

Pleasure and Procreation

ETWEEN the 1880s and the 1920s, the main pillars of expert advice about marriage and maternity were their necessity and mutuality. According to hygienists, sexual advisors, and moralists, female sexuality was inseparable from matrimony and maternity. Updating the ideas of natural historian Comte de Buffon, these experts argued that marriage was "the foundation stone of the social edifice"[1] and that lifelong virginity was harmful to women and men. Many hygienists repeated evolutionary theses that the propagation of the species was paramount and that women were "made for reproduction" of the species.[2] In the 1920s, some experts proclaimed that feminine pleasure (orgasm) promoted good marital relations and fertility. This new marital sexual advice addressed husbands, and so any information reached women, the most interested party, through changes in their husbands' sexual comportment or through spousal instruction in new practices.

In general, medical and hygienic literature represented maternity (pregnancy and delivery) as a duty rather than as an attractive option for women. Once again, internal contradictions undercut the message from sex and hygiene experts to have more babies. Even the medicalization of maternity, which lowered maternal and neonatal mortality, did not significantly alleviate the pain of labor and delivery. In turn, the failure to ease labor and delivery contributed to the failure of the campaign to raise the birth rate.

For some young women at the turn of the century, marriage was an "emancipation" from draconian social and sexual restrictions. For most hygienists, this meant that young women would exhaust themselves and thereby reduce their chance for conception or increase their chance of miscarriage. Almost all health guides for women told wives never to refuse their husbands' sexual advances;[3] marital sexual advisors admonished wives "to be mothers as often as nature wants."[4] Both sets of advisors adopted Adolphe Pinard's dictum about women's physiological need to exercise their reproductive function. Pinard, first chair at the state-of-the-art obstetrical clinic of the Baudelocque Hospital, documented the positive impact of prenatal rest on the birth weight and health of neonates.[5] Best known for inventing *puériculture* (infant and prenatal care), Pinard was a pronatalist and a eugenicist. Like most French eugenicists, he was a Neo-Lamarckian who believed in the importance of environment, including the pregnant woman's health, to fetal and neonatal health.[6]

As fears about (allegedly) hereditary diseases spread in the early twentieth century, marital advice complicated reproductive advice. According to venereal specialists, syphilis caused forty thousand miscarriages annually and twenty thousand stillbirths or neonatal deaths annually.[7] Despite medical controversy over tuberculosis being hereditary, one gynecologist "forbade" tubercular people to wed. Few patients obeyed.[8] Hygienists advised fiancées to have a gynecological examination to detect any vaginal anomalies—"in the presence of a third person, preferably belonging to the girl's family." These recommendations also had little effect. Prof. Couvelaire, son-in-law and successor of Pinard at the Baudelocque, opened the first prenuptial clinic in 1930. Open one morning a week, the clinic tested only fourteen women and sixty-seven men in 1932.[9]

Pleasure

In theory, encouraging women to enjoy sexual relations might have had the desired effect of increasing natality. In practice, French sex experts did assert that women had a capacity for sexual arousal, that the clitoris was an erectile organ similar to the penis, and that penile stimulation of the clitoris produced the most female pleasure. Yet the same medical experts also reported that feminine arousal was unnecessary for conception, that women had a relatively passive role in intercourse, and that they were less easily "inflamed" than men were. Prewar physicians claimed that their opinions were based on "long practice and numerous confidences."[10] Although they did not admit it, most were influenced by popular attitudes toward feminine sexuality and by pronatalist propaganda.

During and after the Great War, a few sexual advisors took more radical stances on feminine sexuality. Jean Marestan (aka Gaston Harvard, mentioned in the preceding chapter) declared that both sexes must exercise their genital organs for their health. He quoted the English advocate of married women's love, Marie Stopes, who advocated sexual intercourse as often as necessary to satisfy both spouses. Marestan went beyond listing the places to kiss and stroke in foreplay, telling men to open and lubricate the vulva and vagina before copulation. To this point Marestan's *Sexual Education* reads like erotic manuals for men interested in perfecting their sexual techniques with no thought about reproductive outcomes. Thereafter, *Sexual Education* deviated, as Marestan espoused a "free love" possible only when women knew how to avoid unwanted pregnancies and "men's ardor was subordinated to women's consent." In his view, nothing should override a woman's right "to remain sovereign mistress of herself and the fecundity in her flanks." Moreover, after criticizing clandestine abortions by unqualified persons, Marestan approved five contraception devices and proposed medical abortions on demand.[11] For his opinions, Marestan, like other Neo-Malthusians, was under constant police surveillance during and after the war.[12]

By contesting sexual hierarchies directly, Marestan used more political and provocative language than Stopes, who argued for contraception to protect women's health. Consequently, Marestan had a less positive effect on French marital advice. Most French experts distanced themselves from his radicalism by using more conservative, male-centered, and natalist rhetoric. These texts prescribed what hegemonic masculine heterosexuality should be and hinted at some troubling realities about bourgeois sexual behavior.

As in the United States and Britain, postwar marriage manuals exhorted husbands to exercise greater restraint and be more attentive to their wives' pleasure, especially, but not exclusively, on the wedding night. Without detailing how female sexuality might be expressed, these manuals assumed that women had a right to sexual pleasure.[13] But French handbooks included this caveat: pleasure was not to be accompanied by contraception. In short, the new French manuals articulated a more expressive version of female heterosexuality and a more considerate version of masculine heterosexuality but only within the parameters of a reproductive feminine sexuality and a masterful masculine heterosexuality.

If the impact of the war on the institution of marriage explains the change in British marital and contraceptive advice, the war had other repercussions in France. The war left many amputees and a new social construction of a disabled person as "a potent man rendered impotent."[14] To counter any doubts about the sexual capacities of the *mutilés de guerre*—doubts that one war memoir ascribed to nurses and, by implication, all women—medical men insisted upon these men's ability to control their bodies and father children.[15]

The loss of life during and after the war also exaggerated existing demographic apprehensions. In the 1920s, a hygiene textbook written by Drs. Courmont and Rochaix reported that France continued to have a lower birth rate than other European countries because of more voluntary restriction of marital fertility. Although Courmont and Rochaix blamed husbands and wives, they believed that they could more easily influence wives,[16] probably because the new ideal of feminine sexual satisfaction separate from reproduction was very controversial.

Dr. Bourgas's postwar manual, called *Woman's Right to Love,* added a biological cast to the new model of feminine sexuality and fertility. Arguing along lines drawn by Moreau de la Sarthe—to wit, that women's sex organs affected their whole bodies—Bourgas claimed that women had more complicated sex lives. Men had not bothered to learn about these complicated creatures, and ninety-nine times out of a hundred, women "put up with rather than participating in the sex act." Bourgas was less orthodox in his belief that human sexual intercourse did not have "reproduction as its only objective." Because humans had the faculty of sexual relations at any time, they developed durable affections that became the "most solid base of society." After proclaiming the right of women to pleasure and the interest of society in that pleasure, Bourgas stipulated how husbands should make love and thereby provided some insight into what might otherwise happen in the marriage bed. He told husbands not to stop foreplay, not to ejaculate prematurely, and not to withdraw before satisfying their wives—not solely to satisfy their wives, but also to ensure conception. Conversely, Bourgas threatened that artificially prolonged intercourse and other "voluptuous refinements" led to "senile impotence" in men and nervous disorders in women. He warned that all forms of contraception caused genital infections in women, degeneration in surviving infants, and depopulation in France.[17]

Neither Bourgas nor anyone else who made statements about women merely tolerating sex could cite any study. Interwar experts did not allude to patient confidences out of heightened concern about confidentiality. Respectable women probably did not tell doctors about their sexual appetites or experiences, given assumptions about feminine passivity and convictions that sexual intimacy was a private affair. To be frankly interested in sex, as opposed to being subtly seductive, must have seemed masculine. In her study of marital breakdowns based on sexual rejection, Anne-Marie Sohn found that wives who refused conjugal relations expressed disgust with sex. Most blamed cold or unloving partners; some specified brutal relations. Wives used both direct and indirect means to avoid sex: they turned their backs or pushed their husbands away; they pled exhaustion or feigned illness or pregnancy as excuses. Real illness and pregnancy were considered legitimate reasons to abstain.[18]

Even the Association for Christian Marriage (ACM) recognized that the newly proclaimed right to female sexual enjoyment put new demands on husbands. Their pamphlets, which were often written by Catholic medical men, were more forthright than prewar Catholic propaganda. They advised husbands to avoid a "brusque" initiation and to consider their wives in intercourse: "To be master of his senses, to delay long enough to permit her to take part in the joy of their union." Nevertheless, the authors insisted that men must not become "slaves of their wives' fantasies"—witness what had happened to Adam and Eve in the Garden of Eden.[19]

Sohn's analysis of more than 150 letters sent to Abbé Viollet (of the ACM) indicated that sexual relations could be a source of unhappiness for Catholic provincials. Several married men wrote to complain about wives refusing conjugal duties or yielding only after repeated advances. Not as many wives wrote of acquiescing to emotional blackmail; one admitted faking orgasm in order to have some peace. By contrast, three neglected wives confessed that they were tormented with sexual frustration. Several others agreed that marriage without sexual compatibility was lamentable.[20]

Secular marital guides for husbands compared male and female sexuality. *The Art of Keeping Love in Marriage* by Dr. Jean Fauconney (now writing as Dr. Jaf, not, as previously encountered, as Dr. Caufeynon) offered observations on women's external sex organs taking longer to get aroused and assurances that this difference should disappear with experience. Dr. Henri Drouin's *Advice for Young Men* (1926) quoted Marie Stopes, saying that women felt desire only shortly before and after their menstrual period. For the rest of the time, Drouin informed young husbands, women's genitals "fall asleep" and require foreplay to awaken.[21] In 1928, a more sophisticated book "on the mechanics of the flesh" focused on the elasticity of women's organs.[22] Even though this kind of information might have reassured virginal brides, the book addressed men. Perhaps the assumption was that the male readers would pass this information on to brides. Certainly, these marital guides for husbands instructed new brides (through their husbands) to contribute to their own and their partners' health by douching. In the prewar, some women douched with an antiseptic solution to prevent "white flowers" from infecting or offending their partners.[23] After the war, most doctors suspected that douching with imperfectly cleaned equipment introduced germs into the vagina, irritated vaginal tissue, and interfered with fertilization. Hygienists recommended douching once or twice a week, using cooled boiled water with a teaspoon of household antiseptic, and postcoital douching only after several hours to avoid any interference with conception. Women hygienists hinted that wives should spare their husbands contact with offensive discharges, but they did not mention menstrual blood. Only one male gynecologist, Dr. Eddé, advised douching after every period to remove all traces of blood.[24] His unstated assumption was that intercourse ceased during the flow.

In the late 1920s and early 1930s, the Parisian publisher Artistic Bookshop specialized in books such as *Manual of Married Love* and *Treatise on Carnal Relations*. Another Parisian publisher launched a series of pamphlets with titles such as *The Genital Organs in Both Sexes* and *Desire, Love, Copulation*. Although these publications addressed both sexes, it is clear that the male authors envisaged male readers. The authors referred to *our* versus *their* sexuality, with *our* being masculine and *their* being feminine. Far more than their predecessors, the authors—all specialists in reproduction—insisted that copulation was good for women and for the nation. Along with their natalist and evolutionary views came a revitalized biological functionalism. This literature defined female sex organs as just another organic system and copulation as just another physiological function. Like most of their peers, these authors accepted the physiological paradigms that all systems are interdependent, that all require regular exercise, and therefore that regular intercourse benefited the entire organism. Few acknowledged that their position contradicted traditional Christian views. Even Prof. Jussey, in his scholarly book *Sexual History of Woman* (1928), only alluded to the contradiction in a statement that "copulation should . . . not be regarded as shameful, but as a physiological and moral necessity."[25]

In the 1920s, sexual specialists responded to the lesbianism that was now chic on the Left Bank in Paris[26] as well as to the number of women practicing contraception. Dr. Drouin wrote another book entitled *Damned Women* to warn about the physiological and psychological costs of women not absorbing the "mysterious equilibrating effects of sperm."[27] Instead of repeating this threat in his marital guide, he and other advisors on marital sex promoted the vaginal or "real" orgasm. They explained that stimulation of the clitoris only initiated sensual pleasure, whereas the erogenous zones in the vagina "bring on the final spasm." According to these male advisors, penetration was the only act capable of bringing "complete pleasure" (*jouissance*).[28]

As Freudian ideas began to infiltrate this literature in the late 1920s, many sex experts expressed incredible concern about the size and sensitivity of the clitoris. Prof. Jussey (who was not a Freudian) cautioned that repeated masturbation enlarged the clitoris to the point that removal of the clitoris becomes necessary. Dr. Bourdon noted unidentified (but Freudian) theories correlating lesbianism with "deficiencies in the erogenous zone" but reassured his readers that "an appropriate [surgical] treatment would cure these deficiencies."[29]

Otherwise, French Freudians had little impact on marriage manuals. Neither the *Bulletin of the Society of Sexology*, with a tiny circulation, nor the *French Review of Psychoanalysis*, with a slightly larger press run of five hundred in 1928,[30] ran articles on female sexuality until the mid-1930s. Then Marie Bonaparte, daughter of Prince Bonaparte and the major financial benefactor of Freudian ventures in France, published articles on Freud's *Three Essays on Sexuality* in the *French Review of Psychoanalysis*. These articles accepted Freud's concepts of penis envy, passivity, masochism, and narcissism as normal components of female sexuality.[31] Bonaparte is infamous for her work on female frigidity, especially her attendance at, and advertisement of, an operation to move a frigid woman's clitoris closer to her vagina. According to Bonaparte, the operation was intended to increase female pleasure, but it also made it easier for the partner to arouse the patient.[32]

None of the chapters on marital hygiene in women's health manuals went into detail about external genitalia or their relationship to sexual gratification. Dr. Anna Fischer's medical drawings of external genitalia in the 1905 edition of her women's health manual provoked such outrage that she eliminated them from the 1924 edition. The publisher left a blank space in the text with the disingenuous caption, "This engraving is of a purely technical order and of medical rather than profane interest."[33] In 1922 and in 1933, specialized gynecological manuals inserted similar illustrations without any information about how these organs might affect sexual pleasure or comfort.[34]

Similarly, none of the marital hygiene chapters in women's health guides gave an account of penetration. Dr. Hélina Gaboriau explained that "further details" should be acquired from other women.[35] It is doubtful that many respectable women would have talked about such a private and personal subject. No women's health manual disputed the primacy of the vaginal orgasm until Nelly Nelfrand's *What Every Young Girl Should Know at Puberty* (1932) announced that the vaginal canal is only "an accessory to orgasm." Nelfrand's guide for girls also stood alone in assuring women who remained unsatisfied after withdrawal that they could and should "finish the job" themselves.[36]

Conception

Throughout the Republic, some specialists and all health guides counseled moderate sexual activity to ensure conception. A Catholic gynecologist, Georges Surbled, cautioned that "vigorous and brief relations," five to six times a month, were ideal. In the interwar, all but a few Catholic moralists approved of sexual intercourse one to three times a week and less often from middle age on.[37] This advice reflected lingering Christian doubt about the probity of sexual intercourse, even in marriage, and tenacious medical opinion about the potential of intercourse to debilitate, both through the draining effects of ejaculation on men and through the damage that vigorous copulation could cause women. Probably the critical factor for most couples was opportunity, given how many married women performed a double workload and how many mothers a triple workload.

Until the 1920s, most marital sexual advice literature devoted many pages to the propitious moment for conception. One reason was that medical researchers still debated the timing of ovulation.[38] *Fin-de-siècle* experts wavered between spontaneous ovulation with no connection to the menstrual cycle and release of the ova during menstruation.[39] Most practicing obstetricians assumed that the eggs dropped into the uterus during menstruation.[40] A 1907 doctoral thesis reported that ovaries removed over the course of the menstrual cycle revealed that ova were released fourteen days after the onset of menstruation.[41] For more than a decade, this important discovery did not alter advice on when to conceive.

Postwar hygienists were less definite about the timing for conceiving and for avoiding conception. In the early 1920s, some still recommended the middle of the menstrual cycle as the safe period. In the late 1920s, Dr. J. R. Bourdon reported that new data on the longevity of the sperm in the vagina showed that safe periods were not so safe.[42] In the early 1930s, the Japanese scientist Ogino invented the method of measuring body temperature to pinpoint when ovulation occurred; practicing French Catholics hoping to reconcile Catholic teaching with economic realities promptly publicized the Ogino method.[43] Other Catholic physicians continued to advocate chastity as the only safe means of birth control.[44]

As Martine Sevegrand showed, the clergy was divided on the issue of a safe period. Faced with the widespread practice of coitus interruptus in the nineteenth century, the French Church did not condemn the women, whom they defined as victims of this male-controlled form of birth control. Periodic abstinence had not been considered a mortal or venial sin since 1880. As knowledge of the Ogino method spread, some Catholic priests accepted the method as respectful of both the sex act and the legitimate secondary purpose of marriage, "mutual aid for concupiscence." Even the initially hostile ACM published a pamphlet allowing for periodic continence.[45] After several years of public silence, Catholic women belatedly entered the discourse. Monique Levallet-Montal accepted that love had two purposes: procreation and "happiness," which did not mean pleasure. Separating the two purposes was sinful, she believed, but under certain conditions, such as difficulties in raising existing children, couples could "space" marital relations. Levallet-Montal approved the new Ogino method for health, not "egotistical" (i.e., contraceptive), reasons. Other means of contraception posed serious danger to the family and "the race itself."[46]

Most sex manuals also discussed frigidity. In the late 1880s, one specialist on impotence in both sexes (meaning, in the case of women, frigidity) explained that feminine indifference to intercourse had no effect on fertility. Quite the contrary, Dr. Moussaud argued, overly passionate women were sterile: "In the ardor and vibrations of epileptic coitus, the uterus, convulsively contracted, closes its entrance to the sperm."[47] One wonders if readers desperate for children tried to curb their wives' ardor. Conversely, experts faulted the most common form of birth control, coitus interruptus, because men complained about frustration and because it left the uterus indifferent to "copulative excitation" and semen.[48] Specialists did identify physical and pathological causes of infertility such as deformities of the vagina or diseases of the fallopian tubes, for which they prescribed douching, hydrotherapy, massage, and electrotherapy.[49] Although sexual advisors mentioned these dubious "cures," they stressed avoiding sexual excess or contraceptive "abuse."[50]

Postwar sexual advisors considered sterility a serious problem—one reported that 15 percent of all couples were sterile and that one third of these cases resulted from "masculine deficiencies"—but subsumed their discussions of infertility in criticisms of contraception. With the exception of Montreuil-Strauss and the Feminine Education Committee, who attributed most infertility to the ravages of venereal, hereditary, and infectious diseases, popularizers did not consider pathological sources of infertility, perhaps because of pessimistic prognoses for a cure.[51] They found it easier to denounce coitus interruptus for leaving the genitals of both partners in a state of pathological hypertension, causing sterility.[52]

Despite folk customs of infertile women seeking fecundating water or wearing fertility charms, none of the sex guides or health manuals blamed childlessness exclusively on women. In 1902, Dr. Marie Schultz reported on recent research demonstrating that men "played almost as important a role" and advised both spouses to get a medical examination (although she conceded that it was hard to get men to accept treatment). Like Mme. Gensse in 1899, Schultz mentioned the possibility of artificial fertilization to correct any physical anomalies. Both women took a more positive approach to artificial fertilization than hygienists had in the 1880s, the latter having had misgivings about unknown prenatal influences as well as about the morality of the procedure.[53] With the Church continuing to criticize the method, artificial fertilization remained extremely rare.

Contraception

As early as 1896, anarchist Paul Robin (1837–1912) founded a Neo-Malthusian league that distributed birth control tracts, held birth control meetings, and sold contraceptives. This League for Human Regeneration was more radical than most Neo-Malthusian organizations. Robin was committed to women's right to decide when to conceive and how to avoid conception as well as to the proposition that control over reproduction was "the essential point of female emancipation." Nelly Roussel (1878–1922) was one of the few feminists to take up the controversial cause of birth control. After difficult deliveries in 1899 and 1901, the latter followed by the death of her second baby, she joined Robin's league and added her own unique focus on reducing maternal pain and linking free choice of maternity to the "right to a complete life" (*la vie intégral*). As Elinor Accampo argued, Roussel was claiming for women the bodily integrity upon which French citizenship had been based since the Enlightenment.[54] For most hygienists, women's control of their fertility and its corollaries, bodily integrity and individuality, was unacceptable.

In the first decade of the twentieth century, one female hygienist and one male sexual advisor discussed female sexuality separate from reproduction, in both cases in relation to attitudes toward the body. As discussed earlier in this chapter, the second edition of Fischer's health manual was censured for its illustrations of genitalia and also of nude bodies. Fischer responded polemically by deploring declining respect for the natural beauty of the human body. In Dr. Mayoux's sex guide, he complained that prevailing esthetic standards, notably about nudity, were "essentially masculine."[55] His work drew less criticism because it was designed to help parents educate their children about sex and was not distributed as widely as Fischer's second edition, which sold nearly 200,000 copies.

After mollifying their critics by affirming that the purpose of sex was procreation, the two doctors stretched the limits of respectability by advocating contraception, albeit for different reasons. Fischer held that the more women developed, the more they understood the need to limit the number of children they bore so they could pursue careers. Fischer disapproved of coitus interruptus because it deprived the woman of "a carnal satisfaction necessary to her health." Furthermore, she had no faith in condoms because she (and several authors of sex manuals) found that men would not use inconvenient methods. Assigning women responsibility for contraception, Fischer assessed available female methods (sponges, rings, douches, and prophylactic peccaries) more optimistically than present-day birth controllers would. She argued that women should impose moderation on their husbands because women were better at controlling their passion. Dr. Mayoux offered more Malthusian reasons for limiting births: to avoid transmitting degenerative diseases and to maintain family finances. He also allotted more responsibility to men and provided information on male- and female-controlled forms of contraception.[56]

Although many hygienists endorsed Fischer's contention that women should impose moderation in sexual activity, most rejected the notion of women imposing contraception and limiting births in order to pursue careers. Mayoux's utilitarian justification for birth control and the male-dominated approach to contraception had more supporters.

In the interwar, two women hygienists subtly supported birth control. Although Hélina Gaboriau only recommended antiseptic douches for infections, savvy readers would have realized that an antiseptic solution could be spermicidal. Shortly after her section on antiseptic douches, Gaboriau informed readers that the cold douches they believed to be spermicidal were ineffective because they were not antiseptic. Houdré-Boursin was bolder but still prudent: she advocated "consensual and prepared procreation" and provided formulas for antivenereal douches that were, but were not labeled, spermicidal.[57]

Very few female physicians openly supported birth control. When the French Association of Women Doctors sent a questionnaire about birth control to its members in the early 1930s, only fifteen members replied; of the forty-six Parisian doctors interviewed, only seven, five of them women, wanted the law against abortion and female contraception revised. Most reported offering their patients "maternity or continence." Some denounced the "licentious propaganda of a society marching toward the folly of ethnic suicide by depraved manners." Challenged by militant birth controller Berthe Albrecht, the investigator retorted, "Going against biological laws is anti-medical."[58]

In 1930, the Papacy issued the Casti Connubii encyclical on marriage, sexual morality, and contraception. The encyclical was a profoundly conservative response to feminists seeking women's "physiological emancipation," eugenicists advocating restrictions on both the right to marry and access to birth control, and to all propagandists "against marriage and its primary purpose, procreation." Sections on the necessity of "conjugal chastity" specified that conjugal relations should not be for "the satisfaction of the senses"; sections on "submission of the wife" clarified that wives remained mistresses of their conscience, especially with regard to procreation. Commentaries were issued and study groups instituted to familiarize Catholics with the encyclical.[59]

In the following decade, French clerics and Catholic doctors elucidated the encyclical. ACM pamphlets taught that "love in marriage is not platonic love, it is human and sexual love regulated by moral and religious law"; nevertheless, women's bodies did not belong to their husbands "without limit," and wives did not have to be a "plaything" for their husbands. In an amalgamation of natalism, nationalism, and Catholicism, Abbé Albert Dubois argued that women owed their country citizens and soldiers and their Church more Christians.[60] Catholic biopsychologist René Biot chimed in that hormonal research would prove that women suffered when deprived not only of sexual satisfaction but also of maternity.[61]

Birth controllers persevered. In 1933, Dr. Jean Dalsace publicized contraceptive methods and, as a result, lost his laboratory position. With the complicity of the socialist mayor of a commune known for its exemplary public health measures, Dalsace set up a center to teach contraception and there distributed diaphragms and spermicidal jellies from England. Simultaneously, Berthe Albrecht made *The Sexual Problem* a tribune for the sexual liberation of women and "free" maternity. Free thinkers debated Abbé Viollet and published pamphlets contending that Catholic doctrine was opposed to the equality of the sexes and the emancipation of women.[62]

Theoretically, the Calvinist minority in France was more open to "the satisfaction of bodily needs." A 1930 thesis on Protestantism and the sexual question posited that marital sex for pleasure "cemented the union." Author T. de Félice argued that men did not have "the exclusive right to take the initiative," that women had the same right to orgasm and, in blunt language, that men should postpone entry until the vagina was dilated and lubricated. Although Félice proclaimed the "duty" of the healthy to reproduce, he insisted that pregnancy must not compromise women's health, and he supported contraceptive devices.[63] In the absence of any comparative religious studies of Frenchwomen's sexual behavior, it is difficult to tell how these attitudes translated into practice. A 1914 inquiry by a Catholic physician, who sent questionnaires to bourgeois and noble families, was able to compare the fecundity of one hundred "believing" and five hundred "unbelieving" families. Dr. Dauchez found that the average "believing" (practicing Catholic) family had 6.2 children, whereas "unbelieving" families had an average of 2.73 children.[64]

Pregnancy

Beginning with Pinard and the other leading prewar obstetrician, Budin (1846–1907), obstetricians redefined pregnancy in a more positive but still paradoxical way, much as their colleagues were redefining puberty. In reaction to medical traditions and popular beliefs, obstetricians denied that pregnancy was a disease, but, in line with their interests, they declared that it was a physiological state that affected the entire organism, predisposed it to fatigue and suffering, and required special discipline. Prenatal care was felt to be essential to the health of the fetus and infant. Fewer added that prenatal care was essential to the health of the pregnant woman and new mother.[65]

Despite the experts' unanimity on the desirability of maternity, two elements of their representations of pregnancy were perverse. First, only female authors of women's health guides reported that many pregnant women felt a new vitality, that save for nausea in the early months, most felt fine throughout the pregnancy, and that some new mothers enjoyed better health after gestation.[66] Second, free brochures distributed to poor women by women's charities blamed pregnant women for neonatal mortality. One brochure cited the high rate of neonatal mortality in France compared with that in Scandinavian countries and claimed that two thirds of the dead neonates should have lived because they had succumbed to preventable diseases. The brochure claimed that the health of pregnant women and nursing mothers contributed to these deaths, for "the blood of the mother transmits antibiotic substances into the blood of the baby." Intended to frighten pregnant women into having medical examinations and treating any conditions,[67] the scare tactic may have had the opposite effect.

Especially in the prewar years, hygienists assumed that nearly all women were ignorant of pregnancy. Certainly, there was not as much knowledge as might be expected in a society where many births occurred at home. Mme.

Lucie's mother told her that parents "bought babies." As late as 1935, Monique Levallet-Montal suggested that mothers tell daughters who realized that babies did not come directly from heaven that God placed the soul in mother's body. Then, when daughters reached twelve years of age, the mothers should add that God placed the body into a mother's body. When her own daughter asked how the baby got out, Levallet-Montal answered, "with great difficulty for mama." Until she was eighteen, her daughter got no more details from Levallet-Montal.[68]

In this literature, hygienists listed such signals of pregnancy as missed periods, swelling stomach, nausea, morning sickness, and bizarre cravings. Later, pregnant women might expect swollen breasts, darker nipples, and facial discoloration, and around the fourth month, feeling the fetus (referred to as the infant) move.[69] Guides for pregnant women specified how to get ready for birth, beginning with preparing nipples for suckling. For three decades, that meant hardening nipples by rubbing them with alcohol; by 1910, it meant softening them with glycerin or other emollients. In 1901, one of Budin's students warned that the peasant custom of preparatory sucking by a midwife or a husband could induce premature labor. Other hygienists continued to patent and promote breast pumps to start lactation.[70]

From the turn of the century, hygienists exhorted pregnant women to have their urine analyzed for albuminuria (indissoluble protein) which might bring on eclampsia, a convulsion caused by toxemia. Recognizing that many women could not consult a doctor, some hygienists reported the symptoms of albuminuria and advertised mail order tests for it. By the war, obstetricians were using urine analysis to detect the presence of glucose, an indication of diabetes. To prepare for difficult deliveries, hygienists urged a pregnant woman to have a medical examination in the eighth month to detect a deformed pelvis or improperly presenting fetus By the 1920s, the pamphlet *You Will Be a Mother* suggested seeing the doctor at the beginning of a pregnancy.[71]

Although the above suggestions were not realistic for most peasant and working-class women, the medicalization of pregnancy did reach beyond the privileged. Beginning in the mid-1880s with Marie Bequet de Vienne, charitable women began founding private shelters to assure rest and a modicum of care for poor, abandoned pregnant women regardless of their marital status. In the next decade, municipal welfare bureaus established public asylums mainly for single servants and garment workers.[72] Free prenatal clinics and medical visits followed, as the Baudelocque and other hospitals added these services. By 1930, poor pregnant women came to the Baudelocque, on average, three times per pregnancy. Because three prenatal visits remained exceptional, reformers tried to generalize the practice. In 1933, the new social insurance system required three free prenatal examinations for insured pregnant women, without which they forfeited their maternity benefits.[73]

Researchers found it difficult to ascertain the length of a pregnancy because most pregnant women considered inquiries about the date of conception "indiscrete and injurious." In the last two decades of the nineteenth century, a series of studies and conferences favored terms of up to eleven months.[74] In the early twentieth century, a norm of nine months emerged. By the 1930s, some hygienists were talking about "wise couples, knowing how to take precautions." Such couples chose the moment of conception to assure a spring birth, so that the woman could avoid suffering from the heat in the last stage of pregnancy.[75]

Hygienists grappled with popular opinion about the "moral influence of the mother on the fetus" into the 1930s. Early hygienists accepted that strong maternal emotions such as fear, anger, or surprise affected fetuses and agreed that a shock could induce miscarriage through the influence of the nerves in the uterus. In 1899, Mlle. Thilo counseled foregoing anything that evoked sadness or other bad feelings during a pregnancy. Generally, hygienists denied folk beliefs that lively emotions or visual impressions, especially of frightening or ugly things, left physical marks on babies or that denying a craving would leave a mark on the infant in the shape of the desired food or object. However, the hygienists retained a belief in "a feticulture, which happens without the mother being conscious . . . and imposes a duty to watch her moral state during pregnancy."[76] Much ink was spilled about widespread anxieties that a woman who had relations with a man of color could later bear a colored child, even if she had been consorting with a Caucasian at the time of conception. By 1930, all hygienists rejected such prejudices, although they still encountered them in their patients.[77]

Pinard and Budin insisted that sexual relations during pregnancy traumatized the uterus and induced premature births and miscarriages. In his huge clinic for pregnant women, Pinard posted a notice that "All pregnant women must refuse sexual relations for their entire pregnancy." Hygienists made unsubstantiated claims that more than half of the premature births were caused by untimely or boisterous sex during pregnancy. In 1913, Dr. Robert Lacasse called intercourse during pregnancy "a little assassination by two, a tiny infanticide." Fortunately, few hygienists were so stringent or sinister. Like most midwives, most hygienists recognized that it was difficult for women to deny their husbands; a few hygienists acknowledged that it might be hard for women to ignore their own desire. Accordingly, the majority of hygienists only prohibited intercourse for women with histories of miscarriages and otherwise recommended restricting conjugal relations after the middle trimester. A few gave sensible advice to abstain when sex was awkward or painful.[78]

Like general health advice, pregnancy advice began with cleanliness, especially lukewarm tub baths. Hygienists divided by sex over douching: male doctors either ignored or limited douching to treating infections or preparing for labor; most women doctors advised douches throughout pregnancy. Presumably most women continued not to douche. After researchers condemned douching for introducing germs into the very vulnerable birth canal in the 1920s, everyone denounced the practice.[79] This advice must have had an impact on the minority of women who had taken up douching.

Hygienists tried to fight traditional medical and folkloric opinion that a pregnant woman should eat for two. Several hygienists advised continuing regular eating habits; more proposed reducing the consumption of stimulants such as tea, coffee, wine, and spirits. Although Pinard endorsed the advice given by most midwives that a pregnant woman should eat "what pleases her," some hygienists condemned any indulgence of cravings. The midwives and Pinard were undoubtedly more influential. Many hygienists counseled eliminating milk from the pregnant woman's diet because milk hardened fetal bones, making for a difficult delivery.[80] Competing advice may have meant little change in pregnant women's eating habits.

According to hygienists, all women were prone to constipation resulting from a woman's shorter digestive tract or from not having regular bowel movements (because of false modesty). Obstetricians worried that constipation would induce labor. Many dietary rules (such as eating fruits and vegetables) were designed to prevent constipation. The manuals repeated guidelines found in general health guides for women: "educate your intestines" to have a daily bowel movement, exercise, massage, and, if necessary, take laxatives, not harsh purgatives.[81]

Everyone recommended walking and light housework to lift spirits, accelerate blood circulation, and regulate digestive and eliminatory systems. Pregnant women were not to sit or stand too long lest they congest the uterine region. Before the war, hygienists condemned long stretches of pedaling sewing machines, which, they claimed, induced contractions or dislodged the fetus in the womb. Because they believed that all vibration of the lower body was traumatic, many proscribed bicycling and horseback riding, and some forbade train or automobile rides.[82] As debate raged about adult women's participation in sports in the late 1920s and early 1930s, a quiet discussion about pregnant women's exercise occurred. Initially, physical educators claimed that the benefits included less abdominal "deformation," shorter labor, and easier postpartum recovery.[83] By 1934, Profs. Ducuing and Guilhem approved physical training to prevent constipation, fat, ptosis, and varicose veins during pregnancy and to tighten stretched abdominal muscles, restore calcium to bones leached by pregnancy, and lose fat after delivery. Although Ducuing and Guilhem adapted their routines to individual women and the stage of their gestation and postpartum recovery, patients demurred.[84] Obstetricians prohibited exercise routines if the women had respiratory or heart diseases or any chance of miscarriage.[85]

Delivery

In the Third Republic, there was a two-tier system of birthing. Those who could afford to give birth at home had a midwife or a doctor-*accoucheur* in attendance. Even a midwife cost more than many working-class women could afford. Religious charities helped married believers pay for midwives; after state subsidies were available in 1886, secular charities assisted women in childbirth regardless of their marital status. Most poor women went to a general hospital or, in Paris, to the Maternity Hospital or a public-welfare midwife. In 1900, patients spent just over a week in the Maternity Hospital, where there was little prenatal preparation, and they rarely received anesthetic. Recurring epidemics of puerperal fever, a contagious postpartum infection, was a major cause of maternal death in the Maternity Hospital, yet every year it turned away approximately one thousand women seeking admission.

Improvements in medical care and facilities lowered the puerperal fever death rate. In 1882, public assistance created a corps of doctor-*accoucheurs* whose education was conducted along Pasteurian lines. In the same decade, medical schools began offering two-year courses, with units on asepsis, to midwives. As part of the implementation of an 1893 law on free hospitalization for the destitute sick, the government ordered medical schools to offer two-year courses to midwives.[86] New specialized maternity wards and birthing clinics were built. These services segregated women in labor from sick patients and healthy from tubercular women in labor. Asepsis and segregation reduced maternal mortality caused by puerperal fever in hospitals to 1 percent in the 1930s. Generally, maternal mortality halved between 1900 and 1925 and then stabilized between 2 and 3 percent. The overall decline was primarily the result of preventive prenatal care.[87]

Throughout the Republic, the medical consensus was that the pain of contractions was the "mode of expression" of deliveries. Brochures written by Catholic women referred to hours of "very intense suffering" in labor. Catholic midwives felt that too much anesthetic was given during birthing, which was simply a physiological act.[88] Compared with their silence about sexuality, Catholic women were verbose about suffering in labor. Many *accoucheurs* and *accoucheuses* quite reasonably criticized Anglo-Saxon use of general anesthetic but less reasonably refused to intervene with local anesthetic, except in particularly difficult or Cesarean deliveries. By comparison, the French Association of Women Doctors was more receptive to analgesics to relieve pain. Conversely, more French than Anglo-Saxon parturients were allowed to remain in the most comfortable position during most of their eight- to twenty-four-hour labors. Although a few interwar obstetricians denounced the tendency to accept perineal tears as normal, tears remained common. According to one study, 30 to 35 percent of primapares had perineal tears, which were often not sutured properly. No wonder women experienced "this sublime function" as an exhausting, even degrading, trial.[89] No wonder they did not relish having many babies.

Conclusions

Natalists were fighting a losing battle. In the 1930s, despite no fewer than fifty monetary and honorary incentives to have large families, most French people could not afford, or chose not, to have many children. The proportion of families with three or more children dropped from one-third in 1911 to one-quarter in 1936.[90] Attitudes toward large families did not improve. Emilie Carles expressed the feelings of a "modern" countrywoman:

> Before the 1914 war, you could count six or seven youngsters to a family. That was a minimum—many had ten or more. No birth control or anything. Once they were married, women had a baby practically every year. Not far from here, a record was even set, through the feats of a person I'll call "that irresponsible man" rather than name him. He married his first wife when she was eighteen or twenty and kept on getting her pregnant until it killed her. She had thirteen and died in childbirth at the age of thirty-three. Then he took a second wife and had ten more with her. A sum of twenty-three kids! That may be a record but it is also a crime when you think of how they had to live.[91]

Chapter 7

Menopause and Loss

$\mathcal{I}$N FRANCE, as in other pronatalist societies, the confusion among women's sexuality, fertility, and feminine identity meant that menopause was perceived as a loss of sex appeal, purpose, and persona.[1] Women who had accepted the primacy of their sexual attractions and maternal role fought the loss of their *raison d'être*, suggesting that they felt the loss of self as well.

Although classical medical literature contains many passages about the climacteric, or change of life, of women as well as men, it tells us little about the menopause other than remedies for retention of the menses. Because humoral medicine construed menstruation as the elimination of "a plethora of morbid humors," termination of menstruation signified retention of poisons. Descriptions of female "disturbances," primarily hemorrhages, during the change, only appeared in the mid-1700s. However, as Germaine Greer notes in *The Change: Women, Aging, and the Menopause*, Mme. de Sévigné's complaints about "flying" and joint pains [and more frequent and "humiliating" attacks of vapors] in her late forties may refer to hot flashes and osteoporotic pain now linked to menopause.[2] Around 1800, several French publications distinguished a menopausal syndrome with physical and mental symptoms. In 1821, Giraudy coined the term *menopause* to replace the phrase *cessation of menses*.[3] Joel Wilbush attributes the medical identification of a menopausal syndrome to the increased reporting of symptoms ensuing from a new rapport between wealthy female patients and physicians and the willingness of these women to consult doctors for intimate "female" complaints. But his principal explanation is the new social status and stresses of bourgeois and aristocratic women after the French Revolution. The intensified "dependence upon appearance, attractiveness, and sexual capacity" of these women meant that more than ever, menopause implied social decline and neglect.[4]

Cultural expectations that middle-aged women should remain beautiful and desirable crystallized in the next century. In the Belle Epoque, many of the titled women who wrote beauty books targeted married, middle-aged women. After the Baroness d'Orchamps and the Countess de Tramar defined beauty as "health, freshness, velvety smooth, unwrinkled skin" and a slender figure, they reassured readers that a woman of forty could be "an opulent, captivating flower"—if she studied the arts of pleasing men and combating age. The baroness proposed a "career of beauty" requiring constant vigilance but promised that a woman who hid her "defects"—wrinkles, gray hair— would be "the most complete instrument of voluptuousness to a thinking man."[5] The divorce law of 1884 put a premium on remaining desirable to keep a husband. Several of the beauty countesses explained that women who lost their looks lost their husbands. Viscountess Nacla (pseudonym for Mme. T. Alcan, wife of the publisher Alcan) argued that wives must remain seductive to stop their husbands from straying.[6] Mme. Lucas, proprietor of the first beauty institute in Paris (opened in 1895), claimed that "a woman can and should be loved until she is seventy-five. . . . To love and be loved, you must be a flower. I am the horticulturalist of women."[7] Untangling cause and effect in prescriptive literature and advertising is notoriously difficult. These books and businesses certainly exploited new sources of disposable income and more time for personal care. They reflected new notions about marriages based upon love and dread of abandonment after the reinstitution of divorce. Whatever the knot of cause and effect, the youthful ideal must have encouraged bourgeois women to mitigate the effects of menopause. Their demand gave an impetus to medical research on menopause.

By exalting maternity, pronatalists and maternalists degraded further the popular image of menopause. Few pronatalists or maternalists acknowledged a postmaternal phase of life other than grandmothering; one, Dr. H. Thulié, considered and rejected another role. Having opposed women in politics because they were "unstable" during menstruation, pregnancy, and childrearing, Thulié also objected to women entering politics during menopause, which brought "intellectual and nervous alterations."[8] Only Beauvoir argued that, by physically freeing women from their fertility and by intellectually liberating them from their link to the family/species, menopause implied that menopausal and postmenopausal women were individuals.

Biomedical Menopause

Moreau de la Sarthe's *Natural History of Woman* (1803) illustrates the historical fusion of biological and esthetic reasoning and the centrality of comeliness, as well as fecundity, in the definition of femininity and the denigration of menopause. Like the Comte de Buffon, Moreau de la Sarthe considered prepubescent girls "equivocal," not fully female beings. The idea that sexual identity was acquired in puberty persisted throughout the nineteenth century. Puberty brought the "menstrual revolution, which is nothing other than an exaltation of sensibility, a lively irritation, a sort of sickness of the uterus." In short, femininity implied uterine domination through the nervous system. The critical age (not yet assigned an average age of onset) involved another internal revolution in which the uterus returned to "its local and limited life," and the woman's constitution "approaches that of the man, as the rigidity of her organs proves." Like other biologists before permanent boundaries were drawn between the sexes,[9] Moreau de la Sarthe was comfortable with the idea of masculinization. Nevertheless, he used the terminology of binary sexuality: the transition was from soft to hard organs. Along with internal atrophy came external decay. "The skin loses its polish and softness . . . wrinkles multiply." The neck thinned, breasts sagged, etc.[10] Like many biomedical men, Moreau de la Sarthe promoted marital intercourse by warning that "the unhappy victim of virginity" had a hard menopause because excess uterine energy upset the entire organism. Such warnings would recur in the medical literature into the twentieth century. Fortunately and typically, Moreau de la Sarthe's hygienic advice was less bleak. He contended that the change was a natural process that could be trouble free if women adopted a retiring lifestyle.[11] His advice sounded what was to become a familiar note about restricted options.

Between the 1800s and 1870s, French researchers grafted studies of menopause onto studies of puberty.[12] The pattern of ancillary research reflected the results of statistical studies showing that women had higher mortality in their thirties than in their forties (then considered the menopausal decade) and had lower morbidity than their male cohort in the fourth, menopausal decade of life. By 1868, Adam Raciborski had studied two hundred cases and could cite several clinical and statistical studies. Aware of the effect of removing ovaries (ovariotomies), Raciborski concentrated on ovarian "metamorphoses" ending ovulation and menstrual discharge. Yet he clung to the idea of a plethora of blood, which he blamed for headaches, palpitations, and other vascular symptoms of menopause. Treatments included bleeding and long walks to eliminate by perspiration poisons no longer expelled vaginally.[13] Like his clinical studies of puberty, his clinical studies of menopause—without his etiology or therapies—were cited into the 1930s.

By the 1880s, researchers recognized that the hospital was not the best place to study menopause because women rarely came there "for the thousand accidents" of menopause. On the basis of a study of atrophied uteruses and ovaries removed from menopausal women, one hospital-based researcher, Ernest Barié, hypothesized that these organs were "not tied to the very existence of women, their functions are essentially limited and temporary."[14] This hypothesis made little impression on the medical community because the leading authority, the first chair of gynecology at the Paris Medical Faculty, Samuel Pozzi, contended that the sexual apparatus was not "an accessory cog in the female mechanism"—unlike, it went without saying, in the standard (male) mechanism.[15] Several clinicians studied women who continued to menstruate after ovariotomies; they only belatedly recognized that menstruation continued after removal of only one ovary or part of the ovary.[16] Like biomedical writers who reported every instance of premenarchal pregnancies, these clinicians were uncomfortable with the new ovarian etiology.

Other researchers studied patients who experienced heart palpitations and breathlessness when they were physically active or who were diagnosed as "mad" during menopause. The conclusions of these researchers resembled those of contemporaries who were studying puberty: the body of a menopausal woman "was a terrain admirably prepared for circulatory and nervous diseases."[17]

In the early twentieth century, endocrinology fused together notions of fecundity and femininity and redefined menopause as an ovarian deficiency entailing a loss of function and identity. As this occurred, specialists in menopause provided more detailed and less appealing descriptions of the change. In addition to menstrual disorders, cancers, tumors, and vascular ailments, physical symptoms now included chronic bronchial, pulmonary, and nasal problems, digestive disorders, constipation, and incontinence. Psychological manifestations were also multiplying and were classified under nymphomania, morbid jealousy, religious delirium, and depression.[18] In the 1880s, hygienists interested in aging had assumed that there were analogies between the critical ages of men and women. Dr. Louis de Seré compared the end of the menstrual flow with a reduction in the quantity and quality of the "seminal liquid."[19] As endocrinologists accepted earlier evidence about continued sperm production and potency into old age, most medical researchers rejected the idea of a "masculine menopause."[20]

By the 1920s, students of midlife emphasized women's earlier deterioration, manifested in loss of beauty and femininity, even though mature women were healthier than men their age. Dr. Arthur Leclercq claimed that the difference between young and old (meaning fifty-year-old) women was greater than the difference between their male counterparts. According to Leclercq, one reason was the "general rule that dominates the organic state, which is that the hormonal glands supplement one another." Ovarian atrophy meant excessive adrenaline, hypo- or hyperthyroidism, and associated problems such as obesity. Nevertheless, feminine character, specifically women's modest appetite and "sober nature," ensured that they experienced less gout, angina, arteriosclerosis, and myocardial, renal, and syphilitic complications than men did.[21] In other words, the prescribed feminine role—with its self-discipline—preserved women's health.

At the turn of the century, endocrinological etiology displaced uterine and nervous etiologies. As late as 1895, two experts on menopause attributed heavy and erratic flow and cardiovascular problems to uterine decay and psychological aberrations to "nervous plethora."[22] Within a decade, Félix Jayle's redefinition of menopause as an "ovarian deficiency" and his associated ovarian extract therapy (described in Chap. 2) were disseminated to practitioners.[23] By 1908, Dr. Charles Vinay argued that ovarian secretions neutralized vascular toxins and regulated blood pressure, metabolism, and the nervous and eliminatory systems. Therefore, ovarian deficiency meant unchecked vascular toxins, higher blood pressure, a lower metabolic rate, and organic disturbances. Hormonally induced "self-intoxication" caused irritability, cognitive loss, erotic fantasies, and hysteria. Vinay linked puberty and menopause as "preferred" ages for hysteria. Pregnancy, labor, lactation, and menopause—times when hormonal production was erratic—made women irascible and delirious.[24] Psychological studies traced neuroses associated with menopause to insufficient ovarian secretion and its contingent physiological manifestations. One psychiatrist, Dr. Gerdussus, attributed irritability, mysticism, insomnia, and moodiness to congestive and goiter problems caused by inadequate ovarian output. Gerdussus prescribed opotherapy, symptomatic treatments, a healthy diet, and reduced sexual relations.[25]

In France, there was a major debate over the medical utility and morality of ovariotomies and hysterectomies. Before 1880, French specialists in "women's diseases" rarely practiced surgery. They took pride in their invention of the speculum and their use of manual examinations. In the 1880s, Pasteur's germ theory suggested external causes of genital complications. Familiar with the idea of miasmatic or airborne poisoning, surgeons accepted disinfection procedures. Because asepsis improved the safety of operations and required costly installations, the number of operations increased.[26] In the United States and Germany, many surgeons performed hysterectomies and bilateral ovariotomies on women in their late twenties and early thirties for a variety of sometimes quite minor menstrual, pelvic, and nervous disorders.[27] Thanks to the French medical tradition of gynecological examination and especially to the opposition by Catholic gynecologists to hysterectomies and ovariotomies (which rendered women infertile), Frenchwomen were spared this operative excess.[28]

Catholic gynecologists who were virulently opposed to "the intrusion of surgical Americanism" shaped public opinion through free brochures, cheap tracts, and an inexpensive journal. Dr. Goupil, who had a talent for invective, waged a propaganda war on this "operative debauchery" (although he accepted hysterectomies and ovariotomies to treat cancer). Public figures such as Victor Hugo and Emile Zola supported Goupil's charity "to protect women against surgical abuse."[29] Other Catholic opponents combined offensives against ovarian "castration" with attacks on abortion.[30] Even the Protestant surgeon Pozzi had reservations about removing ovaries, querying "a mutilation of the patient that is more serious, from a social point of view, than the amputation of a limb." As he put it, "the female organism between puberty and menopause may be said to simultaneously live two lives—that of the individual, and that of the species: or that of the organs in general, and that of the generative apparatus in particular."[31] The first Frenchwoman licensed as both a physician and a pharmacist, Hélina Gaboriau, also campaigned against surgical solutions to women's diseases in *Normal Feminine Medicine,* published in 1904 and 1905. Like many physicians editing health magazines, she advised and advertised alternatives in which she had a financial interest. In her case, she promoted a tonic and unguent manufactured by her husband, who was also a physician and pharmacist.[32]

After the war, researchers tried to distinguish between menopausal symptoms and disorders coterminous with, or exacerbated by, menopause. In 1919, Isabelle Gaboriau, daughter of Hélina, reviewed studies of uterine infections and hemorrhages and determined that many were caused by previous conditions or by the general state of health.[33] But even as this was published, the endocrinological gaze shifted from the gonads to all glands. The emerging consensus on a synergy among all glandular secretions introduced notions of general glandular disequilibrium in mature women resulting from the suppression of ovarian function.[34] Antagonistic or moderating glands had to compensate for the loss of ovarian hormones; glands stimulated by deficient hormones necessarily slowed down. Most research focused on hypothyroidism, or slow metabolism, which often occurred around the same time as menopause. This concentration dovetailed with intensified interest in obesity and weight gain.[35]

By the 1930s, specialists were uncomfortable with the notion of masculinization and more generally, with the notion of an unstable sexual identity. Despite positing that sex differences were most pronounced when the "maternal organs" were active, biologist René Biot reported that experiments with ovariotomies did not confirm widespread assumptions about masculinization. Referring to recent research on sex determination (described in Chap. 2), he insisted that girls were feminine from the time they were conceived.[36] The notion of impermanent sexual identity, a logical corollary of the notion of femininity as fertility, challenged the new canon about permanent sexual identity. In 1929, Dr. Vignes cited research indicating that sex hormones merely activated inherent, likely genetic sexual traits at an appropriate stage in the growth process. Two years later, Dr. Watrin appended data about the prepubescent acquisition of sexual characteristics. Both of these experts denied earlier theories about menopausal virilization, with Vignes positing regression to a prepubescent or "undifferentiated sexual type" and Watrin declaring secondary sexual characteristics irreversible. Like Moreau de la Sarthe and many other biomedical men, however, they spoke of a loss of sexual value and sex appeal.[37]

In *The Second Sex,* Simone de Beauvoir reflects this state of research, albeit with her hallmark existentialist spin. She refers to menopause as "another serious crisis" and to diminished ovarian activity resulting in reduction of "the individual's vital forces" as well as the appearance of fatty deposits and, in some cases, masculinization. However, she credits the metabolic (thyroid and pituitary) glands for compensating for the ovarian deficiency, causing signs of excitation, including increased sexuality. She concludes that "Woman is now delivered from the servitude imposed by her female nature, but she is not to be likened to a eunuch, for her vitality is unimpaired. And what is more, she is no longer the prey of overwhelming forces; she is herself, she and her body are one." She becomes an individual.[38] Other Frenchwomen felt the same way, although they did not express their feelings in existentialist language.

During the interwar, treatments for menopause proliferated and became more intricate. Certain spas continued to specialize in women's, mainly menopausal, problems. Older therapies such as tepid baths, fresh-air cures, bland diets, massage, laxatives, and even bleeding persisted into the 1930s. Increasingly, however, months of mixed ovarian and thyroid extract medication, along with the administration of antispasmodic drugs and radiography, supplanted or supplemented the customary treatments. In 1935, a spa doctor prescribed up to nine and a half grams of ovarian extract or a mixture of ovarian and thyroid extract a day, for twenty days a month, either orally or subcutaneously.[39]

Ovarian hormone replacement therapies became more complex. A twenty-year debate about the anatomical source of the ovarian hormone was re-oriented after the discovery that there were two ovarian hormones. Dutch researchers Zondek and Ascheim found a source of estrogen in the urine of pregnant women, which led to research on other organic sources of estrogen. In the early 1930s, placental extracts were promoted. After tests on animals and international conventions to standardize doses, tests were conducted on seventy women. Initially, the dose was 25 to 150 grams of "fresh organ" a day; later the dose was lowered. The scientists reported favorable results in the form of fewer hot flashes, less perspiration, and less vertigo.[40] By 1939, gynecologists prescribed estrogen for vascular and "nervous" conditions and for vaginal atrophy and dryness in menopause; they also reported that it "refreshed" the skin and firmed the breasts. Although less inclined to prescribe progesterone, gynecologists considered testosterone useful to treat the "subjective symptoms" of menopause.[41]

Researchers moved toward greater specificity about the average age of menopause—forty-eight for European and North American women—but also to a longer "normal" range of between forty-two and fifty-five years of age.[42] Specialists began including some environmental qualification of simple biological reductionism. Throughout, they made the familiar distinctions by climate, race, class, and residence (urban versus rural dwellers). By the 1930s, they also distinguished between extrinsic influences, such as climate, and intrinsic influences, such as heredity. Throughout the interwar, specialists insisted on the impact of reproductive behavior on the onset of menopause, claiming that sterile women entered menopause earlier than mothers of many children, and single women entered menopause earlier than married women. As evidence about the effect of reproductive behaviors, the specialists mentioned personal observations of patients in their own practices.[43] This kind of remark contrasts to the reticence about patient confidences in marital advice literature.

Researchers also refined the stages of menopause. Even before the war, Prof. Siredey distinguished a premenopausal phase beginning as early as thirty to thirty-five years of age. In this phase, lasting up to ten years, women might suffer circulatory disorders in the form of varicose veins or ulcers as well as premenstrual tenderness and "heaviness" in the abdomen and lumbar back. Siredey interpreted these symptoms as evidence that menopause was not solely the cessation of menstruation. Generally, he thought that too many organic disorders were attributed to modifications in the utero-ovarian system and not enough to pre-existing conditions that were merely activated or accentuated by menopause.[44] Here he took a stance similar to that being developed by contemporary researchers of puberty.

Menopausal Hygiene

In the 1880s, medical students learned little about menopause. After several lectures on menstruation and on maternity, Prof. Bernutz of the Paris Faculty devoted one lesson to menopause. He taught that individual conditions such as celibacy, genital infections, and living conditions had a greater effect on menopause than on puberty. In addition to physical symptoms such as irregular periods, anemia, hot flashes, heavy perspiration, and weight gain, Bernutz identified psychological symptoms such as hysteria, "nervous states," and hypochondria and changes in sexual desire, including first a diminishing then a revival of desire. After menopause, he contended, a new life commenced for women, just as it did for men.[45] In the following decades, most experts advised menopausal women to stop sexual relations, although a tiny minority believed in continued desire, based on new theories of a separation of the sexual instinct from the reproductive instinct.[46] Clearly menopausal women with symptoms requiring medical intervention informed the descriptions of menopausal syndromes by medical instructors, but the instructors' conceptions of femininity informed their prescriptions. Both descriptions and prescriptions influenced their students' practice and, in turn, their patients' understanding of the condition.

Feminine hygiene texts addressed to physicians updated practitioners' and accordingly patients' knowledge of menopause. Happily, early texts asserted that menopause was not catastrophic if women followed some simple precepts. In 1894, Dr. Caubet advised a bland diet and a placid life. Aside from avoiding late nights and vigorous exercise, he suggested that menopausal women cease or minimize sexual relations, which he believed excited the nerves. Mild purgatives were useful for infections of the internal sex organs; herbal baths would treat external infections and relieve nervous problems.[47] Like several of his successors, including women doctors, he suggested "suppressing strong feelings," which supposedly exacerbated nosebleeds and other types of displaced menstrual flow.[48] In the next two decades, similar texts identified the age of onset as between forty-five and fifty. These texts listed more physiological and psychological symptoms, including hot flashes, vertigo, neuralgia, and feelings of lassitude. Among the external signs of decay, they listed acne, eczema, and obesity.[49] Only one general study referred to the phenomenon of renewed vigor, or what Margaret Mead later called "menopausal zest," which many contemporary North American doctors discussed. Predictably, Dr. Caufeynon focused on a return to "rosy complexions and youthful freshness." Equally predictably, in order to plug over-the-counter cosmetic drugs he managed to exploit fears that menopause was "the supreme disaster for femininity."[50]

Books on feminine hygiene written for general practitioners continued to differ in their representations of menopause. In the 1920s, there were some optimistic representations. Dr. Eddé underscored that menopause had a positive effect on fibroid tumors. Accepting that menopause could increase "sexual appetite," he counseled continued relations because "forced continence" induced pelvic congestion. However, there were disturbing notes. Eddé prescribed opotherapy preventively, "to give the organism time to get accustomed to the deprivation of the ovarian secretion."[51] French gynecologists did not discourage recourse to the new high-dosage hormone pills for early menopausal symptoms such as hot flashes and migraines until after the Second World War. Then Dr. Hélène Wolfromm rejected any parallel between the onset or degree of hormonal deficiency and the inception or intensity of psychological instability. Instead, she linked psychological instability to fear of aging. For depression about aging (and what she considered irrational acts such as leaving husbands without having "another attachment"), she prescribed isolation and rest cures.[52]

Writing in the 1930s, Dr. Pauchet considered menopause "a veritable physiological crisis" for a woman which "alters her physiognomy, external appearance, voice, and even character." He based his argument on twenty years of glandular research showing that hormones vitalize the system. Without ovarian hormones, he argued, women gained weight, their waists thickened, and their faces bloated. Unlike many physicians in that decade, Pauchet employed the notion of masculinization. As "feminine" features retreated, masculine features advanced: "Sometimes these virile cells take on such importance that the face acquires a masculine aspect: the nose lengthens, the hair of the cheeks, upper lip, and chin become a beard."[53]

This depiction of aging androgynous women reads like depictions of the hag, crone, or witch, with all of their negative connotations. Androgyny was less attractive as one aged. Pauchet and other physicians also made undocumented remarks about the "cantankerous character" of mothers-in-law. This taken-for-granted representation of mothers-in-law assumed general agreement with these physicians' derogatory attitude toward mothers-in-law and mature women.

An early nonmedical popularizer of feminine hygiene, Mlle. Thilo, recommended a diet and lifestyle approach similar to today's "natural menopause" approach. In 1891, Thilo considered the "best preservative a calm and regular life." She rejected drugs for constipation in favor of eating fresh fruits, taking a daily dose of bran, and doing exercise such as gardening.[54] Vegetarians such as Dr. Narodetzki also advised a "regular life," doing fresh-air exercise and avoiding emotions, alcohol, and meat. However, they promoted a variety of products: salts for calming baths, tonics to decongest the veins, elixirs to combat constipation, and sedatives to aid sleep.[55]

No physician wrote hygiene guides specifically addressed to menopausal women. Instead they (and laywomen) taught bourgeois women about menopause in health and beauty manuals that were officially addressed to all women but were, in effect, intended for maturing women. The authors of these manuals found that promising health and beauty "sold" both the books and the services, as well as the products they promoted, better than promising health alone. Accordingly, organotherapy quickly made inroads. Brown-Séquard's dubious findings about male gonadal extracts rejuvenating older men soon appeared in health and beauty manuals—and in pharmacists' advertisements—directed toward middle-aged women.[56] Other endocrinologists devised and marketed diets and exercise programs to combat menopausal obesity. Until the 1930s, specialists did not admit that menopause rarely induced obesity (as opposed to weight gain) and that ovarian hormones did not reduce fat.[57]

Often, medical messages about menopause and how to cope with it reached bourgeois women by way of magazines. By the early twentieth century, practitioners wrote health columns in magazines such as *Figaro Fashion* and *Illustrated Fashion,* where they took a relatively sanguine approach. Dr. Choffé underlined that women had half the mortality rate of men during the critical mid-forties to mid-fifties decade of their lives. Although their mortality rate rose more than that of men in the mid-fifties to mid-sixties decade, it remained lower than the rate of their male cohort. Anachronistically, Choffé attributed menopausal and postmenopausal women's resistance to disease to their highly developed nervous system. Consequently, menopausal women had little need of special hygiene other than tepid baths before going to bed to prevent night sweats and staying active to avoid muscular atrophy (because their muscular system was deficient compared with men's paradigmatic system). Unlike most hygienists writing about menopause, he recommended gymnastics, fencing, biking, and aerobic sports in moderation for menopausal women. Choffé's position on changes in physical appearance was less reassuring. Women had transparent skin and lacked facial hair, or beards, to cover wrinkles. As "precautions," Choffé advised women to use astringent lotions religiously, massage their faces in an upward direction, and smile less. He offered many other commercial and noncommercial suggestions about how to "conserve" beauty.[58]

Feminine hygiene texts written by women doctors represented menopause more optimistically than their male peers did. Most women hygienists asserted that menopause was a normal if sometimes troubled physiological state. Although Marthe Francillon's doctoral thesis compiled the most complete list to date (1905) of sex differences that appeared or accentuated at puberty, her popular hygiene text (1909) offset the usual inventory of symptoms associated with ovarian deficiency with assurances that physical modifications were "barely noticed by healthy women."[59]

But even women who rejected medical definitions of menopause did not question the ill consequences of virginity or infertility for menopausal women. The 1908 translation of an American manual by Dr. Emma Drake criticized medical literature for labeling menopause a crisis and for generalizing from sick women. Drake preferred the metaphor of "a major cleaning to prepare the house for winter." As a maternalist, she warned that women who had danced or exercised too much during their periods, who had used alcohol, drugs, or contraceptives, or who had had abortions could expect a "stormy menopause."[60] Prewar Frenchwomen took the more positive approach of stressing that mothers suffered less during menopause, in only one case adding "as if nature wanted to punish the others."[61] Interwar texts took a less judgmental stance. Dr. Houdré-Boursin reported that healthy women experienced little pain during menopause. Like contemporary colleagues, she advocated walking, moderate gymnastics, and aerobic sports such as golf to keep a youthful appearance.[62]

Experience

Inadequate knowledge of their organic processes and the very adverse image of menopause projected by medical and psychological studies encouraged silence about menopause. In twelve Frenchwomen's journals and memoirs covering the normal age of menopause, there were few reminiscences about menopause. The exceptions involved catty remarks about other women being menopausal and, indirectly, more references to migraines than in the entries for earlier years.[63] However, the silence of these women may have another meaning. Certainly reports that many practitioners never treated anything identified as menopausal problems dovetail with recent surveys showing that most women do not report enough suffering to disrupt their lives or to consult physicians.[64]

For some insight into women's experience of menopause, we must turn to the few medical writers who discuss social factors and to literature. In 1895, Drs. Barbaud and Rouillard, respectively a spa doctor and a clinician, claimed on the basis of clinical observations that "women of the people" welcomed menopause as a deliverance from childbearing and some respite from their husbands' sexual demands. They rather naively believed that "sexual activity is extinguished" in menopausal women, and this deterred husbands from demanding their conjugal rights. Interwar hygienists repeated the description of the reception of menopause by working-class women, without the assumptions of earlier doctors about an end to sexual desire or to spousal demand for sex. Conversely, Barbaud and Rouillard argued that "worldly women" were apprehensive about losing their sex appeal. As the two doctors ominously observed, "Too often, alas, it is the husband who first notices the loss of feminine charm" and "visits the neighbor's bed." Over the next twenty-five years, other doctors agreed that depression was more common in "higher social milieus."[65] Not surprisingly, society ladies denied their condition and concealed their battle against aging (hence the popularity of very expensive books of beauty secrets). Dr. Francillon-Lobre believed that women who feared and fought aging were prone to "deceptive flattery and disappointment," whereas women who resigned themselves gained serenity. She did not advise menopausal women to give up their sex life, just to moderate it.[66] By the 1930s, some specialists accepted new theories about a sexual instinct after menopause and urged gynecologists to convince "worldly women, too attached to their physical charms, that menopause does not deprive them of admiring relationships and voluptuous pleasures."[67]

Literary sources confirm that circumstances and expectations influenced women's experience of menopause and aging. In the early stages of menopause, women of the world were supposed to camouflage the signs and deny the realities of aging. As Colette put it, older women should not break "the contract they signed with beauty." In one of her trademark vignettes about intimate aspects of feminine experience, the first-person narrator finds her friend Alix without her cosmetics and rejects her friend's protest that this is her real face: "No. Your real face is in the drawer of your dressing table, and sadly enough, you have left your good spirits in with it. Your real face is a warm, matte pink tending toward fawn, set off high on the cheeks by a glimmer of deep carmine, well blended and nearly translucent." The narrator expands the argument: "The true Alix is the one who always had a taste for adorning herself, defending herself, and pleasing others, for savoring the bitterness, the risk and the sweetness of living—the true Alix, you see, is the young one."[68]

If this passage seems to take a very superficial view of women of the world, consider the consensus that these women existed to please with their appearance and that most definitions of beauty were very imprecise, except about freshness/youthfulness.[69] Colette herself was knowledgeable about beauty and aging. In the 1930s, she founded a beauty institute, where she spent four hours a day, five days a week.[70] She had decided opinions about the value of cosmetics for menopausal and postmenopausal women: "Since I have cared for and made up my contemporaries, I have not yet met a fifty-year-old woman who was discouraged, nor a neurasthenic sexagenarian. . . . The harder the times for women, the more the woman, proudly, insists on hiding that she suffers."[71]

Moreover, Colette recognized that the struggle to seem young would falter. In two semiautobiographical novels, *Cheri* and *The Last of Cheri*,[72] the older courtesan Léa gives up the struggle to look younger and enjoys the freedom from constant attention to her body. There are consequences. The young lover Cheri notices "two folds of slightly yellow skin" under Léa's chin and decides to return to his young wife, with her "silky young neck."[73] But the consequences are not necessarily sad. In her autobiographical novel, *Break of Day*, the character Colette introduces herself as "no longer forty," an age "when the only thing that is left for her is to enrich her own self." The character Colette has become more masculine, with "a thick neck, bodily strength that becomes less graceful as it weakens." The character and the author understand menopause to mean a loss of "allure" and an escape "from the age when she is a woman." The character (not the author) renounces sexual relationships without regrets. Of course, the character, like the author, had a mother who modeled a self-sufficient maturity full of curiosity about and pleasure in the natural world.[74]

In *The Second Sex,* Beauvoir agreed that what lends importance to the disturbances of "the dangerous age" is "their symbolic significance. The crisis of the 'change of life' is felt much less keenly by women who have not staked everything on their femininity; those who engage in heavy work—in the household or outside—greet the disappearance of the monthly burden with relief; the peasant woman, the workman's wife, constantly under the threat of new pregnancies, are happy when, at long last, they no longer run this risk."[75]

The suggestions that working women were not debilitated by menopause conform to reports of few menopausal "perturbations" in early twentieth-century health manuals for teachers.[76] Like teachers, most working women were physically active, and recent research shows that physically active women suffer less osteoporotic pain. Barbaud and Rouillard's ideas that working women felt less sexual desire may also have some merit. Recent surveys have found that one quarter of all menopausal women surveyed (not just working-class women) temporarily experience discomfort during (heterosexual) intercourse and, if their partners were not considerate, avoided conjugal relations.[77]

Feminist scholars have begun to investigate psychosocial and cultural factors in menopause. Their evidence corroborates the insights of Barbaud and Rouillard that women who do not want more children welcome menopause, whereas women who are not ready to give up their reproductive role are more distressed. Given the overwhelming evidence that Frenchwomen in the Third Republic wanted to limit their families, this suggests that many women did not despair about menopause. Studies today indicate that working-class women have more negative feelings about menopause than middle-class women do.[78] Barbaud and Rouillard's class prejudices may not account fully for the apparent reversal because new career opportunities for middle-class women may have offered these women options that were more attractive than remaining seductive and reproductive.

Conclusions

In the late nineteenth and early twentieth centuries, changing expectations of middle-aged Frenchwomen colluded with political and scientific agendas. Propaganda about depopulation represented women's bodies as exclusively or primarily reproductive. The advertising image was youthful, seductive. Along with this, scientific researchers adopted endocrinological definitions of menopause as a deficiency disease with rapid deterioration of the whole organism. Middle-aged Frenchwomen faced aging and the loss of their reproductive role just as they felt new pressures to prevent wrinkles, trim their bodies, and remain desirable. Paradoxically if predictably, the negative biomedical model of menopause ensured that women did not challenge that degrading image of it.

PART 3

Physical Performance

—◦❯ • ❮◦—

GIRLS AND WOMEN acquire bodily awareness through their physical activities, which act directly upon and through the body. In the Third Republic, most French schoolgirls took physical education classes with a more overt curriculum about bodily discipline and sex differences than Anglo-American girls encountered in their physical education.[1] A small but increasing number of Frenchwomen played sports; more women read the extensive debates over what forms of physical activity girls and women could or should do. Because female bodies had been defined as weak and because physical training had been coded masculine, these debates continued to the end of the Third Republic and beyond.

In Chapter 8 I explore the wholesale criticism of the idleness of bourgeois girls by hygienists and physical educators. Experts favored aerobic exercise because walking, dancing, and rhythmic gymnastics were good for the allegedly sluggish metabolism of girls and improved their coordination; parents liked dance and rhythmic gymnastics because they developed physical traits such as flexibility and grace and were useful social skills for young women to have. Because of the early military history of gymnastics, the public confused it with muscle building and military discipline. To persuade schools to introduce physical education, proponents of gymnastics for girls devised less acrobatic and aggressive programs, with girls being excused from the "difficult" routines in the standard (i.e., boys) program. Meanwhile, purveyors of feminine fitness programs developed a following by promising to sculpt figures like those of classical statues. The boundaries of feminine physical activity expanded only along the familiar biosocial or gender lines.

Women's sports were so subject to controversy that women's sports federations disagreed about whether sports undermined women's femininity and
fertility. Opponents held that competitive and contact sports were masculine
in essence and masculinizing in effect. Instead of scientific research, these critics deployed gender stereotypes, depopulation fears, and dismay at the public
display of female bodies in arenas or stadiums. Even female physicians who
encouraged women to play sports distinguished between feminine sports such
as tennis and masculine sports such as boxing. Athletic women who challenged clichés about feminine weakness overcompensated by stressing their
femininity.

Perhaps the most egregious irony of the discourse on women's bodies was
its neglect of the bodies of working women in a country with a high proportion of women in the labor force. In 1881, more than five million women or
nearly 29 percent of the female population were gainfully employed; in 1936,
more than seven million or 34 percent of all women were employed. According to census data, the proportion of women in the labor force peaked at more
than four tenths in 1921, but estimates for the final years of the First World
War—when nearly four fifths of Frenchmen were mobilized—are far higher.
The participation of British women in the labor force was consistently lower.
Much of the difference can be attributed to the proportions of married women
employed: around four tenths of all married women in France versus one
tenth in Britain.[2]

Nevertheless, occupational and industrial hygiene focused on masculine
workplaces, which reinforced popular opinion that hard labor was intrinsi-
cally masculine. When occupational hygienists noticed women's work, they
fixated on reproduction, which bolstered conventional wisdom that childbearing was the vital feminine function and that paid work endangered that function. Occupational hygienists concentrated on toxic materials, hazardous
technologies, and unsafe plants, or on the contorted postures, gross movements, and physical exertion of heavy labor, done mainly by men. These hygienists criticized the moral failings of working men but emphasized corporeal limitations only when examining women's work. They envisioned female
bodies as weak and vulnerable because of their reproductive role. Accordingly, in Chapter 9 I use other sources to document Frenchwomen's extraor-
dinary work performance and then explore the gender bias running through
the new discipline of occupational and industrial hygiene.

A glaring omission must be mentioned here. Typically, hygienists displayed less concern about peasant girls and women and declared that their la-

bor was healthy because it involved physical exertion in fresh air and sunlight. They did not consider that most rural girls and women did household chores in tiny, ill-ventilated cottages and that some of their outdoor chores were insalubrious. Agricultural laborers walked long distances in their biannual migrations and stooped over for hours hoeing, spreading manure, and stoking grain in the fields.[3] Occupational and industrial hygiene ignored the largest group of women workers because of the variety of tasks performed by peasant women and because no enlightened employer, union, or political interest group sponsored studies of the work of peasant women. Another explanation of the oversight is that the labor of peasant women made a mockery of bourgeois ideas about weak womanhood. As James Lehning suggested, rural women made crucial and recognized contributions to farm productivity.[4] A fourth factor may be that the sturdiness of peasant women's bodies contradicted the ideal feminine body type. In *The Morphological Anatomy of Woman* (mentioned in Chap. 1), Félix Jayle labeled his stocky bio-type a rural woman's body.[5]

Chapter 8

Gymnastics, Sports, and Gender

*I*N THE 1880s and 1890s, French hygienists condemned what they perceived as the indolence of bourgeois girls.[1] Although etiquette books confirm that urban girls stayed indoors, were discouraged from boisterous play, and were allowed only supervised walks in nearby parks, women's memoirs and autobiographical novels depict prepubescent girls running and playing games inside—and whenever possible outside—enclosed gardens in villages and suburbs. As girls entered puberty, many of these liberties were withdrawn, although some adolescent girls swam, skated, and tobogganed[2] (see Fig. 6). In addition, many bourgeois girls danced, and some did a limited kind of gymnastics. Beyond these activities, parents and educators debated what girls could do because girls' bodies had been defined as weak, and physical training had been coded as masculine. To enlarge the range of physical activities for girls required adjustments to popular understanding of girls' bodies as well as to the gender connotations of physical education.

While Baron Pierre de Coubertin (1863–1937) was reviving the Olympic Games in the 1880s and 1890s, he publicized the Arnold of Rugby thesis that athletic games built team spirit and moral fiber in boys.[3] In the late 1880s, sports clubs formed in elite schools for boys, and, after 1900, the clubs took on nationalist and partisan overtones, as sports promoters prodded them to emulate English models, and Catholics and the secular Education League established federations to sponsor athletic meets. By the 1920s, these meets replaced gymnastic *fêtes* as patriotic spectacles.[4] In this context, Frenchwomen took up organized sports decades later than Englishwomen did.[5] Although some "feminine" federations (as they were called) had nationalist goals and Catholic or republican affiliations, supporters of women's sports disavowed

6. Photograph entitled "Quatre jeunes femmes baignant," 1900s.
Bibliothèque Nationale de France

the competitiveness "in vogue among a neighboring people."[6] Instead, feminine federations waged an ideological battle about whether sports undermined women's femininity and fertility.

Dance and Gymnastics

In the 1860s, hygienists preferred maternal supervision of daily walks, skipping, ball games, and simple exercises without equipment to develop agility and poise. Private schools offered deportment classes that inculcated a rigidly straight posture and a graceful (smooth) way of walking. At these schools, exercise meant household chores, nature walks, and games. When the Republic mandated physical education in 1882, many normal schools had no gymnasium, several public schools for girls refused free equipment, and Catholic girls schools stuck with nature walks.[7] Pessimistic about the progress of physical education in the school system, experts urged mothers to arrange for their daughters a quarter or half hour of domestic exercise daily.[8] The reiteration of this advice and autobiographical silence about "domestic exercise" suggest that private exercise remained a pious hope.

For most of the nineteenth century, the only other organized physical activities for girls were private dance classes and orthopedic gymnastics, which hygienists approved because they improved coordination or corrected physical deformities.⁹ Parents sent frail or awkward daughters to dance classes to strengthen them and give them "grace." Some girls loved the opportunity to move in normally forbidden ways. When the Paris Opera ballet school accepted Blanche Kerval and a friend, young Blanche was jubilant: "We jumped for joy and improvised fantastic leaps." Some girls had the right blend of stamina, skill, and talent to perform children's roles at eight or nine years of age and travesty—young men's—roles at eleven or twelve.¹⁰ Until the arrival of the Ballet Russe in 1909, ballet was a ballerina's art form. With refinement of toe work, the ballerina had come to represent the artistry of ballet. As Lynn Garafola remarks, femininity "became the ideology of ballet, indeed, the very definition of the art."¹¹

Ballerinas were hardly ethereal. Professional ballerinas practiced hard to perfect their art and had a bad reputation. Visualize Degas's paintings of ballerinas, with the dancers, like working women, posed as if engaged in strenuous activities. Traits that he added to the wax statuette of the Little Dancer of Fourteen Years (1880–81) were traits that criminologists attributed to the sexual criminal type. Critics suggested that the statuette be displayed at the Museum of Pathological Anatomy.¹² Dance classes could be both physically demanding and sexually exploitative. To be admitted to opera classes, applicants had to pass a medical examination, which more failed than passed. Six days a week, students attended classes composed of stretches at the barre, holding leg and arm positions while arching their backs and maintaining their balance, and practicing classic (not very dynamic) movements. Attentive mothers shielded daughters from the pedophilic men who watched dance classes and from sexual harassment by instructors, but maternal supervision could not shield girls from the immoral reputation of dancers. With regulation in the early twentieth century, ballet school conditions improved, but girls still had little privacy or protection from men who hung around backstage.¹³ Few bourgeois parents encouraged this kind of career.

Because French gymnastics began in the armed forces, the public confused it with military training and muscle building and hence with masculinity. Experts who designed exercise programs for girls had to distinguish their programs from the military prototype and its macho reputation. After the defeat of France at Waterloo (1815), foreign military officers opened private gymnasiums in Paris. A Spaniard, Colonel Amoros, promised that his combination of running, jumping, and acrobatic feats on ropes and parallel bars assured military prowess. Unvarying routines stressed building upper-body muscle. Amoros's method, designed for young men, was scaled down for secondary schools for boys. In the 1830s, a Swiss officer, Clias, proposed gymnastics for primary schools but substituted calisthenics for girls schools. Dozens of communal schools instituted calisthenics because it was consistent with cultural convictions that acrobatics deformed girls' bodies and endangered their reproductive organs (and, pragmatically, because it required no equipment).[14] In the 1880s, Dr. Fernand Lagrange argued that girls and boys gymnastics had different purposes: the former was "to favor regular and harmonious development of the body," the latter to make "agile and hardy saviors, capable of executing the most difficult movements."[15] Not until the 1920s did doctors such as Arlette Gelé de Francony challenge the entwined myths that strength was masculine, and girls did not need physical force.[16]

In midcentury, the French imported Swedish gymnastics, also known as orthopedic gymnastics, a method designed to alleviate back pain by isolating and stretching back muscles. Early French enthusiasts were bodybuilders who isolated and built upper-arm and shoulder muscles.[17] Despite this macho beginning, later advocates of Swedish gymnastics thought that its principles of exercise for health and beauty could be applied to girls.[18] In the 1890s, Dr. Angerstein claimed that spot exercises of the back muscles corrected curvature of the spine, which was common in adolescent girls, and systematic exercise stimulated every organ, which modified "girls' indolent nature." Other supporters claimed that systemic exercise alleviated chlorosis and hysteria, cured shallow breathing, and prevented chronic constipation.[19] In the first decade of the twentieth century, the Feminine League for Physical Culture, founded by militant suffragist Caroline Kauffmann, contended that Swedish respiratory exercises expanded girls' lungs and protected girls from consumption. Boosters of the system promised an elegant carriage, graceful gait, and decisive demeanor. Alluding simultaneously to the new ideal of a slimmer body and the old correlation of femininity with rounded contours, these enthusiasts insisted that exertion reduced but did not eliminate fat.[20]

One of Amoros's students, Napoléon Laisné, experimented with gymnastic routines to music in four women's wards in hospitals. In the 1850s, Laisné adapted his program to fortify "delicate" but not hospitalized girls through games, skipping, light weightlifting, and "dry swimming" on a sawhorse. Designed for apartments, his system called for instructors, preferably women, because instructors had to touch girls' arms and legs to correct their positions.[21] Realizing that few people could afford private gymnastic instructors or equipment, Laisné designed and taught classes in secondary and normal schools for girls in Paris.

After the Franco-Prussian War, a law required gymnastics in public schools and military drills in boys schools to train the next generation of soldiers.[22] Not surprisingly, Laisné's classes were more militaristic than coterminous classes in London. Girls arranged in rows and columns moved in unison on command. Laisné prided himself on his gymnasts' discipline during public demonstrations at the patriotic *fêtes,* where they performed drills beside boys battalions. By the early 1880s, 29,198 girls had attended Laisné's classes in communal schools, and 846 young women had taken his classes in normal school. Graduates were teaching in provincial schools; one wrote an elementary school gymnastics text.[23] In provincial cities, other former military men modified military gymnastics, provided instructors for communal schools, or opened their private gymnasiums to school children.[24]

The hegemony of military models of gymnastics also skewed rationales for girls physical education. For two decades in most of France and longer in the departments bordering the lost provinces of Alsace and Lorraine, gymnastic and drill *fêtes* were held. Military drill instructors boasted that they were "a practical apprenticeship" in military discipline.[25] Advocates of girls' gymnastics devised a complementary rationale: exercise prepared girls to bear better babies and rear sturdier soldiers.[26] Eugenicists endorsed girls gymnastics to combat depopulation and degeneration.[27] Feminists articulated a maternal variation of the eugenics argument. The Feminine League for Physical Culture asserted that women's health was essential to physical regeneration, for "the mother's health is the child's heritage." As late as 1936, Ida See invoked angst about "insufficient cradles" in her protest against a physical education decree that ignored pubescent girls.[28]

Another constraint on physical education for girls was society's moral aversion to mixed-sex activities. Prewar attempts at physical coeducation—other than in village primary schools—were short lived. In 1880, the radical republican board of the Prévost Orphanage appointed Paul Robin (the future Neo-Malthusian mentioned in Chap. 6) as director. An anarchist imbued with Rousseau's ideal of integral—meaning a physical as well as an intellectual and moral—education, Robin included gymnastics, military drills, and manual work in the curriculum. Although the orphanage advertised "education in common," teachers used separate gymnastics texts for girls and boys. Even though the orphans swam in sexually segregated groups, critics were outraged by the fact that they swam naked. In the early 1890s, fifty Catholic newspapers condemned Prévost for "perverse promiscuity" and attempts to "neutralize the sexes." Ignoring a commissioned report praising the Prévost curriculum,[29] the moderate republican government replaced Robin. One of the two other coeducational orphanages founded before the war folded during the war; the other one survived but revised its program after the war.[30]

Physiology and Physical Education

In the nineteenth century, French parents and pedagogues resisted having educational institutions direct children's corporeal development. To change their minds, hygienists and physical educators formulated a pedagogic rationale from Rousseau's ideas about integral instruction. To satisfy the university, which controlled curricula, advocates assembled a physiological rationale using Claude Bernard's theory of a self-regulating internal milieu, Darwinian hypotheses about organs atrophying without use, and Neo-Lamarckian postulates that exercise offset scoliosis and compression of the lungs caused by prolonged sitting at desks. By the 1880s, physiologists had demonstrated that muscular exertion accelerated blood circulation and oxygen consumption.[31] Between 1880 and 1900, biochemical investigations established that muscle contractions promoted deep breathing and perspiration, which, physical educators hypothesized, improved physical health and academic performance.[32]

Before 1880, Christian condemnation of the body and the antagonism of liberal arts toward mechanical arts sustained parental and pedagogical suspicion of physical education in the school. Most parents and educators believed that physical exertion distracted boys from their studies and drained precious resources from intellectual endeavor. Hygienists and physical educators countered with the new concept of the constitution as a closed system that must be in equilibrium. These experts maintained that moving muscles, the heaviest part of the body, engaged the nervous and circulatory system and invigorated all organs, including the brain. After 1880, physical education advocacy was more proactive. Campaigning against the long hours and exclusively academic classes of public schools, advocates asserted that systematic exercise prevented intellectual fatigue and infectious diseases and had an esthetic effect.[33] Interwar experts evoked psychologists such as Freud and Jung on physical education molding character.[34]

Given a widespread belief that "woman draws well-being from her physical traits more than her intellectual talents," the case for gymnastics for girls should have been physiological.[35] Actually, scientific theories about an integrated constitution did not neutralize cultural convictions that pubescent girls had unstable constitutions and must conserve their resources for reproduction.[36]

Until the 1920s, research on the physiological effects of gymnastics focused on young men. In 1866, pioneer kinesiologist Etienne-Jules Marey (1830–1904) was appointed to the College de France. Using photography to track physiological functions, Marey mapped how corporeal energies were transformed while his subjects performed different movements.[37] In 1881, Drs. Chassagne and Dally published 16,330 measurements indicating that systematic exercise increased the chest measurements of military recruits. The two doctors inferred that exercise would prevent anemia, rickets, obesity, and neurasthenia. Although researchers knew that girls were more susceptible than boys to anemia and neurasthenia, subsequent studies used male subjects.[38] A laboratory established by a Marey student, Georges Demeny, demonstrated that aerobic activity expanded lung capacity and increased bone mass in young men; it also identified underutilized muscles. Demeny posited correctly that girls would benefit from exercise because they had smaller lungs, lighter bones, and weaker abdominal muscles than boys and young men.[39]

In the 1920s, exercise during menstruation and puberty finally attracted scientific attention. In 1923, Dr. Gelé de Francony distinguished between prepubescent girls, who did not need special physical education, and pubescent girls, whom she thought should be confined to moderate exercise to regulate menstruation and counteract atrophy of the abdominal muscles, which caused difficult deliveries.[40] By the mid-1930s, an endocrinologist, Dr. F.-A. Papillon, contended that physical education during puberty favored development of the glandular system and corrected menstrual deficiencies. Dr. Henri-Camille Druost reported that about one third of all of the young women who had been studied stopped exercising for physiological or esthetic reasons, and one fifth reduced their exercise regimen during menstruation. Only one fifth of the stalwarts who kept exercising reported any ill effects, mainly lower back pain. Druost concluded that pubescent girls should do "judicious exercises" to stimulate blood circulation in the pelvic region and to tone the abdominal and pelvic muscles.[41]

Women's magazines cited these medical studies as evidence that moderate gymnastics contributed to the overall health of girls, but ambivalence marked most arguments for it. An 1898 textbook declared that exercise was necessary because girls and women rarely "escaped" unhealthy lodgings or breathed fresh air, yet it spared girls from difficult routines because they were "fragile, delicate" beings "not made for work and effort."[42] Interwar theorists amplified the argument about social constraints and reduced the number of exemptions from the male norm.[43] Only Dr. Esther Bensidoun queried assumptions about feminine inferiority. In *Sports and Woman* (1933), Bensidoun noted that studies showing that women had two thirds of men's average muscular strength focused on the upper body, where men tend to excel. She urged development of the abdominal, pelvic, extensor, and abductor muscles, where women have an advantage. She also pointed out that women's muscles performed well by the criteria of flexibility, precision, and speed.[44] Earlier experts who acknowledged that women excelled in flexibility and endurance had explained that these physical traits were "in perfect accord" with household tasks but added that "it was not in woman's nature to develop her muscles."[45]

One theme in the campaigns for physical training was that it cultivated gender-appropriate moral qualities. Baron de Coubertin maintained that physical training of boys instilled "discipline and good manners." Lobbies pledged that girls gymnastics inculcated qualities such as patience, endurance, and attentiveness. When naval Lieutenant Georges Hébert publicized his aerobic method, he promised it would develop the "virile qualities" of will, courage, audacity, energy, and industry. When Hébert adapted his method for girls and women, he emphasized personal emancipation and self-assurance. The first claim for women's "right to movement" appeared in a wartime manual written by another naval officer, Lieutenant Guinet.[46] Few champions of girls gymnastics spoke of emancipation or rights—they had to persuade parents, educators, and officials, not girls. Instead, the case for girls' gymnastics remained esthetic and natalist. Prewar advocates maintained that exercise enhanced beauty and thereby increased sexual attractiveness and reproduction. Postwar advocates mentioned preparing women for the dual role of employment and maternity but emphasized that the fundamental purpose remained esthetic and procreative: training meant good posture, firm breasts, supple movement, and self-mastery—the qualities of "the perfect wife and ideal progenitor."[47]

Public opinion about exercise changed very slowly. In 1934, a Catholic newspaper reported that girls' and women's "special functions . . . are incompatible with intense muscular efforts." During menstruation, pregnancy, and nursing, intense effort caused exhaustion.[48] Popular and scientific prejudices, such as the notion that flexible tissues, necessary for future gestation and birthing, precluded muscle building, impeded physical education for girls long after it was part of the public school program.

School Physical Education

To a far greater degree than in England, where a separate tradition of girls' physical education existed,[49] girls' gymnastics was formulated in relation to that for boys, a militaristic system designed for discipline and disconnected from recreation.[50] Thanks to liberal exemptions, lax implementation, and the inclusion of dance, girls' physical education was less alienating. Of course, it also gave girls fewer opportunities to test or stretch their physical abilities.

Except for the military battalions, the 1880s decrees on physical education applied to girls. Elementary school children had a common curriculum. Retired military men drafted the prepubescent program for girls and modeled it on the program for boys. The version for girls combined orthopedic and military activities without equipment and included indoor running, jumping, and swimming. Educators and parents criticized its militaristic style and complained that it bored girls.[51] After Demeny revised the program in 1891, ten- or eleven-year-old girls danced, sang, and skipped whereas boys their age performed military drills. Prepubescent boys could play twelve games; prepubescent girls, seven games. At the *lycée*, boys could chose from five sports, girls could only play lawn tennis.[52]

Staffing posed major problems. Because most of the thirty-four normal schools for women did not require physical education, only about two hundred women passed the gymnastics examination in 1886.[53] Unlike England, France had no private colleges to supply gymnastics mistresses.[54] Some schools tried to solve the problem by hiring male instructors or assigning untrained female teachers for physical education. Neither was a good solution. Male supervision embarrassed some adolescent girls and offended some parents. Between one fifth and one third of adolescent girls were excused from gymnastics "for family or health reasons," not just "a few days a month" (a euphemism for during their periods), but for entire terms. Louise Weiss offered this unkind description of her untrained gymnastics mistress: "a fat person with flabby flesh held in by a corset with bones that hurt her so much she avoided bending over. Her shiny high heels, the tight armholes on her bodice, her foolish curls cleverly pinned up, kept her from showing us exercises."[55]

Another problem was political: municipalities delayed the construction of girls school gymnasiums for up to three decades.[56] Many senior primary schools and *lycées* simply offered no physical education. Other schools substituted free-form exercise (which did not require space or equipment) for orthopedic routines and sports.[57]

By the 1890s, private organizations tried to fill the gaps. The Gironde League for Physical Education sponsored boys' track-and-field events, for which it received subsidies from the city of Bordeaux. Although in 1892 the league approved the principle of girls' events, it did nothing until 1900, when the Feminine Committee formed. The committee trained gymnastics mistresses and raised money to buy equipment for girls' schools in, and the women's normal school near, Bordeaux. In 1903, the committee held the first girls' track meet, which consisted of stretching routines, conducted with punctilious regard for propriety before an audience of teachers and family members. When the League for Physical Education splintered in 1908, the committee became the autonomous League for the Physical Development of Young Girls and supported gymnastics for local girls for several more years.[58]

In 1900, the women's normal school in Pau (in the Pyrenées) hired Dr. Philippe Tissié to teach his combination of Swedish gymnastics and games. When Mme. Dolle became director in 1903, she authorized Tissié to document the effects of his program on students. By 1907, the *Primary Education Annual* reported that Pau students visited the doctor less often than their peers, especially for menstrual problems and anemia. Every year fifteen to thirty graduates accepted employment in schools throughout the southwest, but Mme. Dolle refused to let her students participate in regional gym *fêtes* or perform at the 1913 International Physical Education Congress.[59] Although school physical education was gradually if grudgingly accepted, gymnastic displays outside the confines of sexually segregated schools remained morally repugnant. The one prewar feminine gymnastics *fête* drew only five hundred participants.[60]

At the turn of the century, the Ministries of War, Public Instruction, and the Interior appointed a commission to advise on the unification of physical training in the army, school system, and athletic clubs. The commission made unrealistic recommendations of one hour of exercise every school day, gymnastics examinations in primary schools, and physical education courses in all secondary schools. The Ministry of Public Instruction did not experiment with daily classes until 1936, and many girls' *lycées* treated physical education as an elective subject through the 1930s.[61] However, the ministry did commission Demeny and other experts to write a new physical education manual. Once again, the manual presented exercises for boys as the norm and excused girls from "difficult" routines. It did not allow prepubescent girls to lift weights, climb rope, or box, and it forbade pubescent girls most track-and-field events. When the girls reached the age of sixteen, the list of activities prohibited to them grew.[62]

Dance teachers complained that the official program had been "set up by men, for boys." Exploiting the cultural consensus that dance was feminine, they contended that girls had "an instinctive taste for music and rhythm" and wanted harmonious proportions and gestures. (Others noted that parents approved of dancing and rhythmic gymnastics as social skills and enjoyed watching them performed.)[63] In this period, Isadora Duncan was performing free-form "antique" dances designed by her brother Raymond.[64] The Duncans inspired Demeny to create "gymnastic dancing"—varied "whole body exercises" to music—for girls. Other systems of rhythmic exercise flourished in private gymnastic academies for girls.[65]

In the prewar decade, a new system of physical training emerged in the navy. Starting with Rousseau's postulate that activity was a law of nature, Hébert advocated "instinctive" and utilitarian movement based on walking, running, and jumping in light clothing in the fresh air. Hébert argued that an hour of aerobic and cardiovascular exercise a day was time efficient. Minus the early twentieth-century elements of testing resistance to cold and other hardships, his "natural method" is an ancestor of the fitness movement popular at the end of the twentieth century. Some public schools adopted Hébert's natural method after the war, primarily because it was inexpensive. After a law making physical education mandatory in all (including Catholic) schools, Hébert opened sections in his three athletic colleges and a college for young women. The college offered two years of instruction in anatomy, physiology, kinesiology, practical hygiene, dance, and physical education, as well as naturism ("the healthy life through fresh air, sun, and natural foods"). Most graduates became dedicated teachers; many were still physical education instructors in the 1950s.[66]

Instead of Hébert's colleges, interested secondary school teachers could attend a one-month summer course that belatedly accepted women in 1905. About ten women and forty men took the course each year.[67] In the 1920s, twelve universities set up physical education institutes to train secondary school teachers and medical students; women filled about half of the 150 seats. With the exception of lessons on female anatomy and physiology, classes were coeducational.[68] English gymnastics mistresses organized separately, but French gymnastics mistresses and monitors formed mixed-sex professional associations dominated by men. One result was a salary gap of twelve hundred to three thousand francs, depending upon rank (only partly due to the longer hours demanded of male monitors).[69]

After the war, the International Physical Education Congress convened to assess physical training systems and approved a mix of aerobics, acrobatics, and orthopedic gymnastics.[70] The Ministry of War issued rules that divided students into elementary, secondary, and adult groups. In the elementary cohort, girls did the same exercises but played fewer games than the boys did. In the secondary group, girls did fewer repetitions and more rhythmic routines than "the program." The rules assumed that adults who did athletics and sports were men.[71] When the ministry adopted the rules in 1929, it spared girls acrobatics, athletics, and sports. Although authorizing short-term suspensions from bars, two-handed fencing, and racquetball, the manual refused any body-contact sports as dangerous to the uterus. From puberty on, the manual explained, the "special physiological functions" of girls were incompatible with "intense muscular effort."[72] With minor modifications, this manual was used to the end of the Republic.[73]

Sports Medicine and Propaganda

Although sports medicine emerged as a specialty before the First World War, very few biomedical studies of the impact of sports on women were published before 1930. In 1913, a professor of gynecology, J. A. Doléris, explained that "the special disposition" of the pelvic bones in prepubescent girls limited their activities—the sacrum, attached to the lumbar spine, was vulnerable to sudden, strenuous, or continuous effort. However, he added, prepubescent girls should develop their pelvic muscles to protect their sex organs, preferably by fencing, because lunges were "the best movements of the pelvic and femoral muscles."[74] Thereafter, experts differentiated between sports appropriate for girls and sports appropriate for women. Most experts believed that playing sports would prevent the full development of girls' bones, but they did accept skating, lawn tennis, and golf as aerobic activities that nourished the entire organism.[75]

By the 1920s, scientists had gauged respiration, pulse, and blood pressure rates before and after exercise to prove that exertion regulated appetite and reduced body fat. Other studies showed that (on average) women inhaled less air than men did.[76] These findings fueled a familiar argument: aerobic exercise improved feminine health and beauty.[77] Even before the war, purveyors of fitness programs had built a following among Parisian women by promising to slim and shape their figures.[78] After the war, Irene Popard advertised that her system of "harmonic gymnastics" fostered "natural qualities of grace and flexibility" and also tightened the abdominal belt and expanded the thorax.[79] In the 1930s, Marguerite Vincelo claimed that fifteen minutes of her aerobic exercises daily trimmed bodies for body-draping dresses. According to her publicity, regular exercise was a prophylaxis for "women of a certain age, who must appear young to avoid being fired."[80]

Opponents of sports for women rarely cited scientific research, as opposed to gender stereotypes and depopulation fears. Many opponents simply declared that sports were dangerous for women's fragile organism.[81]

In the 1880s, pundits had warned that bicycling threatened women's modesty and fertility. In that decade, bicycles, introduced at the 1867 International Exhibition, added horizontal chains and pneumatic tires and became viable vehicles. By 1902, France had one bicycle for every thirty-two inhabitants.[82] Dozens of bicycle manufacturers sprang up; their advertising depicted attractive feminine figures in typical Art Nouveau style, with long, flimsy gowns and long, loose hair[83] (see Fig. 7). Perhaps the utterly impractical attire reaffirmed the essential femininity of female cyclists. Certainly, moralists and physicians in France, as elsewhere, censured female cyclists for abandoning household duties and jostling their reproductive organs. Hygienists warned that sitting astride bicycles ruptured hymens and rubbing against the raised forward part of the saddle seat stimulated the vagina (probably meaning the clitoris). As a few women cyclists donned more practical clothing, journalists made doubly disarming criticisms. On the one hand, they contended that culottes and bloomers, which allowed women to stand with their legs apart, made women "act like men." (It is possible that these journalists, almost all of them men, were uncomfortable seeing women's legs apart.) On the other hand, journalists claimed that bloomers, which magnified female curves, made women ugly. All of the women interviewed for a book on women's views about cycling costumes disliked the "immodest and ridiculous" bloomers, although some were "no longer disgusted" by culottes.[84]

Although the barrage of criticism about proper cycling attire delayed the adoption of more sensible attire, it did not deter women from cycling (see Fig. 8). Over time, opposition waned. By the 1890s, skeptical physicians noted that the medical profession had rejected similar objections about the pedaling of treadle sewing machines damaging (or exciting) the genitalia. Dr. Philippe Tissié advised buying suspended and flexible bicycle seats to reduce bouncing (see Fig. 9). Other physicians endorsed cycling to build girls' and women's muscles.[85] By the 1920s, women doctors only discouraged girls or women who were menstruating or suffering from pelvic diseases from biking.[86]

As bloomers faded from the scene, women journalists wrote about comfort in sports clothing and made fun of men fretting about seeing women's calves. By 1912, a sports manual for women recommended fashionable clothing tailored for each sport. By the 1920s, a short-lived magazine entitled *Women, Sport, Fashion* reported on "a new kind of fashion, sports clothing." A reporter overoptimistically proclaimed that "We are in an epoch when this somewhat masculine attire no longer frightens anyone."[87]

Opponents of women in competitive sports had a more lasting effect when they complained that intense spectator sports masculinized and exposed the female body. After a 1903 marathon race through Paris among several trades, including female garment workers, even proponents of more genteel sports for women deplored the extreme effort and public exposure of female bodies. Women ceased to run in this race.[88] When women competed in same-sex races and other athletic events after the war, critics objected that "women cease to

7. "Cycles Sirius" poster by Henri Boulanger, 1899.
Musée des Arts décoratifs

8. Photograph entitled "Lisette/Gladiator" by Jules Boyer,
no date but likely turn of the century.
Bibliothèque National de France

be women" after prolonged effort and that sweaty, scantily clad runners were unattractive.[89] Given their approval of female gymnasts performing increasingly vigorous harmonic gymnastic routines in skimpy costumes in theaters and arenas,[90] their real target was women in athletic events that had been coded masculine, wearing jerseys and shorts, considered masculine attire.

9. "La Selle Sâr" poster by Maurice Deville.
Musée des Arts décoratifs

After the war, films, plays, and posters encouraged Frenchwomen to take up sports in order to bring them up to the physical standards of English and American women.[91] Conversely, postwar angst about low birth rates revitalized aversion to women in competitive sports. Although Dr. Maurice Boigey (mentioned in the Introduction) approved of sports for corporeal perfection, he disapproved of long-distance running, jumping, and boxing, which he felt melted the fat reserves needed for conception.[92] Feminists and sports enthusiasts responded that noncompetitive sports prepared women for their dual role as mothers and paid workers.[93] In *Sports and Women* (1931), Dr. Yvonne Legrand of Femina-Sport catalogued the benefits of noncompetitive sports, including easing the organic and emotional transition of pubescent girls as well as alleviating the headaches and moodiness of menopause. She recorded the effects of playing sports on her own pregnancy and those of twenty-four other women in sports. All reported that toned abdominal muscles facilitated normal deliveries, postpartum recoveries, and a rapid return to flatter stomachs.[94]

In the 1920s, women physicians remained suspicious of competitive sports. The heroine of the novel *Sportive* by Dr. Marthe Darcanne of Femina-Sport (writing as Dr. Marthe Bertheaume) remained faithful to the sports she took up at the Sorbonne but renounced competitions because her girlfriend died "from competitiveness." However, Dr. Marie Houdré-Boursin, a president of Femina-Sport, was already keeping records about sportswomen. After monitoring girls' and boys' sports for a decade, Houdré-Boursin reported that the main sex difference was that girls relied on agility and coordination and boys on strength and action. In her 1930 health guide for women, she endorsed "feminine" sports such as tennis, racquetball, and field hockey, which fostered decisiveness, cooperation, and team spirit. Unlike most advocates of women's sports, she encouraged women to play simply because they would enjoy sports.[95]

Three years later, Dr. Bensidoun confronted the issue of masculinization, which she defined as excessive musculature and independence. Quoting Social Darwinist Herbert Spencer on the role of beauty in sexual selection, she stressed that beauty was a function of health and slenderness, which sports enhanced. To the classical beauty canon of small, firm breasts and a slightly rounded stomach, she appended new (but now familiar) calibrations such as the depth of the subcutaneous fat that could be pinched on various parts of the body. To arguments that competitive sports were not worth women's effort because women would never beat men's records, she responded that men's and women's swimming records were similar. (In 1934, Dr. Sophie Zabewska explained that thicker subcutaneous fat allowed women to float and tolerate cold better than men.) Responding to criticism about "abuses" such as championships, Bensidoun dryly observed that what was "provisionally good for men, is good for women too." Despite this egalitarian stance, she followed the sports medicine line in prohibiting women's sprints, long-distance running, boxing, and most team sports.[96] In the Third Republic, this was the most progressive position on women's sports.

In the late 1930s, the biomedical community remained divided on the subject of women in sports. After summarizing research on women's pulmonary capacity, bone density, and muscle elasticity in *Women and Bodily Exercise*

(1937), Dr. Martinie-Doubousquet concluded that "the normal woman has harmoniously acquired reserves for a happy racial conservation." Athletic events that required intense or prolonged effort, such as sprints or long-distance running, exceeded their respiratory capacities. "Normal" women who engaged in competitive sports lost subcutaneous fat, their shoulders enlarged, their breasts shriveled, and their hips shrank. In a typical rhetorical shift from verifiable physical conditions to psychological speculation, Martinie-Doubousquet claimed that *sportives* "too often forget the condition of their sex. The ambiance in which they live is charged with an extreme *masculinisme*." Lesbianism was "not foreign" to them. Muscular adult women who could do sports were "clearly pathological." He cited East European Olympic athletes who had had sex change operations. The same year, at the Congress on Medicine Applied to Physical Education and Sports, Robert Jeudon retorted that sports did not alter bio-types and had good gynecological effects.[97]

Sportives *and Sports Organizations*

Sportswomen's feats gradually challenged platitudes about feminine weakness and inertia. In the *fin de siècle,* wealthy women raced automobiles, sailed boats, and flew airplanes. When auto, yacht, and flying clubs refused to admit women, "feminine" associations formed to rent equipment and offer training.[98] As late as 1930, journalists described women drivers as liberated because there were so few women in the increasingly professional sport of racing. Sailing, which remained a wealthy amateur sport, allowed wealthy women to compete with men—and win—in the 1928 Olympics.[99] When such feats received positive press coverage, they inspired less privileged women.

Many sports pioneers publicized their exploits and thereby encouraged other women.[100] Early pioneers used the modesty topos. For example, Mme. Camille du Gast apologized for "the feminine sin of pride" after she described training for the 1903 Paris-Madrid auto rally. She also insisted on her essential femininity by telling about stopping to assist a hurt driver. She added a moral: "Even if a woman drives 120 per hour, she must always stop to care for those who suffer."[101] Most of the second generation of sportswomen were single, employed, and unapologetic. Marie (nom de plume: Meryl) Marvingt of Nancy competed in skating and shooting events as well as in cycling, skiing, and bobsled races. In 1909, she was the only Frenchwoman with licenses to fly balloons and airplanes. Sports magazines called her "the intrepid sportswoman." Rejected as a pilot during the war, Marvingt took nurse training and organized the first corps of flying nurses. After the war, she helped establish a flying health service.[102]

The third generation of sports stars specialized, and a few became professionals. In the mid-1870s, tennis, which had been revived as a sport for ladies, was the most respectable and receptive sport. Early reporting of women's tennis commented upon the elegance of the players' swings and the esthetics of their positions. All media described tennis costumes; a feminist guide called tennis dresses "coquette and smart."[103] As Abigail Feder argues (about a later generation of skaters), the media's emphases on the players' femininity became the players' policy of overcompensating to avoid being labeled masculine or lesbian.[104]

Suzanne Lenglen (1899–1938) was widely recognized as "the best woman tennis player ever." She won several Wimbledon championships between 1919 and 1926 and became a professional player in 1927. Her international success brought national recognition as a "sports diva," partly because she had a forceful forehand and accurate backhand and partly because she beat the English on their own turf[105] (see Fig. 10). Yet reporters paid as much attention to her chic and style. Women's magazines commented upon her midcalf and short-sleeved outfits and her collaboration with the couturier Jean Patou. Newspapers raved that her leaping tennis game belonged "in the dance world"; the Moulin Rouge offered her three thousand francs to appear in a tableau vivant with rackets and balls. Lenglen sensibly rejected the nightclub offer but collaborated in the news coverage. In an interview she said, "I always sought to create an elegant movement, a general equilibrium in a gesture, rather than to set any records." To one reporter, she seemed "so feminine—in all the senses that may have been implied in the past, nonsportsy, emotional, sensitive."[106]

Although Lenglen was playing against a negative stereotype of professional sportswomen, amateur tennis had been accepted as appropriately feminine and bourgeois. With the emergence of Lenglen and another "sports princess"—Mlle. Thion de la Chaume, winner of national and international women's golf cups in 1926—attitudes toward *sportives* began to change. One reporter insisted that the word now implied "Grace, strength, suppleness, beauty, femininity. Nothing brutal, nothing unattractive, a harmony."[107] In this more supportive environment, Lenglen finally wrote about the rigorous training her father had imposed on her as a teenager, as well as her demanding regimen of rhythmic dance, gymnastics, and skipping as an adult. She even

10. Photograph of Suzanne Lenglen, not dated but likely in the 1920s.
Bibliothèque Nationale de France

remarked that tennis required "training similar to a boxer's." Shortly thereafter, a prominent actress, Cécile Sorel, admitted that she boxed to keep her
figure, despite the fact that boxing was "universally dismissed" as too brutal
for women.[108]

Doubts about sportswomen persisted. An article entitled "Our Comrades,
the Sportswomen" in a 1933 supplement, "Today's Women," in *Figaro* ad-
mired women in sports "that are less tests of strength and prowess than cere-
monies." After asserting that sports encouraged a new camaraderie between
the sexes, the reporter, Jeanne Ramon Fernandez, warned that the sportswoman "risks a lot." By adopting men's ways, she predicted, "she will find
herself without defenses when the other woman, the one they call eternal, re-
sumes her rights." The other woman was "distant, mysterious, supine."[109]

Organized amateur sports followed a twisted path. In the 1880s, boys *lycées*
organized running clubs, and alumni organized the French Union of Running
Societies. By 1905, the Union of Athletics Societies represented eight hundred
clubs with sixty thousand members.[110] Five years later, Admiral Paysse proposed a women's auxiliary to his athletic club and, when his club refused, he
helped found Femina-Sport. With the assistance of the Duchess d'Uzes (men-

tioned in Chap. 1), Marie Marvingt, and the car manufacturer André Citroen, the Feminine Sports Federation formed. In 1917, it hosted the first feminine championships, a six-day affair with relay races, jumping events, field hockey matches, and demonstrations of gymnastics and boxing.[111]

After the war, Mme. Alice Milliat, an avid rower, assumed the presidency of the Feminine Sports Federation. Milliat was "the most prominent woman in French and world women's sports between the wars." Unfortunately, she was forced to resign from the presidency over a scandal about a lottery to raise money for a training field.[112] Acquiring practice and playing space was a serious problem. In 1929, just one of the eight stadiums in the Paris region, the Elizabeth Stadium in the suburb of Montrouge, was open to Femina-Sport. Only about 10 percent of state support for amateur gymnastics and sports went to feminine societies, and most of it went to gymnastics societies.[113] With representatives from six other countries, Milliat organized the International Women's Sports Federation, which arranged for the first Women's Olympic Games in 1922. Although French athletes did not fare well in these games, they won the second largest number of medals at the second Women's Games in 1926. By 1928, the International Women's Sports Federation had twenty thousand French members.[114]

The largest women's federation, the Federation of Feminine Gym and Physical Education Societies, was ambivalent about sports. One reason was that Robert Amy, Mayor of Saumer, and other male enthusiasts dominated the executive committee, although some regional committees included several women.[115] When affiliates wanting to play sports seceded in 1923, the federation proclaimed its devotion to "larger, more heterogeneous groups, not forgetting the weak." After a few secessions, the federation continued to grow, reaching 565 affiliates and 25,000 members in the 1930s.[116] The federation sponsored single-sex track-and-field meets. In the mid-1920s, two remarkable women's teams from the northern industrial town of Tourcoing won several regional and national cups. In 1928, one of these teams came in last in the gymnastics "demonstrations" and jumping events at the Women's Olympic Games. After several years of poor showings, the federation eliminated certain events from their meets.[117]

Instead, the federation, influenced by Irene Popard, the only woman on the executive committee, promoted harmonic gymnastics. At its 1926 federal *fête*, most of the girls performed in costumed and choreographed productions. Reporters contrasted the "masculine celebration of strength" of the prewar gymnastics *fêtes* to this "feminine celebration of grace." Most of the press photographs were of rhythmic gymnasts.[118] The following year, the federation ordered affiliates not to participate in masculine *fêtes,* which treated women's events as "a form of exhibitionism." Yet the federation sponsored public performances of symbolic dance, reinforcing the earlier suggestion that opposition to women in spectator sports was really opposition to women in "masculine" spectator sports. In the mid-1930s, members performed symbolic scenes with characters representing hatred, corruption, "and all the horrors that invade France." At the 1939 federal *fête,* one group presented a "fresh-air opera" called "Peace, Work, Fraternity."[119] *Peace* and *Work* were two parts of the motto of the collaborationist Vichy regime under the Occupation.

Conclusions

In the 1930s, France offered less physical education for girls and women than most developed countries did. Experts complained that 98 percent of Frenchwomen neglected physical culture and that the others were revolutionaries or eccentrics. Girls either followed their elders' example of inertia or "consecrated themselves . . . body and soul, without taking into account their personal aptitudes, rational training, or physiological controls."[120] Lobbies for women's fitness only partly allayed anxiety about the instability of female bodies. To persuade schools to introduce physical education, these lobbies had accepted less acrobatic and athletic programs. The perimeters of feminine physical activity had expanded but still existed.

Of course, physical training of girls and women evoked fears other than the frequently articulated ones about threats to femininity and natality. The first self-defense manual for Frenchwomen, which was published (with support from the Duchess d'Uzes) in 1913, tried to assuage these fears. Written by jujitsu instructor Max Pherdac, the manual described open-hand blows to vulnerable points on an attacker's body. Addressing men in the preface, Pherdac explained that women needed to defend themselves against unwanted attentions from suitors, thieves, and gangs. But, Pherdac reassured his readers, women would only learn defensive moves, would remain "physiologically inferior," and would still be good wives and mothers.[121] In short, women's self-defense (like their physical training) would not threaten patriarchy.

Chapter 9

Working Bodies

*I*N Third-Republic France, women were well represented in most sectors of the economy. With the introduction of electric-powered small machinery into the home, the growth of consumer goods industries, and industrial decentralization to avoid labor standards in manufacturing, home-based industries not only survived but also expanded. As Judith Coffin shows, the Singer sewing machine agent, Callebaut, concentrated on home-sized models, sold nearly half of his stock to workers, and, in conjunction with the Dufeyal department store, pioneered working-class purchase of appliances on credit. Recognizing the trend toward female domestic sewing, companies quickly replaced male figures in industrial settings with female figures in domestic settings on their posters and other advertisements. What had been a mixed-workshop occupation became primarily a feminine and domestic occupation[1] (see Fig. 11).

Even before the First World War, many Frenchwomen worked in heavy industries and on heavy equipment (see Fig. 12). What the war changed was women's access to formerly masculine heavy industries and jobs. In metalworking, the number of women workers nearly quadrupled between 1914 and 1939. The big surge occurred during the war, when up to three quarters of some firms' employees were women. Most of these women came from feminine sectors of the economy, drawn by wages twice the average woman's wage of two to three francs a day. After the war, large numbers of these women remained on the job because by that time employers had designed a gendered internal labor market. As Laura Lee Downs demonstrates, employers broke work processes down into distinct tasks, defined these tasks as unskilled, and recast human capacities that had been called *skilled* in men as aspects of feminine nature. The speed and routine of fragmented tasks were linked to women's innately nimble fingers and methodical nature. In this

manner, as Downs notes, employers used gender to enforce Aristotelian principles of hierarchy and authority.[2]

To account for the distinctive trend of continued high female employment
in postwar France, Susan Pedersen points to the wartime social contract
whereby unions were decimated by conscription, and the state delegated the
organization of war production to employers. Unlike British unions, French
unions did not negotiate protection of jobs for demobilized men. Some large
employers took advantage first of the war to redesign their plants and hire
women and then of the devastating aftermath of the war to retain women in
the new, more repetitive jobs. Ultimately, the war confirmed prewar patterns
whereby Frenchwomen remained a normal, if inferior, class of workers,
whereas British women remained temporary workers. Pedersen illustrates her

11. Photograph entitled "Couturière piquant à la machine," 1938.
Bibliothèque Nationale de France

12. Photograph entitled "Fabrication des boîtes métalliques," 1911.
Roger-Viollet

thesis with separation allowances, which the British gave to wives of deserv-
ing servicemen, thereby reinforcing the family ideal of a male breadwinner
and a dependent wife, and the French conferred on dependents in a parental
mode. More unusually, French industrialists introduced 255 private funds for
family allowances. Eventually, some funds dispersed allowances to working
mothers, recognizing them as breadwinners, not dependents.[3] Pronatalists encouraged this development but had little effect in obtaining other programs to
support working mothers.

Despite public discussion of these trends, occupational and industrial hygienists conducted surprisingly few studies of working women's bodies, work
performance, or productivity. Although novelists such as Emile Zola painted
pathetic portraits of tiny, anemic, and nervous seamstresses,[4] most scientific
studies focused on the impact of industrial jobs on working women's pregnancies, deliveries, and babies. Few hygienists went beyond trite remarks
about working women's bodies being smaller and weaker than men's bodies
or equally canonical opinions about women's nimble fingers and aptitude for
repetitive work. Eschewing most of these studies, in the first section of this
chapter I consider one of the better-documented aspects of Frenchwomen's
work.

Endurance

In the 1880s, legislative commissions gathered evidence not only of an "effective" working day of twelve hours, but also of workers spending fourteen or
fifteen hours at the workplace, counting the two to four meals eaten at work.
Only a tiny minority of unionized workers, almost exclusively male, had ten-
or eleven-hour days. In industry, the workweek was six days, with holidays
for major religious observances. Many industries had violent oscillations in
demand, as in the case of haute couture, or in supply, as in the case of seasonal
food preparation. The result was alternating high seasons of one to three
months, when three to four hours of overtime were common, and low or dead
seasons, when underemployment prevailed.[5]

Three quarters of the clothing workforce was female.[6] In Paris, center of
haute couture, women who wanted to work during the low season agreed to
work long into the night, without overtime pay, in the seven hundred shops
where *veillées* were customary during the high season. Nearly one third of the
944 seamstresses who petitioned against *veillées* in 1891 were willing to stay
late if they were paid overtime.[7] Critics of this system blamed the erratic nature of the industry on consumer demand, either by "capricious" ladies want-

ing their ball gowns the next day or, more realistically, by foreign buyers who came twice yearly, placed large orders, and insisted upon rapid delivery.[8] The refusal of employers in the highly volatile high-fashion industry to risk production in advance of orders also contributed to instability.

When Jeanne Bouvier was a young milliner in the early 1880s, she was paid by the piece. In the good season, she averaged thirty to forty francs weekly; in the dead season, she earned only twelve or fifteen francs a week. She liked the millinery workshop because she met other girls her age there. Although she then lived in a sixth-floor attic room without heat or cooking facilities, her neighbors helped one another "like a big family." When Bouvier was a seamstress in the late 1880s, the shop owners regularly kept her and other seamstresses until two in the morning. After going without food from the four o'clock afternoon tea break, Bouvier had to walk three quarters of an hour to her residence in a working-class suburb because buses did not run after midnight.[9]

Fish, fruit, and vegetable canneries hired large numbers of girls and women seasonally and casually, so that girls and women hoping to be hired lined up outside plants as early as 4 A.M. Only the forty-four braid plants in Saint Chamond regularly employed thousands of women (1,866 adults and 1,253 adolescents) from midnight until noon. Given the lack of alternatives in single-industry towns, women in these towns were not opposed to night shifts. In the east, cotton spinners testified to a legislative subcommittee that they preferred night shifts because they could leave their children with their husbands and because there was less supervision at night. Discerning that employers were manipulating these women, the subcommittee disregarded their testimony. Regrettably, the subcommittee also shelved motions to provide on-site day care for day shifts.[10]

Information about mothers spending fifteen hours away from home expedited passage of sex-specific labor laws. The first decade of debates about these laws (1879–89) neither reflected nor generated research into the susceptibility of women to workplace hazards. Instead, politicians made vague statements about women's special vulnerability to allegedly dangerous conditions. The politicians did not seek documentation because few challenged their statements. In the prolonged legislative debates preceding the law, only two discussions about work processes occurred. Both times, rhetoric about long working days keeping women from homemaking interrupted brief descriptions of the accelerated and relentless pace of mechanized work.[11]

During the 1880s, hygienists quoted legislators rather than the other way around. Hygienist Dr. Henri Napias shifted his support of universal labor standards to sex- and age-specific standards, using the rationale of women and children being more affected by long days and unhealthy conditions. He quoted Dr. Theodore Roussel (most often associated with the 1874 law regulating wetnursing) as a legislator whose "arguments relied upon physiology." Roussel lamented the number of young women "unfit to be mothers and nurses" because unregulated industrial labor impeded the muscular and structural development necessary for "the great functions for which nature destined her." When the legislature debated banning women's nocturnal employment, Napias added a familiar moral argument: "women at work, at night, means men in bars and children in the street."[12]

Legislative supporters only sought medical opinion after an 1889 amendment to remove women from the clause on night work.[13] At the request of the Chamber of Deputies, the Academy of Medicine appointed a commission of two hygienists and two obstetricians who promptly reported that nocturnal work was "prejudicial" not only to women's health but to infants' health as well. Claiming that close work in gaslight ruined eyesight, and night shifts exacerbated women's predisposition to anemia and nervous disorders, the commission pronounced nocturnal labor "especially fatal" for females. Although studies had found a high incidence of eyestrain and anemia in workshops employing women at night, neither medical condition was normally fatal. After emotive rhetoric about babies languishing because of their mothers' "continual absence," the commission cited the high rate of infant mortality in France, implying a correlation between maternal employment at night and infant mortality. With very little discussion, the academy resolved that women's nocturnal work had "the most disastrous consequences."[14]

Prof. Adrien Proust (father of the novelist Marcel Proust and chair of hygiene at the Paris Medical School) responded to the political controversy by publishing an article surveying existing knowledge on women's constitution and nocturnal labor. In his general hygiene text, Proust argued that women were more vulnerable because of "native delicacy," but he conceded "that woman is more resistant than man, she supports suffering, privation, and hemorrhages better, and this resistance translates, at least statistically, into lower mortality rates and greater longevity."[15] His article eliminated the concession. Because night work was fatiguing, and women had "a special delicacy," Proust concluded that night shifts destroyed their "already unstable equilibrium"—a discreet reference to their reproductive functions. His only data indicated that working women took more sick days than working men, with no correlation to nocturnal labor or unevenly distributed childcare responsibilities.[16]

An 1892 labor law set a standard of eleven hours of (paid) work for women in industries employing nonfamily members.[17] Excluding family workshops left an estimated 1,199,296 female homeworkers without standards for working hours. The law did not cover two of the three largest employers of women—agriculture and the service sector—and thereby left three quarters of the female labor force beyond the pale of the law. Yet retail clerks and peasant women put in very long days. Emilie Carles reported that peasant women were "busy from morning to night," doing practically everything except plowing on small farms. Before Carles's brother left for the front during the First World War, he taught her how to plow, which was extremely difficult for her because the plow handle was "designed for a man." Every time the plow hit a stone, she "got the handle in the chest or face."[18] In retail stores, a government inquiry documented twelve- to fifteen-hour days because stores stayed open to accommodate customers who had to shop after their workday and because female clerks had to clean the stores after closing. After this inquiry, the legislature passed an act requiring seats for all female employees in commercial establishments, which was never enforced because inspection of the 615,000 shops in France would have overtaxed the inspection service. Only department stores experimented with overlapping shifts to allow a ten-hour workday and a twelve- to fifteen-hour shopping day. After six years of lobbying by the food and retail employees unions and the Church-backed Popular League for Sunday Rest, a 1906 law mandated Sunday closings except for small shops—the majority of all shops. Fewer than one third of all shops closed on Sundays, although a weekly break from paid work became customary.

Laws regarding hours and weekly rest ignored the emerging feminine profession of nursing. As hospitals began to make the transition from religious to lay nursing after 1905, some lay nurses organized and demanded regulation of hours. Because they had to compete with the dedicated nursing sisters, and many had to room and board on site, making it difficult to avoid overtime, lay nurses only managed to obtain weekly breaks.[19] Teaching, the other semiprofession with many women, also did not have standards for hours. Many teachers exhausted themselves preparing lessons, taking courses, and offering evening adult classes.[20] Even Carles, who had plowed fields without ill effect, fell sick from her teaching schedule.[21]

To avoid the eleven-hour day, manufacturers formed split shifts to permit women to prepare raw materials and finish the products made by men working twelve-hour days. After a 1900 law extended standards to men "working with the protected population" and mandated a ten-hour day by 1904,[22] employers segregated men and women in separate shops so that men could work twelve-hour days and women could continue to prepare raw materials and finish products on split shifts. In 1901, the administration outlawed this practice. Although the law prescribed breaks of an hour, employers took advantage of the absence of penalties if workers returned to work before the end of a break. Most women, paid by the piece, had a financial incentive to return to work early. Moreover, many married women wanted to finish their formal workday early in order to find time for housework and childcare, and many single women preferred to work longer hours for five days a week in order to leave early on Saturdays and visit their families in the countryside. To limit the impact of the legal workday, employers eliminated two of the meal breaks, which happened without much resistance. Working women such as Jeanne Bouvier, who valued workplace sociability, were less receptive to employer efforts to end "distractions" such as socializing around the boilers.

Gradually, the workday was rationalized, routinized, and intensified. Women spent less time at the plant, but many working mothers lost some of the flexibility that had eased their triple burden slightly.

Another article of the 1892 law forbade women's paid labor between 9 P.M. and 5 A.M. The article was riddled with exemptions to accommodate female job ghettos. These included sixty days of overtime in seasonal industries and permanent seven-hour shifts in plants with continuous furnaces. As the legislative reporter explained, a sudden end to overtime in the Parisian luxury trades would endanger an important export sector, and women were "irreplaceable" on the night shifts of sugar refineries and glassworks.[23] Administrative rulings authorized five industries to apply for overtime permits. Because clothing was one of the favored five, permits affected 3.5 million women and 200 million woman-days in four years. A few couturiers renounced *veillées* voluntarily, but most cut back to every second day in the good season, which at least allowed seamstresses to get more sleep on intervening nights. By 1912, the administration only granted permits to 249 shops that sewed mourning clothing. Unfortunately, many subcontractors ignored the law. They took advantage of the large pool of women able to sew—thanks to sewing lessons in all Catholic and many public schools for girls[24]—to pay extremely low wages, which forced seamstresses to break the law. Overtime rules fueled the trend to sewing at home, either after legal working hours or full time.

By 1900, most industries observed the partial ban on night shifts. The unchanged ratio of female spinners suggests that relatively few women lost their jobs. Even before France signed the Berne Convention, which ended exemptions for women's night shifts in 1911, the number of women on night shifts had declined to 490. The following year only 14 women worked night shifts. Political consensus on the prohibition of women on night shifts lasted until 1970, except during the war.

Within days of the declaration of war in 1914, the minister of labor lifted the overtime regulations for defense industries and ordered labor inspectors to facilitate the substitution of women and adolescents for mobilized men. In a later, revealing remark, the minister explained that women had to be recruited because of a "deficient labor pool." These and subsequent measures soon saw women working twelve-hour, virtually uninterrupted shifts, including at night and sometimes without weekly breaks.[25] After the war, France signed an international labor convention setting a universal standard of eight hours. The 1919 law implementing the convention mandated a forty-eight-hour week that translated, in practice, into a mix of nine- and seven-hour days each week. Once again there were liberal provisions for overtime, but this time they were for adult men.[26] The 1919 law did not abrogate the sex-specific ban on night work. The administration blocked manufacturers' postwar efforts to keep women on night shifts.[27]

In the twentieth century, domestic labor encountered mounting criticism from organized clothing workers, public health doctors, consumer groups, and feminists.[28] An investigation of lingerie work between 1905 and 1908 revealed sweated labor conditions and generated interest in a minimum-wage solution. The Labor Office interviewed 129 manufacturers, 112 subcontractors, and 2,013 workers. Their testimony indicated working days exceeding ten hours and piece rates equivalent to ten to twenty centimes per hour (and high rates of charitable or welfare assistance)[29] in the countryside. The study found two thirds of the urban workshops to be crowded, stuffy, and dark. Most workers were women who started sewing lingerie after they wed (because many workshops fired married women) or after they had children (because homework seemed compatible with child minding). The report blamed the degraded conditions on the oversupply of labor, competition from convents and women's prisons, and a casual labor market.[30]

After several years of dickering about how to set minimum wages in diverse industries and dispersed work sites, in 1915 the legislature passed an act mandating regional minimums based upon "the ordinary hourly or daily wage of a nonspecialized worker in the region." Later regional committees also considered the cost of living. The act induced some manufacturers to move operations to cheaper, rural regions. Setting minimums for dozens of different items was time consuming; minimums were only revised every three years, yet the cost of living nearly doubled during the war. Many homeworkers found higher paying jobs during the war.[31]

After a decade of postwar criticism, the domestic labor law was extended to men and was based upon an eight-hour workday.[32] Postwar unions of clothing workers condemned both domestic work and the laws regulating it. One feisty activist, Louise Chenevard, denounced "the lie" that domestic employment helped preserve home and children, explaining that few women could simultaneously fill an order, mind children, and take care of the home. After the social insurance laws of 1928 and the labor accords of 1934, as manufacturers turned to domestic work to avoid paying insurance premiums or implementing the forty-hour week, unions lobbied for coverage of domestic workers and wage parity with shopworkers.[33] Here matters stood at the outbreak of the Second World War.

Between the wars, Social Catholics regularly raised the issue of the exhaustion women suffered because of "the uninterrupted succession" of paid and unpaid work.[34] By the 1930s, Social Catholic women's groups were publishing reports on mothers' work inside and outside the home.[35] Their reports presented valuable information about women's endurance, although their interpretations were dubious. When one investigator found only 7 of 140 working women in poor health, she cited figures from the United States and Germany showing that working women were more prone to illness, which she attributed to exhaustion from menstruation, anemia, and extra housework. Typically, a brief section on the impact of work on reproductive organs preceded an extensive section on miscarriages, stillbirths, and the birth rate.[36] At the depth of the Depression, Catholic unions debated the notions of suppressing women's factory work and offering bonuses to wives to stay home.[37] Louise Chambelland, a communist union organizer, asked two pertinent questions: "On what basis?" and "Paid by whom?"[38] No one provided a satisfactory answer before or after the Second World War.

Engendering Occupational and Industrial Hygiene

In the last four decades of the nineteenth century, the number of French treatises on occupational and industrial hygiene increased dramatically.[39] In the 1880s, specialized journals and conference proceedings swelled this literature.

Despite these changes, the new field did not deviate significantly from the historic pattern of concentrating on masculine work. When the new experts did consider women's work, they displayed new interest in reproduction. The combined effect was a more gendered representation of labor, with few positive suggestions about how to lighten women's double or triple workload.

From the beginning, occupational hygiene implied that (paid) productive work was masculine. About 90 percent of Bernardino Ramazzini's *Diseases of Workers*, which was translated, edited, and plagiarized throughout the eighteenth century, was devoted to masculine trades. Ramazzini emphasized trades with many visible deformities and workplace fatalities—trades more often performed by men. Ramazzini's sources skewed his findings: he consulted doctors, who treated only critical illnesses and traumatic injuries, for information.[40] In the nineteenth century, occupational hygienists paid scant attention to women because women were concentrated in trades that were not prone to the catastrophic accidents easily attributed to working conditions. At the end of the century, the ratio of male to female victims of workplace fatalities and traumatic injuries was more than twenty-five to one.[41] By then, the worksites most exposed to cave-ins and explosions—underground mines—employed almost no women underground, and the few exceptions toiled in tiny family exploitations. The small number (2 percent) of mine and quarry workers who were women worked on the surface, where they did arduous jobs such as pulling railcars filled with ore.[42]

The Industrial Health and Safety Act of 1893 removed women from some egregiously dangerous masculine worksites. Besides banning women, adolescent girls, and children from underground mining, the act barred the same groups from sixty-one other "inherently harmful" trades, most of which handled volatile substances such as mercury or polished metal. Fewer than one in ten workers in these trades were female. Another article prohibited women, adolescents, and children from 119 workshops in direct contact with dangerous materials but permitted women in the safer (although not necessarily healthy) preparatory and finishing rooms of the same plants. These articles reinforced masculine domination of dangerous trades and restricted women's access to high-wage jobs in expanding sectors of the economy—for example, in the chemical industry. Conversely, neither the 1893 act nor its amendments over the next decade barred women from new feminine trades such as ceramic lithography, despite the existence of studies showing that lead-silicate powder posed a risk of lead poisoning. Instead, the administration applied regulations that were general, but difficult to enforce, concerning evacuating harmful particulates. (In the 1920s, an amendment to the 1919 law on occupational diseases recognized lead poisoning from ceramic and porcelain decoration.)[43] Further catering to feminine industries, prewar acts allowed exceptions for ten "dangerous industries where we have always employed women because of their patience, attentiveness, manual dexterity, and supple movements." These industries included the manufacture of cartridges and explosives, where 45 percent or more of the labor force was female.[44]

The bruises, sprains, and chronic pain associated with the cramped conditions and repetitive motions of many women's jobs were not recognized as occupational accidents.[45] Women most often sustained abrasions, contusions, and fractures of the hands and arms either because the installation of new machinery in older workshops left little space between machines for women's work smocks or because the women reached inside operating machinery to clean it.[46] Employers did not pay for downtime to brush out the tufts of cotton, linen, or woolen fiber that drifted around textile mills, settled into partially open machines, and clogged them. Labor inspectors recommended locked grills over gears because workers who were not paid for downtime removed protective devices to clean running machinery. Nevertheless, an administrative circular sanctioned the custom of dislodging lint and other waste from running machinery. Although 101 factories voluntarily installed barriers, which reduced the number of accidents, the circular was not rescinded for more than a decade because protective devices increased the cost of machinery by 5 to 10 percent.[47]

When early occupational hygienists, trained in humoral medicine, recognized that women worked, they displayed considerable interest in the effects on the menstrual cycle. Ramazzini's chapter on laundresses mentioned menstrual "deficiencies" from standing in cold water (which, he contended, blocked "gross juices"). Ramazzini's only reference to pregnancy came in a general indictment of the prolonged leaning position involved in weaving.[48] By the late nineteenth century, occupational hygienists influenced by endocrinology (with its internal interpretation of menstrual difficulties) were less interested in menstruation. However, hygienists incorporated new knowledge about pregnancy, and especially about the effects of continual tension in the extensor muscles on pregnant textile operatives, into their texts.[49]

Traditionally, the emergence of industrial hygiene is correlated with the spread of factory production and the formation of associations of industrialists to prevent workplace accidents. Another long-acknowledged factor is the acceptance of germ theory.[50] Although biopolitical interests are rarely acknowledged, they certainly contributed to the gendered character of industrial hygiene.

Industrialization and its accompanying social disruption affected the new experts' attitudes toward working women. Factories made women's work visible and threatening because it seemed to (and sometimes did) displace men and appeared to (but rarely did) undermine the patriarchal family.[51] Employers' patronage of workplace safety had repercussions for the new scientific methods. Experiments dating from the 1860s focused on workplaces rather than workers. Hoping to prevent serious accidents in their plants, enlightened employers financed experiments that privileged engineering problems and solutions. Although this school of industrial hygiene blamed careless workers for accidents, it usually advocated covering moving parts of motors and building more spacious plants rather than intervening in work behaviors.

Microbiology had more complex repercussions. Germ theory reoriented industrial hygiene toward exposure to invisible microbes and industrial byproducts such as cotton dust. As the "strategy of the invisible" gained allies, microenvironmental pollution from chemicals and biological materials as well as microclimatic factors such as temperature and humidity became central concerns.[52] Generally, this orientation did not predispose industrial hygienists to study individual or collective susceptibilities. However, the conception of a human body "porous to invisible invasion by germs" converged with notions of woman's body, with its layer of soft, fatty tissues, as more open to invasion. As gynecologists developed "the scientific conviction that poisons filter through the placenta,"[53] industrial hygienists detoured into reproductive consequences. In his 1880s text, Léon Poincaré stated but did not substantiate that industrial poisoning in factories with women workers increased the incidence of abortions, stillborn, and premature infants, or depopulation.[54]

The publication of birth and death rates directed attention to infant mortality rates. At midcentury, hygienists and obstetricians began to calculate the rates of miscarriage, stillbirths, and infant mortality among lead workers and their offspring. Even though they discovered high rates of stillbirths and neonatal deaths among the offspring of male as well as female lead workers, they found a stronger correlation with maternal lead poisoning. These statistics prompted scientific research into lead residue in fetuses and breast milk. Theories about maternal poisoning through the placenta and the breast were more comprehensible than establishing the more tenuous connection between con-

taminated sperm and fetuses or newborns. The information about lead in fetuses and breast milk, together with the cultural association of reproduction
with motherhood, meant that maternal transmission received more publicity.[55]

Toward the end of the nineteenth century, fears about degeneration infiltrated the interpretation of work-related research. Some hygienists began to
speculate that lead poisoning produced "beings doomed to degeneration
(idiots, imbeciles, and epileptics)." Speculation was "corroborated" by studies
of the effects of lead on pregnancy, not on the infants themselves. A review of
the literature acknowledged that either parent with lead poisoning "contami-
nated" the descendants, yet argued that woman must be "specially protected
for herself, for her organism offers less resistance" to lead poisoning.[56]

In 1875, Dr. Alexander Layet of the Bordeaux Faculty of Medicine published what became, for forty years, the standard reference work in occupational hygiene. Layet located the subject matter between "social hygiene" and
the general practitioner's concern with individual health. Although Layet and
his followers contended that "misery, immorality, carelessness, and brutalisa-
tion predispose workers to illness," they did not consider low wages or living
conditions.[57] This delimitation meant that many diseases endemic in feminine
trades could be attributed to weaker constitutions, poor nutrition, and bad
habits without investigation of the health consequences of earning, on average, half men's wages or of working in crowded workshops.

Tuberculosis was relegated to the realm of public health, which mapped
the incidence of the disease by population density and locality. Prominent
physicians identified a high rate of tuberculosis in the sixth- and seventh-story
lodgings typical of Paris and other cities, but it was socialist investigators who
noted that maids lodged in those tiny, stuffy rooms as a condition of their employment in lower-story, bourgeois apartments.[58] Just the same, the higher
death rate of young women from tuberculosis was traced to "less energy" or
other shortcomings in their systems. Industrial hygienists' dismissal of tuberculosis represented contemporary thinking about its etiology[59] but ignored
evidence about high rates of pulmonary tuberculosis in sweated trades that
were often carried out in garret rooms.[60]

The 1902 public health law mandated a window in every workroom; two
years later, a health and safety decree required seven cubic meters of air per
working woman to improve ventilation and circulation. Because most small
workshops did not meet these standards, neither the owners nor the women
working in them welcomed inspections. The owners feared orders to renovate, and the workers feared unemployment during shutdowns to renovate

or loss of employment if owners chose to cut the number of workers in the existing space. Inspectors did not explain new theories about exposure to invisible hazards to working women, who remained more concerned about drafts and keeping warm.[61]

Some socialists correlated the extent of pulmonary tuberculosis with the length of employment in textile factories filled with organic particles.[62] Industrial hygienists began to correlate similar pulmonary afflictions with other industrial pollutants. By the 1920s, specialists in infectious diseases considered occupational causes of tuberculosis and spotlighted high mortality rates from tuberculosis among women working in textile factories.[63] Yet a 1936 book on occupational pathology in the cotton industry deplored the paucity of French research on tuberculosis. Predictably, the author, Dr. Maurice Oster, found several papers on the impact of textile work on pregnancies and births. These papers proved that pregnant operatives who stood while they worked had 50 percent more premature or forceps-assisted deliveries than those who sat to work.[64]

Layet referred to rates of premature births and of infant mortality in relation to certain maternal work processes and work environments.[65] His brief and allusive references had a long afterlife. As late as 1924, a study of occupational illnesses cited Layet on "miscarriages, premature births, stillbirths, and congenital debility in children" born to women suffering from industrial poisoning.[66] The author, Dr. Piriou, may have cited Layet because subsequent research on the impact of maternal employment on infant debility and death was contradictory. In 1897, Dr. Etienne of Nancy reported that maternal work in a tobacco plant had little influence on infantile mortality unless the mother continued to breast-feed after she returned to work. Etienne based his conclusions on observations of ninety-three pregnancies and a theory about the transmission of tobacco poison through breast milk. About the same time, Dr. Darquier of Toulouse kept records of 507 babies at the crèche attached to the local tobacco plant. Twice as many of the infants who died had been bottle fed rather than breast fed, which Darquier interpreted as evidence of the deleterious effects of bottle feeding and maternal overwork.[67] In the early twentieth century, obstetricians and pediatricians became the experts on the correlations among women's employment, pregnancy, births, and babies. Obstetricians and pediatricians led by Profs. Budin and Pinard lobbied for up to two months of paid maternity leave and won a four-week leave in 1913. Other obstetricians offered pregnant women practical advice about avoiding raw materials that endangered fetuses and infants.[68]

Layet reported that women most often suffered from skin ulcers, eye infections, head colds, sore throats, and gastrointestinal conditions from contact with corrosive materials and other irritants. Because these complaints rarely caused women to quit work abruptly, they were not taken seriously. Yet constant irritation must have worn down resistance to infection. One of the few prewar studies to recognize this established that 15 percent of women who plucked long hairs from rabbit pelts wept continuously, and a slightly smaller percentage had chronically bloodshot eyes. Prof. Heim discovered that organic residue remained in the nasal passages fourteen hours after these women finished work, and he posited, correctly, that this might have long-term health consequences.[69]

Although some general hygienists proclaimed that they were social scientists,[70] sociological investigation had little methodological, as opposed to ideological, impact on industrial hygiene. In the 1830s and 1840s, social hygienists visited workshops, where they talked to workers. These hygienists publicized disturbing details about unhealthy working conditions and introduced moral concerns about "depravity" in mixed-sex workshops other than family workshops. Their intellectual heirs articulated broader concerns about the disruption of family life caused by women's work away from home. After three revolutions and the Paris Commune of 1871, Frédéric Le Play and the social economy movement proclaimed the patriarchal domestic family, with a wage-earning father and a housewife-mother, an essential foundation for social stability.[71] Few late nineteenth-century industrial hygienists followed sociologists' example of observing workplaces and interviewing workers, but most shared their assumptions that women's rightful place was in the home.

Industrial hygienists who observed and conferred with working women gathered precious evidence, and many who began with prejudices about female fragility ended by paying homage to the stamina of working women. Dr. Jules Arnould's study of women employed in cotton-drying sheds where the air was charged with fibrous particles went beyond the usual technique of taking medical histories from doctors' reports. By asking the women about their symptoms, Arnould learned that they had nausea, headaches, conjunctivitis, bronchitis, and emphysema; his report recommended better ventilation. In a rare admission, Arnould acknowledged that it was difficult to determine the effect of women's work on pregnancies and births because most women in unhealthy occupations left work before giving birth.[72]

Respect for the stamina of working women did not prevent hygienists from advising removal of pregnant women from certain worksites. A 1908 study of a rayon mill found that its workers averaged one more sick day per year than workers in a nearby paper plant. Without exploring the implications of the smell of ether on the breath of all rayon workers, the author, Dr. J. P. Langlois, attributed the difference to a larger proportion of women in the rayon plant: "the morbidity of women is always greater than that of men." Observing that babies of rayon workers were pale and that "large numbers" died in their first year, Langlois speculated that the ether passed through the placenta to the fetus and advised that pregnant women be moved to other jobs.[73]

After hours and safety standards were in place, labor inspectors played a role in industrial hygiene. Although most inspectors were petty bourgeois men, and the remainder were petty bourgeois women, they actually visited women's workshops. Although the men's reports repeat clichés about women's delicate organism and married women's employment destroying the family,[74] neither male nor female inspectors were prisoners of their prejudices. When the dry cleaners union criticized women handling heavy irons during recessions in 1897 and 1907, two industrial hygienists and several inspectors investigated. The two hygienists called this "one of the hardest feminine trades" because leaning over ironing boards increased the risks of stomach ptosis and prolapsed uterus.[75] After visiting hundreds of dry cleaners, the inspectors reported that a third of the women complained about the weight of the iron, but they added that three quarters of the women older than thirty had varicose veins; the inspectors recommended chairs for ironers. Similarly, the inspectors directed attention to the heat, humidity, and smell of benzene in the ironing rooms and obtained stricter regulations about ventilation. (In the interwar, hygienists identified a disease known as benzolism with symptoms ranging from headaches to epileptic seizures, to which women "appeared to be more sensitive, probably because they have more fatty tissues.")[76]

In 1906, the government appointed the Consultative Committee on Industrial Hygiene to study diseases "exclusively or clearly caused by work." Experts outnumbered representatives of the interested parties, which included no women.[77] Ostensibly investigating the health of all workers, researchers examined mainly the effects of toxic substances on men.[78] When these researchers did conduct three case studies in the feminine trade of artificial-flower making and corroborated suspicions about lead poisoning among artificial-flower makers, their results did not prevail over work inspectors' doubts about mortality figures and belief that replacing lead dyes would be too costly in flower making. They were unable to procure the suppression of lead dyes in artificial-flower making.[79]

Establishing occupational morbidity rates was difficult because of problems in proving occupational causation.[80] A 1919 act on "acute or chronic diseases," which concerned inflicted workers "habitually employed in industrial occupations," only recognized saturnism (lead poisoning) from working with lead or lead alloys in twenty-two occupations and mercury poisoning in ten occupations.[81] After studies recommending broader coverage, amendments added many chemicals, gases, caustic agents, and x-rays to the list of dangerous substances. Still, the vast majority of cases involved saturnism, and fewer than 10 percent of them involved women. Aside from employer and medical resistance to reporting cases,[82] isolating working conditions as the effective etiology for complex diseases remained a challenge.[83]

Science and Women's Work

Anson Rabinbach studied the European "science of work" which emerged in the early twentieth century. Based upon new physiological theories of work as a form of energy conversion and upon laboratory study of work, the new science considered overexertion and fatigue as medical disorders. The thermodynamic view of the working body allegedly cleansed work of its social and cultural dimensions.[84] But, as integrated into industrial hygiene, thermodynamics did not cleanse women's work of its social and cultural dimensions.

More scientific industrial hygienists invented techniques to measure aspects of work in the controlled setting of the laboratory. Physiologists introduced instruments such as the cardiograph and sphygmograph to register heart and pulse rates and Etienne Marey's chronophotography to analyze movement itself. Marey claimed that the graphic method eliminated researchers' biases.[85] If systematically applied to women as well as men, these techniques might have refuted prejudices about feminine weakness. Unfortunately, few women were studied. Because of the social stigma about probing (unfamiliar) women's bodies, there were constraints upon testing women in the laboratory. Measuring particular processes fed into the scientific tendency toward conceptual dismantling of the human body, which in turn directed attention to certain parts of the body. In laboratories, essentially "worlds without women," more experiments were conducted on upper-body muscle contractions, where men excelled, than on overall muscle elasticity, where women had an edge.[86]

Given skepticism and stereotypes about women's work capacity, generalizing from male subjects had drawbacks. Research on the weights that people could lift illustrates the problem. Most of the initial experiments tested male subjects categorized by their height and shape as well as their working conditions. The experiments showed that different body types and discontinuous effort precluded simple determination of limits. Although the researchers declared the results inconclusive for men, they decided that general data about women's smaller size warranted weight limits for women. When industrialists inconvenienced by these restrictions obtained a postponement, scientists conducted tests on women to determine more realistic limits. These tests were also inconclusive because the investigators finally recognized that they had to acknowledge the variety in women's physiques, musculature, and endurance.[87] In this instance, the stereotype of woman's weak body only delayed acknowledgment that women's bodies varied.

The Human Machine, the prewar compendium of research most often cited in the interwar, presented more figures on sex differences in the unit on "statics" (anthropometry, morphology, and anatomy) than in the units on kinetics (the study of movement) and dynamics (the study of strength and energy). This disparity might have, but did not, raise any doubt about feminine deficiencies in the workplace. In all three units, the author, Jules Amar, declared that deficiencies, such as lower bone density, which made women more susceptible to fractures, disqualified women from certain jobs.[88] Amar's personal and political views obviously distorted his representation of women's work. He interpreted dynamometer tests showing that women mobilized muscle power slower and less consistently than men to mean that "rational feminism" should demand shorter workdays for women, paid maternity leaves, and bonuses for large families. In a paper reporting an experiment involving four women's startled reactions to unexpected loud noises, as recorded on cardiographs and respiratory gauges, he filtered the results through assumptions about women's physical and psychological constitution. Specifically, he concluded that emotions conditioned all women's activities through the branches of the nerves that govern breathing. In his opinion, feminine emotivity was "fixed by heredity in the nervous system" and constituted "a defense mechanism against overwork." Women should not be employed without passing physiological and psychological examinations.[89]

Generally, cultural assumptions about women's physical capacities and appropriate feminine work influenced scientific interpretation. Armand Imbert promoted Taylorism and the "impartial investigative procedures" of experimental physiology to resolve economic and social problems. In addition to laboratory studies, he advocated direct observation and "minute" analyses of work processes to find the most efficient ways of accomplishing tasks with the least expenditure of energy. After an on-site study of women cutting grape-vines with secaters rigged to register muscular effort, Imbert supported the wage demands of these women. Yet his operating hypothesis about "the sexes" was "the inferiority of the physical strength of the female sex." He posited that women's "special physiological functions" required restrictions on their paid work. Citing dubious data on the influence of mothers' work on newborns, he urged studies of the effect of individual occupations on "the essential functions of women."[90]

Fortunately, not all researchers acted upon such prejudices. Jean-Marie Lahy advocated more precision in laboratory experiments, notably in the two professional journals he edited from 1929 until 1944.[91] Lahy, best known as the "most assiduous opponent of the Taylor system in France,"[92] conducted tests on men and women in the same occupations. For instance, he tested memory, concentration, reaction times, and hand strength in six female and five male typists and reported differences, not by sex, but by level of competence (with a fairly even distribution of men and women in each level). In the "masculine" trade of linotype operators, he decisively disproved stereotypes about women being less productive.[93]

During and immediately after the war, because of wartime demand for labor, researchers took less biased approaches. Labor inspectors measured the muscular effort, energy output, and reaction times of female gunpowder workers and found that they had slightly less strength, slightly longer reaction times, and higher pulse rates at the end of the workday than male coworkers. The introduction of hourly five-minute breaks improved the women's output and halved the number of sick days and voluntary absences.[94] Although the report makes no comparisons with male workers, perhaps because this was traditionally women's work, these results stack up favorably to any research done on male workers.

The exceptions to the more open attitude toward women's physical capacities and productivity remained maternity. A 1919 report to the official Committee on Feminine Work summed up this stance:

> Woman's organism, except in a state of pregnancy or lactation, is able to do the same physical work as that of men, with a reservation about the relative inferiority of their muscular power. In other terms, whatever the duration or intensity of the dynamic effort deployed, the organism does not react differently in either sex, except for the persistence, in women, of localized infirmities and special troubles resulting from an earlier, pathological birth.

At least the author, Dr. Bonnaire, expressed some solicitude for pregnant women themselves, along with their fetuses. Thus he described the fatigue, varicose veins, and so on that women experienced from standing still for long stretches of time when pregnant.[95] As it became apparent that married women and mothers would stay in a labor force, the focus of most industrial and occupational hygiene research on women would be how to accommodate maternal obligations, notably breast-feeding.[96]

Conclusions

By the mid-1930s, scientists were asking more precise questions about the effect of paid labor on women's bodies but were still fixated on the reproductive system. For example, two scientists researched whether standing for hours deformed the pelvises of young women or increased the number of varicose veins in pregnant operatives. A third scientist inquired how textile work differed from housework and began a polemic about the "triple burden" of industrial, house, and childcare work. The physician who reviewed the evidence and exchanges decided that more studies were necessary, but he agreed that industrial work must be banned in a pregnant woman's final trimester and her hours reduced in the second trimester. In addition, he recommended that seating, restrooms, and special meals should be provided and women doctors and nurses should visit regularly to check pregnant women.[97] Such recommendations were unrealistic. Even before the Depression, economic considerations took priority over pronatalism among French employers.

Epilogue

ECAUSE of the Western tradition of associating physicality with being or bioreasoning, Europe has a history of thinking about the body in relation to being. In natural philosophy tradition, as incorporated into Hellenized Christianity, there has been an equally persistent correlation of sexual traits with moral character, or in modern parlance, *gender*. Both of these traditions ordered biosocial traits hierarchically, with men as the prototype and women as the deficient variant. In the eighteenth century, natural scientists and anatomists began discerning sex differences in every body part and inferring gendered personalities, allegedly from these differences but actually from presuppositions about gender roles.

In the century and a half after the Enlightenment, French anatomists and physiologists extended the scope of sex differentiation to the level of the cell and many bodily processes. Together with anthropometrists and anthropologists, these biomedical scientists observed women's bodies through lenses warped by assumptions about sexual and social dichotomies. Although focused on the reproductive system, biomedical researchers sought differences in every system and process. Before and after research into physical dichotomies, they contended that women's bodies were soft, their reproductive organs unstable, and their entire organisms suffused with sexuality; therefore women were sensitive, changeable, and seductive. In the last half of the nineteenth century, as researchers relied more upon measurement and statistics, almost all of their calibrations confirmed their original hypotheses about bipolarity. The result was a surprisingly uniform depiction of "woman's body" and feminine character. Scientists demonstrated that women's bodies had a higher proportion of fat, their bones were less dense, and their upper body was weaker than the prototypical (male) bodies, bones, and upper body. Scientists' projections about feminine personality and role were unsubstantiated by evidence because most simply stated that female reproductive organs or cycles made women more nervous and irrational than men and dangerously seductive to men.

In the late nineteenth century, medical specialties such as endocrinology were added to this biosocial concoction. Endocrinology carried the biological reduction of sex differences to the level of hormones, conceived as carriers of sexual identity, and introduced contradictory implications for biomedical understanding of woman's body and identity. On the one hand, endocrinologists did real research about secondary sexual characteristics and the development of sexual identities. On the other hand, hypotheses about hormonally determined sexuality implied impermanent sexual identity, which destabilized the notions of fixed, bipolar sexuality and caused angst. Theories of intersexuality intensified biomedical efforts to bolster an assertive masculine heterosexuality and feminine fertility. Indeed, femininity was reduced conceptually to fertility.

This conceptualization was fraught with contradictions. Each phase of the reproductive cycle—puberty, maternity, and menopause—was treated ambivalently, not as pathological, as physicians had done in the past, but nevertheless as a transitional time when the body was susceptible to disease, and girls and women were prone to irrationality. French physiologists and endocrinologists acknowledged feminine sexuality and identified a critical moment—sexual initiation—in women's life cycle. But virtually all French physiologists and physicians subordinated feminine sexuality to women's reproductive function—and to their own pronatalist and eugenic agendas. This fixation is best illustrated by the new specialty of occupational and industrial hygiene, which paid more attention to the impact of women's work on pregnancies, births, and babies than to the conditions of women's productive labor.

One reason for the consistently reproductive depiction of women in biomedical discourse was the absence of women in the laboratory and the underrepresentation of women in medical schools. Another reason was the high proportion of eugenists and pronatalists among biologists and physicians interested in women. A third explanation for the continuity of the biomedical model of femininity as fertility was the prominence of two biopolitical issues in the Third Republic: degeneration and depopulation.

Degeneration theorists attributed the military defeat of France in 1870 to a lack of vitality in the population and to high rates of infant mortality, both of which thwarted plans for revenge. In both scenarios, theorists implicated women as mothers, and more pragmatic thinkers, including politicians, decided that mothers needed instruction in "maternal science." Similarly, once eugenists identified syphilis as a hereditary disease, they tried to prevent infection of the next generation by providing more information about venereal diseases and promoting (marital) sex education.

Defeat in the Franco-Prussian War and the massive loss of life in the First World War rekindled longstanding anxieties about depopulation. Following the biomedical custom of assigning women responsibility for reproduction, French scientists and society blamed women for low birth rates. In an effort to control the birth rate, governments passed laws such as the infamous anti-abortion law curbing female-controlled contraception. Finally, recurring cultural crises over independent women, who were often single and sometimes feminists, induced scientists and cultural critics to disseminate biomedical notions of sexual dichotomies and social complementarity.

In the Third Republic, French girls and women learned about the biomedical vision of their bodies through physical culture, or the conscious disciplining of the body. Although physical culture ideally meant maternal guidance in the home, the state and experts intervened to direct, supplement, or supplant mothers. The public school system introduced hygiene and home economics courses, and physicians known as hygienists wrote dozens of health manuals for women. Other experts introduced biomedical views in school gymnastics courses and books on sex advice.

Since the eighteenth century, in order to prevent epidemic diseases such as cholera, French hygienists had tried to publicize new ideas about clean air and water. With the advent of Pasteur's germ theory in the 1880s, hygienists put more emphasis on private cleanliness to prevent epidemics and to ensure individual as well as societal health. The new generation of hygienists realized that they had to persuade mothers, who were primarily responsible for housework and childcare, to implement the new practices of domestic and personal cleanliness and to inculcate them in the next generation. To these ends, hygienists wrote dozens of books and thousands of columns in women's magazines on housework, family medicine, and women's health. Initially these books and articles presented elementary anatomy, physiology, and microbiology in dull and intimidating ways. But soon French hygienists recognized that they needed to entice women to apply and teach personal and household cleanliness by promising them something more concrete and personal than family health. Accordingly, they touted cleanliness as a necessary component of beauty and social distinction.

Dedicated to improving the health of French citizens, ensuring social stability, and preparing for the next war, republicans invested in preventive health measures such as hygiene and home economics courses in the school system and public nursing education and services in the community. The school system introduced basic biological notions into hygiene and home economics courses, and the new public nursing school curriculum was based upon asepsis. In turn, educated women and public nurses brought the new hygienic practices into French homes.

Finally, biomedical and hygienic notions infiltrated another genre of nonfiction written for, and often by, women. Many of the original beauty books and beauty advice columns in magazines were written by hygienists who emphasized cleanliness and skin care and offered advice on the corresponding cosmetics: soaps, cleansing lotions, and creams. As cleanliness gradually became a sign of social distinction, nonmedical beauty counselors developed the hygienic theme. But beauty manuals and women's magazines were also driven by commercial considerations, notably those of two major French industries, cosmetics and haute couture.

From the 1880s to the 1940s, this potent blend of biomedical, hygienic, beauty, and fashion promotion supported by state and business interests was fed to French girls and women in increasingly palatable doses. Bourgeois girls and women, who could afford the bathtubs, cleaning products, cosmetics, and clothing involved, adopted many of the associated bodily ideals and practices. Women bathed more often and bought more bath and beauty products because they were attracted by the message that they deserved to take care of their bodies and themselves. Of course, rising incomes and standards of living, and more precarious marital relations, which put more pressure on wives to remain attractive to their husbands, also contributed to women's attention to their bodies.

Conversely, women resisted the principal message in all of the biomedical and hygienic discourse: to have more babies. Another reading of the continued low rate of marital fertility might focus on the role of husbands, given evidence that the main form of birth control was the male-dominated one of coitus interruptus. Certainly, the financial costs of raising children influenced many couples. However, this book has argued that there were other reasons for women's resistance to the natalist message—namely, internal inconsistencies in the natalist agenda and women's own sense of self-preservation.

One inconsistency was the failure of the educational system to include in the curriculums of girls schools units on the anatomy, physiology, and hygiene of puberty, sexual intercourse, conception, or birth. The Catholic Church and most parents opposed the inclusion of this kind of material on what they considered to be private matters. At the same time, the Church and many parents failed to offer girls enough information to correct misunderstandings and to alleviate apprehensions about menstruation, sex, pregnancy, and birth. Even the new subgenre of sex guides for fiancées did not describe the external genitalia, including the entrance to the vagina, or intercourse, despite the fixation of parallel guides for fiancés on defloration, presented as necessarily bloody, with little instruction about foreplay. What emerges from both sets of premarital guides is a picture of a joyless, and possibly brutal, sexual initiation, which can hardly have facilitated first sex or encouraged future sexual congress. It is true that marriage manuals began to entertain the possibility of feminine sexual pleasure and to enjoin husbands to prepare and satisfy their wives sexually. Yet most of these manuals, which were addressed to husbands, admitted that feminine pleasure was unnecessary for conception and that frequent or energetic orgasms on the part of their wives were inimical to conception. Had sex experts taken a cue from the way beauty counselors and hygienists promoted bathing, they might have included the individual incentive of sexual pleasure along with social benefit of procreation.

Compounding these contradictions about sexuality, the burgeoning number of guides for mothers-to-be offered an even more troubling representation of maternity, or more precisely, pregnancy and birth. Because of their medical training, most of the authors of these guides concentrated on the physical problems associated with pregnancy and described labor as necessarily very painful. Although the introduction of asepsis and the new system of maternity wards improved maternal and infant chances of surviving hospital births, the systematic refusal of anesthetic to women in labor did not enhance women's expectations of a comfortable labor and delivery. The state and employers implemented maternity leaves and family allowances for working mothers, but neither significantly improved the situation of working women who were pregnant or carrying a triple workload. Women's desire for self-preservation might well have overridden the few inducements to have large families.

There are other indications of women's resistance to the biomedical and biosocial agenda. One indication is the repetition of advice to women to exercise more, which suggests that earlier recommendations had not been followed. Other indications are found in the health guides written for women by women physicians who refused to reduce femininity to fertility; they accepted, and in two cases approved of, feminine sexual desire. A few timidly endorsed family limitation to maintain women's health, and the same few subtly suggested female-controlled contraception. Several women hygienists advocated more appealing kinds of gymnastics for girls and noncompetitive sports for women.

Other, more ambiguous kinds of resistance can be discerned in the debates about girls gymnastics and women's sports. The proponents of physical education for girls did not challenge the military, muscular, and masculine model of gymnastics as much as adapt it to feminine tastes and feminine stereotypes. The resulting programs did not introduce girls to a full range of physical activities, but they also did not subject them to the authoritarian and regimented program for boys. Thanks to the inclusion of dance and rhythmic gymnastics, girls physical education may have been enjoyable. Similarly, many pioneer sportswomen overcompensated for their physical prowess in "the arena of masculinity" by stressing their femininity, but their feats inspired the next generation of women and expanded the realm of physical expression for less athletic women.

Notes

Acknowledgments

1. For example, "Body/Power," "The Eye of Power," and "The History of Sexuality," in *Selected Interviews and Other Writings 1972–1977*, ed. Colin Gordon (New York, 1980).

2. Pierre Bourdieu, *The Logic of Practice* (Stanford, 1990).

3. Emily Martin, *The Woman in the Body: A Cultural Analysis of Reproduction* (Boston, 1987).

Introduction

1. Daniel Pick, *Faces of Degeneration: A European Disorder, c. 1848–c. 1918* (Cambridge, U.K., 1989) 40 ff.

2. Karen Offen, "Depopulation, Nationalism, and Feminism in *fin-de-siècle* France," *American Historical Review*, 89 (1984): 648–76.

3. Robert A. Nye, *Masculinity and Male Codes of Honor in Modern France* (New York, 1993) 77–83 (quote 93).

4. Theresa McBride, "Divorce and the Republican Family," in *Gender and the Politics of Social Reform in France, 1870–1914*, ed. Elinor A. Accampo, Rachel G. Fuchs, and Mary Lynn Stewart (Baltimore, 1995). See also Anthyme Saint-Paul, *Du Célibat au mariage: Lettre à M. l'Abbé Bolo* (Paris, 1891).

5. Jules Courmont and A. Rochaix, *Précis d'hygiène*, 4th ed. (Paris, 1932) 23–27 and 30–36.

6. Jean Elizabeth Pedersen, "Regulating Abortion and Birth Control: Gender, Medicine, and Republican Politics in France, 1870–1920," *French Historical Studies* 19, 3 (1996): 673–98.

7. Oyeronke Oyewumi, *The Invention of Women: Making an African Sense of Western Gender Discourses* (Minneapolis, 1997) 1–31.

8. Maryanne Cline Horowitz, "Aristotle and Women," *Journal of the History of Biology* 9, 2 (1976): 182–213.

9. Barbara Duden, *The Woman Beneath the Skin: A Doctor's Patients in Eighteenth-Century Germany*, trans. Thomas Dunlap (Cambridge, Mass., 1991) 21.

10. Margaret M. Miles, *Carnal Knowing: Female Nakedness and Religious Meaning in the Christian West* (New York, 1991) 85–144.

11. Thomas Laqueur, *Making Sex: Body and Gender from the Greeks to Freud* (Cambridge, Mass., 1990) 10 and 149 ff.

12. Londa Schiebinger, *The Mind Has No Sex? Women in the Origins of Modern Science* (Cambridge, Mass., 1989) 190–91 and 206.

13. Christine Delphy, *Close to Home: A Materialist Analysis of Women's Oppression* (London, 1984).

14. Laqueur, *Making Sex,* 152.

15. *The Encyclopédie,* ed. John Lough (London, 1971) 468–81. My translations.

16. Lieselotte Steinbrugge, *The Moral Sex: Woman's Nature in the French Enlightenment,* trans. P. E. Selwyn (Oxford, 1995) 24–26.

17. Jean-Jacques Rousseau, *Emile,* trans. Barbara Foxley (London, 1974) 321–22, 324–26, 328, and 331–32.

18. Geneviève Fraisse, *Muse de la raison: La Démocratie exclusive et la différences des sexes* (Aix-en-Provence, 1989) 9 ff.

19. Joan Wallach Scott, *Only Paradoxes to Offer: French Feminists and the Rights of Man* (Cambridge, Mass., 1996).

20. Joan Wallach Scott, "French Feminists and the Rights of Man: Olympe de Gouges's Declaration," *History Workshop Journal,* 28 (fall, 1989).

21. Olwen H. Hufton, *Women and the Limits of Citizenship in the French Revolution* (Toronto, 1992) 3 ff. Hufton does not note the exclusion of men of color and slaves.

22. Scott, *Only Paradoxes to Offer,* 90 ff.

23. Abbé Charles Grimaud, *Aux Mères et à leurs grandes jeunes filles: Futures épouses,* 19th ed. (Paris, 1927).

24. Karen Offen, "Women, Citizenship, and Suffrage with a French Twist, 1789–1993" in *Suffrage and Beyond: International Feminist Perspectives,* ed. Caroline Daley and Melanie Nolan (Auckland, New Zealand, 1994). See also Pierre Rosanvallon, *Le Sacré du citoyen* (Paris, 1992) 395 and 409; Raymond Huard, *Le Suffrage universel en France, 1848–1946* (Paris, 1991) 203–5.

25. Jack D. Ellis, *The Physician-Legislators of France: Medicine and Politics in the Early Third Republic, 1870–1914* (Cambridge, U.K., 1990) 4.

26. Rosanvallon, *Le Sacré du citoyen,* 405 and 410.

27. *Sénat, Documents parlementaires, 1919,* Annexe 563 (Séance 3 Oct. 1919) Rapport, 814–16.

28. Huard, *Le Suffrage universel en France,* 44–46.

29. "The Feminist Movement in France: Public Opinion," in *Feminisms in the Belle Epoque,* ed. J. Waelti-Walters and S. Hause (Lincoln, Neb., 1994) 59–63.

30. Nye, *Masculinity and Male Codes of Honor,* 86–99.

31. E. Sterian, *L'Education sexuelle* (Paris, 1910) 23–24, 36 ff., 50–53, 63–64, 77, and 79 ff. See also Annalise Maugue, *L'Identité masculine en crise au tournant du siècle* (Paris, 1987).

32. Jeanne Stephani-Cherbuliz, *Le Sexe a ses raisons: Instruction et éducation sexuelles* (Paris, 1934) 192–93.

33. Annie Stora-Lamarre, *L'Enfer de la IIIe République: Censeurs et pornographes (1881–1914)* (Paris, 1990) 38 and passim.

34. For example, Emile Laurent, *L'Amour morbide: Etude de psychologie pathologique* (Paris, 1891) 46 ff.; Paul Garnier, *Les Fétichistes pervertis et invertis sexuels* (Paris, 1896).

35. Maurice Boigey, *Sylvie ou la physiologie de la femme nouvelle,* 4th ed. (Paris, 1922).

36. Elaine Showalter, *Sexual Anarchy: Gender and Culture at the Fin de Siècle* (London, 1991) 4–11, 39, and 78.

37. Auguste Preu-Gaillard, *La Femme française: Un Idéal menacé* (Marseille, 1903).

38. Mary Louise Roberts, *Civilization without Sexes: Reconstructing Gender in Postwar France, 1917–1927* (Chicago, 1994) 35–54.

39. P. Vachet, *L'Enigme de la femme* (Paris, 1931).

40. Karen A. Callahand, Introduction, and Ben Love, "Body Images and the Politics of Beauty: Formation of the Feminine Ideal in Medieval and Early Modern Europe," in *Ideals of Feminine Beauty: Philosophical, Social, and Cultural Dimension* (Westport, Conn., 1994) 9, 25, and 28.

41. For example, Gine Maloit, *Guide intime du bonheur de la femme* (Paris, 1939).

42. Institut de la France, *Dictionnaire de l'Académie Française,* 7th ed. (Paris, 1879) and 8th ed. (Paris, 1932).

43. Irene Julier, "Le Maquillage: Pratiques, discours, et interprétations" (Thèse, Paris, 1989). I am grateful to Michelle Perrot for lending me this thesis.

44. Ernest Feydeau, *L'Art de plaire, études d'hygiène, de goût, et de toilette* (Paris, 1873); L. A. Raimbert, *Notions d'hygiène à l'usage de tous les établissements d'instruction* (Paris, 1879) 94.

45. F. W. J. Hemmings, *The Theatre Industry in Nineteenth-Century France* (Cambridge, U.K., 1993) 135–47 and 199–209.

46. Baudelaire, "Eloge du maquillage" from *Le Peintre de la vie moderne* in *Curiosités esthétiques: L'Art romantique,* ed. H. Lemaitre (Paris, 1962) 489–94.

47. Miraille Dottin-Orsini, *Cette femme qu'ils disent fatale* (Paris, 1993).

48. Rose Fortassier, *Les Ecrivains français et la mode de Balzac à nos jours* (Paris, 1988) 139.

49. Cited in Alessandra Borgogelli, "Boldini: Une voie personnelle vers l'Impressionisme," in *Giovanni Boldini* (Rome, 1991) 36.

50. Clara Malraux, *Memoirs*, trans. P. O'Brian (New York, 1967) 159–60 and 238.

51. For example, H. Beque, *La Parisienne: Comédie en trois actes* (Paris, 1885); Alphonse Daudet, *Sappho*, trans. B. Burnham Ives (Boston, 1899).

52. Charles and Anne-Marie Lalo, *La Faillite de la beauté* (Paris, 1923). This is an expansion of a 1913 article in the *Mercure de France*.

53. Léon Groc, "Y-a-t'il une faillite de la beauté?" *Excelsior* (4 Aug. 1913); Polaire, *Polaire par elle-meme* (Paris, 1933) 10 and 116.

54. Octave Uzanne, *La Femme à Paris* (Paris, 1894) and *L'Art et l'artifice de la beauté*, 5th ed. (Paris, 1902) 5–10.

55. For example, E. Monin, *L'Hygiène de la beauté: Formulaire cosmétique* (Paris, 1886); Paul Gastou, *Formulaire cosmétique et esthétique* (Paris, 1913).

56. For example, Vicomtesse Nacla, *Le Boudoir: Conseils d'élégance* (Paris, 1996) 25 ff.

57. N. G. Payot, *Etre belle* (Paris, 1933) 42.

58. Louis Léon-Martin, *L'Industrie de la beauté (dans les coulisses des Instituts de Beauté)* (Paris, 1930) 35–37.

59. Prof. Y. H. Khamed, *Venus Biblion: Arcanes physiologiques. La Beauté conservée et restituée par la science* (Paris, 1899).

60. *Parfum et savon: Annuaire général de la coiffure, de la parfumerie, des produits de beauté* (Paris, 1936).

61. Uzanne, *La Femme à Paris*, 169–73.

62. Comtesse de Tramar (pseudonym for Marie-Fanny de Lamarque de Lagarrigue), *Le Bréviaire de la femme: Pratiques secrètes de la beauté*, 8th ed. (Paris, 1903) 14; Baronne d'Orchamps, *Tous les secrets de la femme* (Paris, 1907) 16.

63. Lucie Delarue-Mardus, *Embellissez-vous* (Paris, 1926–33) 2 and 8.

64. Mary Louise Roberts "Acting Up: The Feminist Theatrics of Marguerite Durand," *French Historical Studies*, 19, 4 (1996): 1103–4 suggests more feminist opposition to Durand's "feminine wiles" than I am able to find.

65. Juliette Sambourg, "L'Attrait féminin le plus durable,"*La Fronde* (17 Oct. 1899) in BMD, "Beauty, Press Clippings"; Miera Saberlys, "Une Question par mois: La coquetterie est-elle un défaut?" in *Organe de la Renaissance féminine*, 47 (1907); *Le Féministe: Revue mensuelle* (1 Nov. 1896).

66. Rose Nicolle, *Une Idée de parisienne par page* (Paris, 1914) 5–6 and 49–51.

67. Suzanne Balitrand, "La Femme, doit-elle défendre sa beauté?", *L'Intransigent* (28 Mar. 1932).

68. Edward Shorter, *A History of Women's Bodies* (New York, 1982). I am grateful to Ruth Roach Pierson, who shared her collection of reviews of this book with me.

69. For example, despite her engaging critique of the female body as a passive construct, Natalie Angier, *Woman: An Intimate Geography* (Boston, 1999), makes liberal use of geographical metaphors.

70. Philippe Lejeune, *Le Moi des demoiselles: Enquête sur le journal de jeune fille*

(Paris, 1993); Leah D. Hewitt, *Autobiographical Tightropes: Simone de Beauvoir, Nathalie Sarraute, Marguerite Duras, Monique Wittig, and Maryse Condé* (Lincoln, Neb., 1990).

71. Catherine Pozzi, *Journal 1913–1934* (Paris, 1987) and *Journal de jeunesse 1893–1906* (Paris, 1995).

72. Jennifer E. Milligan, *The Forgotten Generation: French Women Writers of the Inter-war Period* (Oxford, 1996), found one fictionalized autobiography, Irène Némirovsky, *Le Vin de solitude* (Paris, 1935), which mentioned an abortion.

73. Judith Butler, *Gender Troubles* (New York, 1990) 112.

74. Margaret Atack, "Writing from the Center: Ironies of Otherness and Marginality" in *Simone de Beauvoir's Le Deuxième Sexe: New Interdisciplinary Essays,* ed. Ruth Evans (Manchester, 1998) 41.

75. Elizabeth Grosz, *Sexual Subversion: Three French Feminists* (Sydney, 1989).

Part One. Carnal Knowledge

1. Donald Bender, "The Development of French Anthropology," *Journal of the History of the Behavioural Sciences,* 1 (1965): 140–42; Charles Vidal, *Etude médicale, physiologique, et philosophique de la femme* (Paris, 1912) 3.

2. A. Marie and L. MacAuliffe, "Communication sur la taille et la morphologie générale de la femme française," *Comptes rendus de l'Académie des Sciences* (1911); A. Chaillou and L. MacAuliffe, *Morphologie médicale* (Paris, 1912) 215 ff.

3. Suzanne de Félice, *Recherches sur l'anthropologie des françaises* (Paris, 1958).

4. Joshua Cole, "There Are Only Good Mothers: The Ideological Work of Women's Fertility in France before World War I," *French Historical Studies,* 19, 4 (1996): 639–67.

5. Nancy Leys Stepan, "Race and Gender: The Role of Analogy in Science," in *The Racial Economy of Science: Toward a Democratic Future,* ed. Sandra Harding (Bloomington, Ind., 1939) 359–76.

6. David Le Breton, *Anthropologie du corps et modernité* (Paris, 1990) 8–9, 14, and 25.

7. Michel Foucault, *The Birth of the Clinic: An Archaeology of Medical Perception,* trans. A. M. Sheridan Smith (New York, 1973) 12: 29 and 90, and *The History of Sexuality.* Vol. 1. *An Introduction,* trans. Robert Hurley (New York, 1980) 26, 103–4, and 126.

Chapter 1. Embodying Gender

1. Londa Schiebinger, *Nature's Body: Gender in the Making of Modern Science* (Boston, 1993) 14, 53–55, and 133.

2. Buffon, *Oeuvres complètes.* 3. *Histoire naturelle de l'homme,* ed. H. R. Duthilloel (Douai, 1832) 62 ff.

3. Buffon, *Histoire naturelle de l'homme,* 60–61, 72–73, 96, and 123. For similar passages in art theory, see Melissa Hyde, "Confounding Conventions: Gender Ambi-

guity and François Boucher's Painted Pastorals," *Eighteenth-Century Studies,* 30, 1 (1996): 17–18.

4. Pierre Roussel, *Système physique et moral de la femme,* new ed. (Paris, 1813) 2–4, 19, 38–52, and 141 ff.

5. J.-L. Moreau de la Sarthe, *Histoire naturelle de la femme* (Paris, 1803) 14–15 and 47–55.

6. J. J. Virey, *De la Femme sous ses rapports physiologique, moral, et littéraire* (Paris, 1823) 3, 14–15, and 212–42.

7. Moreau de la Sarthe, *Histoire naturelle de la femme,* 77, 113–19, and 677.

8. Henri Vignes, *Physiologie gynécologique et médecine des femmes* (Paris, 1929) 7, 50–100, and 489; M. Watrin, "Aperçu sur la physiologie et la pathologie sexuelle de la femme," in Albert Hogge et al., *Physiologie sexuelle normale et pathologique* (Paris, 1931) 95–112.

9. Roussel, *Système physique et moral de la femme,* 27–30.

10. Peter Corsi, *The Age of Lamarck: Evolutionary Theories in France, 1790–1830,* trans. J. Mandelbaum (Berkeley, 1988) 98–99 and 172–76.

11. Stephen Jay Gould, *Ontogeny and Phylogeny* (Cambridge, Mass., 1977) 49 and 127.

12. Virey, *De la Femme,* 18–22.

13. Virey, *De la Femme,* 30–32; Dorinda Outram, *Georges Cuvier: Vocation, Science, and Authority in Post-Revolutionary France* (Manchester, 1984) 118–20.

14. Sander L. Gilman, *Difference and Pathology: Stereotypes of Sexuality, Race, and Madness* (Ithaca, 1985) 85 ff. See also Anne Fausto-Sterling, "Gender, Race, and Nation: The Comparative Anatomy of 'Hottentot' Women in Europe, 1815–1817," *Deviant Bodies: Critical Perspectives on Difference in Science and Popular Culture,* eds. Jennifer Terry and Jacqueline Urla (Bloomington, Ind., 1995).

15. Abigail Solomon-Godeau, "Rethinking Erotic Photography: Notes towards a Project of Historical Salvage," in *Photography at the Dock: Essays on Photographic History, Institutions, and Practices,* ed. A. Solomon-Godeau (Minneapolis, 1991).

16. Hollis Clayson, *Painted Love: Prostitution in French Art of the Impressionist Era* (New Haven, 1991) 46; Hubert Damish, *The Judgment of Paris,* trans. John Goodman (Chicago, 1996) 11 ff.

17. F. Cuvier, "Femme de race Baschimanne," in Isadore Geoffrey de Sainte-Hilaire and F. Cuvier, *Histoire naturelle des mammifères* (Paris, 1824) 1–6.

18. Anne Roquebert, "La Sculpture ethnographique au XIXe siècle: Objet de mission ou oeuvre de musée," in *La Sculpture ethnographique de la Vénus hottentote à la Téhura de Gauguin: Les Dossiers du Musée d'Orsay* (Paris, 1994) 9–10 and 24–25.

19. Clayson, *Painted Love,* 2; Charles Bernheimer, *Figures of Ill Repute: Representing Prostitution in Nineteenth-Century France* (Cambridge, Mass., 1989) 173.

20. Linda Nead, *Female Nude: Art, Obscenity, and Sexuality* (London, 1992) 6–8 and 17–18.

21. Peter N. Stearns, *Fat History: Bodies and Beauty in the Modern West* (New York, 1997) 153 ff.

22. Comtesse de Norville, *Les Coulisses de la beauté: Comment la femme séduit* (Paris, 1894) 73.

23. Mme. Coullaud-Minier, *Le Corset* (Paris, 1927).

24. Jeanne Letang, "La Femme et la mode," and Victor Pauchet, "L'Education physique," *La Mère éducatrice: Revue mensuelle d'éducation populaire*, 5, 1 (1921).

25. Londa Schiebinger, *The Mind Has No Sex? Women in the Origins of Modern Science* (Cambridge, Mass., 1989) 178–87 and 191 ff.

26. Dally, "Femmes" in *Dictionnaire encyclopédique des sciences médicales* (Paris, 1888) 429.

27. Philippe Jullian, *Le Nu 1900: Trésors de la photographie* (Paris, 1976) 9 and 89–90.

28. P. N. Gerdy, *Anatomie des formes extérieures du corps humain* (Paris, 1829).

29. Gerdy, *Anatomie des formes extérieures*, 15.

30. Paul Richer, *Nouvelle anatomie artistique du corps humain. II. Cours supérieur: Morphologie de la femme* (Paris, 1920) 37–41.

31. A. Cabuzel, *Proportions harmoniques du corps de l'homme, de la femme, et de l'enfant* (Paris, 1921) 25.

32. Gunter Merken, "Behind the Mirror: Notes for the Portrait in the Twentieth Century," in La Biennale di Venezia, *Identity and Alterity: Figures of the Body, 1895–1995* (Venice, 1995) 40–41; Linda Nochlin, *The Body in Pieces: The Fragment as a Metaphor of Modernity* (New York, 1994) 30–43 and 53.

33. O'Fallowell, *Le Corset: Histoire, médecine, hygiène* (Paris, 1908) 21 ff.

34. Jean Clair, "Impossible Anatomy 1895–1995: Notes on the Iconography of a World of Technologies," *Identity and Alterity*, xxvi–xxvii.

35. Moreau de la Sarthe, *Histoire naturelle de la femme*, 10, 72–73, and passim.

36. Paul Clergeau, *Sur les différenciations adipeuses et pigmentaires du type féminin* (Paris, 1902) 9–61.

37. F. Jayle, *La Dépopulation de la France: L'Impôt du sang transmis* (Paris, 1910) and *Titres et études sociologiques et scientifiques du Dr. F. Jayle* (Paris, 1937).

38. F. Jayle, *La Gynécologie. I. L'Anatomie morphologique de la femme* (Paris, 1918) 40–48, 84–88, and 164–66.

39. Jayle, *La Gynécologie*, 98 ff.

40. André Binet, *Morphologie médico-artistique de la femme* (Paris, 1935) 104 and 106.

41. André Binet, *Souvenirs et propos d'un gynécologue*, 2nd ed. (Paris, 1948).

42. A. D. Quetelet, *Anthropométrie ou la mesure des différents facultés de l'homme* (Brussels, 1870) 177 ff.; quotations from 227 and 240.

43. Paul Topinard, *Etude sur la taille* (Paris, 1876) 6, 12–14.

44. For example, G. Boigey, *Physiologie appliquée à l'éducation physique* (Paris, 1923) 5 ff., and *L'Education physique féminine* (Paris, 1925) 19.

45. H. Thulié, *La Femme: Essai de sociologie physiologique* (Paris, 1885) iii (quote), 183–84, 218–20, and 178 (quote).

46. Alfred Fouillée, "La Psychologie des sexes et ses fondements physiologiques," *Revue des Deux Mondes,* 119 (Sept. 1893): 404.

47. Linda L. Clark, *Social Darwinism in France* (University, Ala., 1984) 11–12, 19, and 37; Madeleine Barthélemy-Madaule, *Lamarck the Mythical Precursor: A Study of the Relations between Science and Ideology,* trans. M. H. Shank (Boston, 1981) 81–85.

48. C. Letourneau, *La Condition de la femme dans les diverses races et civilisations* (Paris, 1903) 389 (quote).

49. Cynthia Eagle Russett, *Sexual Science: The Victorian Construction of Womanhood* (Cambridge, Mass., 1989) 31 ff.; Carl Sagan, *Broca's Brain* (New York, 1969); Elizabeth Fee, "Nineteenth-Century Craniology: The Study of the Female Skull," *Bulletin of the History of Medicine,* 53 (1979) 426.

50. Cited in Russett, *Sexual Science,* 145.

51. L. Manouvrier, *Sur l'Interprétation de la quantité dans l'encéphale et du poids du cerveau en particulier* (Paris, 1885) 256–58 and 266–68.

52. Dr. Emile Galtière-Bossière, *La Femme: Conformation, fonctions, maladies, et hygiène spéciale* (Paris, 1905) 2–3.

53. Madeleine Pelletier, "Recherches sur les indices pondéraux du crâne et des principaux os longs d'une serie de squelettes japonais," *Bulletins et mémoires de la Société d'Anthropologie de Paris,* 5th series, 1, 1 (1900): 509.

54. Paul de Regla, *La Femme* (Paris, n.d.) 20, 46, 61, and 80–81.

55. Charles Vidal, *Etude médicale: Physiologique et philosophique de la femme* (Paris, 1912) 1–19.

56. See Léon de Rosny, "L'Infériorité de la femme d'après l'anthropologie," *Le Valériquois* (24 Sept. 1892). My thanks to Karen Offen for this reference.

57. P. Poirier and A. Charpy, *Traité d'anatomie humaine,* new and revised ed. (Paris, 1931) 597–99.

58. Schiebinger, *The Mind Has No Sex,* 228.

59. Dorinda Outram, "Before Objectivity: Wives, Patronage, and Cultural Reproduction in Early Nineteenth-Century French Science," in *Uneasy Careers and Intimate Lives: Women in Science, 1789–1979,* ed. P. G. Abir-Am and Dorinda Outram (New Brunswick, 1989) 19–30.

60. Joy Harvey, *"Almost a Man of Genius." Clémence Royer, Feminism, and Nineteenth-Century Science* (New Brunswick, 1997).

61. Robert Fox, "The Savant Confronts His Peers: Scientific Societies in France, 1815–1914," in *The Culture of Science in France, 1700–1900* (Aldershot, U.K., 1992) 242 and 258.

62. George Weisz, *The Emergence of Modern Universities in France, 1863–1914*

(Princeton, 1983) 231–32 and 242–46; M. Maurice d'Ocagne, "Les Femmes dans la science," *Journal de l'Université des Annales,* 1, 2 (10 Jan. 1909).

63. Edmée Charrier, *L'Evolution intellectuelle féminine* (Paris, 1937) 152–53 and 203–8.

64. Charrier, *L'Evolution intellectuelle féminine,* 407–8 and 425.

65. J. L. Davis, "The Research School of Marie Curie in the Paris Faculty, 1907–1914," *Annals of Science,* 52 (1995): 321–55.

66. Susan Quinn, *Marie Curie: A Life* (New York, 1995) passim.

67. Jeanne Deflou, *Le Sexualisme: Critique de la prépondérance et de la mentalité du sexe fort* (Paris, n.d.) xvi–xvii, 72–73, 99, and 156.

68. Marius Decrespe, *L'Eternel féminin et le mécanisme de l'amour* (Paris, 1895) 16 ff.

69. Anna Klumpke, *Rosa Bonheur: The Artist's (Auto)biography,* trans. Gretchen van Slyke (Ann Arbor, Mich., 1997).

70. Anne Higonnet, *Berthe Morisot's Images of Women* (Cambridge, Mass., 1992) 22–187.

71. Duchesse d' Uzes, *Souvenirs* (Paris, 1939) 117.

72. Ludmilla Jordanova, *Sexual Visions* (Madison, Wis., 1989) 2.

73. Vanessa Schwartz, *Spectacular Realities: Early Mass Culture in fin-de-siècle Paris* (Berkeley, 1998).

74. Jo Burr Margadent, *Madame le Professeur: Women Educators in the Third Republic* (Princeton, 1990) 101 n.; Sylvie Fayet-Scribe, *Associations féminines et catholicisme: De la Charité à l'action sociale, XIXe–XXe siècles* (Paris, 1990) 161.

75. AMB, "Rapport sur l'Ecole supérieure des jeunes filles" (19 Jan. 1889) and Inventaires, 1873–1904; ADG, Fonds du Rectorat 241, Cours secondaires, Programme 1891; 242, Cours secondaires, Prospectus, 1879–80, and 271, Ecole Normale d'Institutrices, Bordeaux and Pau, Emploi du temps, 1884–86.

76. E. Caustier and Mme. Moreau-Bérillon, *Hygiène et économie domestique à l'usage des élèves de 3me* (Paris, 1908–24) 119.

77. Bruno Beguet, "La Vulgarisation scientifique au XIXe siècle," in *La Science pour tous,* Dossiers du Musée d'Orsay, 52 (Paris, 1994).

78. F. des Malis, "La Science dans l'habillement," *La Science illustrée,* 283–85 (29 Apr. and 6 and 13 May 1893).

79. Maryline Cantor, "Un Musée de province au XIXe siècle: Félix-Archimede Pouchet et le Musée d'Histoire Naturelle de Rouen," in *La Science pour tous.*

80. Beguet, "La Vulgarisation scientifique," and Jordanova, *Sexual Visions,* 44 ff.

81. Henri Marion, *Psychologie de la femme* (Paris, 1900) 41, 49 ff. (quote 51).

82. "She Who Is Always Sacrificed," in *Feminisms of the Belle Epoque,* ed. J. Waelti-Walters and S. Hauss (Lincoln, Neb., 1994) 20 and 36.

83. Anna Lampérière, *La Femme et son pouvoir* (Paris, 1909) 9, 18, 26, 86, 89, and 187.

84. Claude Vento, *Les Peintres de la femme* (Paris, 1888) and Armand Dayot, *L'Image de la femme* (Paris, 1899).

85. Comtesse de Tramar, *Le Bréviaire de la femme: Pratiques secrètes de la beauté,* 8th ed. (Paris, 1903) 134; Baronne d'Orchamps, *Tous les secrets de la femme* (Paris, 1907) 22 and 32; Comtesse de Gencé, *Le Cabinet de toilette d'une honnête femme* (Paris, 1909) 120. See also Emile-Bayard, *L'Art d'être femme* (Paris, n.d.) 144 and 147.

86. Mme. Costau-Pader, *Leçons d'économie domestique et d'hygiène à l'usage des lycées et collèges des jeunes filles* (Paris, 1907) 215; M. Dreyfus, *Leçons d'hygiène et d'économie domestique* (Paris, 1903) 78–79; Jeanne Letang, "La Femme et la mode," *La Mère éducatrice,* 5, 1 (1921).

87. J. Klinger, *La Femme dans la décoration moderne* (Paris, 1900).

88. Debora L. Silverman, *Art Nouveau in Fin-de-Siècle France* (Berkeley, 1989) 186–206.

89. Marcus Verhagen, "The Poster in *Fin-de-Siècle* Paris: That Mobile and Degenerate Art," in *Cinema and the Invention of Modern Life,* eds. Leo Charney and Vanessa R. Schwartz (Berkeley, 1995); Abigail Solomon-Godeau, "The Other Side of Venus: The Visual Economy of Feminine Display," in *The Sex of Things: Gender and Consumption in Historical Perspective,* eds. V. de Grazia and E. Furlough (Berkeley, 1996).

90. Gustave Kahn, *La Femme dans la caricature française* (Paris, n.d.) 281–86.

91. Silverman, *Art Nouveau in Fin-de-Siècle France,* 38 ff.; Gilette Ziegler, "La Beauté féminine à travers l'histoire," *Minerva* (13 Nov. 1935).

92. Max Gallo, *The Poster in History* (New York, 1972) 32–33 and 48–79; E. Feinblatt and B. Davis, *Toulouse-Lautrec and His Contemporaries: Posters of the Belle Epoque* (Los Angeles, 1985) 10–12.

93. Marguerite Moreno, "La Guirlande de beauté," in *Femmes de France* (5 Feb. 1928); Hélina Gaboriau, *Les Trois âges de la femme* (Paris, 1923) 10.

94. Georges Hébert, *L'Education physique féminine: Muscle et beauté plastique,* 2nd ed. (Paris, 1921) 2 and plate 2; "La Beauté facile," *L'Illustration* (2 Apr. 1933).

95. Croisilles, "La Plus belle femme du monde: Un Tournoi international de beauté aux Etats-Unis," *La Revue francaise* (10 Apr. 1927); and Maurice de Waleffe, "Le Tournoi de beauté de Galveston," "Miss France est classée deuxième au concours de beauté," and "A la Recherche de la plus belle femme d'Europe," *Journal* (26 May 1927, 7 June 1928, and 17 Dec. 1928). See also Jean Kolb, "Comment doit être la plus belle femme?" and "Miss France 1929," *Paris Soir* (7 Feb. and 14 May 1929); J.M. "Mais où sont les 'Miss France' d'antan?" *Franc-Tireur* (24 Dec. 1947) in BA, Fo 17.853–17.857.

96. Mme. Léontine Doresse, *Leçons de sciences appliquées à l'hygiène et à l'économie domestique* (Paris, 1922) 8–9.

97. Leon Rioter, *Le Mannequin* (Paris, 1900) 77–78, 94; Nicole Parrot, *Mannequins* (Paris, 1981) 22, 44 ff.

98. René Biot, *Le Corps et l'âme* (Paris, 1938), esp. 119–93.

Chapter 2. Biomedicine and Femininity

1. Françoise Loux, *Le Corps dans la société traditionnelle* (Paris, 1979) 157; "Folk Medicine," in *Companion Encyclopedia of the History of Medicine,* ed. W. F. Bynum and Roy Porter (New York, 1993) 661–75.

2. Une Doctoresse, *Le Guide médical de la femme et de la famille* (Paris, 1933) 137 ff.; N.-G. Payot, *Etre belle* (Paris, 1933) 69 and 72.

3. Loux, *Le Corps,* 136 ff.

4. Evelyn Bernette Ackerman, *Health Care in the Parisian Countryside, 1800–1914* (New Brunswick, 1990) 107–8.

5. Thomas, *L'Art de conserver la beauté par les plantes et les fleurs* (Paris, 1878); Baronne de Vaulx-Soueff, *Les Secrets de la beauté ou l'art de la toilette* (Paris, 1879); Y. H. Khamed, *Venus Biblion: Arcanes physiologiques: La beauté conservée et restaurée par la science* (Paris, 1899).

6. Comtesse de Gencé, *Le Cabinet de toilette d'une honnête femme* (Paris, 1909) 48–49; Marie Earle, *Culture rationnelle et scientifique de la beauté* (Paris, 1909) 4 and 6; E. Adair, *Conférences sur la culture scientifique de la beauté physique* (Paris, n.d.) 18.

7. Baronne d'Orchamps, *Tous les secrets de la femme* (Paris, 1907) 117 ff.; Mme. De Memphis, *Ce que femme doit savoir,* new ed. (Paris, 1933) 126–27.

8. Caufeynon, *Histoire de la femme, son corps, ses organes, son developpement au physique et au moral . . . ,* 1st ed. 1904 (Paris, 1985) v, 11–12, 17–23, 42–45, and 69–77. Fauconney's most obvious antilesbian propaganda was *L'Amour lesbien: Histoire, variétés, causes et origines, désordres, préservation par l'hygiène* (Paris, 1932).

9. A. Le Pileur, *Le Corps humain* (Paris, 1883) 2–11.

10. Anthony Preus, "Galen's Criticism of Aristotle's Conception Theory," *Journal of the History of Biology,* 10, 1 (1977): 65–85.

11. Alfred Fouillée, "Le Tempérament physiologique et moral d'après la biologie contemporaine," and "La Psychologie des sexes et ses fondemens physiologiques," in *Revue des Deux Mondes,* 63 (15 July 1893): 273–80 and 119 (Sept. 1893): 400–6.

12. J.-L. Moreau de la Sarthe, *Historie naturelle de la femme* (Paris, 1803) 183, 186, and 681.

13. Dr. Mure and Sophie Liet, *Résumé d'anatomie et de physiologie pour servir à l'intelligence du médecin du peuple et de l'homéopathie pure* (Paris, 1883) 23.

14. G. Bernutz, *Conférences cliniques sur les maladies des femmes* (Paris, 1888) 3–4.

15. Henri Vignes, *Physiologie gynécologique et médecine des femmes* (Paris, 1929) 4.

16. Thomas Laqueur, *Making Sex: Body and Gender from the Greeks to Freud* (Cambridge, Mass., 1990) 158–60, 175–79, and 211–16. See also O. Cadiot, *Cours de physiologie professé à l'Ecole de Médecine de Paris (1882–1883)* (Paris, 1883) 113 and 129–30.

17. Simone de Beauvoir, *The Second Sex,* trans. H. M. Parschley (New York, 1952) 1.

18. Mikhail Bakhtin, *Rabelais and His World*, trans. Helene Iswolskiy (Blooming-ton, Ind., 1984) 319 (quote).

19. Edouard Brissaud, *Histoire des expressions populaires relatives à l'anatomie, à la physiologie* (Paris, 1888) vii, 2-3, 35, and 70; Marie Schultz, *Hygiène générale de la femme: Menstruation, fécondation, stérilité, grossesse, accouchement, suites de couches, d'après l'enseignement et la pratique du Dr. Auvard*, 2nd ed. (Paris, 1909) 11.

20. Georges Stade, *Nécessité d'enseigner aux jeunes filles l'hygiène et quelques notions de médecine pratique* (Paris, 1900) 15 ff.; Armand Levy, *L'Enseignement de l'hygiène individuelle dans les écoles* (Paris, 1902) 25 ff.

21. E. Aubert and A. Lapreste, *Nouveau cours d'hygiène avec des notions de puériculture: Ecoles primaires supérieures professionnelles. Jeunes filles* (Paris, 1910) 9 ff.; L. Brisset and O. I. Scordia, *Leçons de sciences avec applications à l'hygiène et à l'enseignement ménager: Cours moyen des écoles de filles* (Paris, 1915) 97 ff.

22. Hélina Gaboriau, *Les Trois âges de la femme* (Paris, 1923) 93 and 96.

23. Catherine Pozzi, *Journal 1913-1934* (Paris, 1987) 55-56 and 398-99.

24. William Coleman, *Biology in the Nineteenth Century: Problems of Form, Function, and Transformation* (Cambridge, U.K., 1977) 2 and 14.

25. E. Couvreur, *Les Merveilles du corps humain* (Paris, 1892) 11.

26. Charles Robin, "Sexe," and Rouget, "Ovaire" in *Dictionnaire encyclopédique des sciences médicales* (Paris, 1881) 462 and 724 (quote).

27. Coleman, *Biology in the Nineteenth Century*, 11 and 33; André Senet, *L'Homme à la découverte de son corps* (Paris, 1956) 201 ff.; Claude Bernard, *An Introduction to the Study of Experimental Medicine*, trans. H. C. Greene (New York, 1957) 64, 76, 94-95, and 98.

28. Georges Canguilhem, *The Normal and the Pathological*, trans. Carolyn R. Fawcett and Robert S. Cohen (New York, 1991) 35, 43-45, and 75.

29. Charles Richet, *Souvenirs d'un physiologiste* (Paris, 1933) 7, 3 and 71.

30. Paul Bert, "La Physiologie dans l'éducation," *Leçons, discours et conférences*, 2nd ed. (Paris, 1888) 146-48 and *Leçons de zoologie professées à la Sorbonne: Enseignement secondaire des jeunes filles* (Paris, 1881) i-iii ff.

31. L. Duchesne and E. Michel, *Traité élémentaire d'hygiène*, 3rd ed. (Paris, 1887).

32. E. Brucker, *Hygiène: Classe de troisième* (Paris, 1931); Elie Lazerges, *Le Corps humain: Hygiène suivie de notions de puériculture* (Paris, 1940).

33. Coral Lansbury, *The Old Brown Dog: Women, Workers, and Vivisection in Edwardian England* (Madison, Wis., 1985) 162-63, cited in Kathleen Kete, *The Beast in the Boudoir: Petkeeping in Nineteenth- Century Paris* (Berkeley, 1994) 18.

34. Anne de Réal, "Les Torquemades de science: De la vivisection," in *Le Féministe: Revue mensuelle* 54 (10 Mar. 1910).

35. Richet, *Souvenirs*, 50-53, 100, and 139-54, and Richet, "L'Enseignement de la physiologie," *Revue des deux mondes* (15 Nov. 1923) 365-94.

36. Charles Richet, *En Temps de guerre: Ce que toute femme doit savoir. Conférences faites à la Croix-Rouge* (Paris, 1917).

37. "Les Venins, poisons régulateurs de la vie," and "Le Bactériophage de d'Herelle, virus de guérison," *Figaro* (29 Oct. 1929 and 26–27 Feb. 1930).

38. Pozzi, *Journal*, 401, 407–8, 436, and 482–83 (quote).

39. Jane Maienschein, "What Determines Sex? A Study of Convergent Research Approaches, 1880–1916," *Isis*, 75 (1981): 457–80.

40. Laqueur, *Making Sex*, 162.

41. Augustin Cleisz, *Recherches des lois qui président à la création des sexes* (Paris, 1889) 10–13 and 30–57.

42. M. Caullery, *Les Problèmes de la sexualité* (Paris, 1913) 138.

43. Armand Sabatier, "Contribution à l'étude des globules polaires et des éléments éliminés de l'oeuf en général" in *Recueil des mémoires sur la morphologie et sur la nature de la sexualité* (Montpellier, 1886) 135–235. For a more sophisticated statement, see Lucien Cuénot, "Sur la détermination du sexe chez les animaux," *Bulletin scientifique de la Françe et de la Belgique*, 32 (1899): 462–527.

44. Caullery, *Les Problèmes de la sexualité*, 8–10 and 189.

45. Adrienne Sahuqué, *Les Dogmes sexuels* (Paris, 1932) 31–32, 60–63, and 248.

46. Herbert Tuchman, *Essai de synthèse des idées actuelles sur le problème de la sexualité* (Thèse, méd., Paris, 1935) 10.

47. Michel Delsol and Janine Flatin, "L'Embryologie en France de 1920 à 1950," and Jean-Louis Fischer, "Les Recherches sur l'intersexualité experimentale chez les vertébrés dans l'Ecole française de l'entre-deux-guerres," in *Les Sciences biologiques et médicales en Françe 1920–1950* (Paris, 1994) 143 ff.

48. E. Gley, *Traité élémentaire de physiologie*, 2nd ed. (Paris, 1910) 702 and 714–17.

49. C. Champy, *La Croissance des caractères sexuels et leur regulation* (Coulommies, 1927) and C. Champy, "Genèse des produits sexuels et fécondation," in G. H. Roger and Léon Binet, *Traité de physiologie normale et pathologique. 2. Reproduction et croissance* (Paris, 1934) 3–14.

50. Richard Goldschmidt, *Le Déterminisme du sexe et l'intersexualité* (Paris, 1932); Georges Bohn, *Leçons de zoologie et biologie générale. 2. Réproduction, sexualité, heredité* (Paris, 1934). Morgan's *Embryology and Genetics* was translated in 1936.

51. C. E. Brown-Séquard and A. d'Arsonval, "De l'Injection des extraits liquides provenant des glandes et des tissus de l'organism comme méthode thérapeutique," *Comptes-Rendus de la Société de Biologie*, 9th series, 3 (18 Apr. 1891): 248–50; André Role, *La Vie étrange d'un grand savant: Le Professeur Brown-Séquard* (Paris, 1977).

52. Nelly Oudshoorn, *Beyond the Natural Body: An Archeology of Sex Hormones* (London, 1994) 99–103.

53. L. Dartigues, *Le Renouvellement de l'organisme* (Paris, 1928) 13–108. From 1923 to 1928, he published forty-six articles on glandular grafts in sixteen French journals and six Spanish journals.

54. F. Jayle, "Opothérapie ovarienne contre les troubles consécutifs à la castration chez la femme," *Presse médicale* 4, 38 (1896): 221–22 and "Insuffisance ovarienne," *Presse médicale* 8, 22 (1900): 133–36.

55. For example, André Robin and Paul Dalché, *Traitement médical des maladies des femmes*, 2nd ed. (Paris, 1902); Mauclert, "L'Insuffisance ovarienne," *Journal des praticiens* (1904). For a more complete list, see Gregario Maranon, *The Climacteric (The Critical Age)* trans. K. S. Stevens (St. Louis, 1929) 19.

56. Jane Lewis, "Feminism, the Menopause, and Hormone Replacement Therapy," *Feminist Review* 43 (spring 1993): 19–43.

57. M. Watrin, "Aperçu sur la physiologie et la pathologie sexuelle de la femme," in Albert Hogge et al., *Physiologie sexuelle normale et pathologique* (Paris, 1931) 151–54.

58. E. Monin, *Hygiène et médecine féminines: Secrets de santé et de beauté* (Paris, 1901) 232; M. Boppe, "Ménopause chirurgical," *Maman* 1, 3 (1930); Victor Pauchet, *L'Automne de la vie: L'Homme et la femme à l'âge critique* (Paris, 1932) 39; Charles Platon and Antoine Lacroix, *Le Sauvetage de la femme: Essai de traitement prophylactique des maladies des femmes* (Toulouse, 1934) esp. 16, 125–27, and 537–57.

59. French researchers such as Paul Ancel (1873–1961) of Strasbourg did similar research on testes and later on regulation of the menstrual cycle. See Delsol and Flatin and Fischer articles in *Les Sciences biologiques et médicales en France 1920–1950*, 154–55 and 163–64.

60. This and the following paragraphs draw heavily on Oudshoorn, *Beyond the Natural Body*, 22–36, 43–44, and 89–98.

61. R. Rivoire, *Les Acquisitions nouvelles de l'endocrinologie*, 2nd ed. (Paris, 1935) 138–39.

62. Oudshoorn, *Beyond the Natural Body*, 25–36.

63. Guy Laroche, *Opothérapie endocrinienne: Les Bases physiologiques, les syndromes, posologie de l'opothérapie*, 2nd ed. (Paris, 1933) 3.

64. Guy Laroche, ed., *La Puberté: Etude clinique et physiopathologique* (Paris, 1938) 17–18 and 24.

65. G. Maranon, "Les Etats intersexuels à la puberté," Groupe lyonnais d'études médicales philosophiques et biologiques, *Médecine et adolescence* (Lyon, 1936) 33–48.

66. Henri Allaix, *De l'Inversion sexuelle à la détermination des sexes* (Versailles, 1930).

67. L. Gallien, *La Sexualité* (Paris, 1941); Etienne Wolff, *Les Changements de sexe*, 5th ed. (Paris, 1946).

68. Beauvoir, *The Second Sex*, 8 and 13.

69. N. Pende, "Les Types constitutionnels de fémininité somatique et leur formule endocrinienne," *La Presse médicale*, 103 (27 Dec. 1933).

70. Speeches reprinted in André Binet, *Souvenirs et propos d'un gynécologue*, 2nd ed. (Paris, 1948) 123–75.

71. Pierre Darmon, *La Vie quotidienne du médecin parisien en 1900* (Paris, 1889) 25–27; George Weisz, *The Emergence of Modern Universities in France, 1863–1914* (Princeton, 1983) 246–47.

72. Darmon, *La Vie quotidienne du médecin parisien*, 26; D. Penneau et al., "La Femme médecin à travers les âges et les pays," *Histoire des sciences médicales*, 15, 1 (1981): 339; Maurice Lacomme, "Premières femmes médecins," *Bulletin de l'Académie Nationale de Médecine*, 159, 5 (1975): 759.

73. Edmée Charrier, *L'Evolution intellectuelle féminine* (Paris, 1937) 297–99; "Les Premières femmes médecins et internes," *La France médicale* (1906) 260–61; Penneau et al., "La Femme médecin," 340.

74. Peinard, *La Profession médicale en France* (Paris, 1894) 10 ff.

75. Robert Nye, "Honor Codes and Medical Ethics in Modern France," *Bulletin of the History of Medicine*, 69 (1995): 99–111.

76. *L'Hygiène de la femme et de l'enfant* (1883–85).

77. Charrier, *L'Evolution intellectuelle*, 311–13; Darmon, *La Vie quotidienne du médecin parisien*, 211–15; Mathilde Pokitonoff, *Hygiène de la mère et de l'enfant* (Paris, 1893); *Le Bonheur au foyer: Revue des épouses et des mères de famille* (1898).

78. "Rapport . . . au Congrès international de la condition et des droits des femmes," in S. Bell and K. Offen, *Women, the Family, and Freedom*, 2 (Stanford, 1983) 145.

79. Charrier, *L'Evolution intellectuelle*, 304 ff.

80. C.M., "Un Congrès important," *Revue philanthropique*, 40 (1919): 393–95; Charrier, *L'Evolution intellectuelle*, passim.

81. *Association internationale des femmes-médecins*, 5 (Dec. 1931): 3–30.

82. *Association internationale*, 4 (June 1931): 16.

83. Minerve, "Un Livre pour les femmes," *La Mère éducatrice: Revue mensuelle d'éducation populaire* 6, 10 (1923).

84. Joscelyn Godwin, *The Beginnings of Theosophy in France* (London, 1989) 12–18; Joy Dixon, "Sexology and the Occult: Sexuality and Subjectivity in Theosophy's New Age," *Journal of the History of Sexuality* 7, 3 (1997): 409–33.

85. Marie Schultz, *Hygiène générale de la femme: Alimentation, vêtements, soins corporels, d'après l'enseignement et la pratique du Dr. Auvard* (Paris, 1903) and *Hygiène générale de la femme: Menstruation, fécondation*. Schultz also collaborated in translating the *Bhagavad Gîtâ* and works of English Transcendentalist Annie Besant.

86. *Le Bonheur au foyer*, 1 and 2 (Nov. and Dec. 1898). For details about *Les Trois âges*, see Note 21, this chapter.

87. Anna Fischer, *La Femme, médecin du foyer*, new ed., trans Louise Azéma (Paris, 1924).

88. Nelly Nelfrand, *Ce que toute jeune fille doit savoir à l'âge de la puberté: Education sexuelle de l'adolescence. Petite physiologie génitale de l'hygiène interne de l'homme et de la femme* (Paris, 1932).

89. Marie Houdré-Boursin, *Ma Doctoresse: Guide pratique d'hygiène et de médecine de la femme moderne* (Strasbourg, 1930); Arlette Gelé de Francony, *Santé et beauté de la femme par l'éducation corporelle* (Paris, 1923); *Femina-Sport*, 1, 1 (1926).

Chapter 3. Hygiene and Housewifery

1. Jean-Pierre Goubert, *La Conquête de l'eau: L'Avènement de la santé à l'age industriel* (Paris, 1986) 25.

2. Françoise Loux, *Le Corps dans la société traditionnelle* (Paris, 1979) 97.

3. Georges Vigarello, *Le Propre et le sale: L'Hygiène du corps depuis le Moyen Age* (Paris, 1985).

4. Goubert, *La Conquête de l'eau*, 21, 30, 66–68, 198, 215, and 222–27; Jacques Léonard, *Archives du corps: La Santé au XIXe siècle* (Ouest-France, 1986) 115; Nathalie Mikailoff, *Les Manières de propreté du Moyen Age à nos jours* (Paris, 1990) 170, Table 2.

5. Armand Levy, *L'Enseignement de l'hygiène individuelle dans les écoles* (Paris, 1902) 14.

6. Julia Csergo, *Liberté, égalité, propreté: La Morale de l'hygiène au XIXe siècle* (Paris, 1988) 153–77.

7. Andrew Wear, "The History of Personal Hygiene," in *Companion Encyclopedia of the History of Medicine*, ed. W. F. Bynum and Roy Porter (New York, 1993) 283–84.

8. Claire Salomon-Bayet, "Penser l'histoire des sciences," in *Pasteur et la revolution pastorienne*, ed. C. Salomon-Bayet (Paris, 1986).

9. *La Santé: Organe de vulgarisation des connaissances de médecine et d'hygiène*, 360–73 (15 Dec. 1890–15 Jan. 1892).

10. ADG, Fonds du Rectorat, T99, Faculté de Médecine, Etudes. Hygiène, 1883–85; Jules Courmont and A. Rochaix, *Précis d'hygiène*, 4th ed. (Paris, 1932) ix ff.; Léon Bernard and Robert Debré, *Cours d'hygiène professé à l'Institut d'Hygiène de la Faculté de Médecine de Paris* (Paris, 1927) preface.

11. Jack D. Ellis, *The Physicians-Legislators of France: Medicine and Politics in the Early Third Republic, 1870–1914* (Cambridge, U.K., 1990) 69–70; Yvonne Knibiehler et al., *Cornettes et blouses blanches: Les infirmières dans la société francaise 1880–1980* (Paris, 1984) 41 ff.; Henri Napias, "Rapport sur le recrutement du personnel secondaire des établissements hospitaliers," *L'Assistance* (1899): 40–44; F. Regnault, "Les Ecoles de gardes-malades," *L'Assistance* (31 Mar. 1902): 53–61; Louis Rivière, "Ecoles d'infirmières," *Revue Philanthropique* 9 (1901): 575–91 and 683–85.

12. ADG, 5M582, Ecoles d'Infirmières; 5M583, Ecole d'infirmières-visiteuses. See also Katrin Schultheiss, "La Veritable médecine des femmes: Anna Hamilton and the Politics of Nursing Reform in Bordeaux, 1900–1914," *French Historical Studies* 19 (spring 1995): 183–214.

13. Knibiehler, *Cornettes et blouses blanches*, 61.

14. Bonnie G. Smith, *Confessions of a Concierge: Madame Lucie's History of Twentieth-Century France* (New Haven, 1985) 32.

15. Goubert, *La Conquête de l'eau*, 9–15 and 85–88; Léonard, *Archives du corps*, 66 and 77–80, 234, and 247; Doctoresse Eva, "Les Eaux minérales" and "L'Hygiène des eaux," in *Le Pot au feu: Journal de cuisine pratique et d'économie domestique* (15 Apr. 1894 and 15 May 1896).

16. Goubert, *La Conquête de l'eau*, 183–90.

17. AMB, 808R1, Cours publics d'hygiène, 1872–87.

18. Ellis, *The Physicians-Legislators*, 138 ff.; G. Lefosse, *Précis élémentaire d'hygiène pratique à l'usage des écoles primaires* (Toulouse, 1904) 6–8.

19. Jules Courmont and A. Rochaix, *Précis d'hygiène*, 4th ed. (Paris, 1932) 13–19 and 30–36.

20. Vigarello, *Le Propre et le sale*, 228.

21. E. Littré, *Médecine et médecins*, 3rd ed. (Paris, 1875) 229–84.

22. AMB, 808R1, Cours publics d'hygiène, 1872–87.

23. *Portez-vous bien: Revue mensuelle d'hygiène pratique* no. 1–5 (mid-1890s).

24. Chavigny, *Psychologie de l'hygiène* (Paris, 1921) 32.

25. Goubert, *La Conquête de l'eau*, 113–18.

26. For this analysis, I consulted *Le Journal des femmes* (1891–1910), *Le Féministe* (Nice, 1906–11), *La Chronique féminine* (1911–13), *Féminité* (1912–13), and *La Mode pratique* (1919–39).

27. Vincent Vinikas, *Soft Soap, Hard Sell: American Hygiene in an Age of Advertisement* (Ames, Iowa, 1992) 27.

28. R. Flament, "La Propagande éducative d'hygiène," in *Journées médico-scolaires de l'enfance d'âge scolaire* (Paris, 1935) 250–53.

29. Chavigny, *Psychologie de l'hygiène*, 9–13 and 20–24.

30. See advertisements for hygiène books in *La Mère éducatrice* (1919–26) and *Maman* (1929–33).

31. Goubert, *La Conquête de l'eau*, 24.

32. Rachel G. Fuchs, "The Right to Life: Paul Strauss and the Politics of Motherhood" and M. L. Stewart, "Setting the Standards: Labor and Family Reformers," in *Gender and the Politics of Social Reform in France: 1870–1914*, ed. Elinor A. Accampo, Rachel G. Fuchs, and Mary Lynn Stewart (Baltimore, 1995). For other examples, see the dossier on the Veilleuses de Lyon in the ADR, 4M621, Sociétés religieuses; *Institution des diaconesses des églises évangéliques de la France* (Paris, 1892), and the dossier on the Dames d'Assistance Républicaine in the ADMM, 5M53.

33. BML, Fonds Humbert, ii–18, Unions des Femmes de France; ADMM, 5M53, Union des Femmes de France; *Assemblée générale du Comité de Tours . . . 1907* (Tours, 1907) 5 ff.; *Assemblée générale du groupe de Toulouse . . . 1911* (Toulouse, 1911) 9–10; Roger Colomb, *Rôle de la femme dans l'assistance aux blessés et malades militaires* (Bordeaux, 1903) 94 ff.

34. Knibiehler, *Cornettes et blouses blanches*, 84–112; Margaret Darrow, "French Volunteer Nursing and the Myth of War Experience in World War I," *American Historical Review* 101 (Feb. 1992): 82–106; Duchesse d'Uzes, *Souvenirs* (Paris, 1939): 128–29; Baronne J. Michaux, *En Marge du drame: Journal d'une Parisienne pendant la guerre 1914–1915* (Paris, 1916) 135.

35. Jeanne Leroy, "La Sortie de l'hôpital" and G. Alphen-Salvador, "L'Association pour le Développement de l'Assistance aux Malades," "Les Secours et l'assistance médicale à domicile en 1905," "Bulletin de la Société Internationale pour l'Etude des Questions d'Assistance," and "L'Association pour le Developpement de l'Assistance aux Malades," in *Revue Philanthropique* 9 (1901): 686–90; 21 (1907): 605–9 and 655–58; 22 (1907–8): 302 ff.; and 33 (1913): 292 ff.

36. Pierre Guillaume, *Du Désespoir au salut: Les Tuberculeux aux 19e et 20e siecles* (Paris, 1986) 198–99; dossiers on assistantes sociales in ADN, M229/6 and M229/9 and ADG, M583, and "Le Diplôme d'état d'infirmières et de visiteuses d'hygiène sociale," *Revue Philanthropique* 51 (1930): 81–90.

37. E. Monin, *La Propreté de l'individuel et de la maison*, 4th ed. (Paris, 1884) 25 ff.

38. David S. Barnes, *The Making of a Social Disease: Tuberculosis in Nineteenth-Century France* (Berkeley, 1995) 114.

39. For example, *Le Pot au feu* (Paris, 1893–96); *L'Hygiène au foyer* (Bordeaux, 1907–10).

40. For example, Doctoresse Eva, "La Fênetre ouverte," *Le Pot au feu*, 10 (1 Sept. 1893); "Hygiène," *La Mère éducatrice*, 4, 10 (1921).

41. Goubert, *La Conquête de l'eau*, 95; Léonard, *Archives du corps*, 76.

42. Kristen Ross, *Fast Cars, Clean Bodies: Decolonization and the Reordering of French Culture* (Cambridge, Mass., 1995).

43. Ellen Furlough, "Selling the American Way in Interwar France: Prix Uniques and the Salons des Arts ménagers," *Journal of Social History* (spring 1993): 491–519; Robert L. Frost, "Machine Liberation: Inventing Housewives and Home Appliances in Interwar France," *French Historical Studies*, 18, 1 (1993): 109–30.

44. J. Cazajeux, "Les Ecoles ménagères en France et à l'étranger," *La Reforme Sociale* (16 Dec. 1897).

45. AMB, 620R1, Ecole primaire supérieure de jeunes filles, report by Directrice, 29 Jan. 1889; ADG, Fonds du Rectorat 241, Cours secondaires, Programme, 1889; 276, Ecole normale d'institutrices, Dordogne, requests for books, Feb. 1883; and 208, Ecole normale d'institutrices, Dordogne, reports from directrice, 31 May 1891; and ADMM, T1278, Ecole normale d'institutrices, reports of the directrice, 1889–90.

46. E. Caustier and Mme. Moreau-Bérillon, *Hygiène à l'usage des élevés de quatrième et de cinquième années de l'enseignement secondaire des jeunes filles* (Paris, 1908–24) and Letter from Lydie Martial, *Le Féminisme intégrale: Journal mensuel*, 2, 2 (1914).

47. L. Pastoriaux, E. Le Brun, and Mme. Lasalle, *Les Sciences et l'enseignement ménager* (Paris, 1937).

48. Sylvie Fayet-Scribe, *Associations féminines et catholicisme: De la Charité à l'action sociale, XIXe–XXe siècle* (Paris, 1990) 22–24, 53–57, 81–87, and 155–57.

49. J. Héricourt, *L'Hygiène moderne* (Paris, 1908) 165 ff.; Marthe Francillon-Lobre, *Hygiène de la femme et de la jeune fille* (Paris, 1909) 166 ff.

50. Héricourt, *L'Hygiène moderne*, 49–57; Francillon-Lobre, *Hygiène de la femme*, 20–34; Une Doctoresse, *Le Guide médical de la femme et de la famille* (Paris, 1933) 73 ff.; E. Monin, *La Santé de la femme* (Paris, 1928) 82–85.

51. Thilo, *L'Hygiène de la femme*, 53 ff.; articles by Clemesnel in *L'Hygiène au foyer* (Oct. 1908 and Feb. 1909); *Mère au foyer . . . pour la bonne santé de la famille* (Paris, 1934) 10–11.

52. Cancalon, *L'Education médicale de la femme* (Versailles, 1897); Augusta Moll-Weiss, "La Mère francaise," *Premier congrès d'hygiène scolaire et de pédagogie physiologique, 1903. Rapports et communications* (Paris, 1904) 265–68; Nancy J. Edwards, "Social Science from a Feminine Perspective: Augusta Moll-Weiss and the Domestic Science Movement 1890–1920" (Ph.D. diss., 1997).

53. M. Munié, "Enseignement de l'hygiène aux maîtres, aux élevés, et aux familles," *IIIe Congrès d'hygiène scolaire. II. Résumés de rapports* (Paris, 1910) 434–35.

54. Cherilyn Lacy, "Science or Savoir-Faire? Domestic Hygiene and Medicine in Girls' Public Education During the Early Third Republic, 1882–1914," *Proceedings of the Western Society for French History* 24 (1997): 25–35.

55. "La Maternelle: Université populaire féministe," and "L'Entente internationale des femmes: Programme du mois d'avril," in *La Femme affranchie: Organe du féminisme ouvrier-socialiste et libre penseur*, 9 and 19 (Apr. 1905 and Mar. 1906).

56. Jean Baudrillard, *Seduction*, trans. Brian Singer (Montreal, 1990).

57. Monin, *La Propreté*, 12 ff.

58. A. Debay, *Hygiène médical du visage et de la peau: Formulaire de beauté*, 5th ed. (Paris, 1869); A. Izard, *Hygiène du teint* (Paris, 1881).

59. For example, Joseph Nicolas and A. Jambon, *Hygiène de la peau et du cuir chevelu* (Paris, 1911); Paul Chevallier and Marcel Colin, *Hygiène de la peau* (Paris, 1934).

60. Monin, *L'Hygiène de la beaute: Formulaire cosmétique* (Paris, 1886) 2–3; *Hygiène et médecine féminines: Secrets de santé et de beauté* (Paris, 1901) 62. See also de Lusi, *La Femme moderne: Son hygiène, sa beauté* (Paris, 1906); Léon Bizard, *Conseils d'hygiène et d'esthétique* (Paris, 1924).

61. Louis Bourdeau, "Fards, cosmétiques, et teintures," *Revue de Paris* (Dec. 1895): 902; Ris-Pacquot, *Hygiène, médecine, parfumerie, pharmacie* (Paris, 1894) 17.

62. Marie Schultz, *Hygiène générale de la femme* (Paris, 1903) 267 ff.; Une Doctoresse, *Le Guide médical de la femme*, 117–18.

63. Baronne d'Orchamps, *Tous les secrets de la femme* (Paris, 1907) 240–50; Comtesse de Tramar, *Le Bréviaire de la femme: Pratiques secrètes de la beauté*, 8th ed. (Paris, 1903) 78–88; André-Valdes, *Encyclopédie illustrée des élégances féminines: Hygiène de la beauté* (Paris, 1892) 55 ff.; Mestadier, *La Beauté: Hygiène féminine* (Paris, 1912) 54 and 57–64.

64. Ned Rival, *Histoire anecdotique de la propreté et des soins corporels* (Paris, 1986) 193.

65. Goubert, *La Conquête de l'eau*, 80–81; Csergo, *Liberté, égalité, propreté*, 215 and 221–23.

66. Csergo, *Liberté, égalité, propreté*, 243–45, 172–73.

67. Louise d'Alq, *Les Secrets du cabinet de toilette: Conseils et recettes* (Paris, 1881) 1–50, Baronne Staffe, *Le Cabinet de toilette* (Paris, 1893), Orchamps, *Tous les secrets*, 225 ff.; Tramar, *Le Bréviaire de la femme*, 77–81.

68. *Hygiène et beauté: Affiches du fonds iconographique* (Paris, 1977).

69. Hollis Clayson, *Painted Love: Prostitution in French Art of the Impressionist Era* (New Haven, 1991) 67–79. For prints, see Henri Boutet, *Autour d'elle* (Paris, 1897–98).

70. Comtesse de Gencé, *Le Cabinet de toilette d'une honnête femme* (Paris, n.d) 48; Alq, *Les Secrets du cabinet de toilette*, v and 7; Orchamps, *Tous les secrets*, 224; Tramar, *Le Bréviaire de la femme*, 19–20.

71. Marquise de Garches (pseudonym for Mme. Bindels-Villette), *Les Secrets de beauté d'une Parisienne* (Paris, 1894) 13; Norville, *Les Coulisses de la beauté*, 6; Tramar, *Le Bréviaire de la femme*, 13.

72. Caufeynon, *Les Secrets de la beauté* (Paris, n.d.) 5–6; Jean d'Auteuil, *A Travers la beauté: Hygiène et beauté. Secrets inédits* (Paris, n.d.) 8 and 13.

73. Madeleine Ray, *Notre santé et notre charme* (Paris, 1932), 64–78.

74. Mikailoff, *Les Manières de propreté*, 170, 172, and 174.

75. Goubert, *La Conquête de l'eau*, 83–85.

76. René Martial and Léontine Doresse, *Hygiène féminine populaire* (Paris, 1923) preface.

77. Augusta Moll-Weiss. *Les Mères de demain: L'Education de la jeune fille d'après sa physiologie* (Paris, 1902) 18; Calmard and Laurent, *Enseignement ménager: Hygiène. Puériculteur*, 2nd ed. (Paris, 1939) 9.

78. Isidore Bourdon, *Notions d'hygiène pratique: Education supérieure* (Paris, 1860).

79. Caustier and Moreau-Bérillon, *Hygiène à l'usage*, 3.

80. L. A. Raimbert, *Notions d'hygiène à l'usage de tous les établissements d'instruction* (Paris, 1879) 1; Ernestine Wirth, *La Future ménagère* (Paris, 1882) 384.

81. ADG, Fonds du Rectorat 241, Cours secondaires, Programme 1891; Levy, *L'Enseignement de l'hygiène individuelle*, 48; J. Weill-Mantou, *Hygiène à l'usage des écoles normales primaires* (Paris, 1906) viii–ix; Mme. Costau-Pader, *Leçons d'économie domestique et d'hygiène à l'usage des lycées et collèges de jeunes filles* (Paris, 1907) 141.

82. E. Brucker, *Hygiène: Classe de troisième* (Paris, 1931) preface; Eisenmengher, *Le Corps humain* (Paris, 1932) esp. 300.

83. Chavigny, *Psychologie de l'hygiène*, 25–28.

84. Emilie Carles as told to Robert Destanque, *A Life of Her Own: The Transformation of a Countrywoman in Twentieth-Century France*, trans. A. H. Goldberger (New York, 1992) 226–27.

85. Compare Mlle. M. Dreyfus, *Leçons d'hygiène et d'économie domestique* (Paris, 1903) 124 and Caustier and Moreau-Bérillon, *Hygiène à l'usage*, 63, with Mathilde Pokitonoff, *Hygiène de la mère et de l'enfant* (Paris, 1893) 8 ff. and Jeannine Martay, *L'Hygiène dans les soins de toilette chez la jeune fille et chez la femme* (Paris, 1909).

86. Csergo, *Liberté, égalité, propreté*, 122. See also *Catéchisme d'hygiène à l'usage des écoles de jeunes filles par une institutrice* (Lyon, 1898) 32.

87. André Lucas and M. A. Covillaud, *Amis et ennemis du corps humain* (Paris, 1905) 60–62.

88. Levy, *L'Enseignement de l'hygiène individuelle*, 28–30.

89. Smith, *Confessions of a Concierge*, 20; Raimbert, *Notions d'hygiène*, 96–97; Wirth, *La Future ménagère*, 385–86; J. L. Mora and C. Vesiez, *Nouveau cours d'hygiène* (Paris, 1890) 22; G. Lefosse, *Précis élémentaire d'hygiène pratique à l'usage des écoles primaires* (Toulouse, 1904) 22–23; L. Brisset and O. I. Scordia, *Leçons de sciences avec applications à l'hygiène et à l'enseignement ménager* (Paris, 1915) 291; Calmard and Laurent, *Enseignement ménager*, 9.

90. Monin, *Hygiène et médecine feminines*, 77–83; Schultz, *Hygiène générale de la femme*, 318–23; Martay, *L'Hygiène dans les soins de toilette*, 105–26; Nicolas and Mabon, *Hygiène de la peau et du cuir chevelu*, 66 ff.; Une Doctoresse, *Le Guide médical de la femme*, 119–20; Marie Houdré-Boursin, *Ma Doctoresse: Guide pratique d'hygiène et de médecine de la femme moderne* (Strasbourg, 1930) 180 ff. See advertisements for Sublimoir de Harris and La Blondine Velake in *La Fronde* (25 Feb. and 9 Mar. 1898).

91. Bourdon, *Notions d'hygiène pratique;* Raimbert, *Notions d'hygiène*.

92. Philippe Perrot, *Fashioning the Bourgeoisie: A History of Clothing in the Nineteenth Century*, trans. Richard Bienvenu (Princeton, 1994) 160.

93. C.L., "Modes-Corset de Mme. Léoty," *Journal de demoiselles* (16 May 1881); M. de Thilo, *L'Hygiène de la femme* (Paris, 1891) 18–19.

94. Raimbert, *Notions d'hygiène*, 83; Wirth, *La Future ménagère*, 423–24; L. Duchesne and E. Michel, *Traité élémentaire d'hygiène*, 3rd ed. (Paris, 1887) 215; Pastoriaux, Le Brun, and Lasalle, *Les Sciences et l'enseignement ménager*, 392.

95. *Catéchisme d'hygiène* 36; O'Fallowell, *Le Corset: Histoire, médecine, hygiène* (Paris, 1908) 21–22 and 216–18.

96. Schultz, *Hygiène générale de la femme*, 190–202.

97. Une Doctoresse, *Le Guide médical de la femme*, 184–86; Anna Fischer, *La Femme, médecin du foyer*, new ed. (Paris, 1924) 156–58 and 179–83. On dress reform,

Gabrielle, "La Transformation du costume" and "Mode et hygiène" in *Le Féministe, Revue mensuelle* 22 (22 May 1908) and 42 (9 Dec. 1909).

98. Ernest Léoty, *Le Corset à travers les âges* (Paris, 1893) 102; Gencé, *Le Cabinet de toilette d'une honnête femme*, 50 and 120; Garches, *Les Secrets de beauté d'une Parisienne*, 60–61; Iolande (Marquise Marie Maiocchi-Plattis), *Talismans de jeunesse (Les Raffinements de la femme* (Paris, n.d.) 278; Norville, *Les Coulisses de la beauté*, 59; Orchamps, *Tous les secrets*, 22 and 84.

99. Adolphe Olivier, *Hygiène de la grossesse: Conseil aux femmes enceintes* 2nd ed. (Paris, 1910) 6–7 and 96 ff.; Léoty, *Le Corset*, 97–105; Schultz, *Hygiène générale de la femme*, 225–33; Martay, *L'Hygiène dans les soins de toilette*, 194–95; *La Fronde* (7 and 12 Apr. 1898).

100. See advertisements for maternity belts in *La Mode pratique* (21 Jan. 1921) and in "Dernières nouveautés, Hiver 1931–1932" in the Au Bon Marché catalogues at the Bibliothèque Forney.

101. Une Doctoresse, *Le Guide médical de la femme*, 186; Fischer, *La Femme, médecin du foyer*, 179.

102. "Le Silhouette et le corset," *La Mode pratique* (19 Mar. 1921).

Part Two. Reproductive Rhythms

1. Caroll Smith-Rosenberg, "Puberty to Menopause: The Cycle of Femininity in Nineteenth-Century America," in *Disorderly Conduct: Visions of Gender in Victorian America* (Oxford, 1985).

2. Janet Lee and Jennifer Sasser-Coen, *Blood Stories: Menarche and the Politics of the Female Body in Contemporary U.S. Society* (London, 1996) 86 ff.; Joan Jacobs Brumberg, *The Body Project: An Intimate History of American Girls* (New York, 1997) 5 ff.

3. Carolyn J. Dean, *Sexuality and Modern Western Culture* (New York, 1996).

4. Angus McLaren, *The Trials of Masculinity: Policing Sexual Boundaries, 1870–1930* (Chicago, 1997).

5. Annalise Maugue, *L'Identité masculine en crise au tournant du siècle* (Paris, 1987); Elaine Showalter, *Sexual Anarchy: Gender and Culture at the Fin de Siècle* (London, 1991).

6. Mary Louise Roberts, *Civilization without Sexes: Reconstructing Gender in Postwar France, 1917–1927* (Chicago, 1994); Susan Kingsley Kent, *Making Peace: The Reconstruction of Gender in Interwar Britain* (Princeton, 1993).

7. Dean, *Sexuality and Modern Western Culture*, 19 ff.; Arnold Davidson, "Closing Up the Corpses: Diseases of Sexuality and the Emergence of the Psychiatric Style of Reasoning," in *Meaning and Method: Essays in Honor of Hilary Putnam*, ed. George Boolos (Cambridge, U.K., 1990).

8. Joanny Roux, *Psychologie de l'instinct sexuel* (Paris, 1899) 23–25; A. Hesnard, *L'Individu et le sexe: Psychologie du narcissisme* (Paris, 1927) 12 ff.

9. Charles Robin, "Sexe," in *Dictionnaire encyclopédique des sciences médicales* (Paris, 1881); Remi de Gourmont, *Physiologie de l'amour: Essai sur l'instinct sexuel*, 12th ed. (Paris, 1915) 10 and 33–34.

10. *Sexual Knowledge, Sexual Science: The History of Attitudes to Sexuality*, ed. Roy Porter and Mikulas Teich (New York, 1994).

11. Janet Holland, Caroline Ramazanoglu, and Rachel Thomson, "In the Same Boat? The Gendered (In)experience of First Heterosex," in Diane Richardson, *Theorizing Heterosexuality: Telling It Straight* (Buckingham, 1996) 143 ff.; Susan Bordo, "Reading the Male Body" in *The Male Body: Features, Destinies, Exposures*, ed. Laurence Goldstein (Ann Arbor, Mich., 1997) 258 ff.

12. George Minois, *History of Old Age*, trans. Sarah Hanbury Tenison (Cambridge, U.K., 1987); Lois Banner, *In Full Flower: Aging Women, Power, and Sexuality* (New York, 1992).

13. *The Cultural Construction of Sexuality*, ed. P. Caplan (London, 1987) 22–24.

14. A. Choffé, *Causeries du docteur. Première partie. La Femme, sa beauté, sa santé par l'hygiène* (Paris, 1905) 93–95; *Science News* (12 July 1998): 7.

Chapter 4. Puberty and Purity

1. Sharon Golub, *Periods: From Menarche to Menopause* (London, 1992); Thomas Buckley and Alma Gottlieb, "A Critical Appraisal of Theories of Menstrual Symbolism," in *Blood Magic: The Anthropology of Menstruation* (Berkeley, 1988) 1–8.

2. Marcellin Camboulives, *L'Homme et la femme à tous les âges de la vie: Etude hygiènique, médicale, physiologique, social, et moral* (Paris, 1890) 184; A. Gensse, *Les Quatre âges de la femme au point de vue physiologique* (Corbeil, 1899) 15–16.

3. Georges Houlnick, *La Femme et la fonction menstruelle: Hygiène de la période cataméniale* (Paris, 1926) 54; Yvonne Verdier, *Façons de dire, façons de faire: La Laveuse, la couturière, la cuisinière* (Paris, 1979) 19–46.

4. Hélina Gaboriau, *Les Trois âges de la femme* (Paris, 1923).

5. Camboulives, *L'Homme et la femme*, 171; Gensse, *Les Quatre âges de la femme*, 15–16.

6. Lucie Delarue-Mardrus, *Le Roman de six petites filles* (Paris, n.d.) 155–56.

7. Marie Houdré-Boursin, *Ma Doctoresse: Guide pratique d'hygiène et de médecine de la femme moderne* (Strasbourg, 1930) 126.

8. A. Quint, *Manuel d'hygiène et d'enseignement social* (Paris, 1914) 61; Une Doctoresse, *Le Guide médical de la femme et de la famille* (Paris, 1933) 269.

9. Charles Platon and Antoine Lacroix, *Le Sauvetage de la femme: Essai de traitement prophylactique des maladies des femmes* (Toulouse, 1934) 59.

10. Paul Dalché, *Gynécologie médicale: La Puberté chez la femme* (Paris, 1906) 27; N. Eddé, *Hygiène des maladies de la femme* (Paris, 1922) 75–83; Houlnick, *La Femme et la fonction menstruelle*, 2.

11. Augusta Moll-Weiss, *Les Mères de demain: L'Education de la jeune fille d'après sa physiologie* (Paris, 1902).

12. Linda L. Clark, *Schooling the Daughters of Marianne: Textbooks and the Socialization of Girls in Modern French Primary Schools* (Albany, 1984) 14; Odile Arnold, *Le Corps et l'âme: La Vie des religieuses au XIXe siècle* (Paris, 1984) 81, 90, 135, and 156.

13. Judith Gautier, *Le Collier des jours: Souvenirs de ma vie* (Paris, n.d.) 154 ff.; Liane de Pougy, *My Blue Notebooks,* trans. Diana Athill (New York, 1979) 100.

14. For a Freudian interpretation, see Nancy Friday, *The Power of Beauty* (New York, 1996) 107 ff.

15. C. Pozzi, *Journal de jeunesse, 1893–1906* (Paris, 1995) 120, 126, and 137.

16. Louise Weiss, *Mémoires d'une Européenne.* 1. *1893–1919* (Paris, 1968) 184; Emilie Carles as told to Robert Destanque, *A Life of Her Own: The Transformation of a Countrywoman in Twentieth-Century France,* trans. A. H. Goldberger (New York, 1992) 52.

17. Anne-Marie Sohn, *Du Premier baiser à l'alcove: La Sexualité des Français au quotidien* (Paris, 1996) 85–87.

18. Marie-Victoire Louis, "Sexualité et prostitution," in *Madeleine Pelletier (1874–1939): Logique et infortunes d'un combat pour l'égalité,* ed. C. Bard (Paris, 1992) 112–14; Simone de Beauvoir, *Memoirs of a Dutiful Daughter,* trans. James Kirkup (New York, 1959) 86 and 101; *The Second Sex,* trans. H. M. Parschley (New York, 1952) 24 ff.; Margaret A. Simons and Jessica Benjamin, "Simone de Beauvoir: An Interview," *Feminist Studies* 5, 2 (1979): 330–45.

19. Serge Grafteaux, *Mémé Santerre: A French Woman of the People,* trans. Louise A. and Kathryn L. Tilly (New York, 1985) 28–29.

20. For example, Dalché, *Gynécologie médicale,* 26; Gensse, *Les Quatre âges de la femme,* 64.

21. Adrien Proust, "Le Travail de nuit des femmes dans l'industrie, au point de vue d'hygiène," *Revue d'hygiène et de police sanitaire* 12 (1890).

22. René Martial, *Hygiène individuelle du travailleur* (Paris, 1907) 28–33, 44, 108–14, and 164–70.

23. Georges Stade, *Nécessité d'enseigner aux jeunes fille l'hygiène et quelques notions de médecine pratique* (Paris, 1900) 15.

24. M. de Thilo, *L'Hygiène de la femme,* 62 ff.; E. Monin, *La Santé de la femme* (Paris, 1928).

25. Monin, *La Santé de la femme,* 15.

26. Germaine Montreuil-Strauss, *Tu seras mère: La Fonction maternelle* (Paris, n.d.) 11.

27. David Richard, *Histoire de la génération chez l'homme et chez la femme,* 2nd ed. (Paris, 1883) 164; E. A. Goupil, *Les Trois âges de la femme. Première partie. L'Age de formation* (Paris, 1886) 13–17, 34–35, and 91; Charles Barbaud and Charles Lefevre, *La Puberté chez la femme* (Paris, 1897) 170–75.

28. Samuel Pozzi, *Treatise on Gynaecology Medical and Surgical,* trans. B. H. Wells

(New York, 1894) 548–51; A. Siredey, *L'Hygiène des maladies de la femme* (Paris, 1907) 5.

29. Adam Raciborski, *De la Puberté et de l'âge critique chez la femme au point de vue physiologique, hygiènique, et médical et de la ponte periodique chez la femme et les mammifères* (Paris, 1844) vii–ix, 6–7, 18–72, and 89; Raciborski, *Traité de la menstruation* (Paris, 1868) 15–17, 38–39, and 105.

30. Barbaud and Lefevre, *La Puberté chez la femme*, 32–33 and 68; Dalché, *Gynécologie médicale*, 17–20.

31. M. Derville, *La Puberté et ses accidents chez la femme* (Paris, 1933) 22–23.

32. Jules Arnould, "Conditions de salubrité des ateliers de gazage dans les filature de coton," *Annales d'hygiène publique et de médecine légale* (1879); Charles Mannheim, *De la Condition des ouvriers dans les manufactures de l'état (tabac, allumettes)* (Paris, 1902) 51.

33. Goupil, *Les Trois âges de la femme*, 42; Barbaud and Lefevre, *La Puberté chez la femme*, 5; Marthe Francillon, *Essai sur la puberté chez la femme: Essai de psycho-physiologie féminine* (Paris, 1906) 81; Dalché, *Gynécologie médicale*, 30–32.

34. Goupil, *Les Trois âges de la femme*, 48; Camboulives, *L'Homme et la femme*, 187; Montreuil-Strauss, *Tu seras mère*, 12.

35. Golub, *Periods*, 13 ff.; Buckley and Gottlieb, "A Critical Appraisal of Theories of Menstrual Symbolism," 19 ff.

36. Francillon, *Essai sur la puberté*, 74–81; Eddé, *Hygiène des maladies de la femme*, 59; Gaboriau, *Les Trois âges de la femme*, 77; Houlnick, *La Femme et la fonction menstruelle*, 29.

37. Raciborski, *Traité de la menstruation*, 90–107.

38. Cited in Houlnick, *La Femme et la fonction menstruelle*, 17.

39. Francillon, *Essai sur la puberté*, 2–63; Marthe Francillon-Lobre, *Hygiène de la femme et de la jeune fille* (Paris, 1909) 173; Dalché, *Gynécologie médicale*, 6–9 and 28.

40. Derville, *La Puberté*, 8, 13–15, and 32–34; Madeleine Hirsch, "Les Troubles de la menstruation à la période pubertaire," and Guy Laroche, "La Puberté: Son Evolution normale: Ses Déviations pathologiques," in *La Puberté: Etude clinique et physiopathologique*, ed. Guy Laroche (Paris, 1938).

41. H. Busquet, *La Fonction sexuelle* (Paris, 1910) 15–122; Henri Fischer, *Hygiène d'enfance: L'Education sexuelle* (Paris, 1903) 4, 203 ff., and 248; Serge-Paul, *Histoire naturelle de l'homme* (Paris, n.d.) 69 ff.

42. Richard, *Histoire de la génération*, 139; Camboulives, *L'Homme et la femme*, 138; Edmond Caubet, *Manuel de thérapeutique gynécologique. II. Hygiène de la femme* (Paris, 1894) 22; Eddé, *Hygiène des maladies de la femme*, 75.

43. Richard, *Histoire de la génération*, 143–45; Eddé, *Hygiène des maladies de la femme*, 74.

44. Anna Fischer, *La Femme, médecin du foyer*, trans. Louise Azéma (Paris, 1905) 269; Monin, *La Santé de la femme*, 28; Houdré-Boursin, *Ma Doctoresse*, 131.

45. Wesley D. Camp, *Marriage and the Family in France since the Revolution* (New York, 1961) 52–53.

46. Gabriel Compayre, *L'Adolescence: Etudes de psychologie et de pédagogie*, 2nd ed. (Paris, 1910) 53. I am grateful to Kathleen Alaimo for drawing my attention to this source.

47. Eddé, *Hygiène des maladies de la femme*, 74–80; Paul Godin, *Recherches anthropométriques sur la croissance des diverses parties du corps*, 2nd ed. (Paris, 1935).

48. M. Watrin, "Aperçu sur la physiologie et la pathologie sexuelle de la femme," in Albert Hogge et al., *Physiologie sexuelle normale et pathologique* (Paris, 1931) 114–15.

49. Goupil, *Les Trois âges de la femme*, 111–12; M. de Thilo, *L'Hygiène de la femme* (Paris, 1891) 59–61; Caubet, *Manuel de thérapeutique gynécologique*, ii and 25–27; Gensse, *Les Quatre âges de la femme*, 31.

50. Goupil, *Les Trois âges de la femme*, 47, 54, 96–106, and 112–14; Barbaud and Lefevre, *La Puberté chez la femme*, iii and 125.

51. Sohn, *Du Premier baiser*, 81–82.

52. Dr. Alquier, *La Femme à Vichy: L'Idéal de la thérapeutique vaginale alcaline réalisé par la nouvelle douche en hamac* (Vichy, 1913); Paul Gandy, *Les Maladies des femmes à Bagnères-de-Bigorre du XVIe siècle à nos jours* (Bagnères-de-Bigorre, 1910) 30–31; Grellety, *Les Médecins et les femmes* (Macon, 1896) 3 ff.

53. M. A. Proust, *Rapport général à M. le Ministre de Commerce sur le service médical des eaux minérales de la France . . . 1879* (Paris, 1883); C. Robin, *Rapport général à M. le Ministre de l'Intérieur sur le service médical des eaux minérales de France . . . 1889* (Paris, 1893) 3–5; F. de Ranse, *Quelques considérations sur le traitement hydrominéral des maladies des femmes* (Paris, 1900).

54. Douglas Peter Mackaman, *Leisure Settings: Bourgeois Culture, Medicine, and the Spa in Modern France* (Chicago, 1998) 121 ff.

55. André Robin and Paul Dalché, *Traitement médical des maladies des femmes*, 2nd ed. (Paris, 1902) 461 ff.; G. Bardet, *Notions d'hydrologie moderne* (Paris, 1909); Laboure, "Promenades à travers nos stations thermales, climatiques, et balnéaires," *Maman* (10 May 1931) and subsequent issues.

56. François Cartier, *Traité complet de thérapeutique homéopathique. IV. Maladies des femmes et des enfants* (Paris, 1929) 506–8; Derville, *La Puberté*, 133.

57. Dalché, *Gynécologie médicale*, 69–82; Natalie Sibirtzow, *Contribution à l'étude du traitement kinesthérapique de certaines dysménorrhées* (Lyon, 1905); Hélène Goldspiegel, "Du Traitement manuel des maladies des femmes selon la méthode de Thure Brandt," *Archives de Toxologie* (Nov. 1889); Karl Lange, *Du Massage vibratoire surtout en ce qui concerne les maladies des femmes*, trans. M. Dauphin (Nancy, 1899).

58. Rachel P. Maines, *The Technology of Orgasm: Hysteria, the Vibrator, and Women's Sexual Satisfaction* (Baltimore, 1999).

59. Goupil, *Les Trois âges de la femme*, 120–3; Barbaud and Lefevre, *La Puberté chez la femme*, 177–78; advertisements in the *Journal des desmoiselles* (1880s).

60. Francillon-Lobre, *Hygiène de la femme*, 173. Monin's frequently reprinted *Santé de la femme*, 14, continued to link chlorosis with menstrual disturbances.

61. David S. Barnes, *The Making of a Social Disease: Tuberculosis in Nineteenth-Century France* (Berkeley, 1995).

62. Susan Griffin, *What Her Body Thought: A Journey into the Shadows* (San Francisco, 1999). My thanks to Susan Wendell for recommending this book.

63. Jeanne Angèle Dupasquier, *Ma Fille* (Lyon, 1895). See also Philippe Lejeune, *Le Moi des demoiselles: Enquête sur le journal de jeune fille* (Paris, 1993) 421 and passim.

64. Isabelle Grellet and Caroline Kruse, *Histoires de la tuberculose: Les Fièvres de l'âme, 1800–1940* (Paris, 1983) 144–47 and 163–66; Pierre Guillaume, *Du Désespoir au salut: Les Tuberculeux aux 19e et 20e siècles* (Paris, 1986) 141 ff.

65. Grellet and Kruse, *Histoires de la tuberculose*, 95 ff.; Guillaume, *Du Désespoir au salut*, 107 ff.

66. ADN, M228/5 and M228/6, correspondence from Prefect, 1905, and inquiry into antitubercular fight, also M229/30, Comité de Préservation Antituberculaire, 1925; Françoise Thébaud, *Quand nos grand-meres donnaient la vie: La Maternité en France dans l'entre-deux guerres* (Lyon, 1986) 34.

67. Francisque Jaubert, *Principales causes de mortalité à Lyon.* (Lyon, 1926); Paul Parisot, *Annuaire statistique et démographique 1927* (Nancy, 1928) 4 and end tables.

68. Barbaud and Lefevre, *La Puberté chez la femme*, 173–84.

69. Henri Vignes, *Physiologie gynécologique et médecine des femmes* (Paris, 1929) 92–93; Derville, *La Puberté*, 48–50.

70. H. Mery, "La Préservation scolaire contre la tuberculose," *Conférences du Laboratoire d'hygiène scolaire 1909* (Paris, 1909) 1–32.

71. Catherine Pozzi, *Journal 1913–1934* (Paris, 1987) 44, 58, 70, 89–92, 389–91, 402–5, 409–10, and 645 ff.

72. Vignes, *Physiologie gynécologique*, 99–100.

73. S. Icard, *La Femme pendant la période menstruelle* (Paris, 1890) x–xi, 23–24, 50 ff., and 263–71.

74. Francillon, *Essai sur la puberté*, 189 and 197; Francillon-Lobre, *Hygiène de la femme*, 105.

75. Abbé Chaupitre, *La Santé pour toutes les femmes* (Rennes, 1911) 5–6, 12, and 51–53.

76. Emile Laurent, *L'Amour morbide: Etude de psychologie pathologique* (Paris, 1891) 46–119.

77. Marthe Noel Evans, *Fits and Starts: A Genealogy of Hysteria in Modern France* (Ithaca, 1991) 9–72; André Rouille, *Le Corps et son image* (La Rochelle, 1996) 55 ff.

78. Evans, *Fits and Starts*, 78–105.

79. Jules Rochard, "L'Education des filles," *Revue de deux mondes* (1 Feb. 1888) 651 and 661–63. See also the publications of the "School for Parents" in the 1930s.

80. J.-B. Fonssagrives, *L'Education physique des jeunes filles ou avis aux mères*

(Paris, 1869) v and vii; Hyppolyte Meunier, *Le Docteur au village: Entretiens familiers sur l'hygiène* (Paris, 1880) 3; Caubet, *Manuel de thérapeutique gynécologique,* ii and 1; G. M. Bessède, *L'Instruction sexuelle à l'école et dans la famille* (Paris, 1911) 87.

81. Fonssagrives, *L'Education physique des jeunes filles,* 3; Barbaud and Lefevre, *La Puberté chez la femme,* vi, quoting Fonssagrives; Monin, *La Santé de la femme,* 9.

82. René Biot, *Ce que la biologie nous apprend de la nature de la femme* (Tours, 1928) 27.

83. Gensse, *Les Quatre âges de la femme,* 25; Siredey, *L'Hygiène des maladies de la femme,* vii and 5.

84. Charlotte L. Houlton, "Questions d'hygiène spéciale de la femme," *La Dame à la lampe,* 3, 25 (1924); Montreuil-Stauss, *Tu seras mère,* 12; Houdré-Boursin, *Ma Doctoresse,* 129.

85. Houlnick, *La Femme et la fonction menstruelle,* 80–85; Anne-Maire Chartier and Jean Hébard, *Discours sur la lecture (1880–1980)* (Paris, 1989) 49 ff.

86. Goupil, *Les Trois âges de la femme,* 42; Doctoresse, *Le Guide médical de la femme,* 271. See also Francillon, *Essai sur la puberté,* 194–98; Derville, *La Puberté,* Chap. 4.

87. Caubet, *Manuel de thérapeutique gynécologique,* 2 and 23; Francillon-Lobre, *Hygiène de la femme,* 173.

88. Siredey, *L'Hygiène des maladies de la femme,* 17; Monin, *La Santé de la femme,* 15.

89. Derville, *La Puberté,* 28; Laroche, "La Puberté," 11.

90. A. Hurel, *Les Ecoles de village dans un canton de Normandie: Etude d'hygiène* (Paris, 1879); E. Barotte, *Statistique hygiènique des écoles primaires du Département de l'Aube* (Troyes, 1882).

91. AN, F17 11781, Hygiène scolaire, reports about eye problems in the schools, 1879–81.

92. Gustave Lagneau, *Du Surmenage intellectuel et de la sedentarité dans les écoles* (Paris, 1886) 19–43; Jules Rochard, "L'Education hygiènique et le surmenage intellectuel," *Revue des deux mondes* (1888): 425–55; A. Collineau, *Hygiène à l'école: Pédagogie scientifique* (Paris, 1889) 180 ff.; Emile Barthes, *Manuel d'hygiène scolaire à l'usage des instituteurs, des lycées, collèges* (Paris, 1889) 3–26; Roger Hyvert, *Conférences populaires d'hygiène pratique á l'usage des écoles normales, de l'enseignement secondaire classique* (Paris, 1901) 54–56.

93. AN, F17 11781, Medical Inspection, responses to the 1887 questionnaire on the execution of the 1879 circular.

94. Ministère de l'Education Nationale, *Prescriptions d'hygiène appliquées dans les lycées et collèges de garçons et filles* (Paris, 1934) 3–4; Jules Courmont and A. Rochaix, *Précis d'hygiène,* 4th ed. (Paris, 1932) 38 ff.

95. Robert Dinet, *Physiologie et pathologie de l'éducation* (Paris, 1903) 67 ff., Des-

parmet-Ruello, "Le Progrès d'hygiène realisés au lycée de jeunes fille de Lyon," *Premier congrès d'hygiène scolaire 1903* (Paris, 1903) 253–60.

96. W. Vandereycken and R. van Deth, *From Fasting Saints to Anorexic Girls: The History of Self-Starvation* (London, 1994), find evidence of earlier French medical identification of anorexia, bulimia, and pica, but they acknowledge that these studies had little impact.

97. Cited in Joan Jacobs Brumberg, *Fasting Girls: The History of Anorexia Nervosa* (New York, 1988) 126 ff. and 213 ff.

98. Marcel Labbé, *Maigreur et obesité* (Paris, 1933) 6–22.

Chapter 5. Sexual Initiation and Sex Education

1. An early example of marital advice is A. Debay, *Philosophie du mariage* (Paris, 1865).

2. Vernon A. Rosario, *The Erotic Imagination: French Histories of Perversity* (New York, 1997) 152.

3. Alain Corbin, *Women for Hire: Prostitution and Sexuality in France after 1850*, trans. Alan Sheridon (Cambridge, 1990). See also Marcellin Camboulives, *L'Homme et la femme à tous les âges de la vie: Etude hygiènique, médicale, physiologique, social, et moral* (Paris, 1890) 30 ff. and 253 ff.

4. Louise d'Alq, *Les Secrets du cabinet de toilette: Conseils et recettes* (Paris, 1881) 71.

5. Elizabeth de Gramont, *Souvenirs du monde de 1890 à 1940. I. Au temps d'équipages* (Paris, 1966) 145.

6. Catherine Pozzi, *Journal de jeunesse. 1893–1906* (Paris, 1995) 106 and 154; Lucie Delarue-Mardrus, "Mes Mémoires," *Revue des deux mondes* (12 March 1938): 72–73 and 82–83.

7. L. Duchesne and E. Michel, *Traité élémentaire d'hygiène*, 3rd ed. (Paris, 1887) 162–63; J. L. Mora and C. Vesiez, *Nouveau cours d'hygiène* (Paris, 1890) 26–30; Vicomtesse Nacla, *Il! Le Choisir, le garder* (Paris, 1897) 17–40; Gramont, *Souvenirs du monde de 1890 à 1940. III. Claire de lune et taxi-auto*, chapter entitled Retrospective (1900–14). See also Anne-Marie Sohn, *Du Premier baiser à l'alcove: La Sexualité des Français au quotidien* (Paris, 1996) 207–8.

8. Julie Manet, *Journal (1893–1899)* (Paris, 1979) 133 and 148; Clara Malraux, *Memoirs*, trans. P. O'Brien (New York, 1967) 100–101.

9. Malraux, *Memoirs*, 138–39; Baronne J. Michaux, *En Marge du drame: Journal d'une Parisienne pendant la guerre 1914–1915* (Paris, 1916) 18, 124–25, 135, 185–86, 211, and 232–33; Gramont, *Souvenirs du monde de 1890 à 1940. III. Clair de lune et taxi-auto*, 81–84 and 187–88.

10. Mary Louise Roberts, *Civilization without Sexes: Reconstructing Gender in Postwar France, 1917–1927* (Chicago, 1994) 154 and 183.

11. Simone de Beauvoir, *Memoirs of a Dutiful Daughter*, trans. James Kirkup (New York, 1959) 71 and 171 ff.

12. Liane de Pougy, *My Blue Notebooks*, trans. Dianna Athill (New York, 1979) 37 and 101; Zelia Villeneuve, *Charme et beauté: Recettes merveilleuses et secrets d'une Parisienne révélés à une Americaine* (Paris, 1920) 68–70.

13. See review of Jenny's collection in *Femina* (Feb. 1924), reviews of the collections in *L'Officiel de la couture* (Jan. and Apr. 1924 and Oct. 1928), and F.C. "Pour les sports," in *Le Jardin des modes* (15 May 1925).

14. Roberts, *Civilization without Sexes*, 67–71.

15. Frère Philippe de Jésus, *La Modestie et les modes féminines* (Lyon, 1926).

16. Marcy Ducray, "Nos Robes ont enfin dégagé leur ligne," *Excelsior* (fall 1930) and "Glanez dans les collections d'été," *La Mode pratique* (12 Mar. 1938).

17. Emmanuel Viau, *La Jeune fille moderne et le mariage: Préparation ou imprévision?* (Avignon, 1932) 13, 67–79, and 96–113.

18. Canon Cordonnier, *Causeries familiales*. II. *Le Mariage approche . . . Etes-vous prêtes?* (Avignon, 1935) 45–85.

19. Monique Levallet-Montal, *Pour les vingt ans de Colette* (Paris, 1935) 196–223.

20. Martine Segalen, *Love and Power in the Peasant Family*, trans. Sarah Matthews (Chicago, 1980) Chap. 1; Rachel Fuchs, *Poor and Pregnant in Paris: Strategies for Survival in the Nineteenth Century* (New Brunswick, 1992) 17 and 101 ff.; Sohn, *Du Premier baiser*, 224.

21. Abbé Charles Grimaud, *Aux Mères et à leurs grandes jeunes filles, futures épouses*, 19th ed. (Paris, 1927) 24–25, 31, 140–43, 181, 186, 190–93, and 282. On beliefs about girls' innocence, see Anne Martin-Fugier, *La Bourgeoisie: Femme au temps de Paul Bourget* (Paris, 1983) 56.

22. Pierre de Lano, *Du Coeur aux sens: A Travers le mariage. Libres intimités. Dans le péché* (Paris, 1898) 15; G. Bardet, *Mariage et sexualité: Le Bréviaire de l'amour* (Paris, 1933) 62; Paul Reboux, *Le Nouveau savoir-aimer* (Paris, 1938) 26 and 33–36.

23. Henri Fischer, *Hygiène d'enfance: L'Education sexuelle* (Paris, 1903) 20; Dr. Mayoux, *L'Education des sexes* (Paris, 1906) 10; Jeanne Stephani-Cherbuliz, *Le Sexe a ses raisons: Instruction et éducation sexuelles* (Paris, 1934) 20–27.

24. A. Coriveaud, *Le Lendemain du mariage: Etude d'hygiène* (Paris, 1884) 9–16.

25. For example, A. Siredey, *L'Hygiène des maladies de la femme* (Paris, 1907) 28–29.

26. Georges Bataille, *Erotism: Death and Sensuality*, trans. Mary Dalwood (San Francisco, 1962) 109.

27. Beauvoir, *Memoirs of a Dutiful Daughter*, 163–71.

28. Sohn, *Du Premier baiser*, 26, 35, and 144.

29. Emilie Carles as told to Robert Destanque, *A Life of Her Own: The Transformation of a Countrywoman in Twentieth-Century France*, trans. A. H. Goldberger

(New York, 1992) 71; Bonnie G. Smith, *Confessions of a Concierge: Madame Lucie's History of Twentieth-Century France* (New Haven, 1985) 41.

30. E. A. Goupil, *Les Trois âges de la femme* (Paris, 1886) 6–7.

31. Emilie Lerou, *Sous le masque (Une vie au théâtre)* (Paris, 1908) 162–63.

32. Kiki, *Kiki's Memoirs* (Paris, 1930). I omit the group of lesbians, many of the foreigners, who left autobiographies. On these women, see Shari Benstock, *Women of the Left Bank, Paris 1900–1940* (Austin, Tex., 1986).

33. Elaine Showalter, *Sexual Anarchy: Gender and Culture at the Fin de Siècle* (London, 1991) 3.

34. Frédéric Monneyron, *L'Androgyne décadent: Mythe, figure, fantasmes* (Grenoble, 1996) 14–17 and 38 ff.; *Two Erotic Tales by Pierre Louÿs,* trans. Mary Hanson Harrison (Evanston, Ill., 1995). The cosmetics line called Chrysis was advertised in one of the first beauty magazines, *L'Art d'être jolie* (1904–5).

35. E. Stérian, *L'Education sexuelle* (Paris, 1910) 23–24, 36 ff., 50–53, 63–64, 77, and 79 ff.

36. L. Mathé, *L'Enseignement de l'hygiène sexuelle à l'école,* 2nd ed. (Paris, 1912) 109; V.-J. Pellissier, *Conseils utiles pour le mariage à l'usage des jeunes filles et des jeunes gens* (Draguignan, 1914) 39.

37. Alfred Fournier, *Syphilis et mariage,* 2nd ed. (Paris, 1890) 21–27 and 141–44.

38. Anne Carol, *Histoire de l'Eugénisme en France: Les Médecins et la procréation, XIXe–XXe siècle* (Paris, 1995) 51–63; Yvonne Knibiehler and Catherine Fouquet, *La Femme et les médecins* (Paris, 1983) 221.

39. Léon Blum, *Du Mariage,* in *L'Oeuvre de Léon Blum, 1905–1914* (Paris, 1962) esp. 49, 81, 152, and 167.

40. Marie Lenéru, *Journal, 1910–1918* (Paris, 1922) 45, 48, and 265.

41. *La Nouvelle législation des fiançailles et du mariage: Décret de la Congrégation du Concile, publié par l'ordre de Pie X* (Angers, 1908).

42. Jean Charruau, *Aux Jeunes filles: Vers le mariage* (Paris, 1904) 228 and 288–89; J. Hoppenot, *Petit catéchisme du mariage* (Paris, 1908) 173–78.

43. Paul de Régla, *L'Eglise et le mariage* (Paris, 1910).

44. *Faut-il instruire les jeunes filles des réalités du mariage?* (Saint-Girons, 1912).

45. Mgr. Henry Bolo, *Les Jeunes filles d'aujourd'hui: Trois conférences données à Paris, les 22, 29 mars et 5 avril 1911* (Paris, 1911). See also his *Les jeunes filles* (Paris, 1896).

46. Jean Marestan, *L'Education sexuelle* (Paris, 1916) 10 ff. and 43.

47. Edward Montier, *Le Mariage: Lettre à une jeune fille* (Paris, 1919) 2–18. The AMC published many Montier pamphlets.

48. Patricia J. Campbell, *Sex Education Books for Young Adults, 1892–1979* (New York, 1979) 6–8. Several of Mary Wood-Allen's titles were translated into French.

49. Sohn, *Du Premier baiser,* 62 and 153.

50. Françoise Loux, *Le Corps dans la société traditionnelle* (Paris, 1979) 114–20.

51. Charles Barbaud and Charles Lefevre, *La Puberté chez la femme* (Paris, 1897) 74.

52. Carles, *A Life of Her Own*, 50.

53. Frédéric Passy, *Entre mère et fille* (Paris, 1907); Jeanne Leroy-Allais, *Comment j'ai instruit mes filles des choses de la maternité* (Paris, 1930).

54. Léon Bourgeois, *Conseils pratiques à l'usage des jeunes femmes et des jeunes mères* (Paris, 1908); Marthe Francillon-Lobre, *Hygiène de la femme et de la jeune fille* (Paris, 1909) 125; Maurice Favreau, *Ce qu'il est indispensable de savoir sur l'hygiène de la femme et de l'enfant* (Bordeaux, 1924).

55. J.-R. Bourdon, *Traitement de la froideur chez la femme: Comment choisir sa compagne* (Paris, 1931) 171–72. On novels, see Laure Adler, Secrets *d'alcove: Histoire du couple de 1830 à 1930* (Paris, 1983) 33–35 and 51.

56. Anne-Marie Sohn, "Catholics between Abstinence and Appeasement of Lust," conference paper.

57. Angus McLaren, *Sexuality and Social Order: The Debate Over the Fertility of Women and Workers in France, 1770–1920* (New York, 1983) 44–45; Ralph Gibson, "Le Catholicisme et les femmes en France au XIXe siècle," *Revue d'histoire de l'Eglise de France* 79, 202 (Jan.-June 1993): 63–93. I thank Judith Stone for drawing this article to my attention.

58. Annie Stora-Lamarre, *L'Enfer de la IIIe République: Censeurs et pornographes (1881–1914)* (Paris, 1990) 31 and 38–39.

59. Carolyn Dean, "Pornography, Literature, and the Redemption of Virility in France, 1880–1930," *Différences* 5 (1995): 62–91.

60. Jean de Lardelec, *Les Livres sur l'éducation de la pureté . . . Guide pour leur choix à l'usage des parents, éducateurs, directeurs de conscience, membres de l'enseignement* (Paris, 1930).

61. Alexis Clerc, *Hygiène et médecine des deux sexes* (Paris, 1885) 5; G. M. Bessède, *L'Instruction sexuelle à l'école et dans la famille* (Paris, 1911) 7.

62. H. Abrand, *Aux Parents et aux éducateurs: Education de la pureté et préparation au mariage* (Paris, 1922) 22–34.

63. August Forel, *The Sexual Question: A Study of the Sexual Life in All Its Aspects*, 2nd ed. (New York, 1944) preface to the 2nd ed.

64. Nacla, *Il! Le Choisir*, 80.

65. Anna Fischer, *La Femme, médecin du foyer*, trans Louise Azéma (Paris, 1905) 264.

66. Hélina Gaboriau, *Les Trois âges de la femme* (Paris, 1923) 94.

67. Siân Reynolds makes this point more generally in *France between the Wars: Gender and Politics* (New York, 1996).

68. N. Nelfrand, *Ce que toute jeune fille doit savoir à l'âge de la puberté: Education*

sexuelle de l'adolescence. Petite physiologie génitale de l'hygiène interne de l'homme et de la femme (Paris, 1932) 20–41.

69. Leslie A. Hall, *Hidden Anxieties: Male Sexuality, 1900–1950* (London, 1991); Kevin White, *The First Sexual Revolution: The Emergence of Male Heterosexuality in Modern America* (New York, 1993); Michael S. Kimmel, "Consuming Manhood: The Feminization of American Culture and the Recreation of the Male Body, 1832–1920" in *The Male Body: Features, Destinies, Exposures,* ed. Laurence Goldstein (Ann Arbor, Mich., 1997).

70. Stérian, *L'Education sexuelle,* 77 ff. and 146 ff.; G. J. Witkowski, *La Génération humaine,* 7th ed. (Paris, 1927) 229 ff.; L.-M. Des Préaux, *L'Education des sexes et la répopulation* (Paris, 1907).

71. Lano, *Du Coeur aux sens,* 25.

72. Stephani-Cherbuliz, *Le Sexe a ses raisons,* 127 ff.; Marie Houdré-Boursin, *Ma Doctoresse: Guide pratique d'hygiène et de médecine de la femme moderne* (Strasbourg, 1930) 128.

73. Stérian, *L'Education sexuelle,* 110–19; Georges Surbled, *La Vie à deux: Hygiène du mariage,* 5th ed. (Paris, 1911) 55.

74. Reboux, *Le Nouveau savoir-aimer,* 36, raised the possibility of sadistic readings.

75. See Paul R. Abramson and Steven D. Pinkerton, *With Pleasure: Thought on the Nature of Human Sexuality* (New York, 1995) 39 ff.

76. P. Aulaire, *La Leçon d'amour: Traité d'instruction et d'éducation sexuelles* (Paris, 1930) 118; Marestan, *L'Education sexuelle,* 34; Clerc, *Hygiène et médecine des deux sexes,* 280–81.

77. P. de Bourgogne, *Aux Fiancés: Conseils médicaux d'hygiène pratique. Ce que tout homme doit savoir* (Paris, 1913) 31–36; H. Fischer, *Hygiène d'enfance,* 265–67; Reboux, *Le Nouveau savoir-aimer,* 37; Surbled, *La Vie à deux,* ix, 56–57, and 75–80. See also Michel Bourgas, *Le Droit à l'amour pour la femme* (Paris, 1919) 81 ff.

78. G. Bardet, *Mariage et sexualité,* 62; Reboux, *Le Nouveau savoir-aimer,* 25–36; *Investigating Sex: Surrealist Research, 1928–1932,* ed. José Pierre, trans. Malcolm Imrie (London, 1992).

79. N. Eddé, *Hygiène des maladies de la femme* (Paris, 1922) 96–97.

80. Mayoux, *L'Education des sexes,* 9 and 17, but see also Bourgas, *Le Droit à l'amour pour la femme;* Marestan, *L'Education sexuelle.* On novels, see Mireille Dottin-Orsini, *Cette femme qu'ils disent fatale* (Paris, 1993) 15, 31, and 92 ff.

81. Siredey, *L'Hygiène des maladies de la femme,* 29.

82. Odile Arnold, *Le Corps et l'âme: La Vie des religieuses au XIXe siècle* (Paris, 1984) 81 and 195–97; Mère Marie du Sacré-Coeur, *La Formation catholique de la femme contemporaine,* 2nd ed. (Paris, 1899) 21–32.

83. Abrand, *Aux Parents et aux éducateurs,* 27–34.

84. Camolet-See, "Comment redresser les déviations sexuelles?" in *L'Eglise et*

l'éducation sexuelle (Paris, 1929) 76–85; R. P. Ganay, Dr. Abrand, and Abbé J. Viollet, *Les Initiations nécessaires*, 26th ed. (Paris, 1933); M. Admary, *Initiations par une maman* (Paris, 1938) 42 ff.

85. Georges Stodel, *Nécessité d'enseigner aux jeunes filles l'hygiène et quelques notions de médecine pratique* (Paris, 1900) 10 and 15–20.

86. Bessède, *L'Instruction sexuelle*, 7 ff.; L. Mathé, *L'Enseignement de l'hygiène sexuelle à l'école*, 2nd ed. (Paris, 1912) 14, 21, and 98 ff.; Jablonski, *L'Education sexuelle: Conférence faite à la Ligue d'Hygiène scolaire* (Poitiers, 1913).

87. M. R. Paty, "L'Enseignement de l'hygiène à l'école primaire," in *Journées médico-scolaires de l'enfance d'âge scolaire* (Paris, 1935) 260–64; A. Pizon, *Hygiène: Nouveaux programmes. Classe de 3me, garçons et filles* (Paris, 1927).

88. A. Calmette, *Simple causerie pour l'éducation sexuelle des jeunes garçons de quinze ans* (Paris, 1920) 9 ff.; J. Pouy, *Conseils à la jeunesse sur l'éducation sexuelle* (Paris, 1928) 7 ff.

89. Mme. Avril de Sainte-Croix, *L'Education sexuelle* (Paris, 1918) 4–40. For a similar plan, see Stephani-Cherbuliz, *Le Sexe a ses raisons*, 199 ff.

90. Bourgas, *Le Droit à l'amour pour la femme*, 1–4.

91. Vaucaire, *Ce que toute jeune fille à marier doit savoir* (Paris, 1921) 15 ff. and 39 ff.

92. Carol, *Histoire de l'eugénisme*, 108.

93. Ganay et al., *Les Initiations nécessaires*, 5–7.

94. Aulaire, *La Leçon d'amour*, 7 and 19; Stephani-Cherbuliz, *Le Sexe a ses raisons*, 13–20, 54–55, and 171–78; Léon Eisenstein, "Education sexuelle: Etude biologique et psychique du problème" (Thèse, méd., Lyon, 1939).

95. International Planned Parenthood Federation, *A Survey on the Status of Sex Education in European Member Countries* (London, 1975) 6–7, 19, 22–27, and 46–47.

96. BHVP, Fonds Dr. Germaine Montreuil-Straus, esp. Dr. Aimé Gauthier, "La Femme contre le péril vénérien," *Vers la santé*, 6, 11 (Nov. 1925); Dr. Germaine Montreuil-Straus, *L'Oeuvre accomplie par le Comité d'Education féminine (1925–1935)*.

97. Nelfrand, *Ce que toute jeune fille doit savoir*, 63–66.

98. Charles Platon and Antoine Lacroix, *Le Sauvetage de la femme: Essai de traitement prophylactique des maladies des femmes* (Paris, 1934) 57; Montreuil-Straus "Note relative à l'éducation sexuelle des jeunes filles," in *L'Eglise et l'éducation sexuelle*, 142–46.

99. Sohn, *Du Premier baiser*, 224.

100. Bernard Lanos and Annick Lanos, *Fiancés et jeunes mariés de notre temps* (Paris, 1968) 234 ff.

Chapter 6. Pleasure and Procreation

1. Dr. Serge-Paul, *Physiologie de la vie sexuelle chez l'homme et chez la femme* (Paris, 1910) 111.

2. Hélina Gaboriau, *Les Trois âges de la femme* (Paris, 1923) 92–97.

3. Edmond Caubet, *Manuel de thérapeutique gynécologique*. II. *Hygiène de la femme* (Paris, 1894) 29–30; Marthe Francillon-Lobre, *Hygiène de la femme et de la jeune fille* (Paris, 1909) 126; R. Cotel-Civa, *Le Foyer conjugal: Guide des époux* (Paris, 1929) 11, 30–36, and 46.

4. Michel Bourgas, *Le Droit à l'amour pour la femme* (Paris, 1919) 135–36; René Vaucaire, *Ce que toute jeune fille à marier doit savoir* (Paris, 1921) 95–96.

5. Mary Lynn Stewart, *Women, Work, and the French State: Labour Protection and Social Patriarchy, 1879–1919* (Montreal, 1989) 182 ff.

6. Anne Carol, *Histoire de l'eugénisme en France: Les médecins et la procréation, XIXe–XXe siècle* (Paris, 1995) 38, 43–49, 73–74, and 135.

7. Françoise Thébaud, *Quand nos grand-mères donnaient la vie: La Maternité en France dans l'entre-deux guerres* (Lyon, 1986) 30.

8. E. Monin, *La Santé de la femme* (Paris, 1928) 22; Marie Houdré-Boursin, *Ma Doctoresse: Guide pratique d'hygiène et de médecine de la femme moderne* (Strasbourg, 1930) 131–32; L. Cleisz, *Hygiène de la grossesse* (Paris, 1933) 3–5; Charles Platon and Antoine Lacroix, *Le Sauvetage de la femme: Essai de traitement prophylactique des malades des femmes* (Toulouse, 1934) 24–37.

9. Thébaud, *Quand nos grand-mères donnaient la vie*, 83.

10. For example, David Richard, *Histoire de la génération chez l'homme et chez la femme*, 2nd ed. (Paris, 1883) 63 and 97–98; A. Moussaud, *Précis pratique des maladies des femmes: Impuissance et stérilité* (Paris, 1887) 23 ff.

11. Jean Marestan, *L'Education sexuelle* (Paris, 1916) 34 ff., 67–70, and 118 ff. See also Madeleine Pelletier, *Le Droit à l'avortement* (Lorulot, n.d.).

12. AN, F7 13955, Malthusianisme. Notes, presse, 1907–25.

13. Roy Porter and Lesley Hall, *The Facts of Life: The Creation of Sexual Knowledge in Britain, 1650–1950* (New Haven, 1995) 203 ff.

14. Joanna Bourke, *Dismembering the Male: Men's Bodies, Britain, and the Great War* (London, 1996) 38. Bourke cites an English translation of Dr. Doyan's criticism of the French army medical service on page 261, endnote 12.

15. See "Amours de Ponceau" in Georges Duhamel, *Souvenirs de la grande guerre*, ed. Tony Evans (London, 1985). See also Margaret Darrow, "French Volunteer Nursing and the Myth of War Experience in World War I," *American Historical Review*, 101 (Feb. 1996).

16. Jules Courmont and A. Rochaix, *Précis d'hygiène*, 4th ed. (Paris, 1932) 23–27 and 30–36.

17. Bourgas, *Le Droit à l'amour*, 7, 10, 30, 35, 102–10, 135, and 177.

18. Anne-Marie Sohn, *Du Premier baiser à l'alcove: La Sexualité des Français au quotidien* (Paris, 1996) 281 ff.

19. H. Abrand, *Aux Parents et aux éducateurs: Education de la pureté et préparation au mariage* (Paris, 1922) 27–34.

20. Anne-Marie Sohn, "Catholics between Abstinence and Appeasement of Lust," conference paper.

21. Jaf, *L'Art de conserver l'amour dans le mariage* (Paris, 1921) 10–12; Henri Drouin, *Conseils aux jeunes gens: Esquisse d'un enseignement sexuel à l'usage des jeunes gens et des adultes des deux sexes* (Paris, 1926) 63.

22. Louis Baudry de Saunier, *Education sexuelle* (Paris, 1930) 9 and 99–100.

23. Jeannine Martay, *L'Hygiène dans les soins de toilette chez la jeune fille et chez la femme* (Paris, 1909) 201–5; A. Siredey, *L'Hygiène des maladies de la femme* (Paris, 1907) 33.

24. Une Doctoresse, *Le Guide médical de la femme et de la famille* (Paris, 1933) 280; N. Eddé, *Hygiène des maladies de la femme* (Paris, 1922) 100–101; Gaboriau, *Les Trois âges de la femme*, 34; Houdré-Boursin, *Ma Doctoresse*, 137.

25. H. Jussey, *Histoire sexuelle de la femme* (Paris, 1928) 30–31.

26. Shari Benstock, *Women of the Left Bank, Paris, 1900–1940* (Austin, Tex., 1986).

27. Henri Drouin, *Femmes damnées*, 3rd ed. (Paris, 1929).

28. Jussey, *Histoire sexuelle*, 18–19 and 29; Drouin, *Conseils*, 70.

29. J. R. Bourdon, *Les Rapports sexuels: Guide moderne des époux* (Paris, 1928) 96–98.

30. *Revue française de psychanalyse* (1928) inserts for the Depot legal.

31. Marie Bonaparte, "Introduction à la théorie des instincts," Parts 1, 2, 3, and 4, *Revue française de psychanalyse*, 7 (1934): 218–30, 250–54, 423–24, and 616–18.

32. A.-E. Narjani (aka Marie Bonaparte), "Considérations sur les causes anatomiques de la frigidité chez la femme," *Bruxelles Médical*, 27, 4 (1924) and Marie Bonaparte, "Les Deux frigidités de la femme," *Bulletin de la Société de Sexologie*, 1, 5 (1935): 161–70.

33. Anna Fischer, *La Femme, médecin du foyer*, trans. Louise Azéma (1905) vii and 259–60, and (1924) 259.

34. Eddé, *Hygiène des maladies de la femme*, 8 ff.; Platon and Lacroix, *Le Sauvetage de la femme*, 82 ff.

35. Gaboriau, *Les Trois âges de la femme*, 100.

36. Nelly Nelfrand, *Ce que toute jeune fille doit savoir à l'âge de la puberté: Education sexuelle de l'adolescence. Petite physiologie génitale de l'hygiène interne de l'homme et de la femme* (Paris, 1932) 29 and 36–38.

37. Georges Surbled, *La Vie à deux: Hygiène du mariage*, 5th ed. (Paris, 1911) 80–84; Drouin, *Conseils*, 97; Houdré-Boursin, *Ma Doctoresse*, 138; Sohn, *Du Premier baiser*, 260.

38. Henri Vignes, *Physiologie gynécologique et médecine des femmes* (Paris, 1929) 132–214.

39. M. G. Lemière, *Des Rapports entre l'ovulation, la menstruation, et la fécondation* (Lille, 1888) 5–55.

40. C. Robin, "Fécondation," *Dictionnaire encyclopédique des sciences médicales,* 4th ed., 1 (Paris, 1877) 354; Richard, *Histoire de la génération,* 1–2.

41. H. Busquet, *La Fonction sexuelle* (Paris, 1910) 30–52 and 111–20.

42. Bourgas, *Le Droit à l'amour,* 143; Eddé, *Hygiène des maladies de la femme,* 108; Bourdon, *Les Rapports sexuels,* 94.

43. R. P. Mayrand, *Un Problème moral: La Continence périodique dans le mariage suivant la méthode Ogino* (Couvent S. Dominique, 1935).

44. René Biot, *Ce que la biologie nous apprend de la nature de la femme* (Tours, 1928) 8–18.

45. Martine Sevegrand, *Les Enfants du Bon Dieu: Les catholiques français et la procréation au XXe siècle* (Paris, 1995) 21–38 and 65–81.

46. Monique Levallet-Montal, *Pour les vingt ans de Colette* (Paris, 1935) preface and 152–69.

47. Moussaud, *Précis pratique des maladies des femme,* 231 ff.

48. Antonin Bossu, *Lois et mystères des fonctions de réproduction* (Paris, 1895) 259.

49. E. Hugon, *La Stérilité chez la femme: Son traitement par les agents physiques* (Paris, 1907).

50. Marcellin Camboulives, *L'Homme et la femme à tous les âges de la vie: Etude hygiènique, médicale, physiologique, social, et moral* (Paris, 1890) 277–78; P. de Bourgogne, *Aux Fiancés: Conseils médicaux d'hygiène pratique. Ce que tout homme doit savoir* (Paris, 1913) 99–104.

51. Eyraud-Dechaux, *Grossesse-Hérédité-Stérilité,* BHVP, Fonds Montreuil-Strauss in Brochures; M. Watrin, "Aperçu sur la physiologie et la pathologie sexuelle de la femme," in Albert Hogge et al., *Physiologie sexuelle normale et pathologique* (Paris, 1931) 127–29.

52. Eddé, *Hygiène des maladies de la femme,* 106; Bourdon, *Les Rapports sexuels,* 106.

53. A. Gensse, *Les Quatre âges de la femme au point de vue physiologique* (Corbeil, 1899) 99–100; Marie Schultz, *Hygiène générale de la femme: Menstruation, fécondation, stérilité, grossesse, accouchement, suites de couches, d'après l'enseignement et la pratique du Dr. Auvard,* 2nd ed. (Paris, 1909) 47–76. On the earlier controversy, see Dubut de LaForest, *Documents humains* (Paris, 1888) and V. Meunier, *Les Excentricités physiologiques* (Paris, 1889) 30–32 and 61–63.

54. Angus McLaren, *Sexuality and Social Order: The Debate Over the Fertility of Women and Workers in France, 1770–1920* (New York, 1983) Chap. 6; Elinor A. Accampo, "The Rhetoric of Reproduction and the Reconfiguration of Womanhood in the French Birth Control Movement, 1890–1920," *Journal of Family History* 21, 3 (1996): 351–71.

55. Dr. Anna Fischer, *La Femme, médecin du foyer,* trans. Louise Azéma (Paris, 1905) vi–vii and 256–60; Dr. Mayoux, *L'Education des sexes* (Paris, 1906) 42 and 158 ff.

56. Fischer, *La Femme, médecin du foyer,* 268–303; Mayoux, *L'Education des sexes,* 247 ff. and 189 ff.

57. Gaboriau, *Les Trois âges de la femme,* 97; Houdré-Boursin, *Ma Doctoresse,* 138.

58. *Bulletin de l'Association française des femmes médecins,* 15.

59. *Le Mariage d'après l'Encyclique Casti Connubii: Texte. Plans d'études. Bibliographie* (Paris, 1932).

60. Abbé Albert Dubois, *Jeunes filles! Si vous vous préparez au mariage* (Paris, 1931) 36–42 and 87–91.

61. René Biot, *Les Buts du mariage* (Paris, 1932).

62. Thébaud, *Quand nos grand-mères donnaient la vie,* 18; Yvonne Knibiehler and Catherine Fouquet, *La Femme et les médecins* (Paris, 1983) 270–71; V. des Hêtres, *La Doctrine catholique: Est-elle opposée à l'égalité des sexes et l'émancipation des femmes?* (Herblay, 1935).

63. Pasteur F.-A. Rollier, *De l'Importance religieuse du corps d'après l'Evangile* (Neuchatel, 1883) 8, 11–12, and 26; T. de Félice, *Le Protestantisme et la question sexuelle* (Paris, 1930) 31–63.

64. Sevegrand, *Les Enfants du Bon Dieu,* 20.

65. See my article "Protecting Infants: The French Campaign for Maternity Leave, 1886–1914," *French Historical Studies,* 13, 1 (1983) 79–105; F. A. D'Ammon, *Le Livre d'or de la jeune femme* (Paris, 1891) 5–6; Caubet, *Manuel de thérapeutique gynécologique,* vol. II, 34; Robert Lacasse, *Hygiène de la grossesse: Conseils pratiques aux jeunes mères* (Paris, 1913) vii; Maurice Favreau, *Ce qu'il est indispensable de savoir sur l'hygiène de la femme et de l'enfant* (Bordeaux, 1924) 7; Une Doctoresse, *Le Guide médical de la femme,* 281.

66. Gensse, *Les Quatre âges de la femme,* 52–53; Houdré-Boursin, *Ma Doctoresse,* 3–5.

67. *Comment sauver nos bébés* (Paris, 1926); Germaine Montreuil-Strauss, *Tu seras mère: La Fonction maternelle* (Paris, n.d.) preface.

68. Bonnie G. Smith, *Confessions of a Concierge: Madame Lucie's History of Twentieth-Century France* (New Haven, 1985) 22; Levallet-Montal, *Pour les vingt ans de Colette,* 18–22; M. Admary, *Initiations par une maman* (Paris, 1938) 42 ff.

69. The most complete description is in Lacasse, *Hygiène de la grossesse,* 34–37.

70. L. Bouchacourt, *La Grossesse: L'Etude de sa durée et de ses variations* (Paris, 1901) 184; Adolphe Olivier, *Hygiène de la grossesse: Conseils aux femmes enceintes,* 2nd ed. (Paris, 1910) 105–9; Lacasse, *Hygiène de la grossesse,* 153–55.

71. Olivier, *Hygiène de la grossesse,* 22–25; Schultz, *Hygiène générale de la femme* (1909) 116; Francillon-Lobre, *Hygiène de la femme et de la jeune fille,* 130–31; Lacasse, *Hygiène de la grossesse,* 46–50 and 94–102; Montreuil-Strauss, *Tu seras mère,* 8.

72. Rachel Fuchs, *Poor and Pregnant in Paris: Strategies for Survival in the Nineteenth Century* (New Brunswick, 1992) 88 ff.

73. Thébaud, *Quand nos grand-mères donnaient la vie,* 40–41 and 79.

74. Bouchacourt, *La Grossesse*, preface and 81–121.

75. Cleisz, *Hygiène de la grossesse*, 10–12.

76. M. de Thilo, *L'Hygiène de la femme* (Paris, 1891) 68–71; Caubet, *Manuel de thérapeutique gynécologique*, vol. II, 42–54; Bouchacourt, *La Grossesse*, 158–68; Schultz, *Hygiène générale de la femme* (1909) 105–6.

77. Houdré-Boursin, *Ma Doctoresse*, vol. 2, 16–17.

78. Caubet, *Manuel de thérapeutique gynécologique*, vol. II, 44–45; Bouchacourt, *La Grossesse*, 182–209; Olivier, *Hygiène de la grossesse*, 76–79; Lacasse, *Hygiène de la grossesse*, 121–23; Gaboriau, *Les Trois âges de la femme*, 139; Cleisz, *Hygiène de la grossesse*, 74–81.

79. D'Ammon, *Le livre d'or de la jeune femme*, 18–19; Caubet, *Manuel de thérapeutique gynécologique*, vol. II, 55–58; A. Dumas, *Guide pratique de la femme enceinte* (Paris, 1902) 39–46; L. Bourgeois, *Conseils pratiques à l'usage des jeunes femmes et des jeunes mères* (Paris, 1908) 10; Olivier, *Hygiène de la grossesse*, 38–39; Lacasse, *Hygiène de la grossesse*, 149–51; Francillon-Lobre, *Hygiène de la femme et de la jeune fille*, 28–29; Gaboriau, *Les Trois âges de la femme*, 138; Houdré-Boursin, *Ma Doctoresse*, vol. 2, 20.

80. Thilo, *L'Hygiène de la femme*, 71; D'Ammon, *Le Livre d'or de la jeune femme*, 7–8; Caubet, *Manuel de thérapeutique gynécologique*, vol. II, 50–51; Bourgeois, *Conseils pratiques à l'usage des jeunes femmes*, 7–8; Olivier, *Hygiène de la grossesse*, 38–39; Lacasse, *Hygiène de la grossesse*, 73; Favreau, *Ce qu'il est indispensable de savoir*, 13–14; Gaboriau, *Les Trois âges de la femme*, 136; Cleisz, *Hygiène de la grossesse*, 19–37.

81. Thilo, *L'Hygiène de la femme*, 73; Caubet, *Manuel de thérapeutique gynécologique*, vol. II, 58; Bourgeois, *Conseils pratiques à l'usage des jeunes femmes*, 8–9; Lacasse, *Hygiène de la grossesse*, 77–80; Gaboriau, *Les Trois âges de la femme*, 137.

82. D'Ammon, *Le Livre d'or de la jeune femme*, 15–16; Caubet, *Manuel de thérapeutique gynécologique*, vol. II, 38–40; Bouchacourt, *La Grossesse*, 308–49; Schultz, *Hygiène générale de la femme* (1909) 130; Francillon-Lobre, *Hygiène de la femme et de la jeune fille*, 128–29; Olivier, *Hygiène de la grossesse*, 41–46; Lacasse, *Hygiène de la grossesse*, 107–9; Gaboriau, *Les Trois âges de la femme*, 136–39; Favreau, *Ce qu'il est indispensable de savoir*, 11.

83. Arlette Gelé de Francony, *Santé et beauté de la femme par l'éducation corporelle* (Paris, 1923) 43 and 60.

84. J. Ducuing and P. Guilhem, "Culture physique de la femme enceinte, de l'accouchée et de la mère," *La Gynécologie* (March 1934) 133–43.

85. Felicia M. Ferszt, "Indications et contre-indications de la gymnastique abdominale en gynécologie" (Thèse, méd., Nancy, 1939).

86. ADG, Fonds du Rectorat, T99, Faculté de Médecine, Études, Sages-femmes, and 5M559, Ecole d'accouchement.

87. Fuchs, *Poor and Pregnant in Paris*, 116 ff.; Thébaud, *Quand nos grand-mères donnaient la vie*, 64, 104, and 180.

88. Thébaud, *Quand nos grand-mères donnaient la vie,* 179.

89. Ibid., 256 ff.

90. Ibid., 13.

91. Emilie Carles as told to Robert Destanque, *A Life of Her Own: The Transformation of a Countrywoman in Twentieth-Century France,* trans. A. H. Goldberger (New York, 1992) 32.

Chapter 7. Menopause and Loss

1. *The Cultural Construction of Sexuality,* ed. P. Caplan (London, 1987) 22–24.

2. Germaine Greer, *The Change: Women, Aging, and the Menopause* (London, 1991) 196–97; *Lettres choisies de Madame de Sévigné* (Coulommiers, n.d.) 376 (letter dated 6 Aug. 1675).

3. Joel Wilbush, "La Menespausie: The Birth of a Syndrome," *Maturitas* 1 (1979): 1454–56. Some doctors linked "vapors" to menopause according to Lindsay Wilson, *Women and Medicine in the French Enlightenment: The Debate over Maladies des Femmes* (Baltimore, 1991) 27–28.

4. Wilbush, "La Menespausie," 147–48.

5. Baronne d'Orchamps, *Tous les secrets de la femme* (Paris, 1907) 24–32; Comtesse de Tramer, *Le Bréviaire de la femme: Pratiques secrètes de la beauté,* 8th ed. (Paris, 1903) 27–31. See also Tramer, *Que veut la femme? Etre jolie, être aimée et dominer* (Paris, 1911) and *L'Amour obligatoire: Les étapes de la vie d'une femme, la carrière de l'homme* (Paris, 1913).

6. Vicomtesse Nacla, *Il! Le Choisir, le garder* (Paris, 1897) v and 103; Gabrielle Cavellier, "Comment on gard son mari," *Féminité,* 2, 21 (1913).

7. Louis Léon-Martin, *L'Industrie de la beauté (dans les coulisses des Instituts de Beauté)* (Paris, 1930) 35–37.

8. H. Thulié, *La Femme: Essai de sociologie physiologique* (Paris, 1885).

9. For example, J. J. Virey, *De la Femme sous ses rapports physiologique, moral, et littéraire* (Paris, 1823) 3, 14–15, and 212–42.

10. J.-L. Moreau de la Sarthe, *Historie naturelle de la femme* (Paris, 1803) 47–55, 83, and 413–19.

11. Ibid., 75–79, 89–113, 368 ff., and 413–19.

12. Adam Raciborski, *De la Puberté et de l'âge critique chez les femmes* (Paris, 1844); Georges Houlnick, *La Femme et la fonction menstruelle: Hygiène de la période cataméniale* (Paris, 1926). The four-line entry for "Ménopause" in *Dictionnaire encyclopédique des sciences médicales,* 2nd series, 16 (Paris, 1873) referred readers to the entry on "Menstruation."

13. Raciborski, *Traité de la menstruation* (Paris, 1868) 335–57, with morbidity and mortality data on 343–44 and 348.

14. Ernest Barié, *Etude sur la ménopause* (Paris, 1877) preface and 15–27.

15. Samuel Pozzi, *Treatise on Gynaecology Medical and Surgical*, trans. B. H. Wells (New York, 1894) iv–vi.

16. For example, L-A. B. Ormières, "Sur la Menstruation après l'ovariectomie et hysterectomie" (Thèse, méd., Paris, 1880).

17. E. Clément, *Cardiopathie de la ménopause* (Paris, 1884); H. Guimbail, *La Folie de la ménopause* (Paris, 1884).

18. C. Vinay, *La Ménopause* (Paris, 1908); Gerdussus, *La Ménopause et son rôle en psychiatrie* (Toulon, 1910).

19. Louis de Seré, *La Virilité et l'âge critique chez l'homme et chez la femme* (Paris, 1885) esp. 17–18.

20. For example, Vinay, *La Ménopause*, 114–16.

21. Arthur Leclercq, *Les Maladies de la cinquantaine*, 3rd ed. (Paris, 1922).

22. Charles Barbaud and A. Rouillard, *Troubles et accidents de la ménopause* (Paris, 1895).

23. Mauclert, "L'Insuffisance ovarienne," *Journal des praticiens* (1904).

24. Vinay, *La Ménopause*, 35 ff.

25. Gerdussus, *La Ménopause et son rôle en psychiatrie*, passim.

26. André Binet, *Souvenirs et propos d'un gynécologue*, 2nd ed. (Paris, 1948) 18 and 39. See also Bernard Lécuyer, "L'Hygiène en France avant Pasteur, 1750–1850," and J. Léonard, "Comment peut-on être Pastorien?" in *Pasteur et la revolution pastorienne*, ed. Claire Salomon-Bayet (Paris, 1986).

27. L. D. Longo, "The Rise and Fall of Battey's Operation: A Fashion in Surgery," *Bulletin of the History of Medicine* 53, 2 (1979).

28. A. Beau, "Les Interactions utero-ovariennes," *Revue française d'Endocrinologie* 11, 6 (1933): 431–33.

29. E. A. Goupil, *La Femme, ses organes, ses fonctions et maladies*, 4th ed. (Paris, n.d) 180–241 and 275–81, and 13th ed. (Paris, c. 1908) 295–305.

30. Etienne Canu, *La Castration chez la femme: Ses Résultats thérapeutiques, conséquences sociales et abus de cette opération* (Paris, 1897); Caufeynon, *Collection de psychologie populaire du Dr. Jaf. II. Ovariotomistes et faiseuses des anges* (Paris, 1908); Abbé Chaupitre, *La Santé pour toutes les femmes* (Rennes, 1911) 29–31.

31. Samuel Pozzi, "Leçon d'ouverture du cours de clinique gynécologique (31 mai 1901)" *La Presse médicale*, 45 (1 June 1901); "Des Opérations conservatrices de l'ovaire," *Annales de Gynécologie et d'Obstetrique* (Mar. 1893) and *Treatise on Gynaecology Medical and Surgical*, iv–v, 316–17, and 557–59.

32. *La Médecine féminine normale: La Guérison des maladies des femmes sans opération* (1904–5). On Gaboriau, see Marcel Baudouin, "Les Premières femmes médecins et internes," *La France Médicale* (1906): 261.

33. Isabelle Gaboriau, "Contribution à l'étude des metrorragies dites essentielles de la ménopause" (Thèse, méd., Paris, 1919).

34. J. Tinel, "Étude pathogénique des troubles et accidents de la ménopause," and Madeleine Hirsch, "Douleurs cellulitiques et ménopause," *Journal médical français* (1928).

35. G. L. P. Mondin, "La Ménopause" (Thèse, méd., Bordeaux, 1931) 19–22 and 36–38.

36. René Biot, *Le Corps et l'âme* (Paris, 1938) 119–93.

37. Henri Vignes, *Physiologie gynécologique et médecine des femmes* (Paris, 1929) 314–68; M. Watrin, "Aperçu sur la physiologie et la pathologie sexuelle de la femme" in Albert Hogge et al., *Physiologie sexuelle normale et pathologique* (Paris, 1931) 125–36. See also Vignes and Simonnet, "La Ménopause," in G. H. Roget and Léon Binet, *Traité de physiologie normale et pathologique*. XI. *Réproduction et croissance*, 2nd ed. (Paris, 1934) 143–51.

38. Simone de Beauvoir, *The Second Sex*, trans. H. M. Parschley (New York, 1952) 27–28.

39. Georgette Perrin, "Traitement de l'hypertension de la ménopause," *Revue médicale de France* (Sept. 1935).

40. Bernard Sommillon, *Action des extraits placentaires sur les troubles de la ménopause naturelle et provoquée* (Paris, 1932).

41. Léonce Noel, "Contribution à l'étude de l'hormonothérapie de la ménopause" (Thèse, méd., Paris, 1939).

42. Notably Tessier, "Etablissement de la ménopause" (Thèse, méd., Paris, 1912).

43. Mondin, *La Ménopause*, 11–13; Barié, *Étude sur la ménopause*, citing Leudet (1867) 40.

44. A. Siredey, *L'Hygiène des maladies de la femme* (Paris, 1907) 37–40.

45. G. Bernutz, *Conférences cliniques sur les maladies des femmes* (Paris, 1888) 166–69.

46. Houlnick, *La Femme et la fonction menstruelle*, 127–28.

47. Edmond Caubet, *Manuel de thérapeutique gynécologique*, vol. II. *Hygiène de la femme* (Paris, 1894).

48. E. Monin, *Hygiène et médecine féminines: Secrets de santé et de beauté* (Paris, 1901) 13; Marie Schultz, *Hygiène générale de la femme: Menstruation, fécondation, stérilité, grossesse, accouchement, suites de couches, d'après l'enseignement et la pratique du Dr. Auvard*, 2nd ed. (Paris, 1909) 35 and 39.

49. Charles Vidal, *Etude médicale, physiologique, et philosophique de la femme* (Paris, 1912) 27–37 and 78 ff.; Galtière-Bossière, *La Femme: Conformation, fonctions, maladies, et hygiène spéciale* (Paris, 1905) 51 ff.

50. Lois Banner, *In Full Flower: Aging Women, Power, and Sexuality* (New York, 1992) 279; Caufeynon, *Histoire de la femme, son corps, ses organes, . . .* (Paris, 1904) v, 11–12, 17–23, 42–45, and 69–77.

51. N. Eddé, *Hygiène des maladies de la femme* (Paris, 1922) 109–13.

52. Hélène M. Wolfromm, "Les Troubles psychiques de la ménopause," in Association Internationale des Femmes-Médecins, *La Ménopause: Rapports du 7me Congrès* (Paris, 1954) 83–87.

53. Victor Pauchet, *L'Automne de la vie: L'Homme et la femme à l'âge critique* (Paris, 1932) 29–30 and 170–71. See also Maurice Boigey, *Le Livre de la cinquantaine* (Paris, 1928).

54. M. de Thilo, *L'Hygiène de la femme* (Paris, 1891) 73 and 84–89. See Sadja Greenwood, *Menopause Naturally: Preparing for the Second Half of Life* (San Francisco, 1984).

55. A. Narodetzki, *La Médecine végétale illustrée*, 150th ed. (Paris, n.d.) 101–2.

56. In addition to the works cited in footnote 7, Octave Uzanne, *L'Art et l'artifice de la beauté*, 5th ed. (Paris, 1902) 5–10; Marie Earle, *Culture rationnelle et scientifique de la beauté* (Paris, 1909) 3 and 14; Mathilde Pokitonoff, *La Beauté par l'hygiène* (Paris, 1892) 98–99.

57. E. Monin, *L'Hygiène de la beauté: Formulaire cosmétique* (Paris, 1886) 16 ff.; Dr. Mestadier, *La Beauté: Hygiène féminine* (Paris, 1911) 4; Massala, *Rester mince* (Paris, 1930) 12 and 16; Marcel Labbé, *Maigreur et obesité* (Paris, 19320) 90–91.

58. A. Choffé, *Causeries du docteur. 1re Partie: La Femme, sa beauté, sa saute par l'hygiène* (Paris, 1905) 4 and 93–98.

59. Dr. Marthe Francillon, *Essai sur la puberté chez la femme. Essai de psycho-physiologie féminine* (Paris, 1906) 1–60; Marthe Francillon-Lobre, *Hygiène de la femme et de la jeune fille* (Paris, 1909) 185–95.

60. Emma Drake, *Ce que toute femme de 45 ans devrait savoir (L'Age critique)* (Geneva, 1908) 22–23, 67–70, 87, and 137–41.

61. For example, Francillon-Lobre, *Hygiène de la femme*, 186; Pokitonoff, *La Beauté par l'hygiène*, 101.

62. Marie Houdré-Boursin, *Ma Doctoresse: Guide pratique d'hygiène et de médecine de la femme moderne* (Strasbourg, 1930) 138–42; Une Doctoresse, *Le Guide médical de la femme et de la famille* (Paris, 1933) 279–81 and 308–11.

63. For example, Liane de Pougy, *My Blue Notebooks*, trans. Diane Athill (New York, 1979) 73 and passim.

64. Choffé, *Causeries du docteur*, 93–95; *Science News* (12 July 1988): 7.

65. Barbaud and Rouillard, *Troubles et accidents de la ménopause*, 32 ff.; Hélina Gaboriau, *Les Trois âges de la femme* (Paris, 1923) 179 ff.

66. Francillon-Lobre, *Hygiène de la femme*, 194–95.

67. Watrin, "Aperçu sur la physiologie et la pathologie sexuelle de la femme," 139.

68. "Alix's Refusal," in *The Collected Stories of Colette*, ed. Robert Phelps (London, 1985) 310. This vignette is from *Paysages et portraits*.

69. Lucien Farnoux-Reynaud, "Du Mont Ida à Galvestone," *Gaulois* (26 Jan. 1929) in BA, Ro 17.855.

70. Evelyne Reymond, "Colette et les produits de beauté," *Pays de Bourgogne* 126 (1984): 215; *Letters from Colette,* ed. and trans. Robert Phelps (New York, 1980) 117 and 128.

71. Colette, "Maquillâge" in *Sido et Les Vrilles de la vigne* (Paris, 1973) cited in Irene Julier, "Le Maquillâge: Pratiques, discours, et interprétations" (Thèse, Paris, 1989) 109.

72. Jerry A. Flieger, *Colette and the Fantom Subject of Autobiography* (Ithaca, 1992) 5.

73. *Chéri,* trans. Roger Senhouse (New York, 1951) 13, and "The Pearls" from *The Last of Chéri,* in *The Collected Stories,* 24.

74. Colette, *The Break of Day,* trans. Enid Mcleod (London, 1961) 5-6, 17-18, and 34.

75. Beauvoir, *The Second Sex,* 542.

76. Roger Hyvert, *Conférences populaires d'hygiène pratique à l'usâge des écoles normales de l'enseignement secondaire classique* (Paris, 1901) 69; Maria Dupont, *L'Hygiène de la femme professeur* (Paris, 1913) 47-48.

77. Janine O'Leary Cobb, *Understanding Menopause* (Toronto, 1988) 60-61.

78. Susan E. Bell, "The Medicalizing of Menopause," and Cheryl L. Bowles, "The Menopausal Experience: Sociocultural Influences and Theoretical Models," in *The Meanings of Menopause: Historical, Medical, and Clinical Perspectives,* ed. Ruth Formanek (London, 1990).

Part Three. Physical Performance

1. Martha H. Verbrugge, "Recreating the Body: Women's Physical Education and the Science of Sex Differences in America, 1900–1940," *Bulletin of the History of Medicine* 77 (1997): 273–304.

2. T. Deldycke et al., *La Populations active et sa structure* (Brussels, 1968) 167, 169, 183, and 185.

3. Emilie Carles as told to Robert Destanque, *A Life of Her Own: The Transformation of a Countrywoman in Twentieth-Century France* (New York, 1992) 15 and 45; Serge Grafteaux, *Mémé Santerre: A French Woman of the People,* trans. Louise A. and Kathryn L. Tilly (New York, 1985) 20–28.

4. James R. Lehning, *Peasant and French: Cultural Contact in Rural France during the Nineteenth Century* (Cambridge, U.K., 1995) esp. 22.

5. Félix Jayle, *La Gynécologie. I. L'Anatomie morphologique de la femme* (Paris, 1918) 99–100.

Chapter 8. Gymnastics, Sports, and Gender

1. Victor Lespineux, *L'Education physique des jeunes filles* (Puy, 1885) 4–5; Jules Rochard, "L'Education des filles," *Revue de deux mondes* (1 Feb. 1888): 656–57; M. de Thilo, *L'Hygiène de la femme* (Paris, 1891) 57.

2. Mary Rosalie Fisher, "Models for Manners: Etiquette Books and Etiquette in Nineteenth-Century France" (Ph.D. diss., New York University, 1992); S. Colette, *My Mother's House* (London, 1949) 23–24; Judith Gautier, *Le Collier des jours: Souvenirs de ma vie* (Paris, n.d.) 24 and 46–47; M. Steinheil, *Mes Mémoires* (Paris, 1912) 11; Julie Manet, *Journal (1893–1899)* (Paris, 1979) 34 and 66.

3. John J. MacAloon, *This Great Symbol: Pierre de Coubertin and the Origins of the Modern Olympic Games* (Chicago, 1981) Chap. 3 and 4.

4. *Les Athlètes de la République*, ed. Pierre Arnaud (Toulouse, 1987) 161 ff.

5. Kathleen E. McCrone, *Sports and the Physical Emancipation of English Women, 1870–1914* (London, 1988) 128 ff.

6. Cousine Odette and "Chronique de la Doctoresse" columns in *La Santé par les sports* 2, 14 (1912): 88–90; 2, 17 (1912): 205–6; and 2, 18 (1912): 245–49; Emile André, *L'Education physique et sportive des jeunes filles* (Paris, 1907) preface and 8.

7. Rebecca Rogers, "L'Education des filles: Les Maisons d'éducation de la Légion d'Honneur (1810–1881)" (Thèse, Paris, 1987); AN F17 9771, 1868 Inquiry, F17 11636, 1882 Inquiry into Gym Instruction at Normal Schools; F17 9672, 1882 Gym inspections, Roche-sur-Yon and Chartres. See also ADR, T58, Inspector's report, 16 Apr. 1882.

8. J.-B. Fonssagrives, *L'Education physique des jeunes filles ou avis aux mères* (Paris, 1869) 83–115; E. Angerstein and G. Eckler, *La Gymnastique des demoiselles* (Paris, 1892) 25–26; C. Boissière, *Comment devons-nous élever nos enfants? Principes élémentaires d'Education physique* (Paris, 1910) 52 ff.; Désiré Séhé and François Raspail, *L'Education physique dans la famille* (Paris, 1921) 20 ff.

9. Isidore Bourdon, *Notions d'hygiène pratique: Education supérieure* (Paris, 1860) 83; E. Masson de la Malmaison, *Instituts de gymnastique et d'orthopédie fondés et dirigés depuis 1826* (Paris, 1844).

10. Cléo de Mérode, *Le Ballet de ma vie* (Paris, 1955) 46 ff.; Roger Feral, "Mlle. Blanche Kerval, doyenne des artistes de la danse à l'Opéra," *Paris-Midi* (22 Oct. 1931); Gautier, *Le Collier des jours*, 251–52.

11. Lynn Garafola, "The Travesty Dancer in Nineteenth-Century Ballet," *Dance Research Journal* (1985–86): 35–40.

12. Richard Kendell, "Degas' Discriminating Gaze" and "Working Women," and Anthea Callen, "Anatomy and Physiognomy: Degas' Little Dancer of Fourteen Years," in *Degas: Images of Women* (Liverpool, n.d.) 8–9, 12–15, and 42.

13. Mérode, *Le Ballet de ma vie*, 54–61 and 85; Jane Hugard, *Ces Demoiselles de l'Opéra* (Paris, 1923) 118–19; Denise Moran, "L'Enfance n'est pas assez respectée dans les écoles de danse," *Le Quotidien* (8 Nov. 1928); Suzanne Balitrand, "A l'Ecole avec des petites danseuses de l'Opéra," *L'Intransigeant* (8 Dec. 1930).

14. A. Rauch, *Le Souci du corps: Histoire de l'hygiène dans l'éducation physique* (Paris, 1982) 109–31; Lt. Clias, *Calisthène ou gymnastique des jeunes filles: Traité élémentaire des différents exercices* (Paris, 1830) v and x. See also AN F17 11645, Corre-

spondence from Clias, and "Sur la gymnastique populaire de M. Clias," *Extrait du Bulletin de l'Académie de Médecine* 11 (31 Oct. 1845).

15. Fernand Lagrange, *Physiologie des exercices du corps,* 3rd ed. (Paris, 1889) vii.

16. Arlette Gelé de Francony, *Santé et beauté de la femme par l'éducation corporelle* (Paris, 1923) 71–72; Doctoresse Nadia, "L'Education physique de la jeune fille," *Bulletin mensuelle de la Fédération féminine française de gymnastique et de sports* 78–79 (Aug.–Sept. 1936): 51.

17. Raoul Fabens, *Les Sports pour tous* (Paris, 1905) 20.

18. Gilbert Andrieu, *L'Homme et la force: Des Marchands de la force au culte de la forme (XIXe et XXe siècles)* (Paris, 1987) 103 ff.; L. Bienaimé, *Gymnastique appliquée à l'éducation physique des jeunes filles* (Paris, 1844); *Effets physiologiques et philosophiques de la gymnastique rationnelle* (Neuilly, 1880) 24 ff.

19. Angerstein and Ecker, *La Gymnastique des demoiselles,* 5–22; Emile André, *La Gymnastique suédoise* (Paris, 1901) 11 and 156.

20. BHVP, Fonds Bouglé, Caroline Kauffmann, dossier 3; C. Boissière, *Comment devons-nous élever nos enfants? Principes élémentaires d'éducation physique* (Paris, 1910) 52–54; M. de Soleirol de Sevres and Mme. Lanfant-La Roux, *Manuel de gymnastique rationnelle et pratique (méthode suédoise),* 3rd ed. (Paris, 1912) 6–8.

21. Napoléon Laisné, *Documents précis sur la marche de l'enseignement gymnastique* (Paris, 1886) 1–51 and 61–77, and *Gymnastique des demoiselles: Ouvrage destiné aux mères de famille* (Paris, 1854).

22. AN F17 11639, Decree of 6 July 1882; F17 11644, Circular from Minister of War, 29 May 1882; *Le Siècle* (23 Mar. 1882); Captain Carl Nolander and Edmond Martin, *Manuel de gynmastique rationnelle suédoise à l'usage des écoles* (Paris, 1883) 1.

23. Laisné, *La Gymnastique à l'école maternelle* (Paris, 1882) and *Gymnastique des demoiselles à l'usage des écoles normales* (Paris, 1883). See also ADN, 2T1376, Enseignement de gymnastique: Report of Inspector in the Sommme, 7 Mar. 1881; Marie Boissier, *Enseignement élémentaire de la gymnastique* (Paris, 1881).

24. AML, R, Ecoles Primaires: Enseignement de la gymnastique, 1873–1897, dossier on Portail gym.

25. ADMM, 1M663, Fêtes fédérales, dossier on 14 July 1881–1909; Désiré Séhé, *L'Education morale par l'éducation physique: Psychologie-pédagogie* (Soissons, 1910).

26. A. Bertrand, *Organisation de l'éducation physique des enfants du premier âge* (Paris, 1873); A. Blatin, *Quelques considérations sur la gymnastique* (Clermont-Ferrand, 1876); Michel Arena, "Notes d'hygiène et d'éducation physique," extract from *Revue de la femme française* (Paris, n.d.): 174.

27. Paul Champtassin, *La Gymnastique scientifique* (Paris, 1911) 11; G. Danjou, *L'Education physique de la femme* (Paris, 1913) 1; Philippe Tissié, *L'Education physique de la race* (Paris, 1913). See Doctoresse Gironce, "Chronique de la Doctoresse," *La Santé par les sports* 2, 18 (1912): 206.

28. BHVP, Fonds Bouglé, Fonds Kauffman, Ligue Féminine de Culture Physique,

dossiers 2 and 3, and Ida R. See, "L'Education physique obligatoire," *La Française* (14 Nov. 1936). See also Milliat, "Organisation de l'éducation physique féminine," in Congrès interallié d'hygiène sociale 1919, *Pour les régions devastées par la guerre: La Mère et l'enfant. Hygiène scolaire. Education physique* (Paris, 1920) 289.

29. Paul Robin, *L'Education intégrale* (Paris, n.d.); *Bulletin de l'Orphelinat Prévost;* AN F17 14312, Orphelinat Prévost, 1892–94.

30. Jacqueline Laslouette, "Trois expériences éducatives d'extrême-gauche," paper presented to the Inspecteurs Départementaux de l'Education National (IDEN) in 1982. I am grateful to Mme. Laslouette for giving me a copy of her paper.

31. M. Louis Lenoel, *Traité théorique et pratique de gymnastique à l'usage des écoles* (Paris, 1867) 10 ff.; Charles Rouget, "La Conservation de l'energie et l'évolution des mouvements," *Revue scientifique* 50 (12 June 1880): 1205–9.

32. Georges Van Gelder, *Notions élémentaires d'anatomie et de physiologie du corps humain appliquées à l'étude de gymnastique* (Paris, 1882); A. Collineau, *La Gymnastique: Notions physiologiques et pédagogiques* (Paris, 1884) 130, 144, and 150; Lagrange, *Physiologie des exercices du corps*, 2 ff.

33. Emile Barthes, *Manuel d'hygiène scolaire à l'usage des instituteurs, des lycées, collèges* (Paris, 1889) 23–26; A. Collineau, *Hygiène à l'école: Pédagogie scientifique* (Paris, 1889) 184–94; Colonel Blandin and C. Seignat, *L'Education physique à l'école et dans la famille* (Paris, 1910) 8–15; H. Boulet, *Hygiène: Programme du 3 juin 1925*, 2nd ed. (Paris, 1926) 357.

34. Pierre Nadal, *La Culture physique de l'intellectuel* (Bordeaux, 1918); K. Van Schagen, *Le Rôle de l'éducation physique dans le développement de la personnalité* (Paris, 1933).

35. Robert Jeudon, "Les Gymnastiques féminines," in Marcel Labbé, *Traité d'éducation physique*, vol. II (Paris, 1930) 540.

36. See F. Avouzi, "La Femme comme modèle de la pathologie au XVIIIe siecle," *Diogene* 115 (1981); J. Livi, *Vapeurs de femmes: Essai historique sur quelques fantasmes médicaux et philosophiques* (Paris, 1984).

37. Lisi Guillot-Kahn, "Le Médecin et l'éducation physique à l'école" (Thèse, méd., Bordeaux, 1919) preface; Marta Braun, *Picturing Time: The Work of Etienne-Jules Marey* (Chicago, 1992) 10 ff.

38. A. Chassagne and E. Dally, *Influence précise de la gymnastique sur le développement de la poitrine, des muscles et de la force de l'homme* (Paris, 1881) 11 ff.; Marjon Savornin, *Atlas d'Anatomie et de physiologie élémentaires* (n.p., 1911); Dettling, *Le Corps humain: Anatomie et Physiologie. Influence de l'exercice sur l'organisme*, 2nd ed. (Paris, 1914); L. Roblot, *Principes d'anatomie et de physiologie appliqués à la gymnastique et aux sports*, 7th ed. (Paris, 1925) ix.

39. G. Demeny, *Les Bases scientifiques de l'éducation physique* (Paris, 1902) 5–33; Cercle de gymnastique rationnelle, *Effets physiologiques et philosophiques de la gymnastique rationnelle* (Neuilly, 1880) 16–24.

40. Gelé de Francony, *Santé et beauté de la femme par l'éducation corporelle*, 8, 21–59. See also Marguerite Despaux, "L'Education physique pendant la periode de puberté chez la femme" (Thèse, éducation physique, Gand, 1924).

41. F.-A. Papillon, "Education physique et sports en gynécologie," *Congrès international de la médecine appliquée à l'éducation physique et aux sports* (Paris, 1937) 80; Henri-Camille Druost, "Menstruation et éducation physique" (Thèse, méd., Nancy, 1932).

42. A. Peres and J. Rataboul, *Traité élémentaire des sciences appliquées à la gymnastique à l'usage des candidates du diplôme de maître de gymnastique* (Paris, 1898) 169–70.

43. Georges Hébert, *L'Education physique féminine: Muscle et beauté plastique*, 2nd ed. (Paris, 1921) 10 ff. and *Guide abrégé du moniteur chargé de l'entrainement dans les écoles, les sociétés de sports* (Paris, 1918) 1.

44. Esther Bensidoun, *Le Sport et la femme* (Paris, 1933) 24.

45. Dr. Hoppel, *La Gymnastique ou le maintien et le mouvement de l'homme sain des deux sexes* (Anvers, 1886) 94–96; L. Roblot, *Guide pratique des exercices physiques: Hygiène et résultats* (Paris, 1903) 20.

46. Pierre de Coubertin, *Pédagogie sportive* (Paris, 1922) preamble; Séhé and Raspail, *Guide pratique d'hygiène et de médecine de la femme moderne*, 6; Georges Hébert, *Guide pratique de l'éducation physique* (Paris, 1909) xv–vi; *L'Éducation physique féminine*, iv; Lt. F. Guinet, *Instruction et entrainement physiques de la femme* (Antibes, 1917).

47. Arena, "Notes," 175; Jean-Joseph Pène, "Méthodes modernes d'éducation physique chez la femme et sports féminins" (Thèse, méd., Bordeaux, 1921) 12–20; Labbé, *Traité d'éducation physique*, 540–41.

48. Ruffier, "Education physique," in BHVP, Fonds Bouglé, articles de presse, thèmes, bôite 10, sports; "Page Médicale," *L'Oeuvre* (8 Nov. 1934).

49. Sheila Fletcher, *Women First: The Female Tradition in English Physical Education 1880–1980* (London, 1984).

50. Pierre Arnaud, *Le Corps en mouvement: Précurseurs et pionniers de l'éducation physique* (Paris, 1981) and "Le Sportsman, l'écolier, le gymnaste. 1. La Mise en forme scolaire de la culture physique" (Thèse, Lyon 2, 1986) 1–22.

51. AN F17 11640, circular from Jules Ferry, 21 Mar. 1882; Ministère de l'Instruction Publique, *Manuel de gymnastique à l'usage des écoles primaires et secondaires de filles et des écoles normales d'institutrices* (Paris, 1885); Désiré Séhé and G. Strehily, *Manuel des exercices physiques à l'usage des écoles primaires* (Paris, 1890).

52. Ministère de l'Instruction Publique, *Manuel d'exercices gymnastiques et de jeux scolaires* (Paris, 1891, 1901, and 1909); G. Demeny, *Résumé de cours théoriques sur l'éducation physique* (Le Mans, 1886) and *L'Education de l'effort: Psychologie-Physiologie* (Paris, 1914). For critiques, see Philippe Tissié, *L'Education physique au point de vue historique, scientifique, technique, critique, pratique, et esthétique* (Paris, 1901) xix.

53. AN F17 11636, Examens des candidats du diplôme de maîtresse de gymnastique;

F17 11637, Correspondance, Université de France, 28 June 1886, and Commission de Gymnastique, Examination 1886; F17 11644, Enseignement de la gymnastique dans les écoles normales d'institutrices, and F17 9457, Ecole normale d'institutrices de Pau.

54. McCrone, *Sports and the Physical Emancipation of English Women*, 108 ff.

55. Louise Weiss, *Mémoires d'une Européenne*. 1. *1893–1919* (Paris, 1968) 45.

56. ADR, T54, Écoles primaires supérieures; AML, R, Lycée des jeunes filles, dossier on entretien de bâtiment, 1883–1897; Allerget and Broussin, "Rapport sur l'hygiène des internats des jeunes filles," and Blance, "La Santé de la femme et les associations féminines d'éducation physique," in *IIIe Congrès international d'hygiène scolaire*. I. *Rapports* (Paris, 1910) 116–23 and 385–86.

57. ADG, Fonds du Rectorat 181, Lycée de jeunes filles de Bordeaux, correspondence about gymnastic instruction, 25 Feb., 3 Mar., and 11 July 1885, and 242; Collège des jeunes filles d'Agen: Emploi du temps, 1890–1; AMB, 620R1, École primaire supérieure de jeunes filles: Emploi du temps, 1889; ADMM, T1278, École normale d'institutrices, annual report 1889–90; ADN, 2T 1376, Enseignement du gymnastique, enquête 1890, reports on girls schools in Laon, Soissons, St. Quentin, Jan. 1890.

58. *Statuts de la Ligue Girondine de l'éducation physique* (Bordeaux, 1889); *Revue des jeux scolaires* 1–14 (Dec. 1890–Dec. 1904); ADG, 1R 103, Ligue Girondine, notice, 1909.

59. Philippe Tissié, *Une Oeuvre nationale par les normaliennes de Pau* (n.p., 1913); *Revue des jeux scolaires et d'hygiène sociale* (Aug.–Sept. 1907, Mar.–Apr. and May–June 1909, Apr.–June 1912, and Jan.–Mar. 1913).

60. ADR, 4M610, letter of 11 July 1914.

61. Fernand A. Menier, "Possibilités actuelles d'organisation de l'éducation physique scolaire en France," *Congrès international de médecine appliquée* (1937) 36; Inspection académique de Meurthe et Moselle, *Bulletin départemental de l'enseignement primaire* (1935) 197–99 and (1936) 53–56. See also F.R., "L'Education physique dans les lycées de jeunes filles," *Le Populaire* (Sept. 1930) in BMD, physical education, press clippings.

62. *Manuel d'exercices physiques et de jeux scolaires* (Paris, 1904); Lamy, *Manuel de l'éducation physique (exercices d'ordre) à l'usage des écoles primaires et secondaires de jeunes filles*, 2nd ed. (Paris, 1905).

63. H. Reynier, *L'Harmonie du geste* (Paris, 1913) 2–3; Bensidoun, *Le Sport et la femme*, 7 and 19–21.

64. Isadora Duncan, *Ecrits sur la danse* (Paris, 1927); Raymond Duncan, *La Danse et la gymnastique: Conférence faite le 4 mai 1914* (Paris, 1914).

65. G. Demeny and A. Sandoz, *Danses gymnastiques composées pour les établissement d'enseignement primaire et secondaire de jeunes filles* (Paris, 1908); Congrès international de l'éducation physique, *Principes de méthodes d'éducation physique* (Paris, 1913) 25–34.

66. Hébert, *Guide pratique*, v–9; *Programme des conditions d'admission en qualité d'élève-monitrice au collège gymnique féminin et enfantin* (Paris, 1922?) and *Les Palestres d'hiver et d'été du Collège gymnique féminin* (Paris, 1925). See also AP, D2T1/15, Inspection de l'enseignement primaire: Réponses au questionnaire du 11 avril 1924, and *Hommage à Georges Hébert*, special issue of *L'Education physique par la methode naturelle* (1958).

67. Fernand A. Menier, "De l'Education physique féminine" (Thèse, méd., Bordeaux, 1915) 75–83; "L'Education physique: Conférence par Mlle. Marguerite Despaux," *Revue des jeux scolaires et d'hygiène scolaire* 36, 4–5 (1926): 23.

68. P.-R. Savigny, "L'Institut d'Education Physique de l'Université de Bordeaux" (Thèse, méd., Bordeaux, 1945); P. Chailley-Bert, "L'Institut d'Éducation physique de l'Université de Paris," *Congrès international de médecine scolaire 1937*, 117–20; P. Tissié, "Le Médecin technicien pédotribe," *Revue des jeux scolaires et d'hygiène sociale* 43 (July–Sept. 1933).

69. ADG, 1R 104, Association des Professeurs d'Education physique et de Sports de la Gironde et du Sud-Ouest, reports dated 29 May and 1 June 1923; ADN, 1T 89/80, report, 30 Dec. 1936.

70. Congrès international de l'éducation physique, *Principes de méthodes d'éducation physique* (Paris, 1922 and 1923).

71. Ministère de la Guerre, *Projet de règlement général d'éducation physique: Education physique élémentaire. Enfance* (Paris, 1919) 15 ff.; Ministère de l'Instruction Publique et Minstère de la Guerre, *Projet de règlement général d'éducation physique. 2. Education physique secondaire (jeunes filles de 13 à 18 ans)* (Paris, 1921); Ministère de la Guerre, *Projet de règlement général d'éducation physique. 3. Education physique supérieure (hommes de 18 à 30 ou 35 ans)* (Paris, 1922).

72. *Règlement général*, 16–17.

73. G. Racine, A. Godier, and L. Leroy, *L'Education physique moderne à l'école: La Méthode française adaptée à la vie moderne* (Paris, 1937). The program decreed on 11 July 1938 was hardly instituted before the war. See *L'Education physique dans l'enseignement primaire d'après les données fournies par les Ministères de l'Instruction Publique* (Geneva, 1941) 130–47.

74. Georges Monguilan, "Esquisse du rôle du médecin dans la vie sportive" (Thèse, méd., Paris, 1912); J. A. Doléris, "Les Sports au point de vue de l'hygiène chez la femme et la jeune fille," in L. Bougier, *Les Oeuvres périscolaires* (Paris, 1913) 223–38.

75. Boulet, *Hygiène*, 293; "La Conférence du Dr. Dubeyre," Femina-Sports, *Bulletin officiel du Comité du Nord* 7 (July 1927).

76. A. Hitier, *La Machine humaine: Anatomie, mécanique, physiologie* (Paris, 1916) 147. For further work on this subject, see Jean Aymé, "Gymnastique respiratoire et rééducation" (Thèse, méd., Nancy, 1926) and Henri Garere, "Etude de l'insuffisance

respiratoire chez l'écolier: Son traitement par la gymnastique respiratoire," in *Congrès international de médecine scolaire et d'éducation physique, 1937* (Paris, 1937) 64.

77. See account of the first Medical Congress on Children's and Women's Physical Education, Sept. 1922, in *Revue des jeux scolaires* (July–Sept. 1922).

78. "La Culture physique de la femme: La Recherche de la beauté," and "Chronique de la doctoresse: La femme peut acquérir la beauté antique," in *La Santé par les sports* 2, 22 (1912): 354 and 378–81; Max Pernet, *La Culture physique de la femme: Beauté et santé par la gymnastique rationnelle* (Paris, 1913); Colette, "La Culture physique et les femmes," *Contes des mille et un matins* (Paris, 1970).

79. Irene Popard, *La Gymnastique harmonique* (Paris, n.d.); ADR, 1R 104, École de gymnastique harmonique, statuts, 1923, and Note to prefect, 10 July 1925.

80. Marguerite Vincelo, *Femme, cultive ton corps* (Paris, 1933). See also Professor G. Demarbre, *Soyez-belle, la gymnastique* (Paris, 1939).

81. L. Duchesne and E. Michel, *Traité élémentaire d'hygiène*, 3rd ed. (Paris, 1887) 175–79; Madeleine Ray, *Notre santé et notre charme* (Paris, 1932) 10 ff.

82. Paul Verlin, "Le Vélocipède," in *L'Illustration, années 1885–1891*, 1891, 280–81, and "Le Cyclisme en 1902 d'après les documents du Ministère des Finances," *L'Auto Revue de l'Est* 34 (1903).

83. *La Petite reine: Le Vélo en affiches à la fin du 19è siècle* (Paris, 1979).

84. Raoul Fabens, "Mademoiselle à bicyclette," *Revue pour les jeunes filles* (20 June 1896): 209–15; C. de Loris, *La Femme à bicyclette: Ce qu'elles en pensent* (Paris, 1896); John Grand-Carteret, *La Femme en culotte* (Paris, 1899).

85. Philippe Tissié, *Guide du vélocipédiste* (Paris, 1893) 119–30 and "Les bienfaits de la bicyclette: La femme cycliste," in *La Pédale de l'Est* 84 (29 May 1897).

86. Marie Houdré, "La Bicyclette et les jeunes filles" (29 Jan. 1925) in BHVP, Fonds Bouglé, presse, boîte 10.

87. "Review de la presse" in *Pédale de l'Est* (25 Feb., 18 Mar., 13 and 25 May 1897); Femina-Bibliothèque, *Pour bien faire du sport* (Paris, 1912) 371 ff.; Paulette Bron, "Patineuses" and "Adieu les 'deux pièces'?" and Jane Saint-Roman, "Costumes de chasse," in *La Femme, le sport, la mode* (Jan. and May 1927 and Jan. 1928).

88. Femina-Bibliothèque, *Pour bien faire du sport*, 242, 318, 327, and 347–48; André, *L'Education physique*, 69–70.

89. Articles in *L'Echo des sports* (23 Feb. 1923) and "L'Excès en tout," *L'Education physique et sportive féminine* 9 (31 Mar. 1921) and 49 (1 Feb. 1926).

90. BHVP, Fonds Bouglé, articles de presse, thèmes, boîte 10, sports, E. M. "Démonstration d'Education physique et rythmique," and photo caption "Les Elèves d'Andrée Joly," *Minerva* (1 Mar. 1934 and 16 Mar. 1939).

91. BA, Ro, 17.722, press clippings on women's sports, review of Ena Beaumon's film, "La Culture physique féminine" and Pierre Bret, "Une Démonstration de culture physique en Sorbonne," *Echo* (7 Nov. 1923).

92. Maurice Boigey, *L'Elevage humain*. I. *Formation du corps, éducation physique* (Paris, 1917) 90–95, and *L'Education physique féminine* (Paris, 1925) 63–65.

93. Nelly Roussel, "La Culture physique de la femme," *La Mère éducatrice* (Jan. 1919); Lucie Neumeyer, "La Culture physique féminine," *Eve* (31 Aug. 1924).

94. Yvonne Legrand, *Le Sport et la femme* (Paris, 1931).

95. Marthe Bertheaume, *Sportive* (Paris, 1926); Marie Houdré-Boursin, *Ma Doctoresse: Guide pratique d'hygiène et de médecine de la femme moderne* (Strasbourg, 1930) 314, 331–45, and 388.

96. Bensidoun, *Le Sport et la femme*, 102, 28–31, and 41–43; Sophie Zabewska, "Rapport sur les effets de l'éducation physique sur le développement, le structure, et les fonctions du corps féminin," *3me Congrès quinquennal de l'Association Internationale des Femmes Médecins, 1934*, 3–9.

97. J. Martinie-Doubousquet, *Les Femmes et les exercices du corps* (Paris, 1937) 6–15, 20–23, 37–45; Robert Jeudon, "Le Sport et la femme," in *Congrès international de la médecine appliquée à l'éducation physique et aux sports* (Paris, 1937) 82–86; George Leroy, "Exercices physiques et sports de compétition chez la femme" (Thèse, méd., Paris, 1939) 7.

98. ADR, 4M610, Aero-Club féminin (1935–36); ADMM, 4M86, sociétés sportives, dossier 95.

99. Femina-Bibliothèque, *Pour bien faire du sport*, 349–55.

100. Baron de Vaux, *Les Femmes du sport* (Paris, 1885); A. de Saint-Albin, *Les Sports à Paris* (Paris, 1889).

101. Suzanne Dudit, "Trente-cinq ans d'automobilisme féminin," and Charlotte Raux, "Les Grandes sportives de France et d'ailleurs," *Minerva* (19 Sept. 1932 and 2 Oct. 1933).

102. Rosalie Maggio and Marcel Cordier, *Marie Marvingt: La Femme d'un siècle* (Sarreguemines, 1991), "Les Ballons en Lorraine," "La Coupe féminine," and M. Marvingt, "Mon Premier vol de durée," in *Le Sport, Journal de Nancy* (21 May and 8 June 1910); "La Vie sportive de Mlle Marvingt," *Nancy sportif*, 48 (4 June 1914).

103. Bartall, "The Game of Lawn Tennis" (1880) in *L'Illustration, années 1876–1884* (SEFAG, 1985); "Sports féminins," *Le Sport, Journal de Nancy*, 32 (19 June 1909); *L'Illustration, années 1909–1913* (SEFAG, 1985) 238 (1912); and Femina-Bibliothèque, *Pour bien faire du sport*, 69–70.

104. Abigail M. Feder, "A Radiant Smile from the Lovely Lady: Overdetermining Femininity in Ladies Figure Skating," in *Women on Ice: Feminist Essays on the Tonya Harding/Nancy Kerrigan Spectacle*, ed. C. Baughman (New York, 1995).

105. Angela Lumpkin, *Women's Tennis: A Historical Documentary of the Players and Their Game* (Troy, 1981) 21; Gianni Clerici, *Suzanne Lenglen: La Diva du tennis* (Paris, 1984) 42 and 67–82.

106. Janet Flanner, *Paris Was Yesterday, 1925–1939* (New York, 1972) 187; and

clippings from *Journal* (17 Feb 1926), *La Revue de Paris* (l July 1926); *L'Illustration* (19 June 1926); *Comédia* (9 Sept. 1926); *Le Petit Parisien* (16 Sept. 1926) in BA, Ro 17.797.

107. Tatiana, "Princesses de sport," *Lectures pour tous* (Apr. 1926) in BA, Ro 11.930.

108. "Quelques souvenirs de Suzanne Lenglen," *Je sais tout* (15 Sept. 1921); "Quelques conseils pour jouer au tennis," *Les Annales* (10 July 1921) in BA, Ro 17.797; Michel Georges-Michel, "Une Journée de Cécile Sorel," *Nuits d'actrices* (Paris, 1933) 50–52; Calmard and Laurent, *Enseignement ménager: Hygiène. Puériculture*, 2nd ed. (Paris, 1939) 31.

109. Ramon Fernandez, "Nos Camarades les sportives," *Figaro illustré* (Feb. 1933).

110. E. Manouevrier, *Les Associations athlétiques dans l'enseignement secondaire* (Paris, 1895); Fabens, *Les Sports pour tous*, 21–25.

111. Jany Casanova, "La Vie active et joyeuse des sportives," *Minerva* (11 Aug. 1939); Georges Rozet, "L'Avenement du sport féminin," *Lectures pour tous* (14 Aug. 1919): 1561–66; Marie Eyquem, *La Femme et le sport* (Paris, 1944) 25–27.

112. Eyquem, *La Femme et le sport*, 51–59.

113. AN, F17 14460, list of the principal sports installations in the Paris region, 1929; ADN, 2T 1381, Subventions to five northern departments, 26 Oct. 1931, 14 Dec. 1934, and 15 Dec. 1937.

114. J.A., "Les Premiers jeux olympiques féminins," *Les Sportives, éducation physique, et sport féminin* (21 Aug. 1922); Alice Milliat, "Les Enseignements des IIe jeux mondiaux féminins à Gothembourg," and Pierre Pelletier, "La Femme et les sports olympiques," *Eva* (20 Aug. 1928), in BA, Ro 17.722 and 17.723.

115. ADR, 4M610, letter to the Minister of War, 9 June 1920, and 4M613, Comité regional d'éducation physique féminine du Sud-Est, 1923; *L'Education physique et sportive féminine* (31 Mar. 1921, 1 Dec. 1923, July 1925, Apr. 1929, Nov. 1932, and Dec. 1936–Jan. 1937).

116. *L'Education physique et sportive féminine* (31 Mar. 1921, 1 Dec. 1923, 1 July 1924, June 1926, June–July 1928, April 1929, and Sept.–Oct. 1934).

117. *Bulletin officiel du Comité du Nord* (1 Sept. 1924 and Aug.–Sept. 1925); "Jeux olympiques," and "Amsterdam Olympic Games," *L'Education physique et sportive féminine* (May 1927, May 1928, Oct.–Nov. 1928, and Nov. 1936).

118. BA, Ro 17.723, Concours fédéral de gymnastique féminine 1926.

119. *L'Education physique et sportive féminine* (Aug.–Sept. 1927, Jan.–Feb. 1934, Dec. 1934–Jan. 1935, Dec. 1937–Jan. 1938, and Aug. 1939).

120. Amelia Arato, *L'Enseignement secondaire des jeunes filles en Europe* (Bruxelles, 1934) 213–16; Jeudon, "Les Gymnastiques féminines," in Labbé, *Traité d'éducation physique*, 539–40.

121. C. Pherdac, *Défendez-vous, Mesdames: Manuel de défense féminine* (Paris, 1913).

Chapter 9. Working Bodies

1. Judith Coffin, *The Politics of Women's Work: The Paris Garment Trades, 1750–1915* (Princeton, 1996) Chap. 4 and 5.

2. Laura Lee Downs, *Manufacturing Inequality: Gender Division in the French and British Metalworking Industries, 1914–1939* (Ithaca, 1995).

3. Susan Pedersen, *Family, Dependence, and the Origins of the Welfare State: Britain and France, 1914–1945* (Cambridge,U.K., 1993) 82–92, 103–23, and 227–60.

4. Emile Zola, *L'Assommoir,* trans. L. Tancock (London, 1970); Louis Morin, *Les Cousettes: Physiologie des couturières de Paris* (Paris, 1895) 14.

5. AN, C3364 and C3365, Enquête sur la situation des ouvriers, 1884, and C5517, C5521, and C5526, Enquête sur le travail, 1889–90.

6. T. Deldycke et al., *La Populations active et sa structure* (Brussels, 1968) 174.

7. AN C5515, Commission Supérieure du Travail, testimony on 14 Feb. and 7 and 12 Mar. 1890 and C5517, Enquête sur le travail, petitions from seamstresses.

8. A. P. Juillerat, "La Veillée, abus et responsabilité," in Ligue Sociale d'Acheteurs, *Conférence de Genève, 1908: Compte-rendu, rapports et voeux* (Fribourg, 1909).

9. Jeanne Bouvier, *Mes Mémoires* (Paris, 1936) 46–52.

10. AN C5515, Minutes of the Commission du Travail, 12 Mar. and 2 July 1890; AN F22 442, Travail de nuit des femmes, 1894–97.

11. For more details about the laws, see Mary Lynn Stewart, *Women, Work, and the French State: Labour Protection and Social Patriarchy, 1879–1919* (Montreal, 1989).

12. Henri Napias, *Manuel d'hygiène industrielle* (Paris, 1882); *Rapport et projet de loi et règlements relatifs à la salubrité et à la sécurité du travail* (Paris, 1885); *Enquêtes sur les modifications à apporter aux lois des 9 septembre 1848 et 19 mai 1874* (Paris, 1886) 5–10.

13. *Journal Officiel, Débats,* 1890, 1347, and 1349; AN C5517, letter from Académie de Médecine, 11 Apr. 1890.

14. Jules Rochard et al., "Rapport sur le travail de nuit des femmes dans les manufactures, usines et ateliers," *Bulletin de l'Académie de Médecine,* 3rd series, 23–24 (1890).

15. Robert Le Masle, *Le Professeur Adrien Proust (1834–1903)* (Paris, 1936); Adrien Proust, *Traité d'hygiène,* 3rd ed. (Paris, 1904) 1048–49.

16. Adrien Proust, "Le Travail de nuit des femmes dans l'industrie, au point de vue d'hygiène," *Revue d'hygiène et de police sanitaire* 12 (1890).

17. Dalloz, *Jurisprudence générale: Recueil périodique et critique de jurisprudence, 1893,* 25 ff.

18. Emilie Carles as told to Robert Destanque, *A Life of Her Own: The Transformation of a Countrywoman in Twentieth-Century France,* trans. A. H. Goldberger (New York, 1992) 7 and 60–61.

19. AN F7 13813 and 13814, Services de santé, 1905–34. See press clippings for 1907, 1909, 1912, and 1919–21.

20. Marie Dupont, *L'Hygiène de la femme professeur* (Paris, 1913) 5 and 105.

21. Carles, *A Life of Her Own*, 83–84.

22. Dalloz, *Jurisprudence générale* . . . *1900*, 4th part, 44–46.

23. *Annales de la Chambre des Députés, documents* (1887) no. 2204.

24. Gertrude Willoughby, *La Situation des ouvrières du vêtement en France et en Angleterre* (Paris, 1926) 38 and 47; AN F17 14364, Ecoles professionnelles.

25. AN F22 538–539, Comité du Travail féminin; *Journal Official: Lois et décrets* (11 June 1917).

26. Joseph Girard, *Eléments de législation ouvrière* (Paris, 1925); François Bacquié, *La Loi de huit heures dans les industries du vêtement* (Paris, 1922) and *La Loi de huit heures dans le travail des métaux* (Saint Didier, 1920).

27. Bulletin International du Travail, *Études et documents*, 1st series, *Travail des femmes et des enfants. 1. La Protection internationale de femmes travailleuses*, 4–12; Andrée Lehmann, "De la Règlementation légale du travail féminin" (Thèse, loi, Paris, 1924) 33–34 and 81–107; AN F22 543, Travail des femmes au nuit, dossiers for 1920–22.

28. Association nationale pour la protection légale des travailleurs, *Le Travail à domicile en France* (Paris, 1906); Rey, "Considérations sur l'hygiène du travail à domicile" (Thèse, méd., Paris, 1906); BMD, dossiers on Congrès du travail féminin, 1907; BHVP, Fonds Bouglé, files on The Consumers League and the Congrès International du Travail à Domicile, 8–9 Sept. 1912.

29. J. H. Weiss, "Origins of the French Welfare State: Poor Relief in the Third Republic, 1871–1914," *French Historical Studies* (spring 1983): 25–29.

30. Ministère du Travail, Office du Travail, *Enquête sur le travail à domicile dans l'industrie de la lingerie. 5. Résultats généraux* (Paris, 1911).

31. BHVP, Fonds Bouglé, Travail à domicile, loi du 10 juillet 1915, activité de l'Office français du travail à domicile 1916–1917, Situation du travail à domicile 1921; and ADV, M293, Industries à domicile, correspondence 1916 and 1919.

32. BHVP, Fonds Bouglé, Travail à domicile, Rapport présenté à l'Office du travail à domicile 1928.

33. BHVP, Fonds Bouglé, Couture, esp. "L'Application des assurances sociales aux travailleurs à domicile devant le Congrès de l'habillement," *Le Peuple* (17 Sept. 1930), "Résolution votée par le 18e Congrès de la fédération de l'habillement," *L'Habillement* (1 Oct. 1934), and "Le Travail à domicile au Congrès de l'habillement," *La Française* (13 Nov. 1937).

34. M.B., "Beaucoup de femmes travaillent trop," *L'Oeuvre* (8 Feb. 1923).

35. For example, Dr. Labeaume, *Maternité et travail* (Paris, 1927); Mlle. Butillard et al., *Le Travail de la mère hors de son foyer* (Paris, 1933); Union féminine civique et sociale, *Le Travail industriel de la mère et le foyer ouvrier: Documents d'études du Congrès international de juin 1933* (Paris, 1933).

36. M. Decouvelaere, *Le Travail industriel des femmes mariées* (Paris, 1934).

37. ADN, 77J 2314, Chambre de Commerce de Tourcoing, Campagne de retour de la mère au foyer, reports on Semaine Sociale on women's work.

38. Confédération Générale du Travail, Fédération Nationale des Syndicats d'Employées, *La Femme au travail ou au foyer: Rapport,* in the Musee Social.

39. Jacques Léonard, *Archives du corps: La Santé au XIXe siècle* (Ouest-France, 1986) 28.

40. B. Ramazzini, *Diseases of Workers,* Latin text of 1713, trans. W. C. Wright (Chicago, 1940) esp. 525 ff. on revisions and translations.

41. "Statistique des accidents du travail" for the last quarters of 1903 and 1906, in AN F22 494, Application de la loi du 9 avril 1898, 1899–1921. The figures were 12,926 and 22,889 for men, versus 458 and 837 for women.

42. Commission supérieure du travail, *Rapports sur l'application pendant l'année 1893 des lois réglementant le travail* (Paris, 1894) 21–28; AN F22 440, Mine Service Inquiry into weights lifted and pulled, 1910.

43. *Des Accidents du travail et les maladies professionnelles: Manuel à l'usage de la victime* (Paris, 1924) 34.

44. Stewart, *Women, Work, and the French State,* Chap. 7.

45. Commission d'hygiène industrielle, *Maladies professionnelles: Etude technique sur leur assimilation aux accidents* (Paris, 1903); Olivier Lenoir, "Accidents du travail et maladies des professionnelles," and V. Thebault, "Maladies professionnelles," in AN F22 519, Congrès des maladies profesionnelles, Brussels, 1910. On diffuse symptoms in feminine occupations, see *Encyclopedia of Occupational Health and Safety,* 2308.

46. V. Vandeputte, "La Securité et l'hygiène dans les tissages," *L'Hygiène ouvrière* 2 (Jan.–Feb. 1912).

47. AN F22 441, Reports on cleaning machines dated 8 Feb., 28 Mar., and 24 May 1899; AN F22 553, Original studies by inspectors, M. Boulins, "Les Accidents évitables dans les filatures et dans les peignages."

48. Ramazzini, *Diseases of Workers,* 163–95 and 253–55.

49. Elia Sachnine, *Etude sur l'influence de la durée du travail quotidien sur la santé générale de l'adulte* (Lyon, 1900) 226.

50. Nicole Xardel, *Le Mouvement d'hygiène industrielle* (Aix-en Provence, 1925) 232–35. See also Proust, *Traité d'hygiène,* Introduction to the 3rd ed., 11.

51. Paul Foucart, *De la Fonction industrielle des femmes* (Paris, 1882) 27–32; Paul Gonnard, *La Femme dans l'industrie* (Paris, 1906) 4 and 19–21.

52. *Pasteur et la revolution pastorienne,* ed. Claire Salomon-Bayet (Paris, 1986); Bruno Latour, *The Pasteurization of France,* trans. Alan Sheridan and John Law (Cambridge, U.K., 1988).

53. Charles Platon and Antoine Lacroix, *Le Sauvetage de la femme: Essai de traitement prophylactique des malades des femmes* (Toulouse, 1934) 24–29.

54. Léon Poincaré, *Traité d'hygiène industrielle à l'usage des médecins et des membres des conseils d'hygiène* (Paris, 1886) 72.

55. J. L. Breton, *Les Maladies professionnelles* (n.p., 1911) 126–54 reviews these studies.

56. A. Orliac and E. Calmettes, *La Lutte contre le saturnisme* (Paris, 1912) 62–63 and 287–88.

57. Alexandre Layet, *Hygiène des professions et des industries* (Paris, 1875) 2 ff.

58. R. E. Chalamet, *Les Ouvrières domestiques* (Reims, 1902) 12–13.

59. Pierre Guillaume, *Du Désespoir au salut: Les Tuberculeux aux 19e et 20e siècles* (Paris, 1986) 136 ff.

60. M. Lemozin, *Travail à domicile et relèvement du salaire féminin* (Reims, 1908) 5.

61. AN F22 571, Application du décret du 19 novembre 1904, correspondence from Boulisset, Feb.–May 1911.

62. Léon and Maurice Bonneff, *La Vie tragique des travailleurs: Enquêtes sur la condition économique et morale des ouvriers et ouvrières d'industrie* (Paris, 1914) 29–30.

63. Léon Bernard and Robert Debré, *Cours d'hygiène professé à l'Institut d'Hygiène de la Faculté de Médecine de Paris* (Paris, 1927) 58 and 655.

64. Maurice Oster, *Contribution à l'étude de la pathologie professionelle dans l'industrie textile (industrie du coton)* (Paris, 1936) 7–21 and 32.

65. Layet, *Hygiène des professions et des industries,* 4, 20–58, 195–97, and 489.

66. H. Piriou, *Contribution à l'étude des maladies professionnelles: Loi du 25 octobre 1919* (Paris, 1924) 30.

67. Cited in Charles Mannheim, *De la Condition des ouvriers dans les manufactures de l'état (tabac, allumettes)* (Paris, 1902) 52–53.

68. M. L. McDougall, "Protecting Infants: The French Campaign for Maternity Leave, 1880–1914," *French Historical Studies* 13, 1 (1983); Adolphe Olivier, *Hygiène de la grossesse: Conseils aux femmes enceintes,* 2nd ed. (Paris, 1910) 32–36.

69. F. Heim, *Recherches sur l'hygiène du travail industriel* (Paris, 1912).

70. Jules Courmont and A. Rochaix, *Précis d'hygiène,* 4th ed. (Paris, 1932) preface to 1st ed. (1913).

71. Frédéric Le Play, *Les Ouvriers européens* 2nd ed. (Paris, 1879); A. Béchaux, "Frédéric Le Play à l'occasion de son centenaire," *Revue des deux mondes* 32 (1906): 768–88.

72. Jules Arnould, "Conditions de salubrité des ateliers de gazage dans les filature de coton," *Annales d'hygiène publique et de médecine légale* (1879).

73. J. P. Langlois, "Les Usines de soie artificielle au point de vue des conditions hygiéniques," *Hygiène générale et appliqué* (Nov. 1908).

74. AN F22 441, 1898 survey, 16 Nov. 1898, Laporte, 1st division, and 15 Jan. 1899, inspector, 7th district.

75. AN F22 571, inspection du travail, enquêtes, ironers, 1897 and 1907.

76. Henri Raymondaud, *Hygiène et médecine à l'usine* (Paris, 1939) 105.

77. AN, F22 515–16, Commission d'hygiène industrielle, 1906–26.

78. Heim, *Recherches sur l'hygiène du travail industriel.*

79. AN, F22 519, Intoxication dans l'industrie des fleurs artificielles (1910).

80. Paul Razous, "L'Influence de la profession sur la morbidité," *Revue scientifique* 5th series, 1 (23 Jan. 1904).

81. AN F22 518 Maladies professionnelles: Reports to hygiene committee on proposed modifications; *Application pendant l'année 1934 de la loi du 25 octobre 1919,* listing decrees modifying law.

82. AN F22 517, Correspondence about employer intransigence and medical declarations of occupational illness.

83. Piriou, *Contribution à l'étude des maladies professionnelles,* 10–12.

84. Anson Rabinbach, *The Human Motor: Energy, Fatigue, and the Origins of Modernity* (New York, 1990) 38, 46–47, and 123–24.

85. Etienne J. Marey, *Du Mouvement dans les fonctions de la vie: Leçons faites au Collège de France* (Paris, 1868) preface.

86. Martine Doubousquet, *Les Femmes et les exercices du corps* (Paris, 1937) 8–9; Esther Bensidoun, *Le Sport et la femme* (Paris, 1933) 3–5.

87. Armand Imbert and M. Mestre, "Recherches sur la manoeuvre du cabrouet," and "Etude expérimentale du travail de transport," in *Bulletin de l'inspection du travail* 13 (1905) and 16 (1909); AN F22 440, Application du décret . . . sur les surcharges, 1910–14, esp. notes on the experiments, 24 Feb. 1912, 13 May and 17 June 1913.

88. Jules Amar, *The Human Machine* (London, 1920) 91–222.

89. Amar, "Reflexions d'un physiologiste sur la femme et le féminisme," *Revue bleue* (16 Feb. 1918) 116–21; Amar, "Origine et conséquences de l'émotivité féminine," *Comptes rendus hebdomadaires des séances de l'Académie des sciences* 168 (1919): 67–69. I am grateful to Lou Roberts for suggesting these references.

90. Imbert, "Les Méthodes du laboratoire appliquées à l'étude directe et pratique des questions ouvrières," *Revue générale des sciences pures et appliquées* 22 (30 June 1911): 479–85; Imbert, "Un Nouveau champ d'action en hygiène sociale: L'Etude expérimentale du travail professionnel," *Bulletin de l'Alliance d'hygiène sociale* 26 (1912): 35–84; Imbert, "Tableau méthodique des professions qui appellent des recherches . . . Fatigue et repos," in AN F22 526.

91. S. Pacaud, "J.-M. Lahy (1872–1943)," *Le Travail humain* (1953): 338–43.

92. Rabinbach, *The Human Motor,* 249–50.

93. "Les Conditions psycho-physiologiques de l'aptitude au travail dactylographique," *Le Travail humain* (1913): 826–34, and "Recherches sur les conditions du travail des ouvriers typographes composant à la machine dite linotype," *Bulletin de l'Inspection du Travail* 1 (1910) 98 ff.

94. M. Frois and B. Caubet, *Le Rendement de la main d'oeuvre et la fatigue professionnelle: Le Travail féminin au bottelage des poudres* (Paris, 1919) 57–89 of *Notes et documents de l'Institut Lannelongue d'Hygiène Sociale.*

95. "Rapport de M. le Dr. Bonnaire sur le travail féminin dans les fabriques de munitions dans ses rapports avec la puérperalité," in Ministère de la Reconstitution In-

dustrielle, *Protection et utilisation de la main d'oeuvre féminine dans les usines de guerre* (Paris, 1919) 139–45.

96. See the rubric "Hygiène de l'ouvrière" in International Labor Organization, *Bibliographie d'hygiène industrielle* 1 and 2 (1923–).

97. Oster, *Contribution à l'étude de la pathologie professionelle dans l'industrie textile*, 30–33.

Bibliographical
Essay

Archives départementales de la Gironde (ADG)

Archives départementales de Meurthe-et-Moselle (ADMM)

Archives départementales du Nord (ADN)

Archives départementales du Rhône (ADR)

Archives départementales de la Seine-Maritime (ADSM)

Archives municipales de Bordeaux (AMB)

Archives nationales (AN)

Archives de Paris (AP)

Bibliothèque de l'Arsenal (BA) (Collection Rondel; Ro)

Bibliothèque historique de la Ville de Paris (BHVP) (Fonds Bouglé)

Bibliothèque Marguerite Durand (BMD)

Bibliothèque municipale de Lille (BML) (Fonds Humbert)

In lieu of a very long bibliography, in this essay I will supplement the endnotes to each section of the book by discussing some works that subtly shaped my approach but are not cited in the otherwise fairly comprehensive endnotes. Because there is surprisingly little secondary literature on the history of the female body in modern France, many of these works are from other disciplines or cover earlier periods or different locations. Historians of Frenchwomen, medicine, or hygiene and comparative historians prepared to read French may ask me for a copy of the ninety-five-page bibliography of the primary and secondary sources I consulted, which will provide them with more complete inventories of archival material, newspapers, and other publications. Serious researchers will also find suggestions about archival and library resources in the last section of this essay.

The Acknowledgments to *For Health and Beauty: Physical Culture for French-women, 1880–1930s* enumerates the principal theoretical underpinnings of this text. The idea of studying "expertise" on the body came from Foucault, so it is hardly surprising that studying one group of experts increased my respect for many of his insights into the construction of both bodies and being. My decision to concentrate on experts in "maternal science" and marital relations and on "translations" of these kinds of expertise into women's advice literature, girls school texts, and women's memoirs and journals came from the practice of women's history and women's studies. Women's historians have long paid attention to women's knowledge and experience, and women's studies scholars with social science training have shown considerable interest in girls' development. Theoretical literature on feminist use and misuse of Foucault reinforced my decision to focus on maternal, conjugal, and other diffuse forms of socialization of girls and women. A good entry into this complicated and conflicting literature is Sandra Lee Bartky, "Foucault, Femininity, and the Modernization of Patriarchal Power," in her collection of essays, *Femininity and Domination: Studies in the Phenomenology of Oppression* (New York, 1990). This germinal essay tries to combine feminist, phenomenological, and Foucaultian approaches to women's issues, including body politics. For more critical perspectives on the utility of Foucault's analysis—and of Bartky's applications of Foucault—for feminist studies, see two other philosophical critiques: Jana Sawicki, "Feminism, Foucault, and 'Subjects' of Power and Freedom" and Monique Deveaux, "Feminism and Empowerment: A Critical Reading of Foucault." Both essays are found in a collection of essays entitled *Feminist Interpretations of Michel Foucault*, edited by Susan J. Hekman (University Park, Penn., 1996). That collection also includes Jon Simon's "Foucault's Mother," which only begins to explore the implications of Foucault's neglect of mothers' roles in the process of subjectification.

In addition to the brief passage on the body in *The Logic of Practice* cited in the Acknowledgments, works by sociologist Pierre Bourdieu contributed to my conceptualization of the social bases of hygienic and sex advice. The chapter on lifestyles in Bourdieu's *Distinction: A Social Critique of the Judgement of Taste*, translated by Richard Nice (London, 1984), helped me recognize that bourgeois women's dedication to personal cleanliness was part of a process of self-presentation and an array of social signals of bourgeois status. Similarly, portions of Pierre Bourdieu and Jean-Claude Passer's *Reproduction in Education, Society, and Culture*, translated by Richard Nice (London, 1990), offered clues about the covert and overt curriculum in school hygiene and home economics programs. In "Appropriating Bourdieu: Feminist Theory and Pierre Bourdieu's Sociology of Culture," in *Feminist Cultural Studies II*, edited by Terry Lovell (Aldershot, 1995), Toril Moi argues that feminists can critique and then "take over" Bourdieu's theory. She notes his suspicion of invocations of biology as the cause of any social practice and his assumption that gender is a "socially variable entity," especially in his essays on race and gender. A more empirical model for future research is Béatrix Le Wita, *French Bourgeois Culture*, translated by J. A. Underwood (Cambridge, U.K., 1994). This ethnographic study of contemporary bourgeois culture informed by both Bourdieu's concepts of distinction, practice, and reproduction and the author's "participant-observer" status unveils the subtle "art of detail" in the self-representation and identification by bourgeois women of other bourgeois women.

Another sociologist affected the analytical framework of this book. Before I read Oyeronke Oyewumi (cited in the Introduction) or David Le Breton (cited in Part One) on the "sheer physicality" and individual isolation of Western concepts of (masculine) being, I encountered these ideas in Bryan S. Turner, *The Body and Society* (London, 1984). Turner also offered reflections on the paradox of the Western perception of the body as "a material organism but also a metaphor," on Christian positioning of women as natural, reproductive, and dangerous and on the long afterlife of the biomedical and cultural traditions of classical antiquity.

An essay by Emily Martin might be consulted for alternative interpretations of medical material similar to some of the medical sources used in this book. Instead of analyzing early French sex cell theories as yet another articulation of the Aristotelian dichotomy between active and passive sexes and genders, I might have read some (though not all) of these theories as "romances," as Emily Martin has so engagingly done with more contemporary sexual physiology. "The Egg and the Sperm: How Science Has Constructed a Romance Based on Stereotypical Male-Female Roles" appears in *Situated Lives: Gender and Culture in Everyday Life,* edited by Louise Lamphere, Helena Rogone, and Patricia Zavella (New York, 1997). Finally, one could deconstruct much of the Pasteurian hygiene literature analyzed in this book and some of the medical and popular beliefs about menstruation described in Chapter 4, as Cecil Helman, a medical doctor trained in social anthropology, does in *The Body of Frankenstein's Monster: Essays in Myth and Medicine* (New York, 1991). Helman sees analogies between medical depictions of the body threatened by germs and legends about monsters, as well as similarities between anxieties about premenstrual syndrome and fears about werewolves.

A single citation of Barbara Duden's important historical work, *The Woman Beneath the Skin: A Doctor's Patients in Eighteenth-Century Germany,* translated by Thomas Dunlap (Cambridge, U.K., 1991) hardly does justice to its explication of premodern, nonvisual, and noninvasive medical perceptions of women's bodies. Her chapter on the history of the body describes concisely the fixation of physiologists on "inner female space" and the emergence of a "body politic" based on demography and political economy. Similarly, my two references to Dorinda Outram's works overlook her remarkable history, *The Body and the French Revolution: Sex, Class, and Political Culture* (New Haven, 1989), with its linkage of male bodies to the new public space and attention to at least one woman's consciousness of women's physical exclusion from the new polity.

After reading much literary criticism on the female body in literature to help me "deconstruct" representations of women's bodies in nonliterary texts, I still consider one essay in Helena Michie's *The Flesh Made Word: Female Figures and Women's*

Bodies (New York, 1989) to be the most useful. "Body, Figure, Embodiment: The Paradoxes of Heroine Description" identifies three representational codes for heroines in Victorian literature, two of which are prevalent in nineteenth- and twentieth-century biomedical writing in French. These are: dead metaphors, especially that of woman's body, which denies all non-normative bodily experiences, and synecdoche, or representing women's bodies by internal reproductive organs, once again, eliding individuality and feminine sexuality. Otherwise I found literary criticism of specific French women writers most helpful. To tease out Colette's knotty relationship with autobiographical writing and especially to separate out the mythical in her writing about mother-daughter relations, I resorted to Jerry Aline Flieger, *Colette and the Fantom Subject of Autobiography* (Ithaca, 1992). General studies of women's autobiographies and journals written in English about Anglo-American women's autobiographical writing did not provide many insights into Frenchwomen's much more reticent manner of writing about their bodies. The exception was Sidonie Smith's *Subjectivity, Identity, and the Body: Women's Autobiographical Practices in the Twentieth Century* (Bloomington, Ind., 1993), which explicates the reserve of women writers about their bodies in terms of the contradictions they faced in concentrating on their bodies, so often represented as irrational, while "writing themselves" as rational beings. Both Flieger and Smith borrow from and make more accessible Hélène Cixous's famous and famously difficult essay, "The Laugh of the Medusa."

When Virginia Woolf did some library research on the subject of "woman" nearly a century ago, she was surprised by the number of entries in the catalogs of Oxford University libraries. Accordingly, when I first searched in the subject catalog at the old Bibliothèque Nationale de France (BNF) for books and articles on women's bodies during the Third Republic I was startled to find few entries, many of which proved to be literary exercises in defining the eternal feminine. By a happy coincidence, the staff at the BNF was conducting a slowdown, which sent me to other libraries where I found far more references and suggestions about alternative subject headings. Despite improvements to the subject listing in the Opale-Plus on-line catalog at the new BNF, I still recommend starting a search on this subject at the Bibliothèque de la Faculté de Médecine de Paris (BFMP). There the old subject catalog lists most French biomedical studies and dissertations on women's bodies and women's diseases in the Third Republic and directs researchers to alternative subject headings such as feminine hygiene, maternity, menopause, menstruation, pregnancy, and puberty. Sorting through the cards under these headings leads, in turn, to other topics such as degeneration and depopulation, which one can explore at the BFMP, other medical libraries in major provincial cities, and the BNF. The BFMP also holds some of the manuals on sex advice which were allegedly "*hors d'usage*" for the eleven years (1988–98) that I requested them at the BNF or that had been removed from the BNF during the Vichy Regime. Two other sexual advice manuals (and some popular hygiene texts) turned up only in municipal libraries in Lyon and Lille.

Other specialized libraries supplement the BNF. The Bibliothèque Forney (BF) has an excellent collection of artistic and commercial images of women's bodies, of cultural criticism of these images, and of women's beauty and fashion magazines. The library of the Institute Pédagogique (IP) has many school texts, although the catalog does not list many of the titles cited in this book. Some of these texts can be located in the curricular material stored in the basement of the institute; others are available at the Bibliothèque Sainte-Germaine, local municipal libraries, and, of course, the BNF. The Institute National d'Education Physique et Sportive contains a good selection of published works on the physiology of exercise and sports, on gymnastic methods, and on the debates about the physical abilitites of girls and women.

In addition to its collections of women's personal journals and feminist periodicals, the Bibliothèque Marguerite Durand (BMD) keeps dossiers of clippings from women's and feminist periodicals labeled "Beauté," "Corps," and "Education physique." The Rondel Collection at the Bibliothèque de l'Arsenal (BA) has many more clippings from the popular press reporting and commenting upon bodily display and abilities, in dossiers labeled "Acrobates," "Actrices," "Cinéma," "Concours de beauté," "Danceurs," "Sports féminines," and "Vedettes." Similarly, the Bouglé collection at the Bibliothèque Historique de la Ville de Paris (BHVP) includes many newspaper articles on the subject of women's bodies and bodily activities in dossiers on topics entitled "Danse," "Dépopulation," "Naturism," "Propriété," and "Sports." In the Fonds Marthe Bray, Fonds Caroline Kauffmann, and Fonds Germaine Montreuil-Strauss of the Bouglé collection, there are statutes, petitions, minutes, reports, and pamphlets of women's associations dealing with issues of women health, physical culture, and birth control.

Archival resources on women's bodies are also dispersed. I visited the Archives Nationales (AN), five departmental archives representing different regions and a range of types of physical culture for women, and four municipal archives in major provincial cities. None of them had as much documentation on girls and women's bodies and corporeal activities as they had on boys and men's bodies and activities.

In the Archives Nationales, four series offer compact compilations of material on girls and women's bodies and physical activities. The Ministry of Education's F17 series contains dozens of boxes of documents on women's normal and girls schools, on girls school gymnastics, gymnastic instruction, and sports. The C3300 and C5500 series of the Legislative Assembly have equally many boxes of minutes on and reports to legislative inquires into women's work, and the F22 series of the Ministry of Labor has more boxes of labor inspectors' reports on the application of the sex-specific labor laws.

In the departmental archives, the M and T series provide more primary sources on gymnastic and sports societies, health and hygiene, and public instruction. The Archives départementales de la Gironde (ADG) contains good records on public health, including, in the 5M series, nursing education and, in the Fonds du Rectorat, on the curricula at the Faculté de Médecine. At the Archives départementales de Meurthe-et-Moselle (ADMM) the M and T series have many dossiers on gymnastic fêtes, sports associations, and public health, including annual mortality rates by age and sex. The M series at the Archives départementales du Nord (ADN) is rich in resources on spas, tuberculosis, and women's work in textiles. Finally, the Archives départementales du Rhône (ADR) has far more material on sports associations than I was able to incorporate into the survey on women's sports.

When I first checked for resources at the Archives de Paris (AP), in 1988 and 1989, there seemed to be very little in the obvious series. After repeated searches in the early 1990s, I found some material on girls schooling and health in the VD6 series. Similarly, two visits to the Archives Municipales de Lyon (AML) produced few specific references, partly because much of the documentation on the contemporary period had not yet been catalogued and partly because much of the relevant material was available at the departmental archives. By comparison, the 62R series in the Archives Municipales de Bordeaux (AMB) had very detailed dossiers on gymnastics and curricular material in girls schools and on public hygiene courses. More research could and should be done in these and other departmental and municipal archives.

Index